Company Financial Reporting

The VNR Series in Accounting and Finance

Consulting Editor
John Perrin, Professor and Director of the Centre
for Research in Industry, Business and Administration
University of Warwick

G. A. Lee
Modern Financial Accounting (3 ed.)

T. A. Lee
Income and Value Measurement (2 ed.)

T. A. Lee
Company Financial Reporting (2 ed.)

J. M. Samuels and F. M. Wilkes
Management of Company Finance (3 ed.)

J. M. Samuels and F. M. Wilkes
Management of Company Finance Students' Manual

S. P. Lumby
Investment Appraisal and Related Decisions

Company Financial Reporting

Second edition

T. A. Lee
Professor of Accountancy and Finance
and Head of Department of Accounting and
Business Method
University of Edinburgh

 Van Nostrand Reinhold (UK) Co. Ltd.

© T. A. Lee, 1976, 1982

First published 1976
Second edition 1982
Reprinted 1982, 1983

ISBN: 0 442 30707 1 paper

Published by Van Nostrand Reinhold (UK) Co. Ltd.
Molly Millars Lane, Wokingham, Berkshire, England

Filmset by Vantage Photosetting Co. Ltd.,
Southampton and London

Printed and bound in Great Britain at
The Camelot Press Ltd, Southampton

In memory of JB
a dedicated reader of financial reports

Contents

Contents

8 Company financial reporting problems – 2

Contents

Preface to the first edition

Accounting is essentially a practical exercise concerned with the measurement and communication of useful financial information. It is also a highly complex and technical process requiring, in most instances, the professionalism of an experienced accountant to produce and report on the required data in a meaningful way. Many would also argue that accounting reports, because of their technical nature, require the professionalism of an experienced financial analyst in order that they be used meaningfully.

Whatever the merits of these arguments and assumptions, it is clear that reported accounting information is an extremely important element in economic decision making, and that it requires to be measured and reported in the best way possible. But what is the 'best way possible' and what are the major problems to be overcome before the 'best way possible' is achieved? As I am not aware of any existing text which fully answers these points, the purpose of this book is to explore in depth the main issues of financial reporting, delineating the major problems and offering what appear to be reasonable and suitable answers.

The text is written within the context of company financial reports because I believe these to be the major source of formal financial information about companies available to investors and other interested parties. While the context is essentially British in terms of the legal and fiscal environment, the text maintains a neutrality which should enable non-British readers to follow it without difficulty. After all, the problems associated with producing and using company financial reports are not uniquely British.

If the reader searches the relevant literature of accounting, he will find that the topic of financial reporting is usually treated in a fragmented way rather than as a complete package. For example, there are textbooks on financial accounting practice which broadly discuss the nature of financial reporting but concentrate on the purely mechanical problems of producing the data to be contained in them. Similarly, there are books on accounting theory which discuss at length particular financial reporting problems without fully discussing the context in which financial reports are used. There are also books which describe in detail the process of analysing financial reports but fail to convey to the reader the fundamental measurement and communication problems underlying the analysable data. In other words, the interested student of company financial reporting can find that its problems and solutions are covered in different parts of various texts. Rarely, if ever, are they discussed completely within one text. Hopefully, this text attempts to remedy this situation.

I have divided the text into two distinct parts. The first part (that is, Chapters 1 to 8 inclusive) deals with the nature and problems associated with measuring and communicating accounting data in company financial reports. I would hope that this gives the interested reader what I believe to be a necessary understanding of the strengths and weaknesses of these reports – that is, in the sense that reports cannot be meaningfully used unless such an understanding exists. The second part (that is, Chapters 9 to 13 inclusive) deals with the use which can be made of reported information and discusses this within the context of the different needs of various users.

It is always tempting when writing on accounting matters to get involved in the detailed mechanics of computing reportable data. Indeed, in many instances, it is not only tempting but also necessary. Accountants and related professionals must at some stage in their education learn these basic skills. However, once they have been learnt, there appears to be little virtue in pursuing the matter endlessly, especially if in so doing it is likely to obscure fundamental arguments and points for debate which are of deep concern to both the consumer and producer of reported accounting information. Thus, this text examines the nature, structure and problems of company financial reporting without getting bogged down in such things as double-entry bookkeeping – despite its arithmetical elegance. This does not mean that the text is devoid of figures – this is neither possible nor desirable. Instead, I have attempted to give the reader figure work whenever this is necessary to develop, explain or examine an argument or a problem. For this reason, I hope the arguments and discussions are clearer than they might otherwise be.

Arguably the largest single problem in writing a text is to clearly, honestly and realistically assess the potential readership. This is never an easy task but I hope I am being fair when I suggest that it should be capable of extensive use by the following groups:

(a) University and Polytechnic undergraduate students seeking a detailed study of the company financial reporting system, either at first or second year level, as part of their overall study of financial accounting matters.

(b) Professional accountancy students undergoing foundation or graduate conversion courses.

(c) Students in professions which are major users of published accounting information – for example, trainee bankers, stockbrokers, and investment analysts and managers.

In each of these groups, the students concerned should, at some stage in their course, require to study the company financial reporting system in depth – not only to understand what the information is and how it is measured and used, but also to appreciate the context in which it is measured and used and the related problems and difficulties which arise.

In addition, because the text concentrates to a considerable extent on the users of company financial reports, it should be of interest to students who are required to study investment and financial management as well as financial accounting.

In other words, because of its lack of emphasis on the purely mechanical aspects of the accounting process (which are well covered elsewhere in a large number of texts), I believe this to be a text which can be meaningfully used by non-accounting specialists as well as by would-be professional accountants. Whether the reader is intending to specialize in the preparation of reportable accounting information, or whether he is intending to specialize in its analysis and interpretation, this text should cope with both needs. The ability to compute accounting figures is one thing – the ability to understand fully the problems inherent in the measurement, communication and use of these figures is another. I feel strongly that students should be fully aware of these problems whether they be student accountants, bankers, analysts or stockbrokers.

Finally, it would be wrong to omit any acknowledgement of the various people who have undoubtedly aided me in producing this book. My grateful thanks go to the following:

To Tom Robertson for contributing what is an extremely useful and clear checklist of legal, professional and regulatory provisions covering company financial reporting in the UK. Condensing all the relevant material into such a few pages is a remarkable feat.

To Mick Glautier, John Perrin and Tom Robertson for reviewing original drafts of the manuscript, and for making many useful suggestions for improvement which have undoubtedly added to any merits the book may now have.

To Ken Fox and Peter Ford of Nelson, who, always to my utter amazement, manage to convert a mass of original and amended typescript into the text you are now reading.

To Chris Nash for producing such a clear original manuscript within an almost impossible deadline.

To my ever-patient wife, Ann, who has, yet again, put up with the selfishness, temper and idiosyncrasies of an expectant author.

And finally, and with feeling, to successive Chancellors of the Exchequer who have made it entirely necessary for me to write this book.

Any faults remaining in the book are undoubtedly mine.

University of Liverpool   *T. A. Lee*

Preface to the second edition

It is inevitable that the author of a text will find that, over a number of years, its original content will require amendment and even radical alteration or deletion. In company financial reporting, part of the reason for change results from the almost continuous development taking place in company law and professional accounting pronouncements. It may also result from the fact that more and more students of accounting are not specialists in the subject and, consequently, require a detailed but simplified introduction to it.

Both these reasons lie behind the changes which are incorporated into the second edition of this book. Many technical and other changes have affected the company financial reporting function, and have necessitated substantial alterations to the first edition. In addition, the market for the latter has gradually encompassed a large number of non-specialist students of accounting. Also, to be perfectly honest, the passage of time has made certain features of the first edition less than attractive to me.

The major change has been one of simplification of the style of the book – away from the original detailed references to the thoughts and approaches of leading writers and writings in the various areas, towards a (hopefully) more straightforward explanation and discussion of the main points of issue. The reader is now given a considerable amount of material in the earlier chapters of the book to familiarize himself or herself with the fundamental features of company financial reporting. Chapters 1, 2 and 3, particularly, spell out in plain terms the structure of the main financial statements and the environment in which they are produced. More attention has been paid in this edition to explaining the nature of these statements, and the reader is introduced to the basic elements of current cost accounting and value added statements in this edition (but without being bogged down in the precise detail of these matters). The upshot of this change in approach is the production of a text very much geared to an introduction to company financial reporting rather than its more advanced aspects. The legal and professional requirements underlying the reporting function have been completely updated in light of the Companies Acts 1976, 1980 and 1981, various additional *Statements of Standard Accounting Practice* and *Auditing Guidelines and Standards*.

In order to give the non-specialist reader (particularly) some experience of producing financial statements without the need to learn the detail of accounting procedures, I have included a number of practice exercises (with solutions) at the end of Chapter 3. It is hoped that these will aid lecturers using the text in compiling a course which combines discussion of issues with practical instruction.

Other new features of this edition include the following: a discussion of reporting objectives and user needs within the context of UK thinking (*The Corporate Report* was published at the same time as the first edition); a greater attention to the needs of users other than shareholders; (as previously mentioned) full descriptions of current costs and value added; an expanded discussion of the valuation and allocation problems in accounting; and the effects of current cost accounting and flexibility of accounting on financial ratio production and use. The selected bibliographies have been updated and amended where relevant.

The existence of a second edition owes much to the many purchasers and readers of the first edition. To the latter, I must express my sincere thanks (and also those of my bank manager and family). To Nelson goes my thanks for retaining confidence in the book and myself. To Tina Graham, however, must go the biggest thanks for managing to type the manuscript at a time when having to cope with a new job and new (and demanding) colleagues.

Edinburgh, December 1981   *Tom Lee*

Introduction

Financial information and the public interest

> When a student is told the result of a test, a golfer sees his ball fall into the rough, or a pieceworker gets his pay packet he is getting knowledge of results. There are few actions which have no perceptible result and in most cases knowledge of results is important to the performer and will affect his future behaviour.[1]

Knowledge of results and its effect on human behaviour are essential themes of a text concerned with the issues and problems associated with the production, communication and use of financial accounting information. The reasoning behind this proposition is not obscure, but neither is it simple, as the contents of this book will reveal.

Business activity has developed over the years within the so-called free-enterprise system, with differing types and degrees of risk being taken by various suppliers of capital. As business enterprises have multiplied, in number and size, the supply of capital and the related risk-taking have increased correspondingly. Inevitably, this has created a considerable public interest in business activity, not just in terms of shareholders, lenders, bankers and creditors, but also including employees, customers, the 'news' media, regulatory bodies of various kinds, and government.

This public interest has caused business enterprises to accept social as well as economic, financial and legal responsibilities, and has created, as a consequence, a growing need for the communication of information to account for results which are of considerable interest to a wide range of individuals and organizations. In particular, there is an obvious need for reliable information which they can use to acquire an essential knowledge of the way in which business enterprises are 'behaving' in relating to these various aspects of public interest. By perceiving enterprise behaviour through communicated information, interested parties can use this knowledge to amend or adapt their own behaviour *vis-à-vis* the enterprises concerned.

One of the most significant aspects of the information systems of business enterprises in a developed economy is that which concerns the production and communication of financial data, particularly that describing enterprise profitability and financial position. This information has obtained such a place of eminence because it attempts to portray the economic resources of the enterprise and the financial results which have been achieved by its management when these resources have been put to use. It attempts to reveal how effective management has been in resource allocation and utilization as well as the financial rewards available to compensate for the risks taken by the various suppliers of capital. The importance of this information to these risk-takers increases the more they are divorced from the relevant resource management; the gap between the supplier and manager of capital creates a lack of knowledge of enterprise affairs which needs to be bridged by the periodic supply of formal financial information. Once supplied with this information, the risk-takers are better informed to make decisions and take action concerning their involvement or interest in the enterprise, and this is obviously beneficial to the efficient working of the free-enterprise system.

Financial information and the company

The vehicle for a substantial portion of business activity in a free-enterprise economy is the limited liability company, and the need for formal financial information about enterprise affairs is seen clearly within the corporate structure of relationships and interests. Capital is provided to these entities by shareholders, lenders, bankers and, at least on a short-term basis, creditors. Depending on the nature and size of the companies involved, these 'investors' may terminate their 'investments' by realization – either through sale on an open or restricted market, or by termination of a contracted agreement. The most long-term and risky investment is recognized generally as that of the shareholder and in most developed countries operating under largely free-enterprise principles, this is also recognized legally or governmentally by provisions requiring corporate managements to produce and communicate periodic financial information to shareholders. The relevant financial reports containing this information are therefore the main vehicle by which management communicates to corporate ownership. However, owing to the complexity of the corporate financial structure, more and more individuals and institutions have increasingly become concerned with gaining a knowledge of enterprise profitability and financial position, and this has meant that company financial reports to shareholders have come to enjoy a much wider audience.

Financial information and the accountant

Largely because of the significant expansion in corporate business activity and its related financial reporting function, the accountancy profession has assumed the considerable responsibility for producing and reporting the required financial accounting information. Although in most countries where corporate financial reports are produced, the legal responsibility for regularly presenting these statements is with boards of directors, it is accountants who are concerned with producing the relevant information on the latter's behalf, subject to certain prescribed and acceptable standards of measurement and communication. Accountants are also responsible for examining and giving an opinion on the quality of reported information in their capacity as auditors. The role of the accountant in providing reliable financial information is therefore an important one, and one which is not only onerous but complex.

The main aim of the accountant is to ensure that the public (that is, the relevant and interested public) has the benefit of the best financial reports which can be devised. No accountant would challenge such an objective, but, as the accountancy profession has found over the years, the production of the 'best' financial reports possible is an extremely difficult task which can attract a great deal of criticism and debate.

The purpose of the text

The above introductory comments are given as a prologue to a description of the nature and purpose of the text. It is concerned essentially with the production, communication and use made of the accounting information contained in the periodic financial reports of companies. As such, it is not so much concerned with the detailed techniques and practices employed by the accountant as with the fundamental issues and problems of principle which affect the measurement and communication of information (from the point of view of the reporting accountant) as well as its use (from the point of view of the individual or institution receiving it). There are many such problems and issues of vital importance in a situation where reliable information for decision-making and other activities is necessarily scarce, and where its highly technical nature may well be a constraint to its usefulness. However, they can be divided into the following two identifiable categories.

Issues and problems of a technical nature

For purposes of this text, these may be defined as those relating to the organization of accounting numbers in such a way as to produce useful and reliable accounting messages relating to the financial affairs of companies. They therefore involve the various standards and conventions which are, or could be, adopted in both the production and the use of corporate financial reports. However, it should be noted that the explanations and discussions which will follow are in no way intended to equip the reader with an expert ability to account. The sole purpose is to educate the reader to give him a basic understanding of the technical issues and problems involved in corporate financial reporting – to give him the confidence and awareness he needs when he is faced with accounting figures.

Introduction

Issues and problems of a behavioural nature

Accounting information exists to influence human behaviour and can, in turn, be influenced by human behaviour. As such, the production and the use of corporate financial reports create a series of issues and problems which relate to the human behaviour aspect. These behavioural points will be fully covered where appropriate, and what empirical evidence is available will be looked at where relevant.

Thus, the text can be divided into two distinct parts: the production and communication of accounting information; and the use made of the relevant reports. Each part contains technical and behavioural problems, and these will be separately identified at appropriate stages. First of all, however, the reader will be given an outline of the history and development of the corporate financial reporting system, together with a description of its present form. This will be stated within the UK context but the main steps can be seen in similar developments in the US and the Commonwealth.

Reference

1 J. Annett, *Feedback and Human Behaviour*, Penguin Books, 1969, p. 11.

1
The nature of companies and their financial reports

Introduction

The purpose of this chapter is to explain, in general terms, the nature, structure and form of company financial reports in widespread use today. The intention is therefore to familiarize the reader with the type of accounting information which describes, in aggregate terms, the financial affairs and conduct of companies. With this background, it is hoped that he will be in a position to follow the subsequent discussions of the issues and problems surrounding the production and use of such information.

The nature and form of companies

There are problems in attempting to describe what a company is to anyone who is not familiar with the term. It exists yet it cannot readily be seen or touched. It is, in fact, merely a legal framework devised to allow various persons to come together within an organization or structure which is capable of transacting business with other persons and organizations. Lillie, for example, has defined a company as follows:

> A company is an association of persons formed for the purpose of carrying on some business or undertaking, in the name of the association, each member having the right, subject to the regulations governing the administration of the association, to transfer his interest therein to any other persons.[1]

This definition embodies the main legal characteristics of companies – that, first, they have a legal personality and existence separate from their owners; secondly, their identity is not affected by changes in their owner membership, thereby giving them a theoretically perpetual life; and, thirdly, they can enter into contractual and other relationships with third parties, through their employees and elected officials and managers, without necessarily having to refer to their owners. Therefore, although similar in certain respects to partnerships, they allow for two factors which partnerships cannot entertain: separation of ownership from management; and potential permanency of life. This arrangement has many advantages – the main ones being that the owners of a business need not also be its managers (and vice versa); and, where there are changes in ownership, this need not result in the business having to close and/or be reformed. In other words, it is an arrangement of considerable convenience concerning the combining of business activity.

Companies can be divided into two main categories: those with limited liability and those with either unlimited or guaranteed liability. As discussions on corporate financial reports normally refer to the former category, this text will concentrate on it to the exclusion of the other. The term 'limited liability' can be defined as limiting the liability of the owners of a company for its debts to an amount not exceeding the capital they have contracted to subscribe to it. This capital is normally in the form of units of a certain monetary denomination called 'shares' and, consequently, the capital of companies is described as 'share capital'.

The limitation of ownership liability for the debts of the company has a particular advantage associated with it – its owners cannot lose more than they have put into it, and their other assets are consequently not available to the company's creditors when they are seeking repayment of amounts due to them. This is not the case with unlimited liability or guaranteed liability where the shareholders can have a potential liability well in excess of the amount of their share capital. (It should be noted that the Companies Act 1980 prohibits the formation of new guarantee companies.)

Company share capital and other sources of finance

There are several types of share which a company can have, and to which its owners (termed 'shareholders') can subscribe. Each type has certain rights attached to it – that is, rights relating to such matters as voting, dividends and capital repayments. (There are also certain legislative requirements affecting such capital – for example, as in Sections 14 to 38 inclusive, Companies Act 1980.)

Preferred shareholders hold preference share units and are usually entitled to dividends as a fixed percentage of capital payable before dividends to other classes of share are determined; repayments of capital prior to repayment of other classes of share capital; but no right to vote on company matters. However, if a company's memorandum and articles of association (statutorily-required documents containing the internal rules and regulations governing the company's behaviour) do not provide for prior repayment of capital, all shareholders, whether or not their shares are preferential, are entitled, *pari passu*, to a return of the surplus assets on a liquidation. Similarly, a company's memorandum and articles may not restrict voting rights, in which case preference shareholders are not so prohibited. In certain circumstances, preference shareholders may have cumulative rights to dividends; that is, if preference dividends cannot be paid in any period because of financial constraints, the right to receive them can be carried forward indefinitely until they can be satisfied.

Ordinary shareholders hold ordinary units which may or may not have voting rights attached, and which have no right to any prescribed level of dividends. Their dividends depend entirely on profitability and the availability of cash, and are determined after any prior rights of preference shareholders have been satisfied. Ordinary shareholders can thus enjoy considerable rewards for their investment should company profits be substantial. On the other hand, should profits be poor, they cannot so benefit. The risk associated with their investment can therefore be very high (and certainly much higher than that of preference shareholders).

In certain circumstances, a company may also have deferred shares, which usually have similar rights to ordinary shares but which can only be satisfied after preferred and ordinary rights have been met. They are consequently the shareholders who take the greatest degree of risk amongst company owners.

Companies have the legal right to issue redeemable shares (subject to certain conditions being satisfied at the time of issue and at the time of redemption), and may also purchase their own shares (again subject to similar conditions to those affecting redeemable shares). All shareholders, however, whatever the type of share they hold, normally have the additional right to receive, on an annual basis, financial reports from their companies which describe their recent financial progress and position. It is with these reports that this text is most concerned.

Companies can be financed in ways other than by subscription to share capital. For example, medium-term finance can be obtained from loans made to a company in the form of debenture stock. These loans are often governed by the provision of a trust deed stipulating *inter alia* the appointment of trustees to administer the loan; a fixed rate of interest to be paid before any dividend distributions are made; a similar right regarding capital repayments; and (not in every case) security of repayment by a legal charge on all or certain of the assets of the company. Voting rights are not normally given to such loans, although long-term lenders often have the right to receive the same reported accounting information as shareholders.

Short-term finance is given to companies in the normal course of business through bank loans and overdrafts, and credit facilities from their suppliers of goods and services. Some of these sources (particularly those such as banks) can become very long-term indeed, and judgement has to be exercised as to whether they ought to be classed as short, medium or long-term sources of finance. They may be secured over all or some of the company's assets and, particularly with regard to bankers, the company may be required to provide annual financial reports as a condition of the financing agreement.

Due to inevitable pressures of space, the above paragraphs can only briefly describe the main aspects of company share capital and other sources of finance. Illustration 1 overleaf summarizes these comments, putting the various sources in a descending order of risk and permanency. This table can in no way cover the detailed legal provisions governing the rights of the persons and institutions associated with these sources of

Illustration 1 Sources of corporate finance

Source of finance	Permanency	Dividend/ interest rights	Repayment rights	Voting rights	Information rights	Security over assets
Deferred share capital	Indefinite[1]	After all other dividend and interest claims have been met	After all other repayment claims have been met	Not necessarily provided for	Usually the receipt of the annual report	None
Ordinary share capital	Indefinite	After all preferred and lending claims have been met	After all preferred, lending and credit repayment claims have been met	Usually provided for[2]	Receipt of the annual report	None
Preferred share capital	Usually indefinite[3]	After all lending claims have been met[4]	After all lending and credit repayment claims have been met	Not usually provided for	Receipt of the annual report	None
Loan capital[5]	Long-term[6]	Prior to any dividend claims being met	Prior to any share capital repayments being met[7]	Not usually provided for	Usually receipt of the annual report	Not necessarily[7]
Bank overdrafts	Short-term[8]	Prior to any dividend claims being met	Prior to any share capital repayments being met[7]	None	Usually receipt of the annual report[9]	Not necessarily[7]
Credit from suppliers	Short-term	None	Prior to any share capital repayments being met[7]	None	Not usually	Not usually

Notes

(1) Deferred shares are rarely issued nowadays, and those in issue are frequently converted into ordinary shares.
(2) Non-voting ordinary shares are not an infrequent occurrence in the corporate sector.
(3) They can be classes as redeemable at a certain future date.
(4) Preference shareholders rights to dividends may be cumulative should there be a failure to pay a particular dividend. Preference dividends are usually computed as a fixed percentage of capital.
(5) Including debenture capital, bank loans and property mortgages.
(6) Usually with a fixed repayment date or redemption over a set period of years. Alternatively, they may be convertible into ordinary share capital at a certain future date (or dates).
(7) The repayment of loan stock (and bank overdrafts) may be made before any other repayment on a realization of the company if the lenders or bankers have a security over all or some of its assets. Otherwise, they rank equally for repayment with the creditors of the company.
(8) Overdraft facilities often become a more long-term source of finance for a company if its bank is willing to renew them over time.
(9) Usually provided as part of the agreement to provide overdraft facilities.

corporate finance. However, it provides an insight into the number and diversity of groups to which reported accounting information has increasingly to be directed nowadays. The needs of these users in relation to share information will be discussed at various points in this text.

Private and public companies

Companies in the UK can be divided into two further categories: public and private companies (governed by Sections 1 to 13 inclusive, Companies Act 1980). Such a distinction mainly concerns the issuing of shares to the public (as a result of the provisions of the Companies Act 1980, other previous distinctions have been removed – for example, regarding the transferability of a company's shares).

Every company must have at least two persons originally subscribing for its shares when it was created; and all companies can transfer their shares freely between shareholders so long as their articles of association allow such a procedure. There is now no maximum number of shareholders for any type of company. A public company, however, is a limited liability company whose memorandum of association states it to be public; is named as a public limited company (P.L.C.); and has an allotted share capital of at least £50,000 nominal value. A private company is any company which is not a public company, and Section 15, Companies Act 1980 prevents a private company from offering its shares to the public. Public companies are also affected differently from private companies so far as concerns (a) profit distributions or dividends – the latter being somewhat more restrictive for public than for private companies (this matter is complex, and will be dealt with later in the text); and (b) the allotment of shares (it cannot allot shares unless at least one quarter of the shares' nominal value, and the share premium, have been paid in money or money's worth).

At the present time, the financial reporting requirements affecting companies do not distinguish clearly between private and public companies – Sections 5 to 10 inclusive, Companies Act 1981 allow most private companies exemption from delivering their full annual financial statements to the Registrar of Companies, thus preventing the public at large from having access to them. Instead, these companies (defined either as small or medium-sized) can deliver modified statements which lack the completeness and the detail of the legally required package for shareholders and debenture holders. But this is only a small distinction between public and private companies, and it would appear that the major advantage of the former over the latter is their access to the public for long-term or permanent finance.

Holding and subsidiary companies

The classification of companies can be extended in one further direction which relates to the financial and managerial relationships which can exist between companies. The shareholders of a company in most circumstances appoint a board of directors to manage its financial and business affairs on their behalf. One of the courses of action open to a board so appointed is to develop and expand the company by acquiring or controlling other companies. This can be done by purchasing more than one-half of the share capital of another company, or by becoming a shareholder in it and controlling the composition of its board of directors. In other words, companies can be acquired or controlled without having to purchase their individual assets and liabilities. The controlling company is called the 'holding' company, and the controlled one is called the 'subsidiary' company. A 'group' is the term commonly given to the aggregate entity; the holding company and its subsidiary.

Illustration 2 below describes some of these relationships (H = holding company; and S = subsidiary company):

Illustration 2 Holding and subsidiary companies

(a) A wholly-owned subsidiary

```
H
│ 100%
▼
S
```

(b) A partly-owned subsidiary

```
H
│ 50+%
▼
S
```

(c) Several subsidiaries

```
            H
  ┌─────────┼─────────┐
  │ 50+%    │ 50+%    │ 50+%
  ▼         ▼         ▼
  S₁        S₂        S₃
```

Each of these companies is a separate legal entity and is required to produce annual financial statements relating to its profitability and financial position. In addition, the holding company is required to present group financial statements describing the financial results of all the companies when aggregated, and after allowing for the existence of outside shareholders in subsidiary companies (termed 'minority interests'). Thus, the corporate legal structure goes beyond the individual company and recognizes the group as a separate entity for reporting purposes.

The holding-subsidiary company relationship can become extremely involved with subsidiary companies acquiring other companies in a chain of suitable share purchases. In many instances, a holding company may control a so-called sub-subsidiary company (SS) without owning more than one-half of its share capital. For example, in Illustration 3, if a holding company owns 80 per cent of a subsidiary's capital; and it, in turn, owns 60 per cent of a sub-subsidiary's capital; then the holding company effectively owns 80 per cent × 60 per cent or 48 per cent of the sub-subsidiary – apparently a non-controlling interest. But, because H controls S, and S controls SS, H is deemed to control SS, despite the less than one-half holding, and would be required to include its financial results appropriately in its group financial statements.

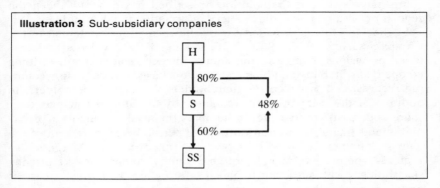

Illustration 3 Sub-subsidiary companies

Regulating company behaviour

In most developed countries, the activities of limited liability companies are strictly controlled by statutory or governmental regulations. There may also be a number of institutionalized regulations. In the UK, all private and public companies are regulated at present by a variety of enactments. However, of most concern in terms of this book on financial reporting matters are the provisions of the Companies Acts 1948, 1967, 1976, 1980 and 1981. Quoted companies are also regulated by the provisions of the Stock Exchange; and, in certain circumstances, companies come under the jurisdiction of the City Panel on Takeovers and Mergers. (The detail of all these provisions will be discussed, where relevant, at various stages in this book.)

UK companies are also required to adhere to certain internal regulations governing their conduct. These are legally required of each company, and take the form of its memorandum and articles of association. The memorandum is mainly concerned with the name, registered office, limited liability and trading objectives of the company. The articles contain more detailed regulations relating to rights of shareholders, transferability of shares, powers and duties of directors, financial statements, dividends and general meetings. All such regulations are in addition to those imposed on companies by statute.

The need for financial information

The fundamental nature of the limited liability company, particularly the separation of management from ownership and its assumed indefinite life, creates the requirement that its shareholders should obtain some measure of protection from possible unscrupulous managers who may be tempted to exploit the gap which exists between the two groups; to their advantage, but to the disadvantage of the shareholders. This problem has been recognized for many years in most countries where limited liability companies exist, and the solution prescribed has generally been the regular provision of periodic financial information for shareholders.

In the UK, this is provided for by the regulations contained in the Companies Acts 1948, 1967, 1976, 1980 and 1981 which include detailed provisions relating to the annual financial statements describing company profitability and financial position, based on adequate accounting records, and provided for shareholders and debenture holders. In addition, if the companies are regulated by the Stock Exchange, their shareholders will receive interim summary financial statements of profitability and financial position during the period between receipt of the annual statements. The City Code on Takeovers and Mergers also requires companies (namely, quoted public companies) to provide shareholders with sufficient financial information with which to assess and decide upon the financial and other arrangements connected with a proposed takeover or merger with which their companies are involved.

Thus, shareholders and, additionally, debenture holders, are provided with regular financial information intended to increase their knowledge of their company's business and financial affairs. Because full annual financial statements of certain companies, and modified statements of other companies, are legally required to be filed with the Registrar of Companies, such information effectively becomes public information and allows other interested persons and institutions to gain access to data about a company's financial progress and position. In recent years, however, company employees have increasingly been formally recognized as another group which could be disadvantaged if financial information were not disclosed to it by company management. Consequently, the Employment Protection Act 1975 and the Industry Act 1975 both contain provisions (subject to certain limitations) requiring information to be disclosed to trade unions for the purpose of collective bargaining and good industrial relations. The Industry Act also gives the government the right of access to financial information when the Minister for Trade and Industry believes this to be necessary.

Corporate business activity

Before proceeding to describe the main financial statements which are produced in response to the afore-mentioned information needs and requirements, it is important to note the underlying business activity which is being described in financial accounting terms. To do this, use is made of the diagrams in Illustrations 4 and 5 below.

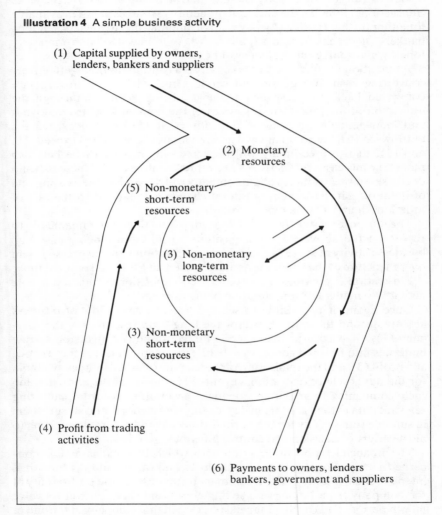

Illustration 4 A simple business activity

(1) Capital supplied by owners, lenders, bankers and suppliers

(2) Monetary resources

(5) Non-monetary short-term resources

(3) Non-monetary long-term resources

(3) Non-monetary short-term resources

(4) Profit from trading activities

(6) Payments to owners, lenders bankers, government and suppliers

As the above diagram reveals, the operational business activity of a company is essentially a continuous flow of transactions – (1) capital is supplied in varying forms by owners, lenders, bankers and suppliers, thus providing (2) the monetary resources and facilities to enable (3) various non-monetary resources to be acquired for trading activity (some with a long-term life and some of a short-term nature). By using these long-term resources to bring the short-term resources to a proper condition for sale, the company (4) can sell the latter for a profit, eventually (5) converting the previous non-monetary resources into a larger amount of monetary resources (larger, that is, by the amount of profit earned on the sales transactions). Finally, the enlarged monetary resources are then available for either further trading (2), payment of amounts due to owners, lenders, bankers, government and suppliers (6), or renewal of non-monetary long-term resources as they wear out (3).

As mentioned above, business activity is a continuous flow – effectively converting cash into goods and services for sale which, in turn, are converted back into cash again, this all being achieved through the utilization of the long-term resources of the company by its employees and management. So long as the inflows at (1) and (4) exceed the outflows at (6), the company will grow in money terms. If (6) exceeds (1) and (4), then the company will be decreasing in size. (Whether such monetary increases or decreases are representative of real increases and decreases in the resources of the company will depend on the existing rate of inflation – if the monetary rate of change is greater than the rate of inflation, there will be a real increase.)

The purpose of the financial reporting function in companies is to report on the above flow and position – profitability being based on business activity at stage (4), and financial position being expressed as an overall picture of the complete activity 'frozen' at a selected point of time.

Illustration 5 provides a more detailed exposition of this reportable activity – a manufacturing situation being assumed.

Once again, it is possible to see the 'cash to cash' flow of business activity around the central core of the long-term resources of the company (1). Of particular relevance is the continuous conversion of raw materials into finished goods for sale (2), the eventual sale of these goods at a profit (3), and the realization of the sales into cash resources available for the next cycle of operational events. It is the job of the accountant in such companies to maintain adequate accounting records: capturing relevant data as they arise from day-to-day transactions, and storing them in suitable totals ready for the periodic internal and external reporting to aid a variety of decision and control functions.

The financial reporting function with which this text is mainly concerned is the annual one to shareholders and others and, as such, it is intended mainly to describe in summary terms only (a) the profitability of the company from buying and selling goods and services over a twelve month period, and (b) the financial position of that company at the end of such a period. In other words, no matter how small or large the company, and no matter how simple or complex its business activity, the end-of-period financial statements must be capable of summarizing such activity

Illustration 5 A more complex business activity

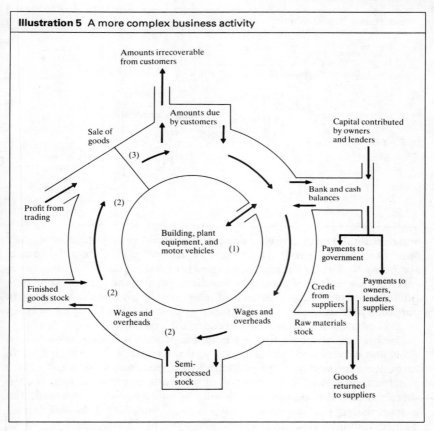

in a relatively few words and figures, using a relatively few accounting conventions and practices. This requires the existence of an effective and efficient accounting function within the company.

The accounting function

The accounting function of a company is the mechanism whereby the detail and volume of its business activity is translated into financial accounting terms in order to produce relevant financial statements and reports. As Illustration 6 seeks to demonstrate, it contains six main sub-functions, three of which can be described as data processing (or bookkeeping), and three of which can be described as information processing (or accounting).

Thus, the business activity of the company, at least of the type described in Illustrations 4 and 5, would give rise to a series of technical exercises designed to produce information of use to the persons inside

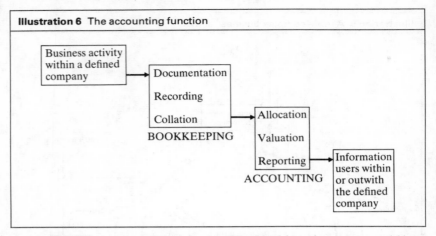

Illustration 6 The accounting function

and outside the company who need it. The bookkeeping stage would be a purely mechanical process to document, record and collate suitable data according to certain generally accepted processing rules (that is, double-entry bookkeeping). This can be handled either manually or by machine (including computers). Although it may provide limited data for control purposes (for example, cash balances or sales totals), the bookkeeping stage is only the foundation required for the accounting stage.

The process of accounting is a complex process requiring professional skills and experience to be brought to it to ensure that the recipients of accounting information are presented with statements and reports of a suitable type and quality. In terms of reporting to external users such as shareholders, the nature and quality of the required information is determined, in part, by statutes such as the Companies Acts, and, in part, by professional accounting recommendations and standards.

The reporting accountant will adhere to these matters when he is preparing the information – that is, when he (a) allocates the recorded data to defined periods of time and selected activities and entities (for example, he may wish to report on the profits of a particular subsidiary company for the six months ending 31 July 1980, in which case he will have to allocate the relevant data for that entity and period); (b) values certain data arising from the allocation process (for example, the inventory of goods on hand in the subsidiary at 31 July 1980); and (c) reports to the eventual users of the information in a form and according to conventions and standards which are believed to be acceptable for the purpose (for example, by presenting a detailed statement of profit for the six months to 31 July 1980). Each of these stages is fraught with diffculties and problems, and it is hoped that the reader will find that the remaining chapters in this text provide a useful appreciation of these matters. Meantime, attention is being given to a major source of information for shareholders and other external users – the annual financial report.

Annual financial reports

At least once every year, UK companies are legally required to present to their shareholders and debenture holders information of their annual financial results. This normally takes the form of a comprehensive report which can be divided conveniently into several distinct sections: (a) the introduction to the financial results; (b) an overview of the financial results; (c) the main financial statements; and (d) the back-up reports to the main financial statements. Derived from the annual report of a large UK public company, Illustration 7 summarizes its structure in these four areas. It should be noted that the amount of detail given in this illustration will vary in practice from company to company – smaller companies tending to present less detailed statements than larger ones. The structure is therefore not intended to convey universal application to the reader.

Introduction to financial results

The notice calling the members to the annual general meeting of the company is legally required and intimates the agenda for such a meeting (including the receipt and adoption of the annual report, the declarations of dividends, and the appointment and reappointment of directors of the company). The list of directors of the company usually gives no more than their names, and whether they hold any named directorial position (such as chairman or managing director). As an information source about directors, therefore, it is of little use.

The summary of financial results for the year is the first indication in the report of how the company has fared in accounting terms. Typically, it will contain figures relating to sales and profits for the year, as well as certain key indicators of performance such as profits per share and dividends per share. Finally, the financial calendar (if given) relates to the dates at which interim and year-end financial results will be announced, and when interim and final dividends will be paid.

The Chairman's report

The chairman's report is included in the financial reports of most companies although, in the UK, it is not legally required to be presented. Its contents are mainly non-quantitative and normally include a review of the year's operations and financial results; particular comments on important projects or parts of the company; news of recent developments; and comments on the progress of the company within the economic, social and political environments prevailing.

For example, in relation to the annual report from which Illustration 7 was derived, the chairman in his latest report covered such matters as the substantial increase in sales and profits which justified a larger dividend to shareholders than in previous years; the specific objectives which can

Illustration 7 Structure of an annual report

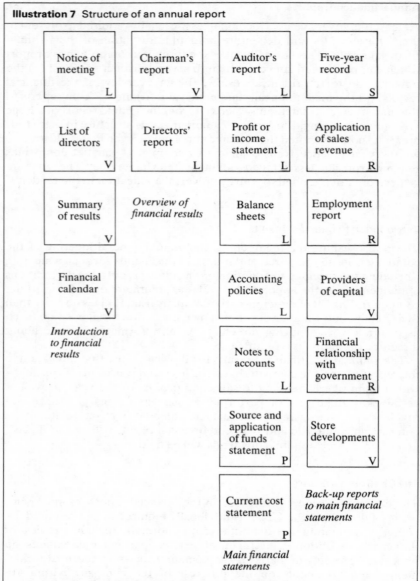

Notice of meeting — L	Chairman's report — V	Auditor's report — L	Five-year record — S
List of directors — V	Directors' report — L	Profit or income statement — L	Application of sales revenue — R
Summary of results — V	*Overview of financial results*	Balance sheets — L	Employment report — R
Financial calendar — V		Accounting policies — L	Providers of capital — V
Introduction to financial results		Notes to accounts — L	Financial relationship with government — R
		Source and application of funds statement — P	Store developments — V
		Current cost statement — P	*Back-up reports to main financial statements*
		Main financial statements	

L = legally required to be reported (as determined by the provisions of the Companies Acts 1948, 1967, 1976, 1980 and 1981).
P = professionally required to be reported (by main accountancy bodies).
R = recommended to be reported (by main accountancy bodies).
S = required to be reported by the London Stock Exchange.
V = voluntarily reported by the company.

only be met if profits are made (for example, quality of goods and services, expansion of operating facilities, and good wages, salaries, pensions and dividends); the care and attention paid by the company to customers and employees; improvements and changes in the goods and services offered to customers; the new operating facilities opened during the year; and the ways in which the company attempted to meet its social responsibilities (in fields such as medicine, art, education and community development).

The contents of the chairman's report are not subject to any verification or attestation by the company's independent auditor. The quantity and quality of the information contained in it will therefore very much depend on the attitude and expertise of the chairman concerned. Some chairmen are less communicative than others, the main fear being the disclosure of information which may be beneficial to a competitor or to a potential acquirer of the company concerned.

The directors' report

The directors' report is a legally required statement in the UK, where the board of directors of a company must give annual information to its shareholders on such matters as significant changes in the company's assets; details of the acquisition by the company of its own shares; company turnover from trading; political and charitable donations; dividend recommendations; names of directors; and directors' holdings in share and loan capital (if not disclosed in the main financial statements). However, the main provisions concern the directors' duty to give a 'fair' review of the development and position of the company, including important events which have occurred since its reporting date; likely future developments; and research and development activities (no definition is given in the Companies Acts of the term 'fair'). Thus, in this statement, shareholders should not only be given interpretive information about past activities, they should also be kept informed about events and activities which have taken or may take place beyond the reporting date of the company. Unlike the chairman's report, there is a legal obligation to have this information verified by the company auditor, his specific responsibility being to observe that it is consistent with the information in the main financial statements and, if it is not, to report this finding in his report to the shareholders.

The main financial statements

The financial statements which companies are legally required to present to their shareholders and debenture holders are, in general terms, the profit statement (hereafter termed the income statement) and the balance sheet. The income statement, as the term suggests, is a fairly detailed report on the overall profits of the company for the defined year. It is supported by a period-end balance sheet summarizing the company's financial position in terms of its accountable resources and obligations at that date. Both these statements are traditionally based on the original values attributable to the underlying transactions, and thus, in these circumstances, the balance sheet will not be described in contemporary terms, and the income statement will only report on profits which have been realized through sale.

For a single reporting company, the income statement and balance sheet are regarded as sufficient, but for a company which owns or controls other companies the situation is somewhat more complex. A holding company is required to produce an income statement and balance sheet relating to its own financial affairs and trading activity, but it must also present an income statement and balance sheet reflecting the aggregate affairs and activity of the group of companies as a whole – that is, inclusive of the financial results of its subsidiaries. These latter financial statements are usually described in the UK as the consolidated income statement and balance sheet. In practice, owing to the accounting techniques of consolidation, it is possible to present the income statement information of a holding company and its group in one statement. Thus the normal practice with a group of companies is to present a consolidated income statement (which incorporates that of the holding company), a holding company balance sheet and a consolidated balance sheet.

The form and content of income statements and balance sheets of companies are legally prescribed, and the information contained in each of these essential statements is legally required to be 'truthfully' and 'fairly' reported, and must be verified and attested by an independent professional accountant (or firm of accountants) appointed as company auditor. The auditor's report should be attached to the reported financial statements.

In addition to these main financial statements, companies must disclose certain other statements in support of them. For example, the notes to the accounts are a legally required series of detailed notes supporting individual accounting figures in the income statement and balance sheet. As such, they prevent the latter from becoming incomprehensible because of the amount of detail disclosed and, consequently, are effectively part of these main statements and thereby subject to audit. The statement of accounting policies is a legally and professionally required report of the main accounting practices and procedures utilized by the reporting accountants when preparing the main financial statements. The reader of these statements is therefore provided with a guidance statement on the way in which the information has been prepared.

Although the income statement provides a picture of periodic profitability of the reporting company, it does not give a complete indication of all the changes which have occurred in its financial position and structure. The source and application of funds statement is designed to fill this gap.

It describes the periodic changes in all the reported resources and sources of finance of the company. It, too, is subject to audit, although this is professionally rather than legally prescribed.

Finally, as a result of recent professional accounting requirements, large quoted UK companies will provide an additional set of financial statements designed to account for the effects of inflation on trading operations and resources. These so-called current cost accounting statements describe periodic income after allowing for the current cost of resources consumed in operational activity, and financial position in terms of the current costs of the resources being held for use and resale at the period end. The auditor is professionally required to examine and report on these statements. However, all companies are legally entitled to present current cost accounting statements if they wish. Any company doing so is legally required to have the statements reported on by its auditor.

(The precise nature and content of all of these financial statements, together with the audit report, will be discussed separately later in this text. For this reason they have only been briefly described at this stage.)

Miscellaneous data

The last category of data in the typical financial report concerns a hodge-podge of miscellaneous items which companies report voluntarily. Practice varies considerably from company to company, but mainly concerns descriptions of company activities and trends of financial results over a number of years.

In the case of the company to which Illustration 7 refers, these descriptions are relatively extensive. There is a five-year statement of sales, profits, dividends and capital employed in the company which is required as a condition of its quotation on the London Stock Exchange. This is supported by a number of financial statements which have been suggested recently for reporting by the professional accountancy bodies in the UK – that is, (a) a statement of application of sales revenue, in which it is shown how much of the latter figure has gone to meet the cost of goods and services, employees' wages and pensions, local and national taxation, and dividends and interest, and how much has been retained in the business to aid its maintenance and expansion in the future; (b) an employment report providing details of employee numbers, income, profit sharing, welfare and pensions; and (c) a statement of the financial relationship of the company with government, in which is described the type and amount of taxes paid and collected by the company for government. Finally, the reporting company also provides voluntarily a detailed statement of the main providers of capital (including shareholders, debenture holders and banks), and a report of new developments during the reporting period in its main activity – retail stores.

Summary

Obviously much depends on the nature and size of the reporting company as to how much information is contained in its annual report. Generally speaking, the larger and more public the company, the more information it is likely to provide. Small, family-based companies, for example, may only produce the bare legal minimum of directors' report, income statement, balance sheet, notes to accounts and auditor's report. Large companies, on the other hand, can provide a substantial package containing many statements – the company in Illustration 7 disclosed nineteen major statements, extending over twenty-eight pages of report.

Increasingly, however, companies of all sizes are being required to disclose more information, not only because of expansion of statutory provisions in this respect, but also because of the increasing requirements of the major professional accountancy bodies. For example, in Illustration 7 it can be seen that, of the nineteen statements, seven were legally required, five were either professionally required or recommended, one was required by the Stock Exchange and the remaining six were voluntarily produced by the company. Thus, the typical UK annual report can be a complex document, describing the financial results of the company from a variety of different standpoints (for example, profits, financial position, funds flow, sales, government transactions and employees), and containing a mixture of legal and professional accounting regulations. It is to these matters that the remainder of this chapter will be directed.

Financial reporting concepts

The above brief description of company annual financial reports, which will be elaborated on later in this chapter, reveals a major source of financial information which is available to a variety of external report users at the present time. As Chapter 4 will reveal, it is a system which has been subject to a great deal of change over the years, despite being based on several concepts and conventions which have remained virtually unaltered until recent times.

First, such financial reports are essentially historical documents, describing the financial results of past company activity. Because of inevitable delays in gathering together the necessary accounting data, the information contained in a financial report is often much out of date when compared with the present situation of the company concerned. Despite this, little has been done over the years to provide information of a deliberately predictive nature in such reports (beyond the occasional vague forecast of activity made by company chairmen in their reports).

Secondly, annual financial reports have been, and still are, legally intended primarily for existing company shareholders. They must also be received by debenture holders irrespective of the provisions of their trust deed but, so far as other interested third parties are concerned, the statements are not legally intended for them. Despite this constraint, these latter persons can obtain and make use of them, particularly since they constitute the primary information source about companies and are available to the public (in full or modified form depending on the size of company) through the Registrar of Companies. In addition, as later sections of this text will demonstrate, the needs of employees and government which are not necessarily met in the annual report are being catered for in other ways – for example, in the Industry Act 1975.

Thirdly, because of the fundamental nature of accountants and accounting, coupled with experiences throughout the history of company financial reporting, the so-called conservatism convention has been for many decades an essential foundation to existing reporting practices. That is, when measuring and communicating accounting data, accountants have adopted reasonable caution, particularly when there is an obvious amount of uncertainty and subjectivity involved in determining the figures concerned.

This particular accounting approach has been in practice for many years, and has resulted in the application of two principles of accounting: (a) the historic cost valuation basis, whereby the accounting information contained in the reported financial statements is measured, in most instances, on the basis of the actual costs of the transactions concerned; and (b) the realization principle where, because of the historic cost basis, no cognisance is usually taken of profits or gains earned by the company until such time as they have been realized either in cash or near-cash terms. In other words, increases in the value of the resources of the company have not normally been accounted for until such time as these resources are realized. Somewhat in contradiction to this, however, value decreases have been accounted and reported before the point of realization, presumably because of the conservatism convention.

Fourthly, despite the conservatism of traditional reporting practice mentioned above, and because of high rates of change in the prices of resources, accountants have increasingly had to examine ways to cope with the effects of inflation as a major part of the financial reporting function of companies. This has resulted in a number of suggestions and recommendations in recent years – the most favoured approach involving an accounting for specific price changes as they arise (thus abandoning the historic cost and realization principles in the financial statements concerned).

Fifthly, the major emphasis in corporate reports has been on providing measures of profit and financial position, these presumably being regarded consistently as the most significant indicators of company performance. This emphasis remains today, although other financial aspects of companies are being reported – for example, its source and application of funds; and its relationships with employees and government.

And finally, wherever possible, accountants have attempted to measure the accounting information reported by companies as objectively as possible. Financial reports, as previously mentioned, are often the only formal financial communication between external interests and internal management, and therefore their credibility is especially important to their users. By ensuring that the information is based, as much as is feasible, on objective and verifiable evidence, the accountant attempts to maximize its credibility. In most developed countries, this concept of information credibility is supported in practice by the audit function – that is, the employment by the company of an independent and usually professionally qualified accountant (or firm of accountants) to examine and report on the quality of the reported information.

The concept of income

The term 'income' is used throughout this text and is synonymous with the alternative terms of 'profit' and 'earnings' so often used in accounting practice. It is felt that it is the one term likely to be accepted by all readers, for the term 'profit' has a particular accounting meaning which is materially different from the meaning given to it by say, economists. 'Income' is an all-embracing term, capable of including elements of gain or value increases.

At the present time, as for many years, the corporate financial reporting function has been centred around the concept of periodic income. For example, the importance of income within the business context is evidenced by its existence as a major business management objective: the maximization of profitability. Although this objective may not now have the same degree of support as it once had, owing to other economic, political and social matters achieving an increased importance to companies and their managers, it is generally assumed to be regarded by investors and other interested parties as an essential indicator of enterprise success or failure – that is, it is believed to be a useful yardstick of how well or badly company management has performed on behalf of its ownership, and can therefore be used as a major means of evaluating the soundness or otherwise of such a performance.

In traditional accounting terms, income is a periodic measure of the difference between an aggregate of the revenues received from the 'sale' of goods or services by a company and a corresponding aggregate of the various costs incurred by it in order to make these sales. In this sense, the net figure, which is reported in the income statement, is a distillation of many significant events and factors which have taken place during a designated period. The accountant will therefore usually define income as a financial gain arising from various buying and selling transactions.

This can be demonstrated in a simple example in Illustration 8. It reveals that, ignoring new contributions of capital or equivalent withdrawals, the effect of income is to increase the economic resources of a company (assuming, of course, a stable price level). Income can therefore be identified, subject to the previously-mentioned qualification, as equi-

---

Illustration 8 Traditional accounting income and capital–1

Assume a very simple business situation. A company was formed at t_0 with capital of £1,000 represented by £1,000 of cash in the bank. It traded during the period t_0 to t_1 by buying and selling newspapers entirely on a cash basis. Its total sales for the period were £8,000, and the cost of newspapers and wages amounted to £6,000. Assuming no other transactions, the income for the period would be calculated as £8,000 − 6,000 = £2,000 (a matching of sales revenues with related costs for the same period). In addition, the cash in the bank will have increased from £1,000 to £3,000 over the period (£1,000 + 8,000 − 6,000), and the figure of £3,000 will now represent the capital of the company at t_1 (the original capital of £1,000 plus the income for the period of £2,000).

Note Because of the simplifying assumption made in this example, there is an inference that income is equivalent to the increase in cash resources. This is the case in this example; it is rarely the case in practice due to credit and other transactions.

---

valent to the periodic increase in the net wealth of the company concerned – in this case, from £1,000 to £3,000. However, much depends on how wealth is defined for reporting purposes, and particularly on how it is valued. Suffice to say at the present stage of the discussion that the value placed upon company resources, and thus on capital, determines the level of reported income, and that differing values will give differing income figures.

The concepts of capital and value

Having stated that accounting income is a residual and temporal measure, usually taken as indicative of company operational success or failure, and which in some way is related to capital and capital value, it is important to state what is meant by capital and value.

During its lifetime, a company will spend money to acquire various goods and services essential to its business activity and to its ultimate survival. Thus, it buys stocks of goods, pays for wages and overheads, purchases plant and machinery, and so on. It finances these acquisitions with monies received from shareholders, lenders and bankers, by credit facilities afforded to it by suppliers, and by earning income from trading which can be 'ploughed back' into the business. Much of the expenditure (for example, on goods, wages and overheads) can be attributed immediately to the measurement of periodic income, being set off or matched against relevant revenues from sales (as was seen in Illustration 8). The remainder, however, is of more long-term benefit to the company, representing resources which it requires to trade or manufacture (for example, buildings, plant or motor vehicles). The aggregate value of these resources, minus any loans and other medium and short-term financing, is equivalent to the measure of shareholders' capital in the company (that is, original subscribed capital plus income retained in the business). This is often described as shareholders' equity, and appears as such in the reported balance sheet. Illustration 9 provides an example of these distinctions.

Illustration 9 Traditional accounting income and capital–2

Assume the same situation given in Illustration 8 with the following amendment – during the period t_0 to t_1, the company purchased a shop for £4,000, financing this acquisition partly by a building society loan of £2,500 and partly by cash of £1,500. Thus, at t_2, the company would have the following resources – a shop which cost £4,000 and cash in the bank of £1,500 (the equivalent figure of £3,000 in Illustration 8 being reduced by £1,500 because of the purchase of the shop) – a total of £5,500. If the building society loan is deducted from this figure (5,500–£2,500), the difference of £3,000 represents the capital of the company as computed in Illustration 8.

The importance of value in the measurement of capital can now be seen more clearly. First, the distinction between expenditure of a long-term nature and that which can be matched immediately against sales revenues is vital to the determination of shareholders' capital and periodic income. Secondly, the value placed upon the resources designated as having long-term use to a company will determine the value of its shareholders' capital. As measured income is a product of the periodic change in the value of such capital then it, too, depends greatly on the values placed upon the underlying resources. It is therefore with these problems of resource valuation, capital valuation and income measurement that the corporate financial accounting and reporting function has to cope. Illustration 10 provides an example of these points.

Illustration 10 Traditional accounting income and capital–3

Assuming the situation and figures arrived at in Illustration 9, what would the position be if the shop were revalued at t_2 to a figure of £5,700? The company's total resources would then be £5,700 plus the cash balance of £1,500, a total of £7,200. Deducting the loan of £2,500, the net figure of £4,700 represents the company's capital – that is, the original capital at t_1 of £1,000 plus the income of the period of £2,000 plus the revaluation surplus on the shop of £1,700 (£5,700–4,000).

In other words, the end-of-period capital of £4,700 was dependent on (a) treating the acquisition of the shop as a long-term resource and not as an expense of the period to be matched against sales; and (b) valuing the shop at £5,700. In addition, the periodic increase in capital from £1,000 at t_0 to £4,700 at t_1 was dependent in part on the value placed on the shop at t_1. Therefore, if income can be regarded as a derivitive of capital value, it is reasonable to suggest that its measurement depends very much on what is treated as capital (and the resources underlying it) and how the latter is valued. This will be seen more clearly in the next chapter dealing with the nature and structure of traditional financial statements.

Reference

1   J. A. Lillie, *The Mercantile Law of Scotland*, Longmans Green, 1956, p. 316.

Suggested discussion or essay topics; and selected bibliography

Because of the inter-relationship of the topics in Chapters 1, 2 and 3, this material is provided at the end of Chapter 3.

2
The traditional financial statements*

The traditional balance sheet

The traditional company balance sheet is a statement of the resources of a company mainly valued on the basis of their original transacted cost, compared with the means by which they have been financed by its shareholders, lenders, bankers, suppliers and income retentions. It is therefore a report on its financial position at one particular point in time – a still photograph of company financial affairs, expressed in accounting terms. Thus, at the end of each financial reporting period, a company will hold certain resources capable of being measured in accounting terms; owe certain sums of money given to it by way of loan, overdraft, or credit; and have its shareholders' interest represented by subscribed capital and retained income. The measured resources represent the various ways in which the funds made available to a company have been employed. By definition, therefore, the sources and employment of funds must equate, and this is represented by the identity

$$L = A \dotfill (1)$$

where $L =$ the liabilities or obligations of the company to its owners, lenders, bankers and creditors; and $A =$ the assets or resources of the company which have been identified and accounted for as such.

This is then the basic financial relationship which is reflected in every reported balance sheet, and Illustration 11 provides a very simple example of it.

Illustration 11 The accounting identity–1

Assume a company has accounted for total assets of £10,000 at t_2. It will therefore also have to account for the £10,000 of liabilities which have financed these resources. Thus, the simplest balance sheet for the company at t_2 would be:

COMPANY LTD

Balance Sheet as at t_2

	£		£
Total liabilities (L)	10,000	Total assets (A)	10,000

---

*The form and content of these statements is stipulated in Schedule 8, Companies Act 1948. In order to explain the structure and composition of these statements for the beginning reader, it has been impossible to adhere to the prescribed layout. However, at the end of the Chapter the completed illustrations are presented in a legally acceptable format.

However, this demands an explanation and definition of assets and liabilities.

The nature of assets

> Assets represent future economic benefits, rights to which have been acquired by the enterprise as the result of some current or past transactions.[1]

In other words, transactions which give rise to the right to expect some future economic benefit from 'properties' of one sort or another can be classified as assets of the company. If there is no likelihood of future benefits to be derived from them, they cannot be classified as assets and any relevant expenditure thereon should be matched against sales revenues when determining periodic income.

Assets can be tangible (for example, plant, machinery, stocks of goods and cash) or intangible (for example, goodwill represented by such factors as the skills of managers and workers, or a reputation for high-quality products; as well as patent rights, trademarks and copyrights). However, for accounting purposes, each must have been part of a past business transaction for which there can be an accounting. In other words, although a company may benefit from the use of public roads, it cannot regard them as reportable assets because they have not been purchased directly by it and there is no exclusive right to the economic benefits involved. Similarly, a company may have considerable goodwill which it has built up over the years but, unless it has formally purchased it from a third party, it would not normally be accounted for.

Fixed and current assets

Assets are usually divided into two main categories for reporting purposes: fixed assets and current assets. Fixed assets are those held for use rather than for resale – that is, assets which the company holds and intends to use on a continuing basis in order to receive economic benefits from their use in manufacture or trade. These would include land, buildings, plant, machinery, motor vehicles, office equipment, and investments in other companies. In traditional accounting practice, they are normally accounted for in terms of their original historic cost, although account is taken of the gradual expiry of their service potential from use and obsolescence. This takes the form of reductions in the original costs, which are then charged against sales revenues when measuring periodic income. This expense, which represents the partial expiry of the usefulness of fixed assets, is termed depreciation. The accounting treatment involved is simply an allocation and charge to income of the original cost of the fixed assets concerned over their useful life. Fixed assets are therefore normally described in the traditional balance sheet at their original cost minus any depreciation written off against sales revenues. Occasionally, companies find it necessary to revalue certain fixed assets, such as land and buildings, in which case they will be reported in the traditional balance sheet at the revalued figure.

Current assets are those assets held by the company for resale and not intended for use on a continuing basis, and are therefore either in the form of cash or resources which can be reasonably expected to be converted into cash in the relatively near future. Included in this category would be stocks of goods (including any work-in-progress), debtors (amounts owed by credit customers), short-term investments of cash surplus to requirements, and bank balances. In the case of stocks, the traditional valuation basis is original cost, although damaged or obsolete stock is often included at its realizable value. Debtors are usually recorded at their expected realizable value minus any allowances for bad or doubtful debts, but investments may well be expressed in original cost terms.

In certain instances, companies find it difficult to classify particular assets as either fixed or current. A frequent example is the intangible asset, goodwill, which, if it has been acquired from a third party, can be treated as a fixed asset, but equally can be disclosed in the balance sheet under a separate category which is neither fixed nor current. Company law in the UK prescribes that such intangible assets should be classified as fixed assets.

Thus, taking the right-hand side of the identity (1) above, it can now be expanded as follows:

$$A = F + C \dots\dots\dots\dots\dots\dots\dots\dots\dots\dots\dots (2)$$

where $F =$ fixed assets of both a tangible and intangible nature; and $C =$ current assets. Illustration 12 represents this in figure terms.

Illustration 12 The accounting identity–2

Expanding the data given in Illustration 11 at t_2, the balance sheet might appear as follows:

COMPANY LTD

Balance Sheet as at t_2

Liabilities	£	*Assets*	£
Total liabilities (L)	10,000	Fixed assets (F)	6,000
		Current assets (C)	4,000
	10,000		10,000

This leaves total liabilities of £10,000 to be explained but, before doing this, the concept and disclosure of fixed asset depreciation ought to be further illustrated. As previously mentioned, depreciation represents the gradual allocation of a committed cost over the useful life of the asset concerned; the various allocations being matched against sales revenue and deducted from the cost as it appears in the balance sheet. Thus, say the net figure for total fixed assets of £6,000 is composed of the following data – £5,000 for plant and £1,000 for an investment in a subsidiary company. If the plant had been purchased at t_1 for £6,000 with an estimated life of six periods and an eventual nil scrap value, then depreciation for the period t_1 to t_2 could be calculated at $\frac{1}{6}$ of £6,000 or £1,000 – giving a net balance sheet figure of £5,000. Similarly, if the investment had been bought at t_0 for £1,000, and it had not been depreciated by t_2, then the total net figure for fixed assets at that point would be £6,000 (£5,000 + 1,000). This is summarized in the traditional company balance sheet as follows (see Illustration 13).

Illustration 13 The accounting identity–3

COMPANY LTD

Balance Sheet as at t_2

Liabilities	£	*Assets*		£
Total liabilities (L)	10,000	Fixed assets at cost		7,000
		Less: aggregate depreciation		1,000
			(F)	6,000
		Current assets (C)		4,000
	10,000			10,000

Note: There are several ways of calculating depreciation, and these will be mentioned later in the text. The practice used above in relation to plant is entitled the straight-line method – that is, a fixed amount of the net cost of the fixed asset concerned (net of the anticipated eventual sale proceeds) is written off against sales revenue in each period of its estimated useful life. In the above example, £1,000 would be written off in each period for six periods. If the original cost had been £6,000, the anticipated sale proceeds £1,000, and the estimated life two periods, then the net cost of £5,000 (£6,000–1,000) would be written off over two periods – that is, £2,500 in each period.

It should be further noted that the illustrations in this section to date have not demonstrated the writing off of depreciation against sales revenue. In fact, this will have been done in arriving at the Total Liabilities figure of £10,000, and the identification of the depreciation write-off will be made when the latter is appropriately examined in relation to income retained in the company.

Liabilities

Liabilities are obligations to convey assets or perform services, obligations resulting from past or current transactions and requiring settlement in the future.[2]

In other words, liabilities are accounting measurements intended to represent amounts owing to persons and bodies outwith a company, including its shareholders. This section will deal only with non-shareholding obligations, and these can be divided into three main categories – provisions (representing liabilities which are likely or certain to be incurred but cannot be determined with accuracy; for example, pensions for employees, and taxation); medium to long-term liabilities (representing amounts which will require to be repaid by the company over a relatively long period of time – say, repayable after more than one year; for example, debenture loans and mortgage loans); and current liabilities (representing amounts due for repayment by the company in the relative short-term – say, repayable in less than one year; for example, credit suppliers (termed creditors), bank overdrafts, dividends proposed, and taxation liabilities). The last two categories of liability are accounted for in terms of the amounts arising from the original transactions concerned. It should be noted, however, that liabilities are transitory items – provisions may become either long-term, medium-term or current liabilities when the amounts due can be determined accurately; and long-term and medium-term liabilities may require to be reclassified as current liabilities as they near their dates of repayment. Equally, current liabilities, which are permitted by the provider of finance to remain outstanding, may require to be treated as medium or long-term (for example, bank overdrafts).

Thus, expanding the left-hand side of identity (1) above:

$$L = E + M + S \dots\dots\dots\dots\dots\dots\dots\dots\dots\dots\dots (3)$$

where E = shareholders' equity (to be explained in the next section); M = medium and long-term liabilities; and S = short-term or current liabilities. Illustration 14 incorporates these definitions in an expansion of the 'Total liabilities' figure used in previous illustrations. For purposes of simplifying explanations throughout the remainder of this text, the identity omits provisions from its explanation of liabilities.

Illustration 14 The accounting identity–4

COMPANY LTD

Balance Sheet as at t_2

Liabilities	£	Assets		£
Shareholders' equity (E)	5,000	Fixed assets at cost		7,000
Medium and long-term		Less: aggregate depreciation		1,000
liabilities (M)	2,000			
Current liabilities (S)	3,000		(F)	6,000
		Current assets (C)		4,000
	10,000			10,000

Shareholders' equity

> Owners' equity is represented by the amount of the residual interest in the assets of an enterprise.[3]

In other words, when deducting the liabilities of a company from its aggregate assets, the net figure is representative of the shareholders' interest in it. This interest is composed of a variety of items – the share capital attributable to the various classes of shareholders; income which has been retained rather than distributed by way of dividend to the shareholders; and sundry other amounts which represent surpluses belonging to the shareholders (for example, asset revaluation surpluses).

Share capital is normally measured on the basis of monies received (or due to be received) from shareholders. It may, however, have been augmented by the translation of income retained in the company or other surpluses into shares; that is, by bonus shares issued to shareholders without further payment on their part. It may also include share issues made in exchange for the acquisition of, or merger with, other companies: for example, when companies or business assets are acquired or merged, the transaction may be satisfied by the issue of shares in the acquiring company, rather than by payment by cash. Share capital arising in these various ways can be described as called up capital.

Share capital figures disclosed in the balance sheet may not represent the full amount paid or assumed to be paid by shareholders. Shares are often issued to shareholders as partly paid up, the remaining monies due being receivable at a later date. The figure representing share capital in the balance sheet, therefore, is that for which shares have been issued irrespective of what has been received. Amounts unreceived are disclosed as an asset in the balance sheet. Called up capital should be distinguished from the authorized share capital figure which appears as a note to the balance sheet, and represents the maximum share capital which the reporting company can issue to its shareholders.

Reserves which form part of shareholders' equity consist mainly of undistributed income which has been realized as part of operational and trading activity. However, it is usually aggregated with other non-trading surpluses (for example, realized gains from the sale of assets such as land and buildings or investments; unrealized gains resulting from the revaluation of certain assets of a similar nature; and sums received from shareholders in excess of the stated nominal value of the share units – that is, share premiums).

Thus, again expanding the left-hand side of identity (1):

$$E = I + R \dots\dots\dots\dots\dots\dots\dots\dots\dots\dots (4)$$

where I = called up share capital; and R = reserves – the term used to cover the above mentioned retained income and surpluses. Identity (4) can be further expanded if it is recognized that the figure for retained income is, in fact, composed of two elements: retained income of the current period to which the balance sheet refers, and aggregate retained income of previous periods. All these points can be seen in Illustrations 15, 16 and 17.

Illustration 15 The accounting identity–5

COMPANY LTD

Balance Sheet as at t_2

Liabilities	£	Assets	£
Called up share capital (I)	2,000	Fixed assets at cost	7,000
Reserves (R)	3,000	*Less:* aggregate depreciation	1,000
	5,000	(F)	6,000
Medium and long-term liabilities (M)	2,000	Current assets (C)	4,000
Current liabilities (S)	3,000		
	10,000		10,000

Illustration 15 demonstrates the split in shareholders' equity between share capital and reserves. Illustration 16 analyses further the composition of the reserves figure.

Illustration 16 The accounting identity–6

COMPANY LTD

Balance Sheet as at t_2

Liabilities	£	£	Assets	£
Called up share capital		2,000	Fixed assets at cost	7,000
Reserves:			*Less:* aggregate	
Share premium	500		depreciation	1,000
Retained income:				6,000
Previous periods	1,300			
Current period	1,200	3,000		
		5,000	Current assets	4,000
Medium and long-term liabilities		2,000		
Current liabilities		3,000		
		10,000		10,000

The analysis of shareholders' equity into its constituent parts is shown in Illustration 16. Obviously, these parts will vary according to the particular circumstances of the company concerned but, for purposes of this text, it has been assumed that the company has issued its share capital at a premium (assuming the share units to be £1 units, then 2,000 units have been issued at £1.25 each: the 25p premium being treated as a reserve of £500 in aggregate). In addition, Illustration 16 reminds the reader of the split between retained income of previous periods and retained income of the current period – the latter figure being the subject of further scrutiny later in this chapter.

Illustration 17 The accounting identity–7

COMPANY LTD

Balance Sheet as at t_2

Liabilities	£	£	Assets	£
Called up share capital		3,000	Fixed assets at cost	7,000
Reserves:			*Less:* aggregate	
Share premium	—		depreciation	1,000
Retained income:				
Previous periods	800			6,000
Current period	1,200	2,000		
		5,000	Current assets	4,000
Medium and long-term				
liabilities		2,000		
Current liabilities		3,000		
		10,000		10,000

In Illustration 17, it has been assumed that the company has made a bonus issue of shares to its shareholders at t_2. The bonus is one share for every two held, thereby increasing the issued share capital from 2,000 £1 units to 3,000 £1 units. The means by which this has been done is to convert the share premium account of £500, and £500 of retained income, into an additional £1,000 of share capital – thereby reducing share premium and retained income by £500 in each case.

The expanded identity

Taking the opening identity (1) of $L = A$, this can now be re-expressed, in light of all of the above comments, as

$$I + R + M + S = F + C \dotfill (6)$$

This then is a simplified model of the company balance sheet; and it is usually found that the accounting data contained in such a financial statement fall into these various categories. It need not, of course, be presented in a form equivalent to identity (6), as this can be rearranged without interfering with the basic relationship. For example, it could be

$$I + R + M = F + (C - S) \dotfill (7)$$

(In this case, short-term liabilities are set against current assets to produce a net current assets aggregate which can be used as a measure of a company's liquidity position – the net figure is often termed working capital.) Or it could be

$$I + R = F + (C - S) - M \dots\dots\dots\dots\dots\dots\dots\dots (8)$$

(In this case, the emphasis is entirely on the interests of the shareholders in the company – that is, reflecting the net assets which support the interests of ownership.)

Illustration 18 represents the balance sheet of a single company. It provides more detail than hitherto of the various categories of assets and liabilities discussed above, but it is presented in summary form, and is not intended to comply with the legal requirements for disclosure which will be discussed later. It is based on the previous illustrations used in this chapter.

Illustration 18 The traditional accounting balance sheet–1

COMPANY LTD

Balance Sheet as at t_2

Liabilities	t_1 £	t_2 £	Assets	t_1 £	t_2 £
Shareholders' equity			*Fixed assets*		
Called up share			Plant at cost	—	6,000
capital	2,000	3,000	*Less:* aggregate		
Reserves:			depreciation	- -	1,000
Share premium	500	—			5,000
Retained income	1,300	2,000	Investment in	—	
	3,800	5,000	in subsidiary		
			company at cost	1,000	1,000
Long-term liability				1,000	6,000
Bank loan	—	2,000			
Current liabilities			*Current assets*		
Creditors	1,100	1,500	Stock	1,800	2,500
Taxation	1,000	1,200	Debtors	600	800
Dividend proposed	200	300	Cash in bank	2,700	700
	2,300	3,000		5,100	4,000
	6,100	10,000		6,100	10,000

Several matters in Illustration 18 require some further comment in order to complete the reader's introduction to the traditional balance sheet based on historic costs: (a) the balance sheet should always remain in 'balance' whatever transactions and adjustments are made to it (that is, the fundamental identity of assets equating with the sources of finance funding them should always remain); (b) the amount of information disclosed in a balance sheet can be voluminous, and the use of notes to the accounts will be seen in practice in order to allow only summarized aggregate data to be disclosed in the balance sheet, with the supporting detail in the notes (in the above example, the detail was not complex enough to require such supporting disclosures); (c) it is legally required that companies provide comparative figures for the previous period, and this has been shown in the above example; and (d) the above financial statement is of the financial position only of a single company – an income statement and (because it is a holding company) a group balance sheet would also be prepared, and the following sections will describe these statements in detail.

The group balance sheet

The reporting treatment applicable to a group of companies is illustrated in Illustration 19. A group balance sheet is presented by taking the balance sheet of the holding company (the figures are based on those in Illustration 18) and substituting the net assets of the subsidiary at the same, or approximately the same, reporting date for the figure £1,000 for 'investment in subsidiary company' (the relevant balance sheet of the subsidiary is shown in Illustration 19 prior to the consolidated statement; it is assumed that the holding company has acquired 100 per cent of the subsidiary's share capital). The result is to inflate each of the main balance sheet categories by the appropriate and equivalent subsidiary company figures. In addition, if the cost of acquiring the subsidiary includes a figure representing its purchased goodwill, then this will also be incorporated in the group balance sheet.

It is not the intention of this book to explain in detail the accounting practices necessary to the production of a consolidated or group balance sheet. However, a number of comments seem pertinent in light of the above illustration.

(a) The figure for fixed assets, current assets, long-term liability and current liabilities are inclusive of data relevant to the subsidiary company – that is, they are based on simple aggregations of holding company and subsidiary company data.

(b) The goodwill figure is that part of the cost of the holding company's investment in its subsidiary representing intangible resources of the latter taken over by it. (In certain instances, it can also represent undervaluations of tangible assets taken over, if these value changes were unrecorded in the records of the subsidiary company.) In this case, the cost was £1,000 and the net assets of the subsidiary when acquired totalled £800 (represented by share capital £500 and reserves £300).

(c) Share capital is the called up capital of the holding company only. Owing to the inclusion of the subsidiary company's net assets in the group

The traditional financial statements

Illustration 19 The group balance sheet

SUBSIDIARY LTD
Balance Sheet as at t_2

Liabilities	t_1 £	t_2 £	Assets	t_1 £	t_2 £
Shareholders' equity			*Fixed assets*		
Called up share			Plant at cost	700	700
capital	500	500	Less: aggregate		
Retained income	400	600	depreciation	300	400
	900	1,100		400	300
Current liabilities			*Current assets*		
Creditors	400	400	Stock	200	600
Taxation	100	100	Debtors	200	200
			Cash in bank	600	500
	500	500		1,000	1,300
	1,400	1,600		1,400	1,600

The above balance sheet, when combined with that of the holding company (see Illustration 18) by means of various aggregations and cancellations, results in the following group balance sheet at t_2:

COMPANY LTD
Group Balance Sheet as at t_2

Liabilities	t_1 £	t_2 £	Assets	t_1 £	t_2 £
Shareholders' equity			*Fixed assets*		
Called up share			Goodwill	200	200
capital	2,000	3,000			
Reserves:					
Share premium	500	—	Plant at cost	700	6,700
Retained income	1,400	2,300	Less: aggregate		
			depreciation	300	1,400
	3,900	5,300		400	5,300
Long-term liability					
Bank loan	—	2,000		600	5,500
Current liabilities			*Current assets*		
Creditors	1,500	1,900	Stock	2,000	3,100
Taxation	1,100	1,300	Debtors	800	1,000
Dividend proposed	200	300	Cash in bank	3,300	1,200
	2,800	3,500		6,100	5,300
	6,700	10,800		6,700	10,800

balance sheet, it is not necessary to include its share capital as well; to do so would be to double count, and it is eliminated by cancellation in the adjustments commented on in note (b).

(d) The retained income figure includes the aggregate retained income for the subsidiary company belonging to the holding company since the date of its acquisition of the subsidiary. (In this case, reserves of the subsidiary were £300 when it was acquired; thus only £100 (£400−300) and £300 (£600−300) have been aggregated with the holding company's reserves at t_0 and t_1 respectively.)

(e) The above illustrations have assumed that the subsidiary is 100 per cent controlled. If control was less than 100 per cent, because not all of the share capital had been acquired, then the group balance sheet would reflect this by disclosing, separately, that part of the subsidiary company's share capital and retained income figure not belonging to the holding company. This would be shown as a group 'liability', presented between 'Shareholders' equity' and 'Long-term liabilities', and usually described as 'Minority interest in subsidiary company'. This would allow the assets and liabilities of the subsidiary to be fully aggregated despite the less than complete control of it by the holding company.

Summary

Summarizing therefore on the traditional company balance sheet, it is clear that it is a statement of financial position, expressed at one particular point of time, and measured in mainly historic cost terms. It is in no way a statement of the present value or market value of a company (or group of companies) as a whole, nor can it be said to be indicative of the market value of shares in the company. It is a record of past transactions giving rise to resources of use to the company in the future, coupled with a statement of the means by which these transactions have been financed. As it is a summary of financial position at one moment in a company's history, it is likely to become almost instantly out of date. For this reason, it requires to be read and used with great care.

The income statement

In one sense, despite its current importance to investors and other interested parties, the traditional income statement is simply a more detailed report on one particular aspect of the balance sheet – that is, the retained income figure for the current period. It is a description and an analysis of the periodic movement in the retained income figure from one balance sheet date to the next. As a source of information about company profitability, however, it is greatly valued by those persons who seek to judge this financial characteristic of company performance.

The traditional retained accounting income identity

Traditional retained accounting income can be identified as $R_a = s - c - t - d$; where s = sales revenues recognized and accounted for; c = various costs relevant to these sales which have been matched with them; t = taxation on the surplus arising from the matching of s and c; and d = dividends paid and proposed to be paid to shareholders. R_a is therefore equivalent to the change in R (reserves) in the balance sheet identity (6) (assuming no other movement in reserve items). As such, it is not the income of the period – that is, the total profits of the company after providing for all expenditures but before distributions to shareholders. Income should therefore be defined as $R_a + d$ or $s - c - t$.

Sales revenues (s) represent monies which have been received, or are about to be received, during the specified period from customers in return for goods and/or services from the company. In certain instances, sales may be recognized before the goods and services are complete or delivered to customers, as in the case of long-term contracts in the engineering industries. However, the normal practice is to recognize sales revenues only when there has been a realization or near-realization in cash terms.

Matched costs (c) are those items of expenditure which can be realistically related to the sales revenues recognized. They include the cost of goods and/or services sold (that is, in terms of raw materials, wages, overheads), as well as interest payments on loans, directors' remuneration, audit fees and so on. They also include depreciation written off fixed assets during the period (that is, the other leg of the adjustment already mentioned in relation to accounting for fixed asset costs in the company balance sheet).

The resultant surplus ($s - c$) represents income from trading operations, and can be augmented by income received from the company's various investments (if any). The total net surplus is used as the basis for computing the company's corporation tax liability. Once the latter figure is computed by applying existing tax laws and rules to the basic operating surplus figure, it is incorporated in the income statement as a deduction from trading income (the adjustments which are made to income for tax purposes mainly relate to items of expenditure which are deducted from sales revenue for reporting purposes but which may not be so deductable for tax purposes). The 'income after tax' figure is then used as a basis for determining the level of dividends to be distributed to shareholders.

The preference dividend (if any) is a fixed percentage of the appropriate share capital, whereas the ordinary or deferred dividends are percentages of capital which depend on the availability of measured income and cash resources; these are determined and proposed by the board of directors, and have to be agreed by the shareholders before they are paid. The computed dividends are deducted from the 'income after tax' figure, leaving a net figure of retained income for the period. This is then aggregated into the retained income figure being brought forward from previous periods.

The traditional income statement can therefore be regarded as a report of the ways in which the measured operational surplus for the period was appropriated; partly to the government by way of tax and partly to the shareholders by way of dividend, the remainder being retained in the company to allow for the necessary maintenance and expansion of its business activity. Illustrations 20 and 21 outline the main components of such a statement (assuming no investment income and no subsidiary companies in the first instance).

Illustration 20 The traditional income statement–1

Following the simple income identity given above of $s - c - t - d = R_a$, the very briefest of income statements to support the balance sheet used throughout Illustrations 11 to 18, inclusive, could appear as follows:

COMPANY LTD
Income Statement for Period t_1 to t_2

	t_0 to t_1 £	t_1 to t_2 £
Sales revenue for the period (s)	20,000	23,000
Less: total costs for the period (c)	17,500	20,300
Total income before tax	2,500	2,700
Less: taxation for the period (t)	1,000	1,200
Total income after tax	1,500	1,500
Less: dividend for the period (d)	200	300
Retained income for the period (R_a)	1,300	1,200

Note: The retained income figures above reconcile with the retained income figures in the balance sheets in Illustrations 11 to 18 as follows:

	t_1 £	t_2 £
Retained income for the period as above	1,300	1,200
Add: retained income for previous periods brought forward	—	1,300
	1,300	2,500
Less: retained income utilized in a bonus issue as per Illustration 18	—	500
Retained income as per balance sheet	1,300	2,000

The above statement, however, provides little information regarding the composition of the cost figures (c) of £17,500 and £20,300, and Illustration 20 can be expanded as follows in Illustration 21.

Illustration 21 The traditional income statement–2

COMPANY LTD
Income Statement for Period t_1 to t_2

	t_0 to t_1 £	t_1 to t_2 £
Sales revenue for the period	20,000	23,000
Less: cost of goods sold:		
stock of goods at beginning of period	2,000	1,800
add: purchase of goods during period	13,400	15,600
	15,400	17,400
less: stock of goods at end of period	1,800	2,500
	13,600	14,900
Gross trading income	6,400	8,100
Less: wages and salaries	2,200	2,300
depreciation of fixed assets	—	1,000
other business overheads	1,700	1,900
loan interest paid	—	200
	3,900	5,400
Total income before taxation	2,500	2,700
Less: taxation on income for the period	1,000	1,200
Total income after taxation	1,500	1,500
Less: dividend proposed for the period	200	300
Retained income for the period	1,300	1,200

Thus, the various expenses of the period can be categorized and suitably matched with sales revenue to arrive at various versions of traditional accounting income – gross trading income (the aggregate measure of the margin added to the cost of goods for sale in order to arrive at a sales price – this cost is determined on the basis of the goods sold and, as can be seen in the example above, allowance has to be made for beginning and end-of-period inventories of goods held ready for sale); income before taxation (arrived at after deducting all expenditures related to the operating of the business during the period concerned; including the cost of financing by borrowing, and the cost of utilizing the fixed assets of the business – the depreciation charge); income after taxation (full account having been made for the tax which will be payable on this period's income, this figure is effectively that upon which the distribution or dividend decision can be made by the board of directors and shareholders); and retained income (the income or profits which are being ploughed back into the business in order to renew and replenish its fixed assets and stocks once they have been used up or worn out, expand its facilities, and cope with the increased cost of replacing its assets during a period of inflation).

The above statement also highlights certain matters about traditional accounting (particularly) and income (generally) which ought to be introduced at this stage, and which will be amplified at various stages later in the text:

(a) The measured income of the period results from an appropriate matching of sales revenue with the cost of those goods and services sold; allowance being made for goods unsold by eliminating their cost from the matched cost of sales figure – for example, the above trading income for the period t_1 to t_2 is £8,100 (matching £14,900 of adjusted costs against revenues of £23,000) and not £7,400 (a figure which would result from a comparison of sales of £23,000 with purchases of £15,600, with no allowance being made for unsold stock at beginning and end of the period). Thus, 'like' is compared with 'like' – X units of sales are matched with the cost of these X units.

(b) The measurement of traditional accounting income is firmly based on the original or historic costs of the assets consumed in earning profits – that is, the cost of goods sold and the other business costs of the period (including depreciation of fixed assets) are based on data valuations which arose at the time of the transactions concerned. Essentially, this means that the use of historic costs results in a measurement of periodic income which describes the profits realized during the period rather than the profits earned during it. For example, the above retained income figures of £1,300 and £1,200 for periods t_0 to t_1 and t_1 to t_2, respectively, conform with this realization principle; they are the profits of these periods which have been realized through sale of goods – no measurement has been made for the profits which may have been earned but which are as yet unrealized on the stocks of goods held at t_1 and t_2. A very simple illustration may serve to clarify this important point, and reveal some of the underlying issues (see Illustration 22).

In this example, it can be demonstrated that, by revaluing closing stock at t_1 at its sale value, £500 of earned but unrealized income has been recognized in period t_0 to t_1 (the period in which the gain took place), and the remaining £400 was accounted for in period t_1 to t_2 (again the period in which it was earned – and also realized). In this way, the income of the period is no longer totally dependent on the realization of assets.

(c) A mixture of factual and judgemental material is utilized to produce traditional accounting income measures – as can be seen from the figures given in Illustration 21. For example, the data used in producing figures for sales, purchases, salaries and loan interest are reasonably factual, based on actual transactions and requiring little more than careful and accurate processing through the accounting system. With other data, however, adjustments require to be made which, although presumably expertly made, nonetheless are little more than personal judgements. In Illustration 21, these would relate to the valuation of stock, wages,

---

Illustration 22 The effect of the historic cost/realization principles

Assume a company buys 10 units of a particular good at t_0 for £1,000. Assume also that it holds these 10 units during period t_0 to t_1 (at t_1 their sale value is £1,500), and that it sold them for £1,900 at t_2. Under traditional accounting practice, the following would be the income for the two periods concerned (assuming no other transactions):

	t_0 to t_1 £		t_1 to t_2 £	
Sales revenue for the period		—		1,900
Less: cost of sales:				
stock of goods at beginning of period		—		1,000
add: purchases of goods during period	1,000		—	
	1,000		1,000	
less: stock of goods at end of period	1,000		—	
		—		1,000
Gross trading income		—		900

Thus, because no realization takes place until t_2, no recognition of income is made until then, and the entire transaction profit of £900 is accounted for in period t_1 to t_2 – irrespective of when that profit was earned or accrued. Period t_0 to t_1 is recorded as having no income on this transaction. However, if the realization principle is relaxed, historic costs abandoned as the basis for accounting, and periodic income recognized as it is earned, the following alternative picture emerges:

	t_0 to t_1 £		t_1 to t_2 £	
Sales revenue for the period		—		1,900
Less: value of stock held or sold:				
stock of goods at beginning of period		—		1,500
add: purchases of goods during period	1,000		—	
	1,000		1,500	
less: stock of goods at end of period	1,500		—	
		(500)		1,500
Gross trading income		500		400

pensions, business overheads, and depreciation of fixed assets. In each case, it can be seen that different figures for these items (different, that is, from those used in the example) would result in different figures for income. This is demonstrated in Illustration 23.

Without wishing to lead the reader into further accounting complications at this stage, it is useful to summarize Illustration 23 as follows:

(a) Entirely similar trading activities for period t_1 to t_2 could result in entirely different income figures describing them – originally, the 'income before tax' figure was £2,700; different accounting procedures have increased it to £3,900.

Illustration 23 Judgement and traditional accounting income

Assume that, for the period t_1 to t_2, £1,000 of wages and £1,000 of overheads could be attributed directly to putting stock in a proper condition for sale. Assume also that the stock at t_1 was valued at £2,400 (not £1,800) and that the stock at t_2 was valued at £4,500 (not £2,500) – in both cases, a proportion of total wages and overheads being allocated to stock valuation because it was believed such a proportion of these costs have been expended on the goods held for sale at those dates (a matter of judgement which becomes more obvious and acute when a manufacturing process is involved regarding stock). In addition, instead of providing for £1,000 of fixed asset depreciation ($\frac{1}{6}$ of the plant cost), management felt that it should be written off over five years – that is, $\frac{1}{5} \times$ £6,000 = £1,200 should be provided for. The effect of these changes on income for period t_1 to t_2 would be as follows:

COMPANY LTD
Income statement for Period t_1 to t_2

	£	Notes
Sales revenue for the period	23,000	
Less: cost of goods sold:		
stock of goods at beginning of period	2,400	(1)
add: purchase of goods during period	15,600	
wages and overheads expended on stock		
during period	2,000	(2)
	20,000	
less: stock of goods at end of period	4,500	(3)
	15,500	
Gross trading income	7,500	
Less: wages and salaries	1,300	(4)
depreciation of fixed assets	1,200	(5)
other business overheads	900	(6)
loan interest paid	200	
	3,600	
Total income before taxation	3,900	
Less: taxation on income for the period	1,900	(7)
Total income after taxation	2,000	
Less: dividend proposed for the period	300	
Retained income for the period	1,700	

Notes:
(1) Original valuation of £1,800 plus £600 addition for wages and overheads expended in period t_0 to t_1 in getting stock at t_1 to its then current condition.
(2) The wages and overheads directly attributed to trading in stock.
(3) A similar adjustment as in (1) for stock held at t_2–the addition for wages and overheads attributed directly to trading in stock (as in (2)) are also attributable to that stock remaining unsold at t_2.
(4) The remaining wages not directly attributable to the trading stock.
(5) The depreciation figure has been raised from £1,000 to £1,200 because of the different estimate of the useful life of the plant.
(6) The remaining overheads not directly attributable to the trading stock.
(7) The original tax figure has been amended to allow for the above changes.

(b) The different accounting procedures are mainly a matter of personal judgement which cannot be fully 'legislated' for – for example, with regard to the life of the plant. (As later chapters will reveal, accountants are attempting to standardize matters which can be standardized – for example, stock valuation.)

(c) The various changes in the income statement would also have an equivalent influence on the balance sheet – for example, at t_2, the stock valuation under current assets would be £4,500 (originally £2,500); the fixed asset figure for plant would be £6,000 − £1,200 = £4,800 (original-ly £5,000); and the tax provision under current liabilities would be £1,900 (originally £1,200). Thus, different accounting procedures alter not only the income statement but also the balance sheet position – all due to matters of accounting allocation (attributing accounting data to par-ticular assets, activities and periods).

(d) The reporting of accounting data is therefore open to managerial manipulation unless there are various devices to minimize this possibility – the two which are designed for this purpose, and which will be discussed at various times in this text, are accounting standards (prescribed by the professional accountancy bodies) and the audit function (prescribed by company legislation).

Traditional income statement characteristics

The following further comments support the above descriptions of the income statement.

(a) The income statement is a dynamic report in the sense that it discloses information of business activity over time. The balance sheet, on the other hand, is a static report reflecting a position at one point of time – that is, the ending date for the income statement's reporting period. Each must therefore be taken and read within these contexts and subject to these limitations – the income statement is for one past period; and the balance sheet is of a fleeting moment in time. Nevertheless, as later chapters will reveal, each has its considerable uses when properly and carefully used.

(b) The traditional income statement is legally intended as a report of realized income. The basic data contained within it should be supported by relevant notes to accounts providing additional information and explanation.

(c) The operational activities of the company are, on occasion, affected by extraordinary items of revenue and/or expense. These exceptional and non-recurrent data should be separately reported in the income state-ment, together with the tax data relevant to them.

(d) As with the balance sheet, the income statement should report figures relating to the previous as well as the current period.

(e) Again, as with the balance sheet, the income statement should relate to both the reporting company and the group of companies owned by it (where relevant).

The group income statement

Illustration 24 relaxes the assumption of no subsidiary companies, and shows the income statement for a group of companies in outline. As in Illustration 19, the details of the existing legal disclosure requirements have been ignored meantime.

The consolidation procedures involved in producing a group income statement are similar in principle to those involved in producing the equivalent balance sheet; namely, the aggregation of similar data and the specific highlighting of group data which, in fact, 'belong' to the holding company. In this respect, two specific comments should be made:

(a) The normal practice in the UK is to combine the data from the holding company's income statement with those from subsidiary company statements in such a way that there is no need to produce a separate holding company statement; thus, the required disclosure of the headings 'Income attributable to the holding company', 'Income retained in holding company', and 'Income retained in subsidiary company'.

Illustration 24 The group income statement

Assume the following income statement for Subsidiary Ltd which is 100 per cent owned by Company Ltd at t_2.

SUBSIDIARY LTD
Income Statement for Period t_1 to t_2

	t_0 to t_1 £	t_1 to t_2 £
Sales revenue for the period	5,000	6,000
Less: cost of sales[1]	3,800	4,300
Gross trading income	1,200	1,700
Less: depreciation of fixed assets	100	100
other business overheads	900	1,300
	1,000	1,400
Income before taxation	200	300
Less: taxation for the period	100	100
Retained income for the period	100	200

[1] Calculated in the normal way with opening and closing stocks.

Taking the above data, and combining them with their Company Ltd equivalents given in Illustration 21, the following group income statement can be proposed for the latter entity.

Illustration 24 *continued*

COMPANY LTD

Group Income Statement for the Period t_1 to t_2

	t_0 to t_1 £	t_1 to t_2 £
Sales revenue for the period	25,000	29,000
Less: cost of sales	17,400	19,200
Gross trading income	7,600	9,800
Less: wages and salaries	2,200	2,300
depreciation of fixed assets	100	1,100
other business overheads	2,600	3,200
loan interest paid	—	200
	4,900	6,800
Group income before taxation	2,700	3,000
Less: taxation on group income for the period	1,100	1,300
Group income after taxation attributable *to holding company*	1,600	1,700
Less: dividend proposed for the period	200	300
Retained income of the group for the period	1,400	1,400
Of which:		
Retained in holding company	1,300	1,200
Retained in subsidiary company	100	200
	1,400	1,400

(b) Following on from (a), the requirement to disclose the holding company's periodic and retained income involves the recognition of income attributable to minority interests (if any). The illustration has assumed that no minority interests exist, but if they had, there would have been a deduction from the 'income after tax' figure representing the proportion of it belonging to minority interests.

Legal requirements

The form and content of company income statements and balance sheets are prescribed (with some flexibility only) in Schedule 8, Companies Act 1948. At the present time, these mainly relate to the financial statements of single companies, although holding companies are recommended to produce group financial statements with the form and content prescribed by Schedule 8 – at least so far as is practicable. The previous illustrations have attempted to give the reader examples which comply as nearly as possible with the prescribed form and content whilst retaining the policy of amending it when necessary for purposes of explanation. It might be useful, therefore, to take the group balance sheet (in Illustration 19), and the group income statement (in Illustration 24), and present them in a way compatible with Schedule 8. In this respect, Format 1 (for the balance sheet) and Format 2 (for the income statement) of Schedule 8 have been adopted.

Illustration 25 outlines the balance sheet.

Illustration 25 Form and content of group balance sheet

COMPANY LTD
Group Balance Sheet as at t_2

	t_1				t_2	
	£	£	£	£	£	£
Fixed assets						
Intangible asset						
Goodwill			200			200
Tangible asset						
Plant			400			5,300
			600			5,500
Current assets						
Stock		2,000			3,100	
Debtors		800			1,000	
Cash at bank		3,300			1,200	
		6,100			5,300	
Creditors: amounts falling due within one year						
Creditors	1,500			1,900		
Taxation	1,100			1,300		
Dividends	200	2,800		300	3,500	
Net current assets			3,300			1,800
Total assets less current liabilities			3,900			7,300
Creditors: amounts falling due after more than one year						
Bank loan			—			(2,000)
			3,900			5,300
Capital and reserves						
Called up share capital			2,000			3,000
Share premium account			500			—
Profit and loss account			1,400			2,300
			3,900			5,300

Illustration 26 outlines the income statement.

Illustration 26 Form and content of group income statement

COMPANY LTD
Group Profit and Loss Account for the Period t_1 to t_2

	t_0 to t_1	t_1 to t_2
	£	£
Turnover	25,000	29,000
Change in stocks	(100)	1,100
Purchase of goods	(17,300)	(20,300)
Wages and salaries	(2,200)	(2,300)
Depreciation of fixed assets	(100)	(1,100)
Other business overheads	(2,600)	(3,200)
Loan interest paid	—	(200)
Profit before taxation	2,700	3,000
Tax on profit	(1,100)	(1,300)
Profit after taxation	1,600	1,700
Dividend proposed	(200)	(300)
Retained profit	1,400	1,400
Of which:		
Retained in holding company	1,300	1,200
Retained in subsidiary company	100	200
	1,400	1,400

The formats outlined in Illustrations 25 and 26 follow the wording of Schedule 8 – for example, profit and loss account instead of income statement and profit instead of income. They also reveal that the layout does not appear to be as informative as in the earlier illustrations – particularly in the case of the income statement (for example, the change in stocks is the difference between opening and closing stock, and has been separated from the purchase of goods figure; by adding the two figures together, the cost of sales figures for the two periods of £17,400 and £19,200 are revealed – as described in Illustration 24).

Finally, it should also be noted that Illustrations 25 and 26 provide only the minimum content legally required for both financial statements. Schedule 8 also prescribes additional information to be disclosed in the notes to accounts. These provisions would include *inter alia*: a statement of the main accounting practices used in preparing the main financial statements; and, in relation to the balance sheet – full details of share capital and debentures; fixed assets, including purchases, disposals and aggregate depreciation provisions; investments, including the market value of Stock Exchange-listed items; movements in reserves and provisions; current, medium and long-term liabilities, particularly with reference to repayment timing; and contingent liabilities: and, in relation to the profit and loss account (or income statement) – details of loan interest payments; investment income and rentals from land; hire payments for plant; auditor's remuneration; taxation; turnover; employees; and extraordinary items.

References

1   R. T. Sprouse and M. Moonitz, 'A Tentative Set of Broad Accounting Principles for Business Enterprises', *Accounting Research Study 3*, American Institute of Certified Public Accountants, 1962, p. 8.
2   ibid.
3   ibid., p. 9.

Suggested discussion or essay topics; and selected bibliography

Because of the inter-relationship of the topics in Chapters 1, 2 and 3, this material is provided at the end of Chapter. 3

3
Other main financial statements

The funds statement

In addition to the traditional income statement and balance sheet, companies are increasingly presenting a further statement in the annual financial report – that is, the funds statement. Usually described in the UK as the source and application of funds statement, it reveals the periodic inflow and outflow of financial funds of a company. As such, it is composed of the periodic movements in balance sheet items – that is, changes in that statement from one reporting date to the next. It can therefore be described in notation form, using a simplified version of the balance sheet identity previously described in Chapter 2:

$$\Delta I + \Delta R + \Delta M + \Delta S = \Delta F + \Delta C$$

where Δ = the measured movement in each item over the defined period.

The construction of the funds statement thus involves identifying and measuring these periodic movements and arranging them in a sensible report form. So far as measurement is concerned, it can be seen that ΔR is, to a large extent, already explained in terms of the income figures disclosed in the income statement (that is, R_a) – although other items such as new share capital receipts, revaluations of assets, bonus share issues, etc. are likely to occur.

Other periodic movements, therefore, are not disclosed in the income statement and are not revealed directly in the balance sheet which, by definition, is static rather than dynamic. The balance sheet is thus intended to reflect the end-result of these movements, and the income statement describes only one particular change. The funds statement is intended to fill this information gap, and its main objective can be described as the need to report on the financing and investing activities of the company, including the extent to which it has generated funds from operations during the period, and to provide a complete disclosure of all changes in its reported financial position during the period. It therefore supplies answers to questions which investors and other interested parties may ask of the company and which are related particularly to the new sources of finance it has obtained during the period (for example, from share and loan issues, bank borrowings, additional credit from suppliers and income retained), and the various ways in which these additional funds have been employed (for example, in the acquisition of fixed assets and stocks, and in the giving of additional credit to customers).

Presentation of funds data can take several forms, there being in practice no generally accepted format (although professional bodies do make recommendations from time to time). For example, the various sources and uses of funds can be reconciled to the periodic movement in cash balances or to the periodic movement in working capital (current assets minus current liabilities). Alternatively, the statement can simply equate total sources with total uses. In addition, practice varies as to the amount of funds data included in the statement – some companies give a great deal of information relating to all the financial events they have been concerned with (including those of a non-cash nature, such as the acquisition of a subsidiary company for shares or loan stock); whereas others give relatively little but concentrate on, say, cash transactions only. The problems and issues associated with this will be discussed later in the book but, meanwhile, Illustration 27 is intended to describe an outline funds statement. It will follow the relatively simple notion of identifying periodic changes in the main balance sheet items mentioned above.

Illustration 27 The funds statement

Assuming the group data provided in Illustration 19, the following figures can be identified for purposes of preparing a funds statement for the period t_1 to t_2 (in this case a funds statement reflecting the financial flows of a holding company and its 100%-owned subsidiary).

COMPANY LTD
Basic Group Data For Funds Statement: Period t_1 to t_2

	t_1 £	t_2 £	Δ t_1 to t_2 £
Plant – cost	700	6,700	+ 6,000
Plant – aggregate depreciation	(300)	(1,400)	− 1,100
Stock	2,000	3,100	+ 1,100
Debtors	800	1,000	+ 200
Cash in bank	3,300	1,200	− 2,100
Goodwill	200	200	—
	6,700	10,800	+ 4,100
Called up share capital	2,000	3,000	+ 1,000
Share premium	500	—	− 500
Retained income	1,400	2,300	+ 900
Bank loan	—	2,000	+ 2,000
Creditors	1,500	1,900	+ 400
Taxation	1,100	1,300	+ 200
Dividend proposed	200	300	+ 100
	6,700	10,800	+ 4,100

The figures in the Δ column represent the basic flows from which the funds statement for the group can be constructed. But, first, there are a few further adjustments to be made:

Illustration 27 *continued*

(a) The increase in share capital of £1,000 was due to a bonus issue made by converting the share premium of £500 and £500 of income retained into share capital, and does not represent a flow of funds – merely a bookkeeping adjustment. Thus, the movement in retained income relevant to trading activities (and representing an inflow or source of funds) ought to be £900 + £500 = £1,400 (the total retained income figure for the group given in Illustration 24). The latter datum will be used for purposes of the funds statement, and the figures of + £1,000 (share capital), – £500 (share premium), and + £900 (retained income) can be ignored from now on.

(b) Defining working capital as current assets minus current liabilities, the change in working capital for the period t_1 to t_2 can be defined for purposes of the funds statement as:

	£	£
Change in stock		1,100
debtors		200
cash		−2,100
		− 800
Less: change in creditors	400	
taxation	200	
dividends	100	700
		− 1,500

In other words, working capital has decreased by £1,500 over the period. This information can be highlighted in the funds statement.

(c) The writing off of depreciation of fixed assets (the increase in £1,100 in the aggregate depreciation provision) does not, in itself, represent a funds flow. In fact, in this sense, it is part of the trading income of the period which has been set aside to allow for the eventual write off of the plant concerned when its useful life has expired. As such, it represents profits retained in the business, and should be added to the income retained figure of £1,400 in order to produce a total of £2,500 (£1,400 + £1,100) for the funds statement.

The above adjustments having been made, the resultant figures, together with those remaining in the Δ column above, can be put in a suitable funds flow format, emphasizing sources and uses of funds. The sources can be identified in this case as:

	£
Total income retained (as above)	2,500
Bank loan received	2,000
Decrease in working capital	1,500

and the uses of funds were as follows:

	£
Purchase of plant	6,000

This can now be put in the form of a funds statement:

Illustration 27 *continued*

COMPANY LTD
Group Funds Statement for Period t_1 to t_2

	£
Sources of funds were obtained from:	
Trading income	2,500
Bank loan received	2,000
Reduction in working capital*	1,500
	6,000

	£
Use to which these funds were put	
Purchase of plant	6,000

*Details of the computation of this figure could be disclosed.

Although of considerable use in evaluating how the company financed its purchase of plant, the above statement provides only limited information. It is possible to extend the disclosure of data by making further adjustments:

(a) The £2,500 income figure in the above statement is the retained one, before deduction of depreciation, but after deduction of two provisions – taxation £1,300 and dividends £300. Thus, the income figure before all such deductions was £2,500 + £1,300 + £300 = £4,100.

(b) By ignoring the dividend and taxation provision in the income statement by using the figure of £4,100 for income in the funds statement, it is possible to also ignore them in the working capital figures – that is, the changes over the period of £200 for tax and £100 for dividends. Instead, the payments for tax and dividends made during t_1 to t_2 can be substituted and included in the funds statement – that is, £1,100 for tax and £200 for dividends (these were both provided for at t_1).

(c) The remaining changes in working capital figures (stock, £1,100; debtors, £200; cash £(2,100); and creditors, £400) can be separately identified in the funds statement (as can the loan of £2,000 and the plant purchase of £6,000, as before).

If the above adjustments are made, the alternative funds statement can be described as follows:

COMPANY LTD

Group Funds Statement for Period t_1 to t_2

Sources of funds included:	£
Trading income realized	4,100
Bank loan received	2,000
Additional credit given by suppliers	400
	6,500
The *uses* to which these funds were put included:	
Payment of taxation	1,100
Payment of dividends	200
Purchase of plant	6,000
Replacement of stock	1,100
Additional credit given to customers	200
	8,600
Resulting in a *reduction* of cash resources of	2,100

The above statement therefore reveals that the majority of the company's additional funds came from trading activity (£4,100), a bank loan (£2,000), and utilization of existing cash resources (£2,100). These went to pay for its obligations to the Inland Revenue and the shareholders, and to acquire needed plant and stock. This gives much more information than the earlier funds statement, and considerably more than the income statement and balance sheet. Also, it should be reasonably obvious from the above data that funds statements can be produced in a variety of ways, according to which adjustments are made and what figures are disclosed.

It can be seen from the presentation in the illustration that a suitable reconstruction of the figures can produce a funds statement which emphasizes the change in working capital – that is, by the aggregation and netting off of stock, debtor, creditor and bank figures. Equally, the emphasis can be placed on cash resources and liquidity. Whichever approach is adopted, the funds statement is clearly a financial report which presents an overview of the financial management of the company. It reveals not only that such an entity has to be profitable to survive, but also that it requires to raise funds from a variety of sources in order to maintain, replenish and develop its existing asset structure, and meet its various obligations on their due dates. However, as it is presently reported as a by-product of the traditional income statement and balance sheet (both based on historic costs and the principle of realization), it is equally based on these conventions, and therefore subject to all the problems and doubts associated with them.

The relationship between the main financial statements

The balance sheet, the income statement and the funds statement form the basis for regularly informing shareholders and other interested parties of the financial affairs of companies. As such, they have a significance which is recognized throughout the business world. They are not all subject to legislative provisions; the funds statement, for example, is not subject to such regulations in many countries. Thus, the degree of emphasis placed on them can vary considerably.

Generally speaking, the income statement is usually given primary emphasis because it is so widely regarded as an important indicator of company success or failure. The balance sheet and funds statement therefore appear to be regarded as 'back-up' statements, giving additional information for assessing the 'quality' of companies and their income. However, it must be remembered that the three statements are very much related to one another; the balance sheet reveals the 'end-result' of company operations and activity over a defined period of time; the funds statement analyses how that 'end-result' came about through the receipt and use of funds of various kinds; and the income statement analyses the source of funds derived from operational activity. It is therefore quite wrong to regard any one statement as more important than the other two. Each has its role to play in informing its user, and the latter person cannot possibly obtain an overall picture of a company's financial progress and position without referring to all three statements. They are complementary rather than competing or exclusive alternatives. However, in addition, there are several other financial statements which increasingly are becoming a required feature of company reports (particularly of larger companies). The first of these concerns accounting for increasing costs.

Accounting for increasing costs

As the previous sections have indicated and explained, traditional accounting income (and its supporting balance sheets) are based on the twin principles of historic cost and realization. As also explained, both principles have consequential effects on the reporting of traditional statements of company profitability and financial position – that is, profits are mainly those realized during the period, and financial position is stated in mainly original cost rather than contemporary value terms. Assuming no capital receipts or repayments during a period, income in these terms is therefore the increase in the historic cost-based capital of the company, after allowing for its renewal in historic cost terms where relevant (by means of such adjustments as depreciation of fixed assets). In other words, the capital of the company is maintained in terms of the original costs of the assets concerned. Illustration 28 attempts to describe this.

The shaded box represents at t_1 the capital of the company, measured in terms of the historic cost of its underlying assets minus its short and medium to long-term liabilities, and maintained in these same terms at t_2. The unshaded area at t_2 represents the increase in capital over the period t_1 to t_2 which has mainly resulted from the realization of assets and which,

Illustration 28 Maintaining historic cost capital–1

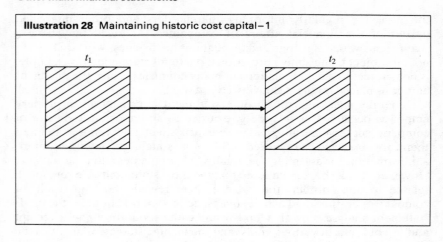

following the historic cost principle, is available to be described as income of the period. In other words, if the company has properly provided for the renewal of its fixed and current assets, by means of accounting for their diminution in value or expiry of useful life in terms of their original cost, then it ought to have sufficient funds available to replace them at their original cost. This can be explained in simple terms as in Illustration 29. The horizontal format is used to facilitate understanding by the reader.

Hopefully, this example, despite its oversimplification, will allow the reader to appreciate the strengths and weaknesses of historic cost income and capital – that is, although they are based on the relatively objective measurement of realized asset transactions, they fail to reflect unrealized value changes, and also assume as a result that price-levels will remain static. For example, using the figures in the last balance sheet at t_2, it should be relatively clear that the £1,000 of cash in the bank is available to purchase a replacement item of stock for £1,000 – thus, maintaining not only the historic cost capital but also the physical substance of the business underlying such capital (in this case, the one item of stock).

But this assumes that the price of the item of stock has remained constant at £1,000. If it has not, then too much or too little income may have been taxed and distributed. For example, if the stock item at t_2 cost £800 to replace then the company could have distributed a further £200 of dividend without impairing its capital position and ability to replace the stock (that is, it would be left with £200 of cash (£1,000 – 800) surplus to requirements after replacing the stock for £800). On the other hand, if the cost of replacing the stock item was £1,200 at t_2, the company would be unable to undertake the required replacement without borrowing £200 (presumably from the bank if it were willing to lend the money). In

---

Illustration 29 Maintaining historic cost capital – 2

Assume a company holding one asset (one item of stock); and that this represents its capital at t_1, there being no other assets and liabilities. Thus:

COMPANY LTD

Balance Sheet as at t_1

Liability	£	*Asset*	£
Share capital	1,000	Stock at cost	1,000

Also assume that, during the period t_1 to t_2, the item of stock was sold for £1,500, providing a profit on the transaction of £500 and a cash balance in the bank of £1,500. The balance sheet at t_2 would be as follows:

COMPANY LTD

Balance Sheet as at t_2

Liability	£	*Asset*	£
Share capital	1,000	Cash in bank	1,500
Retained income	500		
	1,500		1,500

The consequences of the above balance sheet are: (a) a realized, historic cost-based income of £500 has been recognized; (b) this is then available for taxation and dividends; and (c) even if such a profit were completely taxed and distributed, it would mean that £1,000 of cash was left in the company for stock replacement purposes. Thus, assuming the income of £500 for the period to have been completely taxed and distributed (and that the latter payments have been made), the resultant balance sheet at t_2 would be as follows:

COMPANY LTD

Balance Sheet as at t_2

Liability	£	*Asset*	£
Share capital[1]	1,000	Cash in bank[2]	1,000

(1) Retained income = income, £500 − tax and dividends, £500 = nil.
(2) Cash in bank = sale proceeds, £1,500 − tax and dividends payments, £500 = £1,000.

---

the one case, therefore, too much capital has been maintained; in the other case, too little capital has been maintained.

The problem in practice, of course, is normally one of price increases and coping with them in a world of continuous inflation. In other words, over a number of years companies have increasingly had to make provision for replacing their assets at prices often well in excess of their original costs. The problem can be described in the form of Illustration 30.

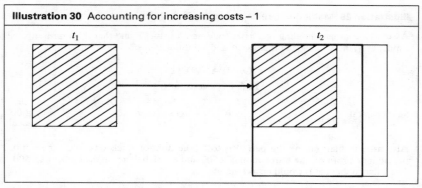

Illustration 30 Accounting for increasing costs – 1

The above diagram is almost the same as that in Illustration 28 – the shaded areas are the historic cost capital positions being maintained from t_1 to t_2; and the unshaded area at t_2 represents the increase in capital due to realized gains during the period. However, one other matter has been introduced – that is, the dark-edged box representing the current cost of replacing the assets which have been consumed by the company during the period t_1 to t_2. The unshaded area within this box indicates the additional capital which requires to be maintained if the company is to replace its assets at prices in excess of their original cost – that is, the amount required over and above the traditional historic cost figure. The remaining unshaded area can loosely be described as the income of the period which has been measured after allowing for the cost of replacing assets used in the various processes of the company's operational activity. It is therefore this figure which is available to meet the taxation and dividend provisions which the company will make should it be decided to maintain its capital in terms of the physical resources underlying it, and in terms of the current cost of replacing these resources. The major accounting problem is one of determining how best to measure income and capital in such current cost terms.

There are essentially two main ways of attempting to account for the increasing costs of replacing a company's assets – that is, within the existing financial accounting framework of statements of profitability and financial position. The first is to do what many companies have been doing for years, and that is to make an informal accounting of the increased cost of replacement by prudently transferring amounts from realized income to reserves, and by making conservative distributions. This policy leaves much to the individual judgement of boards of directors, and provides no specific measurement of how much income is required to be retained in order to replace assets. In other words, the measurement of the black box in Illustration 30 would, under this scheme, be no more than an arbitrary judgement, and the assessment of suitable dividend levels could be fraught with the danger of under or over-distribution.

The alternative solution to the above is to account for the current cost of replacing the reporting company's assets. There are several versions of this, both in terms of the adjustments made, and the means by which these adjustments are computed and disclosed. The following comments attempt to follow in broad principle the system currently in operation amongst the larger companies in the UK.[1]

Current cost accounting statements

On examining the financial statements of a company, it is possible to identify a number of matters for which some adjustment should be made in order to account for the increased cost of replacing its assets. These are as follows:

(a) The assets which will typically require adjustments to account for their current costs are fixed assets (such as land and buildings, plant and machinery, and motor vehicles) and current assets (such as stock and temporary investments).

(b) Two types of adjustment will typically require to be made in each period – first, adjustments to allow for the change in current costs of both assets bought during the period and held at the end of the period, and assets held throughout the period (that is, for *unrealized* current cost changes in the period); and, secondly, adjustments to account for changes in current costs during the period on assets bought and sold in it, or held at its beginning and sold during it (that is, for *realized* current cost changes during the period). In other words, current cost gains and losses are accounted for as unrealized so long as the assets concerned continue to be held by the company; and as realized during the period in which the assets concerned are sold. For example, Illustration 31 explains a simple example involving one item of stock which was purchased at t_0 for £50; held at t_1 when its current cost of replacement was £75; and sold at t_2 for £95 when its current cost of replacement was £80. Assume no other assets, liabilities or transactions.

The increase in current cost of the stock is accounted for as an unrealized gain of £25 until it is realized at t_2. At the latter date, the total unrealized gains of £30 are translated into realized gains of the same amount, and the necessary income adjustment for this (as an additional deduction from historic cost income) is made in the current cost income statement. The reader should also note that it is recommended in the UK that all current cost gains should be taken to a current cost reserve, thereby making them unavailable for distribution and, hopefully, maintaining the operating capability of the company. (In this case, at t_2, and ignoring taxation, if the company distributed its current cost income of £15 to its shareholders, this would leave £80 (£95 − 15) available to meet the cost of replacing the item of stock at its then current cost of £80; no new financing would therefore be needed, and the operating capability of the company, as defined in terms of this stock, would be maintained.)

Illustration 31 Current cost accounting – 1

COMPANY LTD
Current Cost Income Statements from t_0 to t_2

	t_0 to t_1 £		t_1 to t_2 £	
Sale of stock		—		95
Less: original cost of sale:				
opening stock at cost	—		50	
add: purchase of stock	50		—	
	50		50	
less: closing stock	50		—	
		—		50
Historic cost income		—		45
Less: additional current cost of sales		—[1]		30[2]
Current cost income		—		15

(1) No further adjustment is needed in this period regarding realized income because no stock was sold during it.

(2) The current cost of the stock at time of sale t_2 was £80; £50 had originally been accounted for, and this adjustment accounts for the remaining £30.

COMPANY LTD
Current Cost Balance Sheets as at t_0, t_1 and t_2

Liabilities	t_0 £	t_1 £	t_2 £	Assets	t_0 £	t_1 £	t_2 £
Share capital	50	50	50	Stock	—	75[3]	—
Current cost reserve	—	25[4]	30[4]	Cash	50	—	95
Retained current cost income	—	—	15[5]				
	50	75	95		50	75	95

(3) The stock was revalued from £50 to £75 at t_1, because it remained unsold at that date.

(4) The unrealized revaluation surplus at t_1 of £25 would be put to a current cost reserve, and a further unrealized surplus of £5 (£80 − 75) would be accounted for in the same way at t_2 (representing the increase in t_1 to t_2 of the current cost of the stock).

(5) The retained income figure of £15 is that which is calculated above in the current cost income statement for t_1 to t_2.

The UK professional requirements are effectively supported by Schedule 8, Companies Act 1948, which stipulates that, should a company produce its main financial statements on a current cost basis, any current cost adjustments and provisions should be taken to a revaluation reserve (the legal equivalent of the current cost reserve). This reserve may be reduced by transfers to the income statement if, in the opinion of the company's directors, the amount of the transfer is no longer required to fulfill the company's accounting policies, the income statement had been previously charged with it, and it represents a realized gain.

In order to familiarize the reader further with the type of current cost accounting statement already being reported and likely to be seen more widely in the UK over the next few years, Illustration 32 outlines an income statement and balance sheet, based on the historic cost data for period t_1 to t_2 provided in Illustration 19 (balance sheet) and Illustration 24 (income statement). Both statements are for the group (that is, in this case, a holding company and its 100 per cent controlled subsidiary company), and follow the main recommendations of the most recently published practice.[1] Where relevant, they attempt to comply with the form and content provisions of Schedule 8, Companies Act 1948. Although each of the main adjustments is explained in terms of its meaning, the precise nature of the computations has been omitted because this is a matter which can vary from company to company – depending on the circumstances, generally, and the availability of data, particularly.

Illustration 32 Current cost accounting – 2

COMPANY LTD

Group Current Cost Income Statement for the Period t_1 to t_2

	t_0 to t_1 £	t_1 to t_2 £	
Historic cost income before deduction of interest and taxation	2,700	3,200	(1)
Less: current cost operating adjustments:			
additional cost of sales	900	800	(2)
provision for increase in monetary working capital	50	60	(3)
total provision for increased cost of working capital	950	860	(4)
additional depreciation of fixed assets	20	140	(5)
	970	1,000	
Current cost operating income	1,730	2,200	(6)
Add: gearing adjustment	—	300	(7)
Less: loan interest paid	—	200	
	—	100	
Current cost income before taxation	1,730	2,300	
Less: taxation on group income for the period	1,100	1,300	(8)
Current cost income attributable to shareholders	630	1,000	(9)
Less: dividend proposed for the period	200	300	
Current cost income retained	430	700	(10)

Illustration 32 *continued*

Notes

(1) In this current cost income statement, the starting point is historic cost income before deduction of taxation, interest on borrowings, and dividends to shareholders; but after deduction of historic cost of sales and historic cost depreciation. If this statement was presented by the company in fulfilment of the requirements of Schedule 8, Companies Act 1948, it would require to give the detailed accounting data comprising the historic cost income figures in a form and with a content similar, for example, to that given in Illustration 26.

(2) The first deduction relates to the additional cost of sales made during the periods concerned, caused by the replacement price of stock increasing during the period in which it has been held. In other words, it represents in aggregate the differences between the historic costs of these sales and their replacement costs (at the time of each sale).

(3) This provision is made in order to retain profits to fund the periodic price increase in monetary working capital (usually defined for this purpose as debtors minus creditors; but also occasionally including cash balances and bank overdrafts if they can be regarded as part of the same operational activity to which debtors and creditors relate).

(4) The periodic price increase in total working capital is now provided for by the reduction of historic cost income by the two adjustments in (2) and (3).

(5) The replacement cost of depreciable assets having increased during the periods concerned, these additional sums require to be deducted in order to provide for depreciation in terms of the current replacement costs of the assets concerned.

(6) The current cost operating profit represents the realized income of the company for the periods concerned after allowing for the effects of inflation (in replacement cost terms) on depreciable fixed assets, stock, and monetary working capital.

(7) The gearing adjustment is made in order to recognise that the future funding of the replacement of fixed assets and working capital (at prices greater than those originally expended) may well be made in the proportions which currently exist within the financial structure of the company – that is, the existing assets have been funded by shareholders' capital (including retained income) and long-term borrowings, and it may be reasonable to presume that their replacement may be funded in the same gearing proportion (borrowing to capital). Thus, the gearing adjustment is intended to represent that part of the current cost operating adjustments which may reasonably be assumed to be funded by long-term borrowing; and this leaves, after taxation is deducted, current cost profit attributable to shareholders.

(8) The taxation figures deducted are those based on historic cost income, no allowance being made for the various current cost adjustments. Existing UK tax legislation does not make such allowances.

(9) Current cost profits attributable to shareholders are measurements of the income which is potentially available for distributions, but which should not be regarded as automatically free for dividend purposes. It may allow for the increased cost of replacing the company's assets, and for the part funding of such increases by long-term borrowing, but other matters will enter into the dividend decision (for example, the need to retain funds to expand the company's business activities).

(10) These figures represent the adjusted profits which have been retained within the company. They will appear as part of the reserves section of the relevant end-of-period balance sheets.

COMPANY LTD

Group Current Cost Balance Sheet as at t_2

	£	t_1 £	£	£	t_2 £	£
Fixed assets						
Intangible asset						
Goodwill			200			200
Tangible asset						
Plant at valuation		840			7,560	
Less: aggregate depreciation		360	480		1,650	5,910 [(11)]
			680			6,110

Current assets					
Stock		2,100		3,400	(12)
Debtors		800		1,000	
Cash at bank		3,300		1,200	
		6,200		5,600	
Creditors: amounts falling due within one year					
Creditors	1,500		1,900		
Taxation	1,100		1,300		
Dividends	200	2,800	300	3,500	
Net current assets		3,400		2,100	
Total assets less current liabilities		4,080		8,210	
Creditors: amounts falling due after more than one year					
Bank loan		—		(2,000)	
		4,080		6,210	
Capital and reserves					
Called up share capital		2,000		3,000	
Share premium account		500		—	
Revaluation reserve		1,190		2,670	(13)
Profit and loss account		390		540	(14)
		4,080		6,210	

(11) These figures are stated at their current replacement cost net of the appropriate proportion of depreciation.

(12) These figures are stated at the current replacement cost of the stock concerned.

(13) This reserve is composed of revaluations of assets held at each balance sheet date (including depreciable and non-depreciable fixed assets and stocks); and relevant current cost accounting adjustments deducted from historic cost income in the income statement (net of any gearing adjustment). It also includes additional deductions from retained income for depreciation under-provided in previous periods because the most up-to-date current cost of depreciable assets was not known in these periods (this is usually termed 'backlog' depreciation, and ensures that full allowance is made for the replacement cost of depreciable assets when measuring income). No revaluation can be made of the other monetary working capital items held at each balance sheet date as it would be illegal to restate amounts due by customers, cash balances, and amounts due to suppliers, etc. The exact composition of the reserve above is as follows:

	t_1 £	t_2 £
Revaluation of plant (net of relevant depreciation)	80	530
Revaluation of stock held at period-end	100	200
Current cost transfers from income statement (net of gearing)	970	700
Transfer from retained income for backlog depreciation	40	50
	1,190	1,480
Add: balance brought forward from previous period	—	1,190
	1,190	2,670

(These figures are intended as illustrative only, although the interested reader can trace their origin from the data already given in this illustration as well as in Illustrations 19 and 26.)

Illustration 32 *continued*

(14) Profit and loss account represents retained income. Figures are as given in the current cost income statement minus that proportion in each period (represented by backlog depreciation) which is required to be reserved in order to provide fully for the current replacement cost of depreciable fixed assets. This can be summarized as follows:

	t_1 £	t_2 £
Current cost retained income	430	700
Less: backlog depreciation	40	50
utilized in bonus issue	—	500
	40	550
	390	150
Add: balance brought forward from previous period	—	390
	390	540

The above income statements and balance sheets are the main current cost accounting statements which can be reported. It is also possible to produce a related funds statement – that is, by comparing the current cost balance sheet at the beginning and end of a period, a funds statement can be prepared for that period. However, in so doing, the required adjustments will include the elimination of any transactions which do not involve a flow of funds – that is, purely bookkeeping allocations such as depreciation of fixed assets and the bonus share issue explained in Illustration 27. In a current cost accounting system, these adjustments would also include (a) transfers from the income statement to the current cost reserve in the balance sheet (additional cost of sales; additional depreciation; provision for monetary working capital: the gearing adjustment; and backlog depreciation transfers); and (b) revaluation adjustments in the balance sheet to assets being held when their replacement cost changes (mainly fixed assets and stocks, the revaluations being transferred to the current cost reserve).

The effect of all these eliminations is to leave in the funds statement only these transactions which represent actual fund flows. Thus, no matter what current cost accounting adjustments are made in the main financial statements, the current cost statement should be basically the same as its historic cost equivalent (similar, that is, except for the adjustments required to obtain the funds flow data). This can be demonstrated by taking the data in Illustration 32, and producing the relevant funds statement. As can be seen, the end-result is the same as the funds statement shown in Illustration 27. Illustration 33 describes the various adjustments for readers who are interested in tracing the figures through.

Illustration 33 The current cost funds statement

COMPANY LTD

Group Current Cost Funds Statement for the Period t_1 to t_2

	t_1	t_2	Δ t_1 to t_2	Non-fund transactions (HCA)	Non-fund transactions (CCA)	Funds flow transactions
	£	£	£	£	£	£
Plant–current cost	840	7,560	+ 6,720	—	– 720[1]	+ 6,000
Plant–aggregate depreciation	(360)	(1,650)	+ (1,290)	+ 1,100[2]	+ 190[1]	—
Stock	2,100	3,400	+ 1,300	—	– 200[1]	+ 1,100
Debtors	800	1,000	+ 200	—	—	+ 200
Cash in bank	3,300	1,200	– 2,100	—	—	– 2,100
Goodwill	200	200	—	—	—	—
	6,880	11,710	+ 4,830	+ 1,100	– 730	+ 5,200
Share capital	2,000	3,000	+ 1,000	– 1,000[3]	—	
Share premium	500	—	– 500	+ 500[3]	—	
Revaluation reserve	1,190	2,670	+ 1,480	+ 500[3]	– 1,480[1]	
Retained income	390	540	+ 150	+ 1,100[2] + 1,300[4] + 300[5]	+ 700[1] + 50[1]	+ 4,100
Bank loan	—	2,000	+ 2,000	—	—	+ 2,000
Creditors	1,500	1,900	+ 400	—	—	+ 400
Taxation	1,100	1,300	+ 200	– 1,300[4]	—	– 1,100
Dividend proposed	200	300	+ 100	– 300[5]	—	– 200
	6,880	11,710	+ 4,830	+ 1,100	– 730	+ 5,200

Notes

(1) Elimination of current cost accounting transfers and revaluations incorporated into the current cost reserve – see Illustration 32, Note (11).
(2) Elimination of historic cost accounting for fixed asset depreciation – see Illustration 27.
(3) Elimination of bonus share issue transfer – see Illustration 27.
(4) Adjustment to include the tax payment in the funds statement – see Illustration 27.
(5) Adjustment to include the dividend payment in the funds statement – see Illustration 27.

63

Other main financial statements

The statement of value added

One further major financial statement is being evidenced increasingly in the annual reports of UK companies, and that is the statement of value added. This financial statement is essentially a modified form of the income statement, reflecting the income of the company attributable to employees, government, and the providers of its capital (including lenders and shareholders). In other words, reported profits are conceived in terms of a much broader spectrum of interested parties than the traditional income statement prepared for the shareholders. The company is viewed more as a cooperative of owners, lenders, employees, and government, and this can be demonstrated by referring to the previously defined income identity of:

$$R_a = s - c - t - d$$

where R_a = retained income; s = sales revenue; c = matched costs; t = tax on profits; and d = distribution to shareholders (assuming the conventional system of accounting measurement based on the historic cost and realization principles).

Item (c) above is capable of being expanded to include the cost of bought-in materials and services (b); employee wages (w); fixed asset depreciation (f); and loan interest (i). Thus, $R_a = s - b - w - f - i - t - d$.

This last identity represents the basic data which are contained in the traditional accounting income statement. However, by rearranging them suitably, the identity can reflect the data required to describe the value added of the reporting company:

$$s - b - f = w + i + t + d + R_a.$$

Each side of the identity represents the net value added of the company – that is, the additional income which has been realized through operational activity during the reporting period $(s - b - f)$, and is available to pay for wages, interest, tax and dividends, as well as for retaining in the company for replacement and new investment $(w + i + t + d + R_a)$.[*]

Illustration 34 below (utilizing the income statement data in Illustration 26) outlines a value added statement based on the above identity. It clearly indicates the additional realized funds from operational activity which are 'distributed' to the various participants in the company – (t_1 to t_2 figures) 40 per cent to employees, 25 per cent to government, 9 per cent to the providers of the capital, and 26 per cent being retained in the business. It provides some indication of the size of the company (in terms of its net value added), and it enables employees and others to see the stake they have in it (in terms of their participation in its net value added).

---

[*] There is a debate that depreciation ought not to be treated as a deduction in arriving at value added but, instead should be included with R_a as part of the income retained in the company. However, as value added can only be created by the consumption of materials, services and fixed assets, it is felt that the above approach is the more acceptable.

Illustration 34 Statement of value added

COMPANY LTD

Group Value Added Statement for the Period t_1 to t_2

	t_0 to t_1 £		t_1 to t_2 £	
Sales revenue for the period (s)	25,000		29,000	
Less: bought-in materials and services (b)	20,000		22,400	
depreciation of fixed assets (f)	100		1,100	
	20,100		23,500	
Net value added	4,900		5,500	
Distributed as follows:	£	%	£	%
To employees for salaries, wages and				
pensions (w)*	2,100	43	2,200	40
To government for:				
corporation tax (t)	1,100		1,300	
social security contributions (w)*	100		100	
	1,200	24	1,400	25
To providers of capital for:				
loan interest (i)	—		200	
dividends (d)	200		300	
	200	4	500	9
For reinvestment in the company:				
retained income (R_a)	1,400	29	1,400	26
	4,900	100	5,500	100

*Part of the wage cost representing payments made by the company to the government for employee social security has been included as a payment to government, and not as payment to employees.

The statement of value added can also be expressed in current cost terms by deducting the various current cost adjustments from sales revenue and income retained figures. That is:

$$s - b - f - cca = w + i + t + d + (R_a - cca)$$

where $cca =$ the cost of sales, additional depreciation, and monetary working capital adjustments net of the relevant gearing factor (that is, the net allowance for inflation made when determining current cost income attributable to shareholders). Using the data already used in Illustration 32, this identity is presented in Illustration 35.

It can be readily seen that these figures are compatible with those used in Illustration 34 (assuming historic cost accounting) and reconcile with those in Illustration 32 (assuming current cost accounting). Judgements can be made therefore both of the value added achieved after allowing for the effects of specific price inflation and of the resultant allocation of that value added between various participating groups in the company. In particular, it is revealed that with less net value added being created by

Illustration 35 Current cost statement of value added

COMPANY LTD

Group Current Cost Value Added Statement for the Period t_1 to t_2

	t_0 to t_1 £		t_1 to t_2 £	
Sales revenue for the period	25,000		29,000	
Less: bought-in materials and services	20,000		22,400	
depreciation of fixed assets	100		1,100	
current cost accounting adjustments:				
cost of sales	900		800	
monetary working capital	50		60	
depreciation of fixed assets	20		140	
gearing	—		(300)	
	21,070		24,200	
Net value added	3,930		4,800	
Distribution as follows:	£	%	£	%
To employees for salaries, wages and				
pensions	2,100	53	2,200	46
To government for:				
corporation tax	1,100		1,300	
social security contributions	100		100	
	1,200	31	1,400	29
To providers of capital for:				
loan interest	—		200	
dividends	200		300	
	200	5	500	10
For reinvestment in the company:				
retained income	430	11	700	15
	3,930	100	4,800	100

the need to allow for the increased cost of replacing materials, services and fixed assets, a larger percentage of value added goes to each of the participating groups, and less is available for reinvestment in the company.

Other sources of reported information

It should be made clear at this stage that the annual company financial report is not the only source of reported information about a company available to its shareholders and other interested parties. Besides their annual reports, Stock Exchange-quoted companies in the UK are required, as a condition of their quotation, to deliver to their shareholders an interim report of profitability and financial position. This report usually covers the six-month period since the last annual report, and is given in summary form only (occasionally it may be issued on a quarterly basis). In addition, it is not subject to independent audit. The aim of these reports is to provide shareholders with up-to-date information about their companies so as to alleviate the disadvantage of the significant time lag between annual reports. It should be noted that the provision for this type of financial information does not usually extend beyond quoted companies in the UK, though the practice is much more extensive in the US.

In addition to the afore-mentioned source of information – which is by definition historical in nature – company shareholders are provided occasionally with information of a predictive nature. This may well occur when company management produces data relating to an issue of new shares (UK company law requires that a prospectus be published if the shares are being offered to the public) or on an acquisition or merger with another company or companies (in the UK, there are strict quasi-governmental or professional regulations covering such activities). The financial reports presented in these relatively infrequent situations usually contain historical summaries of profitability and financial position, but may also contain forecast data relating particularly to trading income (although there is no specific provision to report such data). These predicted data are obviously far less objective than historic data but, when reported, are covered by a report on their quality by an independent accountant.

Finally, a number of large companies in the UK publish annual financial statements to their employees (they are also usually reported to their shareholders together with the annual report). These statements provide the annual financial results of the company in summary form, supporting the main figures of income, financial position, funds flow and value added with pictorial representation to provide a comprehensible financial message to employees (and shareholders) who are not trained in the complexities of accounting. The publication of such statements is voluntary and there are no specific legal or professional provisions as yet governing their content.

Other sources of information

It would be wrong to leave the reader with the impression that the only financial information available is that contained in the required annual, interim or *ad hoc* reports produced by companies. There are, in fact, several other sources to be mentioned, some of which make use in part of reported company information.

(a) There is the analysed information provided by financial service organizations such as Moodies and Exchange Telegraph which is based on company financial reports. These analysed and summarized data are extremely comprehensive and give an in-depth summary of the past financial record of companies.

(b) Companies frequently give interviews to investment analysts who can use this information source as a background to produce up-to-date reports which are either circulated to very large investor clients (normally institutions such as unit trusts, pension funds, investment trusts and insurance companies) or to stockbrokers who, in turn, produce summary reports for investing clients. This form of information system is usually intended to update the formal reported historic data in company financial statements.

(c) Information about large company activity can also be obtained either in advertisements or in public relations material. Because of its general nature, it is not always of immense use to investors and others, although it should be noted that the lack of such information may indicate that the company concerned wishes to maintain a low profile because of financial or other difficulties.

(d) There is a great deal of economic and industrial information available to aid the user. This information, usually in aggregate statistical form, is inevitably historical in nature, and is contained in various industry and trade journals (including those of government departments, and a number of financial reviews published by the main UK clearing banks). This type of information is useful in building up a picture of a particular industry's position and state of affairs. It therefore helps to provide an essential background to a similar type of assessment of an individual company.

The audit function

Much of the formally reported annual financial information from companies in the UK and similar countries is required to be examined and reported on by a suitably qualified independent accountant. This is the so-called audit function, and the independent accountant is described as the auditor. In practice, the auditor is normally not an individual but a firm of professionally-qualified accountants. The aim of the audit (at least so far as concerns annual financial statements) is the creation of rational belief and confidence in the accounting information contained in the company's annual financial statements. It is legally conducted on behalf of the shareholders in order that they may read and use the information without doubting its reliability or validity. Because the quality of the information is attested in this way, the audit should also be of benefit to other users of the financial statements such as lenders, bankers, employees, and government departments. Thus, the auditor attempts to lend credibility to the reported information by examining and verifying the way it has been produced and reported.

Hopefully, this process gives its potential users greater confidence in its quality, and will encourage them to use it without suspicion. The auditor's comments on the information are contained in a formal report which, following Section 14(3), Companies Act 1967, and recommended professional practice, takes the following form (assuming a funds statement is also produced and therefore reported on):

> We have audited the financial statements on pages – to – in accordance with approved auditing standards. In our opinion, the financial statements (which have been prepared under the historic cost convention) give a true and fair view of the state of affairs of the company at t_2 and of its income and source and application of funds for the period t_1 to t_2, and comply with the Companies Acts 1948 to 1981.

If current cost-based financial statements are published, the auditor concerned is required by either the Companies Act 1967 and/or the main professional accountancy bodies[2] to report on them. The form of his report will vary according to whether the current cost statements are presented as the main statements or as supplementary statements to those based on historic costs. If they are the former or supplementary but classed as unabridged and non-experimental, then the audit report should take the afore-mentioned 'true and fair view' form, suitably amended to cover current cost accounting:

> We have audited the current cost financial statements on pages Y to YY in accordance with approved auditing standards.
>
> In our opinion, these statements have been prepared in accordance with the accounting policies and methods described in notes X to XX and give, under the current cost principles described in Statement of Standard Accounting Practice 16, a true and fair view of the state of the company's affairs at t_2 and of its income and source and application of funds for the period t_1 to t_2, and comply with the Companies Acts 1948 to 1981.

If they are abridged, or unabridged and of an explicitly experimental nature, however, then a compliance style of report should be given as follows:

> In our opinion, the abridged supplementary current cost financial statements set out on pages Y to YY have been properly prepared, in accordance with the policies and methods described in notes Z to ZZ, to give the information required by Statement of Standard Accounting Practice 16.

In addition, the auditor is professionally required to state in his legally required report on the traditional financial statements that current cost statements have not been produced in circumstances where they should have been presented.

A number of factors should be noted from the above brief reports:

(a) The auditor is not a paid employee of the company; instead he is independent of it, and is responsible for an unbiased audit of the main financial statements.

(b) The audit report is an expression of a professional judgement and opinion, and is not intended as a certificate which guarantees the accuracy or otherwise of the reported figures. (This is inevitable owing to the many problems inherent in the production of financial statements.)

(c) The auditor merely states his opinion. He does not report on what he has done or found during his audit. This makes his audit report a relatively sparse statement so far as the use of financial reports is concerned.

(d) The auditor is not responsible for producing the audited financial statements – only for examining and reporting on their quality. (He may however, in certain instances, be employed by the company to produce these statements, but this is not part of the audit function. In the UK, it is the company's board of directors which is solely responsible for the production and quality of the required information.)

(e) The auditor is legally required to give a 'true and fair view' opinion on the annual income statement and balance sheet. He must report on whether or not they are in accordance with the accounting and disclosure provisions of the current Companies Acts. He is also required by the main UK professional accountancy bodies to apply the same procedures to the funds statement (although this is not legally required).

(f) The auditor is also required to report, where relevant, on current cost-based financial statements. He will usually do so in terms of either a 'true and fair view' type of opinion (when the statements are legally required to be so attested or are substantial enough to warrant this) or as a compliance report (when they are of a limited nature). Because of the provisions of Schedule 8, Companies Act 1948, current cost statements can be designated by the company as the main statements and can thus be subject to the legally required audit opinion on their truth and fairness.

References

1 'Current Cost Accounting', *Statement of Standard Accounting Practice 16*, 1980. The system of current cost accounting contained in this *Statement* is based on a relatively complex valuation principle involving net realizable values and future cash flows as well as replacement costs. It is therefore not just about accounting for the current cost of replacing assets. However, in most cases in practice, it is replacement costs which will be applicable and, as the text is intended only to provide a brief introduction to the topic, this and succeeding sections on current cost accounting have been simplified to examine the system in terms of replacement costs only. It should not be forgotten, therefore, that other current values may also require to be applied.

In addition, it should be noted that, as a result of the provisions of Schedule 8, Companies Act 1948, it is permissible for any UK company to produce current cost accounting statements to comply with the reporting requirement of that Act. If this is done, the form, content and disclosure requirements will apply, although there is little prescription of the accounting practices to adopt. Thus, the above-mentioned *Statement* is of vital importance to these companies.

2 'Auditors' Reports and SSAP 16 "Current Cost Accounting",' *Auditing Guideline 502*, The Institute of Chartered Accountants of Scotland, 1980.

Suggested discussion or essay topics (covering Chapters 1, 2 and 3)

1 A major disadvantage of the limited liability company is its potential to separate ownership from management. Explain.

2 Distinguish between share and loan capital in a limited company.

3 What are the essential differences between public and private companies in the UK?

4 Compare and contrast holding companies, subsidiary companies and groups of companies. What implications do they have with regard to company financial reporting?

5 The concept of the limited liability company creates a need for financial information. Why?

6 Describe the different stages to be found in the accounting function of a company in relation to the production of its annual financial report.

7 The annual report is more than a description of the annual income and periodic financial position of the company. Discuss.

8 The annual financial report of a company is the single most important source of information about it. Discuss the validity of this statement.

9 Distinguish between the directors' report and the chairman's report.

10 Explain the apparent dichotomy between the historical nature of the company annual financial report and the concern for the future of the company which is said to be held by shareholders and other interested parties.

11 The concept of income is no more than a man-made conventional symbol or indicator of economic conduct. It is not based on any known natural laws. Discuss the significance of these statements, explaining, in general terms, the nature of the traditional accounting measures of income which are contained in company financial reports.

12 Income cannot exist without capital, and capital depends entirely on the process of valuation. Explain within the context of company financial reporting.

13 The balance sheet is a valuation statement. Comment.

14 Explain the importance of assets in financial reporting. Are all assets of the company capable of being measured and disclosed in its annual financial report?

15 What is meant by the term 'shareholders' equity'?

16 Distinguish between fixed and current assets. What is the relationship between current assets and current liabilities?

17 What is the income statement intended to describe? In what way does it differ from the balance sheet? What is the fundamental relationship between these documents?

18 What are the main effects of the application of the historic cost and realization principles in the measurement of company income and financial position?

19 Producing measures of income and financial position is as much about judgement as it is about the application of accounting rules. Comment.

20 A knowledge of the future is essential to the proper measurement of past income and financial position. Comment.

21 Highlight the main differences between the financial statements of a single company and the financial statements of a group of companies. What is the most important reason for producing consolidated financial statements?

22 What purpose is served by the funds statement? How does it relate to the income statement and balance sheet?

Other main financial statements

23 Why should changes in the prices of specific assets in a company be a major accounting and reporting problem?

24 Explain the main current cost accounting adjustments which can be made to reported accounting income.

25 The statement of value added is no more than an alternative version of the income statement. Discuss.

26 The audit function is a fundamental prerequisite to the existence of a free capital market. Discuss this statement with particular reference to annual financial reports.

27 The auditor's report on the annual financial statements of a company is a limited document. Comment.

Practice exercises (covering Chapters 2 and 3)

Assume in all cases whatever conventions are felt to be appropriate regarding the timing of the eventual repayment of liabilities. The objective of these exercises is to provide the reader with an opportunity to practise the compilation of the main financial statements, and the solutions need not conform with the form, content and disclosure provisions of Schedule 8, Companies Act 1948 (although that would be desirable).

1. Derive outline balance sheets from the undernoted data.

(a) AB Ltd

Assets and liabilities as at t_1

	£
Stock	800
Debtors	120
Trade creditors	350
Shop fittings	450
Bank overdraft	960
Shop premises	4,000
Cash in hand	20
Mortgage loan	2,500
Share capital	1,000
Reserves	580

(b) CD Ltd

Assets and liabilities as at t_1

	£
Debtors	1,250
Trade creditors	225
Cash in hand	85
Stock	1,150
Mortgage loan	600
Motor van	500
Taxation outstanding	200
Bank overdraft	195
Share capital	1,000
Reserves	?

(c) EF Ltd

Assets and liabilities as at t_1

	£
Bank overdraft	6,350
Plant and machinery at cost	6,500
Accumulated depreciation on plant	3,600
Inventory of stock	1,200
Inventory of work-in-progress	3,707
Debtors	2,000
Trade creditors	880
Share capital	200
Retained income (beginning of period)	600
Rent	240
Wages	1,200
Electricity	83
Cost of goods sold	5,500
Sales	9,500
Depreciation for period	700

2. From the undernoted data, you are required to prepare the draft income statement of XY Ltd for the period t_1 to t_2 and the corresponding draft balance sheet at t_2.

	£
Sales	116,400
Office and general expenses	3,340
Running and maintenance costs of delivery trucks	1,600
Property, plant and equipment at cost	26,100
Office equipment at cost	530
Cash at bank and on hand	3,800
Profits retained in business in previous years	4,720
Long-term loans	6,000
Aggregate depreciation on property	
plant and equipment	15,040
office equipment	270
Depreciation charge for current year	1,090
Trade creditors	6,800
Stock of goods for resale	19,000
Trade debtors	16,730
Share capital	20,000
Cost of goods sold	97,040

3. PQ Ltd has been in business for several years, and the following figures appear in its accounting records at t_2.

	£
Called up share capital	416,000
Revaluation reserve	298,196
Retained income at t_1	1,213,295
Land and buildings at valuation	504,371
Plant and equipment at cost	908,602
Plant and equipment aggregate depreciation	517,094
Investments in market securities	21,865
Stock and work-in-progress	753,431
Debtors	1,220,114
Bank balances and cash	527,540

Other main financial statements

Trade creditors	455,872
Tax payable	518,283
Dividend payable	74,256
Bank loan	1,281
Turnover	2,455,422
Change in stock t_1 to t_2	61,307
Depreciation on plant	86,926
Interest on bank loan	1,347
Wages and salaries	300,888
Other business overheads	290,763
Cost of goods purchased	914,152
Taxation provided	406,751
Dividend provided	74,256

You are required to prepare the company's draft income statement for the period t_1 to t_2 and its draft balance sheet as at t_2.

4. The following data have been produced in order to provide a funds statement for ST Ltd for the period t_1 to t_2. You are required to prepare such a statement.

	£
Purchase of plant and equipment	120,000
Taxation paid	8,000
Increase in stock and work-in-progress	12,000
Sale of investments	3,000
Depreciation on plant for the period	17,000
Increase in long-term loans	30,000
Increase in debtors	10,000
Reduction in bank balances	41,000
Dividends paid	4,000
Disposal of plant	27,000
Increase in trade creditors	15,000
Income before taxation	21,000

5. Derive a funds statement for VW Ltd for the period t_1 to t_2 from the undernoted data.

	t_1 £	t_2 £
Shop premises[(1)]	4,000	5,500
Shop fittings[(2)]	450	750
Stock	800	900
Debtors	120	130
Cash	20	20
	5,390	7,300
Share capital	1,000	1,000
Reserves[(3)]	580	1,200
Mortgage loan[(4)]	2,500	3,000
Trade creditors	350	300
Bank overdraft	960	1,800
	5,390	7,300

[(1)]Additional premises purchased for £1,500
[(2)]Changes during the period were as follows:

	£
Opening figure	450
Add: purchases	600
	1,050
Less: depreciation	300
Closing figure	750

[3] Changes during the period were as follows:

	£
Opening figure	580
Add: retained income for period	620
Closing figure	1,200

[4] An additional loan of £500 was obtained during the period to finance the purchase of additional premises.

6. Derive a funds statement for XY Ltd for the period t_1 to t_2 from the undernoted data.

	t_1	t_2
	£	£
Factory buildings[1]	100,000	—
Plant and machinery[2]	65,000	82,000
Stock	234,000	260,000
Debtors	59,000	71,000
Investments[3]	—	10,000
Bank and cash	3,000	9,000
	461,000	432,000
Share capital	50,000	50,000
Reserves[4]	180,000	200,000
Mortgage loan[5]	60,000	—
Trade creditors	171,000	182,000
	461,000	432,000

[1] The buildings were sold for £100,000 during the period.
[2] Changes during the period were as follows:

	£
Opening figure	65,000
Less: sale proceeds equivalent to book value	15,000
	50,000
Add: purchases during period	40,000
	90,000
Less: depreciation	8,000
Closing figure	82,000

[3] Investments purchased during the period for £10,000.
[4] Changes during the period were as follows:

	£
Opening figure	180,000
Add: retained income for the period	20,000
Closing figure	200,000

[5] The mortgage loan was repaid during the period.

Other main financial statements

7. Assuming the following current cost accounting adjustments for the period t_1 to t_2 and current cost valuations at t_2, prepare a current cost income statement and supporting balance sheet for PQ Ltd using the data given in Exercise 3, above.

	£
Period t_1 to t_2	
Additional cost of sales	94,060 X
Provision for increase in monetary working capital	16,329 X
Additional depreciation of fixed assets	47,187 X

	£
t_2	
Current cost valuation of:	
Land and buildings	721,000 X
Plant and equipment	1,236,345 X
Aggregate depreciation on plant	(704,717) X
Investments in market securities	24,766 X
Stock and work-in-progress	848,201 X

The gearing factor should be ignored in this case, as should backlog depreciation.

8. The following are the draft historic cost statements of ABC Ltd for the period t_1 to t_2. (Ignore the question of taxation.)

Income Statement for the Period t_1 to t_2

	£
Sales	26,500
Less: cost of goods sold	13,500
	13,000
Less: depreciation of fixed assets	4,000
Income retained	9,000

Balance Sheet as at t_2

	£	£
Fixed assets		
Plant at cost		80,000
Less: aggregate depreciation		24,000
		56,000
Investments		10,000
		66,000
Current assets		
Stock	5,900	
Debtors	26,500	
Cash	27,000	
	59,400	
Current liabilities		
Trade creditors	6,400	53,000
		119,000

Capital and reserves	
Called up share capital	50,000
Retained income	69,000
	119,000

Notes:

1 The current cost of goods sold for the period was £16,100.
2 The monetary working capital provision for the period was £700.
3 The plant was purchased some time ago. The current cost of the plant in its original condition was £86,000 at t_2.
4 Current cost depreciation for the period was £4,300.
5 The current cost of investments at t_2 was £20,000.
6 The current cost of stock at t_2 was £7,500.

Prepare current cost-based statements for the period t_1 to t_2 using the above data. Ignore the question of backlog depreciation.

9. The following is a draft income statement for LM Ltd for the period t_1 to t_2. Prepare a net value added statement for that period using the data provided.

LM LTD

Income Statement for the Period t_1 to t_2

	£
Turnover	204,000
Change in stocks t_1 to t_2	7,000
Purchase of goods	(134,000)
Wages	(26,000)
Depreciation of: motor vehicles	(7,000)
plant	(14,000)
Other business overheads	(7,000)
Income before taxation	23,000
Tax on income	(11,000)
Income after taxation	12,000
Dividends proposed on: preference capital	(700)
ordinary capital	(3,500)
Transfers to reserve	(2,000)
Retained income	5,800

Selected bibliography for Chapters 1, 2 and 3

This and the remaining bibliographies at the end of each chapter are intended to give the interested reader an opportunity to explore the relevant topics beyond the limits imposed by the writer. However, the selection of additional reading material to support such a general introduction has not been easy, and it should be noted that the following references are only some from among a great many which could have been chosen.

H. W. Bevis, 'The Accounting Function in Economic Progress', *Journal of Accountancy*, August 1958, pp. 27–34. The role of accounting and accountants generally.

P. Bird, *Understanding Company Accounts*, Pitman, 1979, pp. 1–55. A basic introduction to company financial statements.

Other main financial statements

J. L. Carey, *Getting Acquainted with Accounting*, Houghton Mifflin, 1973. The nature of accounting (pp. 1–9); the financial reporting function (pp. 29–41); and the audit function (pp. 55–67).

T. A. Lee, *Company Auditing* 2nd edition Gee & Co., 1982, Chapter 1. The need for financial information, the financial reporting function and the audit function.

T. A. Lee, *Income and Value Measurement*, 2nd edition, Nelson, 1980. An overall explanation of the nature of income, capital and value (pp. 6–19); and an explanation of current cost accounting (pp. 109–12).

M. Moonitz, 'The Basic Postulates of Accounting', *Accounting Research Study 1*, American Institute of Certified Public Accountants, 1961, pp. 8–20. The environment of accounting.

A. M. C. Morison, 'The Role of the Reporting Accountant Today–1', *The Accountant's Magazine*, September 1970, pp. 409–15. The nature of accounting and auditing.

K. Most, *Accounting Theory*, Grid Publishing, 1977, pp. 211–93. A review of the balance sheet, income statement and funds statement.

4
The early history and development of company financial reporting

The pre-limited company era

The formation of companies by joint subscription for shares has a history which is well over 350 years old. The need to provide large amounts of money to finance extensive trading and commercial operations created, for example, the East India Company (in 1600), the Hudson's Bay Company (in 1670) and the Bank of England (in 1694). These unlimited liability companies were formed either by special Act of Parliament or by Royal Charter, without managerial accountability to ownership by means of published financial statements. This created opportunities for fraud and embezzlement, and managers speculated and lost vast sums of money belonging to shareholders.

Thus, in 1719, the Bubble Act was introduced, limiting any form of partnership to six members in the hope that this would reduce the incidence of financial mismanagement. The success of the Act in this respect is difficult to ascertain. Certainly, it did not provide for adequate measures of control which might have protected the interests of owners and creditors. In 1825 it was repealed and a maximum limit of twenty members was then placed on partnerships.

This notwithstanding, there were at the time a number of factors influencing governments to allow a more diffuse ownership in business enterprises, and these included the rapidly increasing industrialization of the UK; and, particularly, the development of railway systems in the first half of the nineteenth century. These changes were creating an ever-growing need for funds to finance the cost of the ventures concerned. They also created an immediate need to provide measures with which legally to protect the providers of the finance from unscrupulous management. In other words, the problem was to encourage investment in private enterprise while, at the same time, adequately protecting the investors.

The railway example

An excellent way of highlighting the movement towards the provision of adequate legal protection for investors and other persons involved with companies is to examine the development of railway accounting. The

Railway Age in the UK occurred between 1830 and 1870 and, for the first time, the world saw the emergence of multi-million-pound enterprises, with large numbers of lay shareholders. It was a period of some chaos, but from it came the basis for the present-day system of corporate financial reports.

The significance of railways in economic development came to fruition with the opening of the Liverpool and Manchester Railway in 1830. Following this, other railway lines were opened by companies incorporated by Acts of Parliament, particularly in the 1830s and 1840s. These Acts of Parliament (one for each railway company) gave the authority to build the line concerned and also to raise funds to meet the costs of construction. Interestingly, most of these private Acts required accounting records to be kept, but made no provision for published financial statements or audits (for example, Section 56, Stockton and Darlington Railway Act 1821). In other words, not only were shareholders not provided with financial statements, they were even denied the right to examine whatever accounting records the companies did keep.

Gradually, however, the Acts took greater cognisance of investor needs, and the provision of formal accounting could be evidenced – for example, the Great Western Railway Act 1835 provided for the presentation of half-yearly financial statements at the appropriate general meetings of shareholders. The numerous enactments were eventually consolidated into the Companies Clauses Consolidation Act 1845, which *inter alia* provided that:

> On the books being so balanced an exact balance sheet shall be made up, which shall exhibit a true statement of the capital stock, credits, and property of every description belonging to the company, and the debts due by the company at the date of making such a balance sheet, and a distinct view of the profits or loss which shall have arisen on the transactions of the company in the course of the preceding half-year.

The balance sheet was examined by at least three directors, signed by the chairman or his deputy and produced at general meetings, but it was not circulated to every shareholder. There was also provision for an audit by a shareholder who was not to be an officer of the company. The balance sheet was then required to be sent to the government department dealing with railways.

This therefore was the situation existing by the mid-1840s. The public could subscribe to these companies and were, in turn, given some measure of protection by the receipt of an audited balance sheet. But these provisions did not apply to companies incorporated before 1845. On the face of it, however, the accounting and reporting provisions, at least for post-1845 railway companies, appear to satisfy the conditions of stewardship defined by Bird:

> Every steward is held accountable to the person or body which entrusted resources to him, whether the latter is a 'superior steward' or the ultimate

owner. Accountability places two obligations upon a steward; he must render an 'account' of his dealings with the stewardship resources, and then he must submit to an examination (usually known as an 'audit') of that account by or on behalf of the person or body to whom he is accountable.[1]

Nevertheless, the stewardship-orientated railway accounting of the mid-1800s must be treated with a great deal of caution, for the following reasons: (a) shareholders were required to be provided with a balance sheet only, while there was no corresponding provision for an income statement; (b) the balance sheet provided was not widely circularized to shareholders, inspection having to take place at the company's registered office; (c) there were no generally accepted standards of accounting available to ensure that published information had been properly measured (the main controversy of the time concerned the treatment of expenditure – what should be matched against sales revenues when determining periodic income, and what expenses should be treated as assets for balance sheet purposes); and (d) auditing standards were extremely poor since few auditors were professionally-qualified accountants. In other words, there still remained a great deal of latitude in company accounting and reporting; much was left to the discretion of company directors, thereby increasing the chances of abuses of shareholder rights. Shareholders in railway companies were not therefore in a particularly strong position to protect their interests.

The Regulation of Railways Act 1868 attempted to remedy this, especially with regard to the accounting treatment of expenditure. Prior to this Act, the major abuse in railway accounting and reporting was undoubtedly the arbitrary treatment and classification of expenditure in such a way as to overstate income in bad financial years, and understate it in good years; this being done in either case to justify the payment of certain levels of dividends to shareholders. As Pollins has stated:

> However, there is some evidence to suggest that many railway directors as well as shareholders wished to have regular rather than fluctuating dividends, and the entries in the final accounts may very well have been influenced by the desire for a record of stable earnings and dividends. The fact that many items appearing (or not appearing) in the revenue accounts involved personal judgments, and that there was not yet a generally accepted body of accounting doctrine, made it easy for the preparation of the final accounts of even the most conscientiously conducted company to be influenced by considerations of management policy.[2]

In other words, the poorly developed system of accounting and reporting for these early railway companies provided opportunities for their directors to manipulate reported income to justify payment of dividends and, at the worst extreme, dividend payments were made when income did not really exist to justify them (high dividends being paid in order to attract more investors who would provide funds to alleviate financial difficulties caused by poor or fraudulent management). The 1868 Act provided for the publication and filing with the Board of Trade of detailed accounting statements including a revenue account (an early form of income statement) and balance sheet in prescribed forms. In particular, the Act required the distinction between depreciable and non-depreciable assets, and created an accounting uniformity amongst railway companies which had not existed previously.

Summarizing, therefore, on the example of railway development, it is clear that the need for investor protection through provision of relevant accounting information was recognized reasonably early, but the relative lack of acceptable accounting standards, coupled with inadequate legal regulations, allowed unscrupulous managements to abuse the system at will. Consequently, by the 1860s, there was an obvious need not only to tighten up the related law, but also to introduce a consistency and uniformity in railway accounting and reporting practices.

The legislative development of company financial reporting, 1844–1900

As already indicated, companies had existed in the UK for some time prior to the mid-1850s. The effects of the Industrial Revolution, with its emphasis on mechanization, manufacturing and the factory system, had given rise to the ever-increasing need of companies for finance from the public. This came in part from subscriptions from shareholders, but a great deal also came from bankers, lenders and creditors. The failure of less formally structured partnerships was caused, in part, by a lack of sufficient finance, and business enterprises were therefore looking more widely to the public for the necessary funds.

Incorporation by registration (as distinct from formation by Act of Parliament) was introduced by the Joint Stock Companies Act of 1844. It had a relatively modern outlook – for example, the provision for accounting records to be kept; the presentation of a balance sheet to each ordinary meeting of shareholders; the balance sheet normally to be sent to shareholders before such meetings; and the audit of the records and balance sheet. Unfortunately, however, the Companies Bill 1844 provision to present half-yearly income statements to shareholders was not incorporated in the 1844 Act. No legal prescription existed regarding the form of the balance sheet, nor was there provision for incorporating companies with limited liability. The main aim of these provisions was therefore limited, as has been summarized by Edey and Panitpakdi:

> (a) To provide the creditors and shareholders of companies with statements of assets and liabilities that would give indications of the solvency of the companies, and (b) in the case of some classes of companies to prevent actual and potential shareholders or creditors from being misled as the result of dividend distributions made out of capital – which, in effect, means made at the expense, in some sense, of the future of the company without this fact being known.[3]

The lack of adequate disclosure and auditing provisions in the 1844 Act (for example, auditors were not required to be professionally-qualified accountants) was not remedied by the subsequent Joint Stock Companies

Act 1855 which did, however, introduce the concept of limited liability. As a result, shareholders of limited companies could only lose what they had invested in them. This particular idea was brought into being because it served as a warning to creditors and lenders not to over-extend their credit and lending facilities to companies. In other words, limited liability appeared to be no more than a governmental move to curb abuses then taking place in the corporate sector.

The 1844 and 1855 Acts were eventually consolidated into the Joint Stock Companies Act 1856, with one important amendment: the compulsory reporting and audit provisions were omitted. Edey and Panitpakdi postulated that this was because of a feeling that such arrangements should be made privately between shareholders and directors if they were felt to be necessary.[4] Thus, at a stroke, the legislative development of the company reporting function was arrested.

However, Table B of the 1856 Act, containing model articles of association, outlined voluntary reporting and auditing provisions for companies if this was felt necessary. These included *inter alia* the keeping of proper accounting records (details of these were given); the presentation to an annual general meeting of an annual income statement (details of the contents of which were stipulated); a similar provision for a balance sheet; and the communication of these reports to shareholders at least seven days before the relevant general meeting. In addition, there were audit provisions relating to the published financial statements – that is, they were to be examined and a report was to be given on the balance sheet in particular:

> The auditors shall make a Report to the Shareholders upon the Balance Sheet and Accounts, and in every such Report they shall state whether, in their opinion, the Balance Sheet is a full and fair Balance Sheet, containing the particulars required by these Regulations, and properly drawn up so as to exhibit a true and correct view of the State of the Company's Affairs . . .

Table B also contained a standard form of balance sheet for the guidance of company directors and accountants. No similar provision existed for the income statement. This, then, was the corporate financial reporting situation that was to remain until 1900 for the majority of companies (banks and insurance companies had minimum accounting provisions reintroduced long before 1900): that is, a policy of no state interference in such matters through legislation.

There are two other events before 1900 worth noting. First, all company laws (that is, for all types of companies) were consolidated into the Companies Act 1862 which contained, in its Table A, model reporting and auditing provisions similar to those in the 1856 Act. And secondly, there were several attempts between 1862 and 1900 to reintroduce compulsory reporting provisions, mainly as a consequence of the growing importance of the company in economic activity and of the market in company shares. However, in 1900 a new Companies Act was introduced. There were no provisions for compulsory accounting and reporting, but an annual audit of accounting records and the balance sheet was required for all companies along the lines contained in Table B of the 1856 Act and Table A of the 1862 Act. Therefore, although many companies did in fact produce financial statements for their shareholders prior to the early 1900s, little doubt exists that the present system of reporting owed little to its inauspicious beginnings in the mid to late-nineteenth century. This can be seen more clearly in the illustration given below.

Illustration 36 (pages 86–7) is intended to demonstrate an example of early company financial reporting. It is the 1881 report of The Distillers Co. Ltd, a UK company which is still very much in business today. The example reveals financial statements well ahead of the then current practice, yet lacking the detailed disclosure and presentation required and expected today.

Illustration 36 is worthy of a number of comments: (a) none of the statements included in the report was legally required at the time of reporting; (b) the audit report and balance sheet only became legally required in 1900 – 19 years later – and the profit and loss account (or income statement) became legally necessary in 1929 – 48 years later; (c) the balance sheet was merely a listing of assets and liabilities – there was little classification, apart from assets being in an order of realizability and liabilities in an order of payability; (d) no detailed data supported the bare figures in the statement – for example, in relation to depreciation of fixed assets; (e) depreciation was accounted for not by allocation of cost but by appropriation of income to a reserve; (f) very little detail was given as to the composition of reported income; (g) no previous year figures were made available; (h) the auditor's report gave a 'true and correct view' certification of the reported figures – not an opinion as is expected today; and (i) the presentation of the financial statements was made as a straightforward copy of the balances as then existed in the ledger of the company (generally in the case of the balance sheet, and particularly in the case of the profit and loss account). Thus, these statements can be regarded as very limited in comparison with those of today, yet were many years ahead of their time in terms of the then generally accepted practice.

The legislative development of company financial reporting, 1900–1948

It is quite clear that the philosophy behind financial practices prior to 1900 was one of maintaining as much secrecy about corporate affairs as company managements regarded as necessary. The informational needs of shareholders, creditors and lenders were apparently pushed into the background; management was left to manage; and, unless company directors felt inclined to do otherwise, shareholders were deprived of formal information concerning profitability and financial position. Indeed, even in situations when financial information was communicated to shareholders, this normally centred around a summarized balance sheet providing a listing of various assets and liabilities which equated with shareholders' equity. The income statement, if one was produced, was simply a disclosure of income available for distribution, dividends paid and income retained in the company. Any income figure disclosed was intended as a statement of what the directors regarded as the maximum dividends which could be distributed. In other words, the objective of company financial reporting at the time was to justify the level of dividends paid to shareholders and to provide creditors with an assurance that the company was solvent, properly managed financially, and not overdistributing income to their detriment.

This particular approach was recognized formally in the Companies Act 1907 when all companies, with the exception of private companies, were required to produce an annual audited balance sheet. No particular format was prescribed nor were there specific regulations dealing with the content of these statements. The emphasis remained apparently very much on creditor protection rather than providing information for shareholders in general, and for investment decision-making in particular. There were still no formal arrangements regarding professional qualifications for auditors. The Companies Act 1908 then consolidated all previous enactments.

The idea that company shareholders should only be interested in the market price of their shares, and the level of their dividends, persisted for many years, with only public company shareholders being guaranteed the supply of regular information. Even then, the information was limited to a summary balance sheet which hid as much as it revealed owing to the accounting manipulation that took place in its production. It was regarded as a virtue to understate the financial position considerably; and to do the reverse in bad years. The use of so-called 'secret reserves' was widely practised prior to the 1930s and was regarded as necessary to the creation of financial stability for the benefit of creditors and lenders. The neglect of shareholders' interests in this respect is usefully illustrated by Hannah in his study of takeover bids prior to 1950.[5] Commenting on the relative lack of takeover bidding in the inter-war period (partly because of the concentration of shareholdings either in private family hands or in large blocs controlled by company directors), he reveals that bids were normally made through the board of directors without reference to shareholders. He quotes one accounting authority of the day in this respect:

> This was the usual form of merger between two quoted companies and it therefore seemed quite natural for an accountant to insist in 1925 that 'the negotiations must obviously be conducted by the Directors. In order to preserve proper secrecy, it is not possible for the Directors to acquaint the shareholders of the matter.' Almost invariably, the shareholders were passive agents in the decision-making process, and the history of their attempts to thwart the decisions of directors and achieve a better bid price is largely a study of failure.[6]

Illustration 36 Example of an early company financial report

THE DISTILLERS COMPANY (LIMITED)

General Balance Sheet as at 14th May 1881

LIABILITIES

To Capital Account—		
65,000 Shares of £10 fully paid up,		£650,000 0 0
" Depreciation and Reserve Account,		43,500 0 0
" Registered Office Accounts—		
Debentures,	£202,000 0 0	
Sundry Creditors,	107,697 15 7	309,697 15 7
" Distillery Accounts—		
Sundry Creditors,	21,596 14 9	
Carriage on Spirits in Bond,	6,366 17 5	27,963 12 2
" Profit and Loss Account,	75,727 19 1	
Less Interim Dividend paid 1st January 1881,	25,350 0 0	
Less Income Tax,	50,377 19 1	
Less transferred to Depreciation and Reserve Account,	10,000 0 0	40,377 19 1
		£1,071,539 6 10

ASSETS

By Land and Buildings,		£287,966 7 11
" Plant and Utensils,		235,377 1 4
" Phoenix Park Distillery,		110,697 15 0
" Distillery Accounts—		
Sundry Debtors	93,828 15 0	
Cash in Hand and Bank,	14,142 19 0	
Stock of Spirits,	254,974 14 1	
Grain,		
Bills Receivable on Hand,	54,545 4 3	417,491 12 4
" Registered Office Accounts—		
Sundry Debtors,	12,123 15 2	
" Cash on Hand and in Bank,	7,882 15 1	20,006 10 3
		£1,071,539 6 10

Profit and Loss Account, for Twelve Months Ending 14th May 1881

Dr.	£	s.	d.	Cr.	£	s.	d.
To Income Tax and Directors' Fees,	3,103	12	6	By Balance from last Account,	72,547	16	4
" Charges Account, including Registered Office Salaries, Law Expenses, Auditor's Fees, and Head Office Expenses,	2,287	12	1	Less Dividend paid 1st July 1880,	71,500	0	0
" Interest and Discount Account,	12,230	4	10		1,047	16	4
" Depreciation and Reserve Fund,	10,000	0	0	Balance from the Distillery Working Accounts,	92,272	19	8
" Balance being Net Profit for the Year ended 14th May 1881,	74,680	2	9	Registration Fees,	28	12	6
" And Balance from the Year ended 15th May 1880,	1,047	16	4				
	75,727	19	1				
Less the above sums transferred to Depreciation and Reserve Account,	10,000	0	0				
	65,727	19	1				
	£93,349	8	6		£93,349	8	6
				By Balance	65,727	19	1
					£65,727	19	1

Glasgow, 7th July 1881. – I have Audited the Books and Accounts of the Distillers Company (Limited) for the Year ending 14th May last, and have found them correct, and I certify that the foregoing Profit and Loss Account and Balance Sheet exhibit a true and correct view of the state of the Company's affairs at that date.

ALEX MOORE, C.A., Auditor.

In addition, as Hannah has pointed out, the quality of reported information was poor when it was made available to shareholders:

> One tentative explanation of the failure of contested direct bidding to emerge in its modern form is the quality of information available to shareholders and potential bidders in the inter-war years. . . . Neither balance sheets nor profit and loss accounts gave adequate indications either of assets and liabilities or of trading profits. For a variety of reasons – commercial secrecy, preservation of credit status, reduction of trade union wage pressure, discouragement of new entry – directors sometimes published figures which understated or overstated the true position of their company. The imperfect state of the law relating to company accounts, and in particular to secret reserves and holding company accounts, allowed common resort to such malpractice.[7]

In other words, the period following the 1908 Act saw the limited publication of financial information on a compulsory basis, and the possibility of manipulated information being presented in published reports. There had therefore been little advance in this respect since the Joint Stock Companies Act 1844. There appeared to be a feeling that shareholders were content if they knew that their capital was being kept intact, and that their dividends were being maintained. Shareholders were regarded very much as sleeping partners in companies and, in any case, the majority of companies were family businesses with shares closely controlled by persons who were also directors (Board of Trade statistics reveal that, by 1930, there were 16,263 public companies and 95,598 private companies).

The above notwithstanding, the consolidating Companies Act 1929 introduced one important change, at least for public companies. It required them to present an annual income statement to their shareholders. There was no guidance given regarding its, or the balance sheet's, contents, nor was it required to be audited. In fact, it was a very small step in the direction of providing adequate financial information for shareholders and other interested persons. It should be stated that, despite the gradual merging of companies into larger entities during the inter-war years, there was no legal provision for the publication of consolidated financial statements reflecting the profitability and financial position of groups as a whole. This obviously helped to mask the state of affairs of companies considerably, as only financial results of the holding company needed to be disclosed. This can be seen by examining the financial statements of The Distillers Co. Ltd for 1939 (Illustration 37, pages 90–1).

The disclosed financial results related to the holding company; no results were given separately or within group statements for its subsidiary companies – even though these investments constituted 69% of the recorded values of the holding company's assets. Thus, a considerable amount of information was missing from this report. It can also be shown that the reporting practices of The Distillers Co. Ltd had changed little in 58 years from those demonstrated in 1881 (Illustration 36). The same omissions remained, and evidently generally accepted practice may well have caught up with the company.

The 1930s and 1940s, however, witnessed a considerable increase in the number of companies and a consequential increase in share ownership. In 1939 there were 160,655 companies (13,920 public and 146,735 private); by 1949 the number had increased to 243,518 (12,075 public and 231,443 private). The need to review safeguards for company investors was recognized governmentally and, in 1943, the Cohen Committee on Company Law Amendment was formed. The Committee sat for two years, and its report, published in 1945, resulted in the consolidating Companies Act 1948, which radically changed the legal requirements for financial reporting and which now forms the basis for present-day company financial statements. The main changes in the 1948 Act can be summarized as follows:

(a) Every company was required to present annually to its shareholders an income statement and balance sheet, both of which had to be audited and reported on.

(b) The Eighth Schedule of the Act contained a list of items of information which every company was required to disclose, where relevant, in its financial statements. In other words, this was the introduction of a legally-enforceable minimum disclosure level, although some companies (for example, in banking and insurance) were exempted from certain of the provisions because of the nature of their business.

(c) Holding companies were required to present to their shareholders consolidated financial statements for the group as a whole. These statements were to be subject to audit and were also subject to the minimum disclosure requirements.

(d) Company auditors were required to be professionally-qualified accountants except in the case of the small family company, defined as an exempt private company.

(e) The auditor's rights, duties and powers were clearly laid down in the Act. In particular, he was required to give an opinion on the truth and fairness of the reported information.

The 1948 Act therefore gave companies the basis with which to provide shareholders and other interested persons with meaningful information about their financial affairs. It will be discussed further in relation to present-day practice in the next chapter.

The legislative development of company financial reporting, 1948 to date

Since the Companies Act 1948, there have been four amending Acts – in 1967, 1976, 1980 and 1981. Each has extended the company financial reporting function. The Companies Act 1967, for example, extensively

Illustration 37 A further example of an early company financial report

THE DISTILLERS COMPANY LIMITED

Balance Sheet as at 15th May 1939

Capital				
Authorised	£15,000,000 0 0			
Issued				
£10,690,962 Ordinary Stock	£10,690,962 0 0			
£2,200,000 6% Cum. Preference Stock	2,200,000 0 0			
		£12,890,962 0 0		
4½% Irredeemable Mortgage Debenture Stock, 1902–				
Held by Subsidiary Company	1,750 0 0			
Held by other Stockholders	148,250 0 0			
		150,000 0 0		
6% Irredeemable Stock, 1907		120,000 0 0		
Reserve Fund		5,200,000 0 0		
Reserve for Equalisation of Dividends		250,000 0 0		
Fire Insurance Fund		500,000 0 0		
Superannuation and Provident Fund		900,000 0 0		
Subsidiary Companies–				
Current and Loan Accounts		8,340,922 8 7		
Associated Companies–				
Current and Loan Accounts		2,042,512 16 1		
Sundry Creditors, Reserves for Taxation and Contingencies, and Credit Balances		2,910,244 17 3		
Carriage on Spirits in Bond		149,482 4 3		
Provision for proposed Final Dividends and Bonus		1,210,492 2 4		
Profit and Loss Account		436,898 7 8		
Contingent Liability–				
Uncalled Liability on Investments, £55,417				
		£35,101,514 16 2		

Land and Buildings–				
At cost, less amounts written off				£403,300 0 0
Plant and Utensils–				
At cost, less amounts written off				246,777 0 0
Sundry Investments, including British Government Securities–				
At or under cost, *less reserve*				6,133,111 10 6
Subsidiary Companies–				
Investments therein, at or under cost, *less reserve*		£16,825,922 13 3		
Current and Loan Accounts		7,008,389 11 10		
				23,834,312 5 1
Associated Companies–				
Current Accounts				110,247 2 10
Stocks of Spirits, Grain, Warehouse Rents etc. as certified by officials of the Company				899,699 3 0
Sundry Debtors				234,354 12 0
Cash in Bank and on Hand, at Home and Abroad				3,239,713 2 9
				£35,101,514 16 2

On behalf of the Board – FORTEVIOT, Chairman
ALEX WALKER, Director

Glasgow, 29th June 1939. – We have to report to the Members that we have examined the Books and Accounts of The Distillers Company Limited for the year ended 15th May 1939, and have obtained all the information and explanations we have required. In our opinion the foregoing Balance Sheet is properly drawn up so as to exhibit a true and correct view of the state of the Company's affairs according to the best of our information and the explanations given to us, and as shown by the

Profit and Loss Account for Year ended 15th May 1939

	£ s. d.	£ s. d.	£ s. d.
To Directors' Fees (including Income Tax thereon)	12,289 15 0		
Less recovered from Subsidiary Companies	760 8 9		
		11,529 6 3	
Note:– Fees from Subsidiary Companies retained by the Directors of this Company – Nil			
" Balance, being Net Profit for Year carried down		2,482,201 12 2	
		£2,493,730 18 5	
To Reserve Fund		400,000 0 0	
" Fire Insurance Fund		150,000 0 0	
" Superannuation and Provident Fund		100,000 0 0	
" Interim Dividends for Year:–			
On Preference Stock	47,850 0 0		
On Ordinary Stock	581,321 1 2		
		629,171 1 2	
Provision for Final Dividends for Year:			
On Preference Stock	47,850 0 0		
On Ordinary Stock	968,868 8 7		
		1,210,492 2 4	
To Provision for Bonus on Ordinary Stock		193,773 13 9	
To Balance carried to Balance Sheet		436,898 7 8	
		£2,926,561 11 2	

	£ s. d.	£ s. d.
By Profit from Trading after writing down Buildings, Plant and Investments, providing for Debenture Interest, Management Remuneration, Head Office Expenses, Taxation and Contingencies, and including Interest and Dividends from Investments		2,492,719 6 11
" Registration Fees		1,011 11 6
		£2,493,730 18 5
By Balance brought down		2,482,201 12 2
" Balance brought forward from last year		444,359 19 0
		£2,926,561 11 2

extended the disclosure requirements in Schedule 8, Companies Act 1948, and amended the latter's audit requirements – the auditor in all cases was required to be professionally qualified, and the wording of the audit report was simplified to exclude any description of the scope of the audit.

The Companies Act 1976 continued the changes in financial reporting and auditing – the reporting period was precisely defined; accounting records to be maintained by the company were specified; and the provisions for the appointment, removal, resignation, remuneration and qualifications of the auditor were strengthened. The audit function was extended in the Companies Act 1980 – the auditor was required for the first time to issue a separate report as to whether any qualified opinion he had on the main financial statements had materially affected any distribution of profits based on these statements. In addition, the Act amplified the provisions concerning the disclosure of transactions involving the company's directors.

The 1967, 1976 and 1980 Acts, therefore, were largely concerned with strengthening and extending the original provisions of the Companies Act 1948. The Companies Act 1981, however, marked a considerable change in the legislation of the company financial reporting function. For the first time in the history of the latter, the form and content of the income statement and balance sheet were prescribed as a requirement to provide the true and fair view of income and financial position. In addition, certain general accounting practices, and various historic cost and current cost accounting rules, were legislated for – again for the first time in company history. The Act allowed certain companies defined as small and medium-sized to deliver abbreviated financial statements only to the Registrar of Companies, supported by an audit report that the size criteria had been satisfied. This is a recent example of changing views as to the relevance of Companies Act provisions to all companies – that is, smaller companies particularly may not require to adhere to all of the extensive provisions which are relevant to larger companies.

Finally, the 1981 Act included the directors' report as part of the package of financial statements to be reported on by the auditor, and significantly extended its content to include a fair review of the development and position of the company (including future development). Thus, the reporting function is seen to extend itself beyond the confines of information about past activities, and to include the auditor in this extension. Certainly, the reporting accountant and the auditor now need to concern themselves much more than hitherto with prediction and the uncertainty of the company's future.

Case law and the early development of company financial reporting

Arguably, some of the most significant developments in company accounting and reports took place in the courts of law – that is, particularly during the period from about 1890 to 1930. All of these cases concern the measurement and reporting of periodic income and especially its relationship to the payment of dividends. The reason for this phenomenon was undoubtedly the lack of guidance on these matters in company law, and the lack of a generally acceptable common body of accounting knowledge (this latter point will be dealt with in detail in the next section).

Relatively early in the history of the limited company, it was decided that dividends should not be paid out of subscribed capital[8] – that is, dividends should only be paid out of surpluses over and above the share capital subscribed to the company. However, with that principle established, there remained the problem of putting it into practice; particularly with regard to the calculation of distributable income elements. A number of cases were decided over the intervening years, each of which presumably had an important influence on accounting practice. The following comments relate to the most significant of these cases.

In *Lee* v. *Neuchatel Asphalte Co. Ltd* (1889) 41 Ch. 1, it was held that a company empowered to do so by its articles of association, may distribute dividends without providing for depreciation of its wasting assets. (A wasting asset, in this context, is one which is being depleted through extraction; for example, as in mines and quarries.) In other words, distributable income could be calculated before deducting such depreciation. The judge, in fact stated: 'There is nothing in any of the Companies Acts prohibiting anything of the kind. . . . It has been judicially and properly left to the commercial world to settle how the accounts were to be kept.'

In *Bolton* v. *Natal Land Colonisation Co. Ltd* (1892) 2 Ch. 124, it was held that a company can declare a dividend out of current income without providing for losses caused by exceptional reductions in the value of assets such as land. In other words, it was proper to pay dividends out of trading income before providing for infrequent reductions in asset values.

In *Lubbock* v. *The British Bank of South America* (1892) 2 Ch. 198, it was held that a gain made on the sale of part of a company can be distributed as a dividend, if the articles of association do not prohibit it. Thus, an element of non-trading income was held to be distributable to the shareholders.

In *Verner* v. *General and Commercial Investment Trust Ltd* (1894) 2 Ch. 239, it was held that, as in the *Bolton* case above, an investment trust company can distribute income before providing for decreases in certain asset values.

In *Wilmer* v. *McNamara and Co. Ltd* (1895) 2 Ch. 245, it was held that a company can declare a dividend out of current income without providing for the depreciation of fixed assets. This case hinged on whether depreciation of goodwill and leased property was to be regarded as expenditure which should be deducted from sales revenues in determining distributable trading income. It was held not to be.

In *Foster* v. *The New Trinidad Lake Asphalte Co. Ltd* (1901) 1 Ch. 208, it was held that a realized gain on an asset taken over by a company at its formation is not distributable income, unless such a surplus remains after a revaluation of all other company assets. This decision seems to be contrary to the previous judgement in the *Lubbock* case above.

In *Bond* v. *Barrow Haematite Steel Co. Ltd* (1902) 1 Ch. 353, it was held that preference shareholders cannot compel directors to pay a dividend without retaining income in the company when the articles of association demand that such retentions be made. This judgement comes nearest to the modern practice of prudent financial management by retaining a proportion of available income before declaring dividends to shareholders.

In *Ammonia Soda Co.* v. *Chamberlains* (1918) 1 Ch. 266, it was held that it is not necessarily illegal for the directors of a company to pay dividends out of current income without taking cognisance first of past aggregate losses. In other words, if the value of shareholders' equity in the balance sheet is less than that originally subscribed because of cumulative losses, it is still proper to pay dividends out of current income rather than out of any surplus left after deducting past losses from current income. The judge in this case stated: 'In my opinion this alleged restriction has no foundation in law. . . . I am, of course, far from saying that in all such cases dividends can properly be paid without making good the previous loss; the nature of the business and the amount of the loss may be such that no honest and reasonable man of business would think of paying dividends without providing for it.'

In *Stapley* v. *Read Bros. Ltd* (1924) 40 T.L.R. 442, it was held that a company can pay a dividend out of current income where accumulated previous losses have been written off by the revaluation of goodwill. This rather follows the previous judgment given in the *Ammonia Soda* case above.

In *Rex* v. *Kylsant and Morland* (1932) 1 K.B. 442, the chairman of the Royal Mail Steam Packet Co. Ltd was found guilty of presenting false financial statements to shareholders with an intent to deceive them. In particular, this involved the manipulation of accounting data through undisclosed secret reserve movements. The judge had this to say of secret reserve accounting: 'We have heard a great deal about the keeping of secret reserves, and we have heard a great deal about the commercial troubles which may flow from that practice. It may work very well in many cases; no doubt it does. It is a practice which is being followed, no doubt by many concerns, of the highest standing. On the other hand, it may be the subject of almost intolerable abuse. It is said to be a matter of domestic concern between the company and the shareholders, but if the shareholders do not know and cannot know what the position is, how can they form any view about it at all?'

The answer to this question came very soon after the *Kylsant* case when, owing to the nature of its findings and judgments (the auditor was found guilty of aiding and abetting with regard to the false information), the practice of secret reserve movements began to disappear from the then generally accepted accounting practice.

Summarizing on the above cases, it is clear that the courts of law had a considerable influence on practices concerned with the measurement of income and asset values for reporting purposes. The particular concern appears to have been with the determination of income figures with which to justify dividend payments, rather than with figures required for general reporting purposes. However, as the reported income statement of these times appears to have been used mainly to justify dividend payments, it is very clear that measurement practices used for dividend purposes would also be those used for general reporting purposes. It should also be said that most of these judgements should not be regarded as representative of current best accounting practice; though they would have been mirroring that of the time in which they took place.

History and development of accounting standards

Ross has summarized the aim of accountants in relation to company financial reports as follows:

> Our essential service to the public thus boils down to assuring they have the benefit of the best financial statements we can devise; and this in turn boils down to producing the most useful accounting principles that we can and getting them generally accepted.[9]

This almost self-evident statement pinpoints one of the most important aspects of financial statements: the need for a generally acceptable body of practices with which to measure the required accounting information. In other words, if financial reports are to contain reliable data, they must be the subject of known and proven principles or standards (to use the contemporary term) of measurement and communication. These can be defined following the Littleton formula;

> A standard is an agreed upon criteria of what is proper practice in a given situation; a basis for comparison and judgment; a point of departure when variation is justifiable by the circumstances and reported as such. Standards are not designed to confine practice within rigid limits but rather to serve as guideposts to truth, honesty and fair dealing. They are not accidental but intentional in origin; they are expected to be expressive of the deliberately chosen policies of the highest types of businessmen and the most experienced accountants; they direct a high but attainable level of performance, without precluding justifiable departures and variations in the procedures employed.[10]

The development of accounting standards has generally taken place within the context of professional development, particularly that of the professional accountancy bodies. Indeed, as the following paragraphs will reveal, government and the courts have tended to take second place to the accountancy bodies in this process. Nevertheless, although these bodies came into being in the second half of the nineteenth century, it was not until the mid-1920s that the debate about adequate accounting standards commenced. However, it has not receded since.

The reason for the lateness of the standards debate, in comparison to the much longer history of company financial reports, may probably be put down to the fact that the earlier professional accountants were concerned primarily with bankruptcies, liquidations and taxation, rather than with the accounting and auditing problems inherent in company financial reporting. In addition, the poor legislative requirements for disclosure of accounting information did not create the appropriate pressure to make the professional bodies look for a generally acceptable and coherent body of relevant practices. However, by the 1920s and 1930s they were becoming aware of deficiencies in the then accounting and reporting practices and were, on both sides of the Atlantic, beginning to look for ways to remedy the situation.

In the US, the then American Institute of Accountants commenced discussions with the New York Stock Exchange concerning the most obvious of the problems in financial reporting which were being publicly commented on. From these discussions, the Institute formed the Committee on Accounting Procedure (1930) and the Committee on the Development of Accounting Principles (1933), the aim of which was to reduce the number of alternative accounting practices available for any one given business situation. This was done by codification and recommendation through published *Accounting Research Bulletins*.

A similar procedure took place in the UK, the Institute of Chartered Accountants in England and Wales being particularly active with its published *Recommendations on Accounting Principles*. This series of pronouncements, commencing in 1944, contained relatively simple statements of the main problem areas in accounting, together with recommended solutions. They were advisory by nature and, as with the *Accounting Research Bulletins*, merely helped to add to the number of available practices in certain defined areas of accounting. This flexibility, coupled with the lack of a mechanism for the abandonment of bad or obsolete practices through time, created criticism of accounting and reporting practices, particularly when it was realized by the financial and investment communities that it was possible for a company to produce a number of alternative income statements and balance sheets, each based on the same transactions and so forth, but each different because of the various accounting practices applied.

In the US, the criticism led to the formation, in 1959, of the Accounting Principles Board of the American Institute of Certified Public Accountants. This was supported by a Research Division, and several *Accounting Research Studies* were published concerning the fundamental truths and ideas in accounting. In other words, the initial approach was to pronounce on what should be rather than what was being accounted for. This produced such radically different forms of accounting that the Board was forced back to the previous system of *ad hoc* problem-solving.

In addition, the recommended practices in *Accounting Principles Board Opinions* were eventually made mandatory on members of the American Institute. However, this created even more public criticism of accountants and their practices, and the Institute set up its Financial Accounting Standards Board in 1973 to replace the Accounting Principles Board in an attempt to produce accounting standards in a normative but acceptable fashion, backed by adequate research. So far, the new Board has published more than 30 *Statements of Financial Accounting Standards* on various aspects of reporting practice. In addition, the Securities Exchange Commission (SEC) in the US has published numerous *Accounting Series Releases* which stipulate accounting practices to be followed by SEC-registered companies (these generally following the SEC policy of allowing the American Institute to initiate, formulate and issue statements on generally accepted practice). Increasingly, however, the SEC has found itself in very recent years advocating reporting practices in advance of bodies such as the Financial Accounting Standards Board – thus leading to some conflict between these bodies.

Generally speaking, the UK experience has been different from the American one. Prior to 1969, the various accountancy bodies produced their individual research reports and recommendations, each of which failed to carry any mandatory provisions. Public criticism grew over the poor 'state of play' regarding accounting standards and, in 1969, the Institute of Chartered Accountants in England and Wales published its *Statement of Intent on Accounting Standards in the 1970's*. Its main aim was to publicise the new attempt to narrow the number of alternatives in accounting practices and, in light of this, the Accounting Standards Committee was formed with members from all the major accountancy bodies in the UK. Since then, the Committee has initiated research in certain key areas, published *Exposure Drafts* of proposed accounting standards for public discussion and comment, and eventually issued a number of *Statements of Standard Accounting Practice*, the contents of which are required to be implemented by members of the major professional accountancy bodies responsible for the production or auditing of company financial statements. If individual circumstances dictate that implementation of a particular standard is not appropriate, then the reasons for this must be fully explained to the shareholders in the relevant financial statements. These standards will be discussed in more detail in the next chapter.

Finally, it would be wrong to describe the history of accounting standards as they affect company financial reporting without making mention of the development of the complementary auditing standards. The audit of company financial statements was little regulated prior to 1980. In fact, the first official recommendations were made in 1961 when the Institute of Chartered Accountants in England and Wales commenced its guidance series entitled *Statements on Auditing*. However, in

1980, the main UK professional accountancy bodies introduced a mandatory series of *Auditing Standards* supported by several *Auditing Guidelines* – each designed to outline what is regarded as best practice and aid the auditor in giving his *true and fair view* opinions. Thus, they assist and ought to improve the quality of the company financial reporting function of which the audit is an essential part.

Conclusions

The present system of financial reporting by companies in the UK is primarily a legally-based one, that base being the Companies Act 1948 and its amending Acts. In addition, it is being supported by a series of mandatory professional provisions which have the strength of the major professional accountancy bodies behind them (though they do not have the same legal status of a Companies Act). Case law has also had a part to play in fashioning reporting practice.

The Companies Act 1948 has been amended significantly by the Companies Acts 1967, 1976, 1980 and 1981, particularly with regard to accounting and disclosure requirements, and it is to these specific present-day provisions that Chapter 5 will be directed. The current professional requirements will also be examined.

References

1 P. Bird, *Accountability: Standards for Financial Reporting*, Accountancy Age Books, 1973, p. 2.
2 H. Pollins, 'Aspects of Railway Accounting Before 1868', in A. C. Littleton and B. S. Yamey, *Studies in the History of Accounting*, Sweet & Maxwell, 1956, p. 354.
3 H. C. Edey and P. Panitpakdi, 'British Company Accounting and the Law: 1844–1900', in Littleton and Yamey, op. cit., pp. 356–7.
4 Edey and Panitpakdi, op. cit., p. 361.
5 L. Hannah, 'Takeover Bids in Britain Before 1950: An Exercise in Business "Pre-History"', *Business History*, January 1974, pp. 65–77.
6 ibid, p. 68.
7 ibid. p. 69.
8 e.g. in *Flitcroft's Case* (1882), 21 Ch. D. 519.
9 H. I. Ross, 'The Current Crisis in Financial Reporting', *Journal of Accountancy*, August 1967, p. 66.
10 A. C. Littleton, *Structure of Accounting Theory*, American Accounting Association, 1953, p. 143.

Suggested discussion or essay topics

1 A knowledge of the historical development of company financial reporting is necessary for an understanding of its present state and problems. Discuss.
2 The nineteenth-century development of the limited liability company created the need, first, for creditor protection and, secondly, for shareholder protection. Comment on this statement, indicating the means by which protection was afforded.
3 Comment on the significance of railway accounting and reporting in relation

to later developments in company financial reporting.

4 Early company income statements were no more than reconciliation statements to justify proposed dividend payments to shareholders. Discuss.

5 How important was the creditor or lender in the early legal and voluntary provisions for company financial reporting?

6 Up to the end of the nineteenth century there appears to have been a tendency, even in the minds of directors, to assume that outside shareholders needed to know little more than creditors. Discuss.

7 The balance sheet was the primary financial statement prior to the 1930s. Since then, the income statement has gradually gained in importance. What reasons can be given for this change in emphasis?

8 Undoubtedly, until the *Kylsant* case, company financial statements were subject to the abuses of secret reserve manipulation. Discuss the implications of these practices from the point of view of statement users.

9 What impact did court case decisions have prior to the 1930s on the development of company financial reports?

10 The Companies Act 1948 marked a major landmark in company financial reporting. Explain this, comparing the 1948 Act with earlier major enactments.

11 Discuss the significance of audit provisions contained in company legislation prior to the Companies Act 1948, with particular reference to the quality and credibility of company financial statements.

12 The accountancy profession has moved from a completely *laissez faire* system to one of compulsion with regard to accounting practices used to produce company financial reports. Discuss this, describing the relative disadvantages of each system.

Selected bibliography for Chapter 4

W. W. Bigg, *Practical Auditing*, HFL Publishers, 1965, pp. 314–48. Covers many of the relevant legal cases in some detail.

H. C. Edey and P. Panitpakdi, 'British Company Accounting and the Law: 1844–1900', in A. C. Littleton and B. S. Yamey, *Studies in the History of Accounting*, Sweet & Maxwell, 1956, pp. 356–79. A description of the legal development in the stated period.

R. W. Gibson, *Disclosure by Australian Companies*, Melbourne University Press, 1971. A detailed study of Australian practices from 1829 to 1969, which follow the UK example closely.

L. W. Hein, *The British Companies Acts and the Practice of Accountancy*, Arno Press, 1978. A detailed study of the impact of company legislation on company accounting practice.

T. A. Lee and R. H. Parker (editors), *The Evolution of Corporate Financial Reporting*, Nelson, 1979. A selection of readings on various aspects of UK and US developments in financial reporting.

A. C. Littleton and V. K. Zimmerman, *Accounting Theory: Continuity and Change*, Prentice-Hall, 1962, pp. 72–102. An overall review of the topic, including pre-company history.

H. Pollins, 'Aspects of Railway Accounting before 1868', in Littleton and Yamey, *Studies in the History of Accounting*, pp. 332–55. A detailed study of the earliest practices.

S. A. Zeff, *Forging Accounting Principles in Five Countries*, Stipes Publishing, 1972, pp. 1–90: The UK development of accounting standards, and pp. 110–268: The US development of accounting standards.

5

Present-day requirements for company financial reporting

The current legal requirements for annual reporting

Financial accounting and reporting by companies in UK are governed by Sections 149 to 158 inclusive of the Companies Act 1948; Sections 3 to 8 inclusive of the Companies Act 1967; Sections 1 to 12 inclusive of the Companies Act 1976; (indirectly) Sections 39 to 45 inclusive and (directly) Sections 54 to 61 inclusive of the Companies Act 1980; and Sections 1 to 21 inclusive of the Companies Act 1981. Certain of these provisions have been amended by succeeding Acts of 1976, 1980 and 1981 where relevant. The main requirements concerning the form, content, accounting principles and rules, and disclosure pertaining to company financial statements are contained in Schedules 8 and 8A of the Companies Act 1948 (as provided in Schedules 1 and 2 of the Companies Act 1981). In addition, company auditing practices are legislated for in Sections 161 and 163 of the Companies Act 1948; Sections 13 and 14 of the Companies Act 1967; Sections 13 to 20 inclusive of the Companies Act 1976; Section 43 of the Companies Act 1980; and Sections 7, 11, 12, 15, 43 and 55 of the Companies Act 1981. Again, certain of these provisions have necessarily been amended by the succeeding Acts of 1976, 1980 and 1981 where relevant. The following paragraphs give a brief description and summary of the main contents of these sections.

Accounting records

Section 12, Companies Act 1976, stipulates that companies must keep adequate accounting records, particularly with regard to data essential for the production of financial statements of the type discussed in Chapter 1. Paraphrasing the various sub-sections 1 to 12, the following are the main features of Section 12:

(a) The accounting records must be sufficient to disclose with reasonable accuracy the financial position of the company at any time, and to enable its directors to produce income statements and balance sheets with the required true and fair view of income and financial position.

(b) The accounting records must contain daily entries describing the nature and amount of monetary receipts and expenses of the company; a record of its assets and liabilities; and, where relevant, detailed stock records of goods bought, sold and held by the company (including the identity of its customers and suppliers).

Thus, the adequacy of a company's accounting records is judged effectively in terms of their ability to provide data which have the legal qualities of truthfulness and fairness. Unfortunately, and this is a matter which will be discussed in detail later in this text, none of the Companies Acts 1948, 1967, 1976, 1980 and 1981 define the meaning of the phrase 'true and fair view' in relation to reported accounting information.

Financial statements

The requirement to provide shareholders annually with financial statements is contained in Sections 1 to 7 inclusive, Companies Act 1976. The following is a summary of its main provisions:

(a) The directors of the company must prepare and lay before the company in general meeting an income statement for each of its defined accounting reference periods, together with a balance sheet prepared by them as at the end of each such period.

(b) These financial statements should be supported by a relevant audit report and directors' report, and the complete package must also be delivered annually to the Registrar of Companies. However, as noted below, the Companies Act 1981 provides for certain exceptions to this general rule.

(c) The accounting reference period shall normally be taken to be a twelve-month period, ending on 31 March unless the company has notified the Registrar of Companies of a different period-end.

(d) The defined accounting reference period can be subsequently changed on due notice being given to the Registrar of Companies.

(e) The financial period to which the income statement relates is deemed to be the financial year of the company (whether or not it covers a year), and can be no more than seven days shorter or longer than the defined accounting period, which itself must begin the day after the end-date of the previous income statement.

(f) The directors must normally produce their required financial statements for the general meeting within ten months (for private companies) or seven months (for public companies) of the end of the defined accounting reference period.

Sections 5 to 10, inclusive, Companies Act 1981 contain certain provisions exempting companies and groups of companies from delivering their full annual financial statements to the Registrar of Companies. The entities exempted in this way are defined as small and medium-sized (a small company or group has to satisfy at least two or more of the following conditions – turnover does not exceed £1.4m, gross assets do not exceed £0.7m, and number of employees does not exceed 50; a medium-sized company or group's corresponding figures are £5.75m, £2.8m and 250). They must not be public companies, banking, insurance or shipping companies, or members of an ineligible group. A small company or group should deliver to the Registrar a summarized balance sheet, and a medium-sized company or group should supply a summarized income statement and a full balance sheet. In both cases, the directors must make a statement that the entity concerned is exempt, and the auditor must supply a special report to accompany his full report on the financial statements to the Registrar, giving an opinion on whether the requirements for exemption have been satisfied.

Section 11, Companies Act 1981 governs the publication of annual financial statements in abridged form – for example, as in the national press. If they are given in a form other than the full or modified forms relevant for delivery to the Registrar of Companies, then they must be accompanied by a published statement by the company or group stating that the statements are not full ones; whether or not full statements have been delivered to the Registrar of Companies; and whether an auditor's report has been made and, if so, if it was unqualified.

The effect of these provisions is relatively straightforward – the shareholders of the company must receive an income statement for each accounting reference period, supported by a relevant balance sheet, directors' report and audit report. The financial period covered by these statements will usually be one of twelve months (although this can be varied by several days). The company must define its reference period but can redefine it at a later date. In addition, the company must deliver its full or modified annual financial statements to the Registrar of Companies, and state publicly that this has been done if it publishes abridged statements.

Section 149, Companies Act 1948 (as provided in Section 1, Companies Act 1981), states the nature and qualities to be attributed to annual financial statements:

(1) The accounts of a company prepared under section 1 of the Companies Act 1976 shall comply with the requirements of Schedule 8 to this Act (so far as applicable) with respect to the form and content of the balance sheet and profit and loss account and any additional information to be provided by way of notes to the accounts.

(2) Every balance sheet of a company so prepared shall give a true and fair view of the state of affairs of the company as at the end of its financial year, and every profit and loss account of a company so prepared shall give a true and fair view of the profit or loss of the company for the financial year.

Once again, the phrase 'true and fair view' is used, without further definition, and the accountants responsible for producing the relevant financial statements are left to interpret it as best they can.

In this respect, Section 149(3), Companies Act 1948 places an onerous responsibility on these accountants. In it, it is stipulated that the requirement for a 'true and fair view' overrides the requirements of Schedule 8 of the Act, and all other accounting and disclosure requirements of the Companies Acts 1948 to 1981 as they affect company financial statements. If the 'true and fair view' is not given, even if all the requirements are satisfied, then additional information must be disclosed. Equally, if satisfying any Companies Act requirement prevents the 'true and fair view' being given, then that requirement must be departed from. The departure, however, must be disclosed, and the effect of it, and the reasons for it, fully explained in a note to the financial statements (Section 149(4)).

However, the main contents of these financial statements are governed by the 'minimum accounting and disclosure' requirements of Schedule 8, Companies Act 1948 (as specified in Schedule 1, Companies Act 1981), which states the majority of items of information which must be disclosed, where relevant, in the published income statement, balance sheet and notes to accounts. Schedule 8 also specifies the form and content of financial statements and certain general accounting rules; as well as specific historic cost and current cost accounting rules, which should or can be applied by reporting companies.

In Part I of Schedule 8, the form and contents of single company income statements and balance sheets are specified in some detail – with a choice of two formats for the former, and four for the latter. The balance sheets prescribed generally speaking follow a vertical layout – either fixed assets plus current assets minus current liabilities equating with longer-term liabilities plus provisions, and share capital and reserves; or fixed assets plus current assets equating with an aggregation of all liabilities plus share capital and reserves. The income statement formats are all vertical in style, but vary according to whether the emphasis is on type of expenditure or type of operation. The chosen format must be adhered to consistently. If a change is made, this should be disclosed in a note to accounts, together with a statement of the specific reasons for the change. Comparative figures (adjusted where necessary to give comparability) should be presented.

Preliminary expenses, share issue expenses and research costs are specifically excluded in Part I from being treated as assets, and the income statement should reveal income before tax, dividends and transfers to and from reserves. In the balance sheet, the most significant features new to company law are the treatment of intangible assets such as goodwill as fixed assets, and the need to differentiate between liabilities due for repayment in less than a year from these due in more than a year.

In addition, in Part II, Section A, the general accounting principles include the presumption in accounting that the company is a going concern; its accounting practices will be applied consistently; prudence will be exercised in accounting (only realized income should be included in the income statement but all known liabilities and losses up to the date of signing the balance sheet should be accounted for in it); and the revenue and expenditure of a particular year should be accounted for without regard to the dates of receipt and payment. The company's directors are required in a note to accounts to disclose any departure from these principles, the reasons for it, and the effects of it on the financial statements.

In Part II, Sections B and C, the rules to be applied in historic cost and current cost accounting are specified – the reporting company being free to report on either basis. The historic cost rules include, for example, the following requirements: (a) fixed assets to be accounted for and depreciated, if of limited useful life, on the basis of purchase price or production costs (direct costs attributable to production plus indirect costs reasonably attributable to it); (b) provision to be made for permanent diminution in value of fixed assets (including investments); (c) development costs only to be included as a fixed asset if there is a special reason (which should be disclosed); (d) non-group goodwill to be written off over its useful life; (e) current assets to be based on purchase price or production cost, with a reduction to net realizable value where necessary; (f) the cost of stock to be determined using one of a variety of bases, including latest prices and, if material, the difference between its historic cost and replacement cost (or latest historic cost) should be stated in a note to accounts.

The current cost rules permit an accounting for fixed assets (except goodwill) and stock. Investments can be accounted for at market or estimated directors' valuation. Depreciation on a historic cost basis, however, must also be disclosed, as must the historic cost of each balance sheet item (except stock). A revaluation reserve is required to handle these current cost adjustments.

Part III of Schedule 8 contains the basic minimum disclosure requirements as they affect the notes to the financial statements – that is, if not given in these statements directly. They can be divided into the following main areas: (a) the main accounting practices adopted by the company in its financial statements should be given; (b) the balance sheet should contain details of share capital and debentures (including new series), fixed assets, investments, reserves and provisions, borrowings, and financial commitments; (c) the income statement should contain details regarding interest received and paid, auditor's remuneration, tax, turnover and profit (allocated between different classes of business), and particulars of staff.

Further additional information which must be disclosed, where relevant, is provided for by Sections 3 to 8 inclusive of the Companies Act 1967 (identity and details of subsidiary and associated company shareholdings, particulars of directors' entitlements in £5,000 bands, and particulars of employees salaries in £5,000 bands if more than £20,000); and paragraph 39(2), Schedule 3 and Sections 54 to 61 inclusive of the

Companies Act 1980 (details of transactions involving directors).

Lastly, Section 3(1), Companies Act 1967 requires a holding company to disclose in a note to its financial statements full details of its shareholdings in subsidiaries. Section 4, Companies Act 1981 extends this requirement to non-subsidiary shareholdings of more than 20% of the allotted capital, with the additional disclosure of the aggregate capital and reserves of the non-subsidiary company at the latest balance sheet date, and its income for the period ended that date. This information should be given in a note to the financial statements. Section 4, Companies Act 1967 (extended by Section 3, Companies Act 1981) provides for companies identifying in notes to the financial statements details of investments of more than 10% in other companies (these not being subsidiaries).

Group financial statements

Reporting requirements for groups of companies are contained in Section 150, Companies Act 1948 (as amended by Section 8(1), Companies Act 1976). The effect of these provisions is that, where the company has subsidiaries at the end of its financial year, it is required to produce group financial statements for the accounting reference period concerned, dealing with the income and financial position of the company and its subsidiaries. These group statements will be required to be laid before the company in general meeting and also filed in full or modified form with the Registrar of Companies (depending on the size of company – Sections 9 and 10, Companies Act 1981). These statements are in addition to the main statements already dealt with in the previous section of this chapter.

Section 150(2) contains several exceptions to the above general provision for consolidated income statements and balance sheets, meaning that no such statements need be produced when, for example, the holding company is itself a wholly-owned UK subsidiary, or when to produce group statements would be, in the opinion of the directors, immaterial, impractical, harmful or misleading or would cause unnecessary delay in publishing the financial statements.

The form of the group financial statements is outlined in Section 151, Companies Act 1948 (as amended by Schedule 2, Companies Act 1976):

(1) . . . the group accounts of a holding company prepared under Section 1 of the Companies Act 1976 (taken with Section 150 of this Act), shall be consolidated accounts comprising –
(a) a consolidated balance sheet dealing with the state of affairs of the company and all the subsidiaries to be dealt with in group accounts;
(b) a consolidated profit and loss account dealing with the profit or loss of the company and those subsidiaries.

If the holding company directors feel that this group financial information could be better presented, they can present more than one set of consolidated statements covering individual group companies or separate sub-groups within the group (Section 151(2), Companies Act 1948).

The quality of the information contained in the required financial statements of groups of companies is governed by Section 152, Companies Act 1948 (as provided in Section 2, Companies Act 1981), and again contains the undefined 'true and fair view' phrase:

> (1) Subject to the following provisions of this section, the group accounts prepared by a holding company under Section 1 of the Companies Act 1976 (taken with Section 150 of this Act) shall comply with the requirements of Schedule 8 to this Act (so far as applicable to group accounts in the form in which those accounts are prepared) with respect to the form and content of those accounts and any additional information to be provided by way of notes to those accounts.

> (2) Those accounts (together with any notes to those accounts) shall give a true and fair view of the state of affairs and profit or loss of the company and the subsidiaries dealt with by those accounts as a whole, so far as concerns members of the company.

Thus, the provisions apply, as much as is practicable, to the accounting and disclosure requirements of Schedule 8. However, it should be noted that Schedule 8 applies in the first place to the financial statements of single companies. However, Part IV makes specific provision for holding companies and their subsidiaries – first, in relation to the holding company's statements, full details of its investments in its subsidiaries must be disclosed, together with any inter-company balances; and secondly, the group financial statements shall be prepared and comply as much as is practicable with the requirements of Schedule 8 and any other requirements of the Companies Act 1948 to 1981.

Part IV also supports Section 151(2), Companies Act 1948. It allows a holding company to provide financial statements for its group in unconsolidated form, provided it discloses the reasons for this treatment in a note to the financial statements, together with any audit qualification (and related details) pertaining to any subsidiary's financial statements. Subject to certain exceptions, such a holding company should disclose its investment in subsidiaries at a value based on their existing share capital and reserves.

Section 153(1), Companies Act 1948 provides that, wherever possible, the financial years of the holding company and its subsidiaries should coincide for reporting purposes. If they do not coincide, Part IV, Schedule 8, Companies Act 1948 provides that the holding company should disclose in a note to its financial statements the relevant dates and the reasons for the timing differences. Finally, Section 152(3), Companies Act 1948 makes a similar provision regarding the overriding nature of the 'true and fair view' to that relating to single company statements – that is, it overrides Schedule 8 of the Act and any other requirement of the Companies Acts 1948 to 1981 in relation to group financial statements.

Thus, summarizing, each UK company will usually present annually to its shareholders an income statement and a balance sheet; and if it also happens to be a holding company which is not a wholly-owned subsidiary, it will usually present annually a consolidated income statement and balance sheet. These group statements are subject to the same 'true and fair view' and accounting and disclosure requirements as the holding company's own financial statements (at least where practicable). However, certain subsidiary company data can be omitted from group statements if conditions warrant it. Lastly, group statements can be incorporated into the holding company's own statements if this is felt to be more convenient than producing separate consolidated information.

Section 154, Companies Act 1948, defines the terms holding company and subsidiary company to allow company directors to decide whether or not they have to comply with the group financial statement provision.

> (1) For the purpose of this Act, a company shall ... be deemed to be a subsidiary of another if, but only if, –
> (a) that other either –
> > (i) is a member of it, and controls the composition of its board of directors; or
> > (ii) holds more than half in nominal value of its equity share capital; or
> (b) the first-mentioned company is a subsidiary of any company which is that other's subsidiary.

In other words, there has to be control of one company by another, usually by holding more than half of the equity capital, but also on occasion by controlling the board of directors of the subsidiary.

Miscellaneous provisions

The Companies Act 1948 also contains several miscellaneous provisions relating to the provision of regular financial information for company shareholders. For example, Section 155 (amended by Schedule 2, Companies Act 1976 and Section 7, Companies Act 1981) requires every company balance sheet (and every copy thereof laid before the general meeting or delivered to the Registrar of Companies – whether full or modified) to be signed by two directors (thereby acknowledging directorial responsibility for the production and quality of the financial statements).

Section 157 (amended by Section 13, Companies Act 1981) provides that a report of the directors must be attached to the balance sheet (and should include, *inter alia*, a fair review of the development of the business of the company and its subsidiaries, and its financial position, the recommended dividend figures, as well as information regarding changes in the nature of the business conducted by the company). Sections 16 and

19 inclusive of the Companies Act 1967, as amended by Sections 13, 14 and 16, Companies Act 1981, added to these requirements providing, *inter alia,* for the disclosure of information pertaining to important events occurring between the end of the reporting period and the time of presenting the financial statements; likely future developments and research and development activities; significant fixed asset changes; directors' interests in the shares and debentures of the company (unless stated in a note to the financial statements); and political and charitable donations. Section 158 (amended by Schedule 2, Companies Act 1976) provides that:

> (1) A copy of every balance sheet, including every document required by law to be annexed thereto, of which a copy is to be laid before a company in general meeting, together with a copy of the auditors' report, shall, not less than twenty-one days before the date of the meeting, be sent to every member of the company (whether he is or is not entitled to receive notices of general meeting of the company), every holder of debentures of the company (whether he is or is not so entitled) and all persons other than members or holders of debentures of the company, being persons so entitled.

Thus, every shareholder and debenture holder of the company is provided with the required reporting package in advance of the general meeting at which it is to be presented for approval. This gives the distinct impression that the reporting function is not intended merely for the shareholders; it is also designed for long-term lenders to the company. In addition, even its creditors are catered for – Section 5, Companies Act 1976 provides them with the right to take the company to court should it fail to register its required financial statements with the Registrar of Companies.

Transactions involving directors

Section 190, Companies Act 1948 prohibited loans or guarantees on loans by a company to its directors (except in very limited circumstances). Section 197 of the same Act required disclosure in the main financial statements of any allowable loans to directors and officers of the company. These curbs on directors' behaviour have been extended considerably by Sections 54 to 61 inclusive, Companies Act 1980 (which effectively repealed the provisions in the Companies Acts 1948 and 1967). The new provisions are complex, but the following provide a summary (of the main points:

(a) The matters requiring disclosure in the main financial statements (not the directors' report as previously) include all transactions in which there could be a conflict of interest between directors and their companies – for example, long-term service contracts, substantial transactions and loans.

(b) The disclosure provisions relate to all companies (although there are certain exemptions for recognized banks); 'directors' include directors and persons connected with them (for example, members of their families); and apply to all relevant matters, wherever made, and whether legal or illegal.

(c) Considerable details require to be disclosed where relevant (for example, outstanding loan amounts, the value of credit and other transactions, the nature of directors' interests in the disclosed transaction, etc.).

(d) Officers of the company, who are not directors, are also subject to these disclosure provisions, although they need not be named.

(e) Because the relevant disclosures are required to be made in the main financial statements, they are subject to the examination and opinion of the reporting company's auditor.

Maintenance of capital and distribution of income

Sections 39 to 45 inclusive, Companies Act 1980 introduced a new concept to company financial reporting in the UK (mainly to bring the latter into line with EEC legislation). This concerns the maintenance of company capital and the distribution of its income, and mainly relates to defining what can or cannot be distributed to shareholders. The following is a summary of these various relevant sections of the Act as amended by Section 84, Companies Act 1981.

(a) No company can distribute an unrealized profit and, generally speaking, realized losses must be offset against realized profits before a distribution can be made. No guidance is given as to when a profit is realized, although depreciation in excess of historic cost depreciation is to be so regarded. Realized losses are to be regarded as any provision (as defined in Schedule 8, Companies Act 1948) except as arising as a loss following an overall revaluation of the reporting company's fixed assets. (It should be noted that the problem of having no effective legal definition of realized profit has been continued in Part II, Section A, Companies Act 1981 in which it is provided that only realized profits should be included in the income statements. Para. 90, Part IV, Schedule 1 states that realized profits should be determined in accordance with generally accepted accounting principles – but does not define the latter.)

(b) Unrealized losses need not be taken into account in determining the distributable income of a private company (development costs should be treated as an unrealized loss if they are accounted for as an asset – unless the company's directors can justify otherwise). Public companies, therefore, will treat distributable income as realized profits less realized and unrealized losses (a somewhat more restrictive definition). These provisions, however, relate to all individual companies, and not just to groups of companies.

(c) All profits and losses are to be treated without the former distinction between capital and revenue (unless the reporting company is an investment company). Distributions should exclude share capital reductions and bonus issues, and share premiums and capital redemption reserves are not distributable.

(d) The provisions are retroactive, and therefore every reporting company will require to separate out its retained income and reserves between realized and unrealized income elements. Because of this, and despite any specific disclosure requirements, the implication is that a reporting company's disclosed reserves will require to distinguish between realized and unrealized amounts. The company's auditor is required to report on distributions in particular circumstances (this will be covered in the next section).

The audit function

The above are the main provisions dealing with the publication and presentation of annual financial statements to company shareholders, and, where relevant, to debenture holders. In each instance, the Companies Acts 1948, 1967, 1976, 1980 and 1981 provide for punishment by fine or imprisonment if directors fail to comply with them. Company financial reporting, however, is not simply a matter of legislating for the production of financial statements. In the UK, as in many other developed countries, such statements are also required to be audited by professionally-qualified accountants. Provision for this is contained in the Companies Acts 1948, 1967, 1976, 1980 and 1981.

Section 161, Companies Act 1948, as amended by Section 13(1), Companies Act 1967 and Section 13, Companies Act 1976, deals with the qualifications required of a person whom it is proposed to appoint as company auditor. He must be a member of a recognized UK professional accountancy body (that is, either a chartered or a certified accountant) or have been recognized by the Secretary of State for Trade and Industry as having adequate knowledge and experience to act as auditor (the Secretary also has the power to change the list of professional bodies, having given due notice of his intention to do so; and he has the specific power to decide on the adequacy of professional qualifications obtained outside the UK). When the auditor is, in fact, a firm of accountants, these provisions apply to each member of the partnership concerned. In addition, no person can act as auditor if he knows he is disqualified from doing so, and he must vacate his office if he finds, following his appointment that he has been disqualified (Section 13(5), Companies Act 1976). In particular subsection 2 of Section 161 states:

None of the following persons shall be qualified for appointment as auditor of a company —

(a) an officer or servant of the company;

(b) a person who is a partner of or in the employment of an officer or servant of the company;

(c) a body corporate.

Thus, company directors and managers, and their partners and employees, are barred from holding the office of company auditor, as is a limited liability company.

Sections 14 and 15, Companies Act 1976, govern the appointment and removal of auditors. Every company is required to appoint, at each general meeting at which the required package of financial and other statements is presented, an auditor to act as such from then until the next general meeting at which such a package will be presented. The directors of the company can appoint an auditor prior to the first such general meeting, or on a subsequent casual vacancy, and the Secretary of State for Trade and Industry can make an appointment if one has not been made by the company or its directors.

There is one exception to these general provisions. Section 12, Companies Act 1981 covers situations where no relevant accounting transaction has been put through the company's accounting records during the financial period. Defined as a dormant company, it does not require to appoint an auditor so long as it is a defined small company which is not a holding company. The directors must state, however, in its modified financial statements to the Registrar of Companies that it has been dormant through the financial year and since the year-end.

Section 14(6), Companies Act 1976 states that the auditor can be removed from office before the due termination date by ordinary resolution of the company in general meeting – this being notified to the Registrar of Companies within fourteen days of it being approved. Section 15, Companies Act 1976 states that a special notice is required for a resolution at a general meeting either to appoint an auditor other than the retiring one; to fill a casual vacancy; to reappoint a retiring auditor previously appointed to fill a casual vacancy by the directors; or to remove an auditor before the due termination date. Details of these resolutions must be sent to all concerned – that is, to the 'new' and 'old' auditors. Any retiring auditor, or auditor about to be removed, can make written representations to the shareholders on notice of his retiral or removal (although the court may be asked by the company to prevent this happening if the representations are defamatory). Any auditor being removed has the right to attend the appropriate general meeting, to receive all relevant notices of such a meeting, and be heard at the meeting (Section 15(6), Companies Act 1976).

Thus, generally speaking, the auditor is appointed by the shareholders, and can only be removed by the shareholders. He has a great deal of protection regarding such a removal (particularly with regard to stating his case), and these procedures extend to his retirement at the end of his term of office when he is being replaced. The auditor therefore cannot be summarily dismissed; nor can he expect tenure in office. His remuneration (including his expenses) is usually fixed by the company in general meeting or in such manner as the company in general meeting may determine (Section 14(8), Companies Act 1976).

Equally, the auditor may resign his office, and Sections 16 and 17, Companies Act 1976 cover this aspect of the audit function. He does this by sending a notice of resignation to the company, containing either a statement that there are no circumstances connected with his resignation which he considers should be brought to the attention of the shareholders or creditors of the company; or a statement of such circumstances (again, the court may be asked to stop the circularization of the latter statement if it is felt to be defamatory). If such a statement is given, the auditor can request an extra-ordinary general meeting to consider his resignation. A copy of the statement must be sent to every shareholder prior to the meeting if it has been received in time. The auditor has the right to attend such a meeting and to be heard at it. Thus, as with retiral and removal from office, the Companies Act 1976 gives the resigning auditor ample scope to make his case, if there is one to be heard in general meeting.

Section 14, Companies Act 1967, outlines the duties and rights of the auditor, once appointed, as follows:

(1) The auditors of a company shall make a report to the members on the accounts examined by them, and on every balance sheet, every profit and loss account and all group accounts laid before the company in general meeting during their tenure of office.

(2) The auditor's report shall be read before the company in general meeting and shall be open to inspection by any member.

(3) The report shall —
(a) .... state whether in the auditor's opinion the company's balance sheet and profit and loss account and (if it is a holding company submitting group accounts) the group accounts have been properly prepared in accordance with the provisions of the principle Act and this Act and whether in their opinion a true and fair view is given ....

(*Note* Paragraph 41(3), Schedule 3, Companies Act 1980 and paragraph 27, Schedule 3, Companies Act 1981 has extended 3(a) above to include the Companies Acts 1976, 1980 and 1981.)

In addition, Section 14 instructs the auditor to carry out sufficient investigations to form such an opinion, and particularly to see that proper accounting records are kept and are in agreement with the published financial statements. If this is not the case, then the auditor must report to the shareholders accordingly. The auditor is also given the right of access to all evidence and information necessary to the audit, and all auditors are entitled to attend general meetings, to receive notices relevant to general meetings, and be heard at such meetings regarding business affecting their audit functions.

Sections 18 and 19, Companies Act 1976 have recently extended the rights and duties of the auditor. Section 18 gives him the right of access to subsidiary companies and their auditors for information and explanations required for purposes of his duties as auditor of the holding company. Also, as Section 19 states, it is now an offence for an officer of a company to unknowingly or recklessly give false or misleading information to the auditor. Both these sections are intended to strengthen the position of the auditor so far as concerns his gathering information for purposes of giving his opinion.

Section 43(3)(c) and (6)(c), Companies Act 1980 requires auditors of both public and private companies to prepare a second report on the latest audited financial statements which have been used to justify a distribution of income, in circumstances where these statements have been qualified by the auditor. The second report must state if the qualification is material to the distribution. This requirement will, of course, only affect situations in which dividend distributions have been related to annual financial statements (these being audited whereas interim statements are not), but it represents a further extension in the company audit function.

The concept of additional audit reports by the company auditor has been extended in the Companies Act 1981. Section 7 requires a special report to be included with modified financial statements, stating that the company size requirements to enable modified statements to be delivered to the Registrar of Companies have been complied with. Section 55 also provides for a separate report – in this case, when a private company purchases or redeems its shares out of capital, the auditor is required to report that he has inquired into the company's state of affairs (financial position), the purchase consideration has been properly determined, and is not aware that the directors have made unreasonable statements regarding the purchase or redemption.

Finally, the Companies Acts 1980 and 1981 add two more functions of auditing to the list provided above – Section 59 Companies Act 1980 requires the auditor to include in his report any disclosures relating to transactions of directors which have not been disclosed as required in the audited financial statements; and Section 15, Companies Act 1981 brings the directors' report within the scope of the main audit report – the auditor being required to observe that the directors' report is consistent in its content with the main financial statements and, if it is not, to state this in the audit report.

Thus, company financial statements and the directors' report are required to be examined and reported on by expert and qualified accountants, who are legally entitled to access to all matters necessary to the conduct of such an audit. Their report to the shareholders is expressed in terms of the truth and fairness criteria legally required of the financial statements. It is essentially a function organized on behalf of the shareholders, although other interested groups may also benefit.

Current legal requirements for employees

As mentioned above, the present framework for company financial reporting appears to be orientated towards the shareholder and, to a far lesser extent, the debenture holder and the creditor. However, in recent years in the UK, the information needs of company employees have been recognized in various Acts of Parliament. Although none of these Acts has a major bearing directly on the financial reporting function being described in this text, it would be wrong not to mention the main provisions because many contain sections giving employees the right to receive financial information.

The first such Act is the Health and Safety at Work Act 1974 which requires companies to provide to their employees full information about their health and safety policies and programmes. The Health and Safety inspectorate also has the responsibility of passing on information on health and safety practices to such employees. Specifically, Section 79 of the Act states that the published directors' report must contain information concerning the company's arrangements to secure the health and safety of its employees and of other persons affected by the work of employees.

The Employment Protection Act 1975 obliges companies to disclose information to trade unions to aid collective bargaining and what it describes as good industrial relations practice. Section 18 provides for certain exemptions to this general requirement (for example, information which either would be against the interest of national security or could be regarded as confidential). Also, the company need not produce information if the effect of doing so would exceed the value of it to collective bargaining. The type of information is not stipulated but companies should refer to the Code of Practice of the Advisory Conciliation and Arbitration Service (this includes data on pay and benefits, conditions of service, manpower, operational performance, and financial performance). The latter type of information includes items going much beyond that required to be disclosed in company financial reports (for example, cost and price structures).

Finally, the Industry Act 1975 contains provisions enabling relevant government ministers and trade unions to be supplied by the company with information which the relevant minister believes to be necessary for either national economic policy making or consultations between government and workers. This enactment, however, appears to relate only to companies making a substantial contribution to manufacturing industry. There is a great deal of discretion, despite this, in the hands of the government ministers concerned – the information required may well include forecasts as well as past data.

Each of these Acts has widened the disclosure requirements of companies. Indeed, it could be argued that they go well beyond the existing provisions for shareholders and debenture holders. Thus, employees (through their trade unions) may be in possession of information which is not given to these other groups.

The current legal requirements for prospectuses

Occasionally, companies require additional finance and make share or debenture issues to raise the necessary funds. If these securities are offered to the public, the Companies Act 1948 requires the directors of the company concerned to publish a prospectus in which full details of the offer are contained. Sections 37 to 46 inclusive of the Act (but excluding Section 42) contain the relevant provisions regarding the dating, contents, registration etc. of such a document. The Fourth Schedule of the Act contains details of all relevant matters which must be disclosed in it.

Part I of the Fourth Schedule states the 'matters to be specified' in the prospectus, and these include *inter alia* details of the directors of the company; full particulars of the share or debenture issue being made; and particulars of any property being acquired with the proceeds of the issue. Part II specifies the reports which must be contained in the prospectus, including:

(1) A report by the auditors of the company with respect to –
(a) profit and loss and assets and liabilities . . .; and
(b) the rates of the dividends, if any, paid by the company in respect of each class of share in the company in respect of each of the five financial years immediately preceding the issue of the prospectus . . .

So far as (a) is concerned, income figures should be given for the last five financial years (they should be those of the group if a group of companies is involved), and assets and liabilities should be stated as at the end of the last preceding financial year (again, being those of a group where relevant). In addition, if the proceeds of the share or debenture issue are to be used to acquire shares in another company, or another business, then the accountant's report containing data relating to the last five years' income of the company or business concerned (as well as its last reported assets and liabilities) must be included in the prospectus. So far as the reporting accountant is concerned, Part III of the Fourth Schedule contains the following provisions:

Any report by accountants required by Part II of this Schedule shall be made by accountants qualified under this Act for appointment as auditors of a company . . . and shall not be made by any accountant who is an officer or servant, or a partner or in the employment of an officer or servant, of the company or of the company's subsidiary or holding company or of a subsidiary of the company's holding company; and for the purposes of this paragraph the expression 'officer' shall include a proposed director but not an auditor.

Therefore, when a company seeks funds from the public, it must also make public data relating to its last five years' income (where possible) and its latest reported asset and liability situation. These data must be reported on by expert professional accountants.

The current professional requirements

Undoubtedly, the major influence on annual financial reporting by companies comes from the requirements of company legislation. Recently, however, an additional and powerful influence has appeared. This is connected with the programme of standardization currently being undertaken by the major professional accountancy bodies in the UK. Their *Statements of Standard Accounting Practice* are intended to notify reporting accountants of the prescribed practices which should be adopted in particular accounting situations. Thereby it is hoped to bring about a greater uniformity of practice, especially between companies with similar accounting problems. As a result of the Companies Act 1981 amendments to Sections 149 and 152, Companies Act 1948, any *Statement of Standard Accounting Practice* which is issued explicitly to aid the legally required 'true and fair view' in company financial statements is effectively required to be considered by the reporting accountant as part of the legal provision in these sections that the 'true and fair view' quality overrides the accounting and disclosure requirements of Schedule 8, Companies Act 1948 and all other relevant provisions of the Companies Acts 1948 to 1981.

To date a number of *Statements* have been issued,[1] of which the second in the series is most relevant to this particular part of the text.[2] *Statement of Standard Accounting Practice 2* defines the general principles behind the process of standardization and, in particular, states that:

> The accounting policies ... followed for dealing with items which are judged material or critical in determining profit or loss for the year and in stating financial position should be disclosed by way of note to the accounts. The explanations should be clear, fair, and as brief as possible.[3]

('Accounting policies' is the term adopted in these *Statements* for the particular accounting practices or methods adopted by the company when measuring its reportable accounting information.)

This requirement is supported by a similar, if wider, legal provision in paragraph 36, Part III, Schedule 8, Companies Act 1948 (the terms 'material' and 'critical', for example, are not used in the latter requirement). The legal and professional need to disclose accounting practices is supported by an auditing standard[4] which requires that the auditor should be satisfied that all relevant *Statements of Standard Accounting Practice* have been complied with (unless impracticable or misleading), and that all other practices not the subject of such *Statements* are appropriate to the circumstances of the business. The auditor does not require to state in require to state in his report that he concurs with a departure from a *Statement* – only if he does not so concur.

The auditor's professional duties in relation to attesting the reporting company's compliance with *Statements of Standard Accounting Practice* has been further extended by an auditing guideline related to current cost-based financial statements.[5] He is recommended, depending on the manner and extent to which current cost data are disclosed, either to give a 'true and fair view' opinion or to state whether or not there has been compliance with the relevant *Statement of Standard Accounting Practice*.[6]

Thus, through these various standards and statements, professionally qualified accountants responsible for producing and auditing company financial statements are required to ensure that prescribed accounting practices have been followed and have been adequately disclosed to shareholders. The number of these prescribed practices is increasing over the years owing to the work of the Accounting Standards Committee, and the penalty for not adhering to them (or failing to disclose non-adherence) takes the form of disciplinary action against the offending accountant by his professional accountancy body. This could mean loss of his professional designation and status, and so the sanction is heavy, even if it lacks the full weight of law.

The requirements of the Stock Exchange

The Council of the Stock Exchange has stated its role as follows:

> The Stock Exchange provides a market for the purchase and sale of securities. The efficient operation of such a market depends primarily upon adequacy of information, a quantity of securities whose distribution is sufficiently wide to provide marketability, and certainty of procedures for the settlement of business.
>
> Information is secured initially by the publication of a prospectus in a form approved by the Stock Exchange . . . Thereafter the company is required . . . to maintain a regular supply of information to its shareholders and the investing public.[7]

In other words, of particular concern to the Stock Exchange is the provision of reliable information from the point at which a company first seeks to market its shares, and thereafter throughout the subsequent period of its share quotation. The need for such information is seen in a much wider sense than is the case with the Companies Acts – existing and potential investors are obviously regarded as the primary users.

The information required to be disclosed in the prospectus seeking quotation is contained in Chapter 3 and Schedule II, Parts A and B, of *Admission of Securities to Listing*,[8] and includes *inter alia* particulars of share and loan capital; identification of directors, auditors, bankers etc.;

details of the nature of the company's business; a statement of the last five years' sales turnover or gross trading income, suitably analysed between activities; a statement of the financial and trading prospects of the company; where thought necessary, a trading income forecast together with a statement of the commercial assumptions on which it has been based; an audit report on the accounting adequacy of such a forecast; a statement by the directors on the adequacy of the company's working capital; a report by the auditors of the company covering *inter alia* its trading income during the last five completed financial years, and its balance sheet at the end of the last financial period; a similar audit report on the financial results of any other company which the reporting company has or is about to acquire since the end of its last financial period; particulars of any changes or issues of share capital of the company or its subsidiaries during the last two years; and details of directors' shareholdings, aggregate emoluments and material interests in company assets or contracts.

Details of the information which the Stock Exchange requires listed companies to provide to shareholders and potential investors is contained in its *Listing Agreement.*[9] This includes *inter alia* notification to the Quotations Department of the Stock Exchange of any information necessary to enable the shareholders and the public to appraise the position of the company and to avoid the creation of a false market in its securities; details of proposed and actual dividends and preliminary trading income announcements; changes in share capital; material acquisitions or realizations of assets; changes in its directorate; and any changes in the general character of business. The quoted company must also prepare half-yearly income reports for shareholders, which must be disclosed in the press, and it must issue its annual report within six months of its financial year-end. In addition, the directors' annual report to the shareholders must include *inter alia* the following data: a statement giving reasons for any departures from prescribed *Statements of Standard Accounting Practice*; a geographical analysis of sales turnover; details of shareholdings of more than 20 per cent in other companies; a statement detailing the repayment timetable for bank loans and overdrafts and other borrowings; a statement giving details of directors' shareholdings in the company; a similar statement of directors' interest in company contracts; and details of dividends and emoluments waived by directors or shareholders. The latter details regarding directors' interests cover the period up to one month before the date of the relevant report.

Thus, the Stock Exchange follows the fundamental reporting structure laid down in the Companies Acts and the mandatory provisions of the professional accountancy bodies. It also attempts to make these provisions more relevant to the investor by updating, where possible, to the date of reporting rather than to the date to which the financial statements etc. are drawn up. At the time of writing, however, the accounting and disclosure requirements of the Stock Exchange in its *Listing Agreement* do not contain any reference to the accounting and disclosure requirements in the Companies Act 1981.

The requirements of the Panel

As previously mentioned, the Panel on Takeovers and Mergers was set up at the request of the Bank of England to regulate takeover and merger transactions. *The City Code on Takeovers and Mergers* contains the various rules and regulations which companies must follow if involved in a takeover or merger. This in particular includes the provision of relevant information to all shareholders concerned in the transaction.[10] Shareholders must be notified immediately by press notice of any firm offer to take over or merge that is made to their directors. In particular, and this applies to all statements given to the shareholders:

> Any document or advertisement addressed to the shareholders . . . shall be treated with the same standards of care as if it were a prospectus within the meaning of the Companies Act 1948.[11]

This is interpreted in terms of the relevant facts and opinions being 'fair' and 'accurate'. For example, the *Code* states:

> Shareholders must be put in possession of all the facts necessary for the formation of an informed judgment as to the merits and demerits of an offer. Such facts must be accurately and fairly presented and be available to the shareholders early enough to enable them to make a decision in good time.[12]

The *Code* particularly draws attention to the need to apply these standards to any trading income forecast and asset valuations which may be contained in the offer document.[13]

The commercial assumptions upon which the forecasts are based must be stated, and the accounting practices utilized in their preparation must be reported on by the auditors or consultant accountants concerned. Any named financial advisor must report on the income forecast as a whole. Also, whether or not income forecasts are reported (and there is no specific requirement that they be so), the latest unaudited income figures, since the last date of formal reporting up to the date of the offer, must be disclosed. Thus the *Code* attempts to provide for the production of up-to-date financial data which are relevant to the decisions of the shareholders who are being faced with an offer to buy their shares. Income forecasts will relate to the offeror company, but may also relate to the offeree company if its shareholders feel that the offer should be rejected. Therefore, shareholders of the offeror company may be presented with information relating to both companies involved in the possible takeover or merger. Whatever the situation, the documents received by the shareholders must contain details of the shareholdings of the offeror company in the offeree company and, where relevant, holdings of the offeree in the offeror. In addition, directors' shareholdings in both companies must be disclosed. Finally, full details of the means by which the offer is to be satisfied must be given.

Concluding remarks

The above paragraphs have attempted to give an outline of the main statutory and other provisions governing the supply of financial information to shareholders and others interested and involved in company affairs. They reveal that the major provision is for annually reported information of a general-purpose nature relating to profitability and financial position. Certainly, the legal intention is that such information be part of the stewardship function to be exercised by company directors.

Other provisions for disclosure of information are, by contrast, concerned with providing specific-purpose information relevant to the making of investment decisions by existing or potential shareholders – that is, particularly concerning the publication of forecast income data. The remainder of this text, however, is mainly concerned with annually reported information, although reference will be made, where relevant, to other sources of reported data.

References

1 These include statements dealing with such topics as accounting for associated companies, earnings per share, extra-ordinary and prior-year adjustments, taxation, stock and work-in-progress, funds statements, depreciation, research and development, and group statements.
2 'Disclosure of Accounting Policies', *Statement of Standard Accounting Practice 2*, November 1971.
3 ibid., p. 3.
4 'The Audit Report', *Auditing Standards and Guidelines*, The Institute of Chartered Accountants of Scotland, April 1980, p. 17.
5 'Auditors' Reports and SSAP 16 "Current Cost Accounting"', *Auditing Guideline 502*, The Institute of Chartered Accountants of Scotland, 1980.
6 'Current Cost Accounting', *Statement of Standard Accounting Practice 16*, 1980.
7 *Admission of Securities to Listing*, Stock Exchange, revised edition, April 1979 (revised 1981), p. 3.
8 ibid., pp. 55–64 and 186–95.
9 ibid., pp. 21–43.
10 *The City Code on Takeovers and Mergers*, Issuing Houses Association, 1981, principle 3.
11 ibid., rule 12.
12 ibid., rule 15.
13 ibid., rule 16.

Suggested discussion or essay topics

1 What is meant by the legally required 'true and fair view' in company financial reporting?
2 Comment on the main features of the 'minimum disclosure' provisions of the Companies Act 1981. In what ways do they benefit shareholders and other users of financial statements?

3 In what circumstances are holding companies not required to publish consolidated financial statements which incorporate the financial results of all subsidiary companies?
4 The company auditor is a suitably qualified accountant who is given certain legal rights and privileges. Discuss.
5 Explain and discuss the role of the company prospectus in investment activities.
6 The professional accountancy bodies have a duty to seek improvements in accounting and reporting practices when legal provisions are inadequate. Discuss.
7 Comment on the provisions of the Stock Exchange and the City Panel in relation to financial reporting. How useful have their contributions been, particularly to the investor?

Selected bibliography for Chapter 5

The Companies Act 1948, HMSO, 1948. The basic accounting and auditing legal requirements.

The Companies Act 1967, HMSO, 1967. The first amendments to the Companies Act 1948.

The Companies Act 1976, HMSO, 1976. Further amendments to the Companies Act 1948.

The Companies Act 1980, HMSO, 1980. Recent amendments to the Companies Acts 1948 and 1967.

The Companies Act 1981, HMSO, 1981. Important amendments to the accounting and disclosure requirements of the Companies Acts 1948 and 1980.

City Code on Takeover and Mergers, Issuing Houses Association, revised edition, 1981. Details of requirements regarding relevant accounting reports for takeovers and mergers.

Admission of Securities to Listing, Stock Exchange, revised edition 1979 (revised 1981). Details of Stock Exchange requirements.

6
The objectives, uses and users of company financial reports

Introduction

What Chapters 1 to 5 have attempted to describe in some detail is the nature of company financial reports as they are constituted presently in the UK. From this analysis, the following points have emerged:

(a) A major part of the information relates to company profitability and financial position, with an increasing emphasis apparently on profitability.

(b) Most of the accounting measures are historic by nature, relating to past periods of company activity.

(c) By far the most significant source of information is contained in the annually and, where relevant, semi-annually published financial reports.

(d) The reported accounting information is measured in accordance with certain accounting practices and conventions which are prescribed legally and professionally.

(e) Most of the reported accounting information is subject to an expert audit and report by independent and professionally qualified accountants so as to assess its credibility.

(f) The reported accounting information which is required to be published is usually specifically designated for company shareholders, although others may use it.

(g) The impetus for reporting on the financial results and affairs of companies comes mainly from company legislation, supported by professional and other regulatory provisions.

Thus, a major intention of corporate financial reporting in the UK appears to be to provide shareholders with regular reports of past income and financial position. In this way, shareholders can be identified as the primary users of such information, and the assumption is that the nature of the prescribed information is relevant to their particular needs. However, it is clear that shareholders are not the only potential users of company financial reports (indeed, existing company legislation occasionally recognises debenture holders and creditors), and that very little is known of their specific information needs, or of the needs of other identifiable users for that matter.

The purpose therefore of this chapter is to look in more detail at the potential users of reported company information so as to establish its broad objectives and the major uses to which it might be put. Because of the main emphasis of the book, the discussion will be within the context of regularly reported accounting information, particularly that which is contained in the annual financial statements. It will be based largely on several recent professional and governmental publications which have attempted to combat the lack of previous attention to identifying users and uses of reported accounting information.[1]

The concepts of utility and relevance

It almost goes without saying that company financial reports must be useful; otherwise there is little point in publishing them. The concept of utility is therefore fundamental to financial reporting. However, it suffers from an obvious vagueness which requires the recognition of more explicit and understandable reporting concepts. In particular, the concept of relevance appears appropriate in this context. Whereas the concept of utility provokes the general questions of useful to whom and for what purpose, that of relevance stipulates that reported accounting information must be capable of influencing the behaviour of its potential user. If it does not do this, it cannot be said to be useful – particularly when he ignores it completely. But for such information to be a useful influence in this sense, its potential users must be identified and their information needs fully explored. Once user needs are established, information can be reported which is relevant to those needs. In this way, the role of accountants should be fulfilled, given the necessary distinction between the provision of information (which is part of the function of accounting) and the use of it (which is part of the 'investment' function in its broadest sense).

The general-purpose approach

Despite the fact that company financial statements are mainly intended legally for shareholders, it is clear that they can be, and are, used for a number of different purposes. The annual financial statements of a company can not only aid its management to regulate the prices of its goods and services and follow a reasonable dividend policy, but can also help its external interests to be reasonably informed about its profitability and financial position; for example, existing and potential shareholders when evaluating the investment potential of the company's shares; creditors and lenders when assessing its credit-worthiness and liquidity; and government departments in administering the system of taxing companies. In addition, they can be of use to employees concerned about such matters as collective bargaining and employment prospects in the company. It is arguable whether one set of financial statements, of the type described in earlier chapters, can be of equal use and relevance to each of these groups of users. It may well be that some will find the information of more relevance than others, because of its emphasis on overall and past company profitability and general financial position. Unfortunately, this is a problem in accounting as yet unresolved, but it will be returned to at a later stage.

The increasing attempt to satisfy several different user groups with the same accounting information does indicate that they all may have something in common so far as their needs are concerned. Indeed, this is the case, since all groups with a potential interest in companies are concerned with making decisions affecting their involvement or investment in such entities. These decisions are economic by nature (that is, they all involve assessments concerning the efficient allocation of scarce economic resources) and they all, by definition, must involve evaluations of the future. Thus, the basic aim of corporate financial reporting is the provision of information about company performance and resources to aid the making of various economic decisions.

In other words, reported accounting information must be capable of having a bearing on economic decisions if it is to be relevant to its users. Identifying the nature of these economic decisions is therefore essential to the proper reporting of information to them. This is the case whether the system is the present one of a general set of financial statements aimed at a heterogeneous group of users who are largely unidentified (with the possible legal exceptions of existing shareholders and the Inland Revenue) or an alternative one of providing specific information for each defined sub-group of users. It is not good enough to identify several groups as being possible users of company financial statements, and hope that the latter's general-purpose nature is sufficiently all-embracing to be of some relevance to them all.

The problem is a complex one which can be summarized as the requirement to identify those persons and bodies having reasonable rights to information from companies; to specify their particular information needs; to determine the feasibility of producing the information likely to meet these needs; to report the required information; and to monitor its acceptance and use by those to whom it has been addressed. At the present time of writing, these matters remain at a relatively primitive stage, and all that can be discussed at this point are the presumed users and uses of reported financial information about companies. In particular, distinctions will be made between management and non-management users.

Management and company financial statements

The annual financial statements of companies are usually regarded as primarily for the use of persons and bodies not involved in the day-to-day management of corporate business activity. However, it would be unfair to imply that company management, and particularly boards of directors, have no use for such reports. It is true to say that the data they contain are relatively 'old news' to company managers, who should in any case be provided with a regular flow of relevant data throughout the financial year, via the management information system. Nevertheless, income statements, balance sheets, funds statements, and value added statements (all in both historic and current cost terms) can give managers and directors an overall review of a company's financial position and progress.

This is in one sense the use of financial statements in a 'feedback' role; the data either confirming or rejecting managerial impressions and expectations of the company's performance throughout the year. Specifically, this type of information should be of general help in evaluating past decisions and making current decisions in such areas as, for example, pricing goods and services and determining profit margins; establishing dividend payments; assessing the means by which the company is financed; making investment decisions; tax planning; credit control; and collective bargaining. Although annual financial statements lack the detail of internal information for these purposes, they can give an overview of the position and should not therefore be ignored entirely.

Accountability and company financial statements

As indicated in Chapter 4 on the history of financial reporting, the early objective of financial statements was to satisfy management's stewardship functions with ownership (and also creditors). Company directors were, and still are, placed in a position of responsibility and trust by shareholders and had, and have, an ethical and legal responsibility to account for their actions. The publication of annual financial statements is therefore intended as a major part of such an accounting. The disclosure of financial information has consequently been aimed at protecting shareholders from, originally, fraudulent practices and, in more recent times, inefficient financial management. At the risk of curbing the freedom of company directors to manage as they see fit, the shareholder has been given a significant source of information with which to hold them accountable for their actions. Accountability must, therefore, still be thought of as a major objective of financial reporting.

There has, however, been a significant change in the direction in which the 'accountability' objective has been moving over the years – that is, away from the original fraud prevention aim into the area of management efficiency. Because of the growing public interest in companies, accountability must now be extended still further to encompass the broader social and economic responsibilities of the company. This can be evidenced in the recent disclosures in company financial reports in the UK of data relating to such socio-economic matters as export sales and pollution costs. Such a trend has been well summed up by the Trueblood Study Group:

> Accountability extends beyond the element of stewardship involved in the safe keeping of assets entrusted to custody. It encompasses the use and conversion of those assets as well as decisions not to use them. Management is accountable for the values of assets as well as their costs. Enterprise managers are also accountable for actions taken to hedge against the economic impacts of inflation and deflation and technological and social changes.[2]

This is the general trend towards public accountability by companies, away from the narrow confines of their legal responsibilities to shareholders (and, occasionally, debenture holders and creditors). It obviously encompasses the interests of persons other than existing shareholders. In other words, because of its significant place in society, a company (through its directors) has a major responsibility to account in financial terms to its shareholders, creditors and lenders and employees, as well as to the public at large (including potential shareholders, etc.).

One of the major ways of judging the quality of financial management is believed to be the evaluation of the profitability of the company – the greater its ability to generate income, the more able it will be to provide sufficient cash to maintain and expand its operations, agree to claims for higher wages and salaries, pay lenders and creditors, and distribute reasonable dividends. Thus, it seems fair to suggest that one of the major objectives of company financial statements has been, and continues to be, the provision of sufficient and relevant accounting information with which directors can inform shareholders and other interested users of the effectiveness of their managerial policies and actions. In this way, the statements not only inform but also protect the various interests of the shareholders and other users. Although this is an enlarging of the traditional stewardship function, it can also be regarded as decision-orientated in the sense that the information may cause its users to exercise their various legal rights against the directors if necessary. Such action inevitably involves decisions. Companies have a custodial role to play in the community regarding the use and safeguarding of corporate economic resources and interests. They must recognize their responsibilities to account for this position of trust. Annual and other financial statements have a considerable part to play in this function.

Investment decisions and company financial statements

By far the most significant general development in company financial reporting has been the use of accounting data by investors when making investment decisions. Over the years, the gradual increase in the disclosure of accounting information by companies has undoubtedly provided investors with increased data with which to evaluate investment potential. This is obviously extending the provision of relevant information beyond the traditional limits of shareholder protection in the stewardship function discussed above. Indeed, it can be argued that by increasing accounting disclosure, and thereby reducing investor uncertainty about company activity and progress, investors can be attracted to above-average companies where investment uncertainty is relatively low owing to a higher-than-average disclosure of information. If this is true, and it has yet to be empirically shown, then the need to increase shareholder protection, which is a matter of public policy, has aided the efficiency of the capital market by encouraging the available capital to go to the more profitable and efficient companies.

Information and prediction

The nature of an investor's decisions requires a consideration of the advantages and disadvantages of the alternative courses of action open to him: to invest or to refrain from investment; to continue to invest or to terminate the investment. These alternatives are generally accepted as requiring the appraisal of the dividend and realization cash flows that are to be expected from the shares concerned (the value of shares being based on the present value of these anticipated cash flows).

In other words, the usefulness of reported accounting information is very much related to its predictive qualities so far as the determinants of the investment decision are concerned. Therefore, reported company accounting information may be said to be useful if it helps investors to predict future cash returns from investments. It should also be noted that, beside being useful for predictive purposes, reported information must also be useful to the investor in a 'feedback' capacity by helping him to judge the soundness and accuracy of his earlier predictions and, possibly, causing him to amend his existing predictions in the light of published financial results.

The ability of reported accounting information to aid the investor in his role of predictor is, as yet, a little unclear, as empirical evidence has not been replicated sufficiently to draw any general conclusions. The predictive ability of different types of accounting information is, therefore, a relatively questionable factor – that is, either whether or not they can be used to predict future events generally: or whether or not particular accounting measurements can be used to predict with reasonable accuracy future accounting measurements of the same type. Because most reported information relates to past events, the main problem in this respect is whether it can be used to anticipate the future. Indeed, it can be argued that reported accounting information was never intended to predict and cannot predict. This may be true in the sense that historic information relates to a past which may not repeat itself in the future. However, the past can be useful as a guide to the future, despite the inherent uncertainties; and if reported information is used for investment purposes, then it must inevitably be involved in predictions of future investment returns.

Use of information

If the 'prediction' evidence is inconclusive, it is reasonably clear that investors do make use of company financial statements and their contents. This has been shown in a number of studies and, despite the lack of generalized conclusions, published accounting information clearly has some degree of influence on investment decisions, and thus on share prices.

Most of the studies involve statistical analyses of the relationship between the reporting of accounting data and the subsequent share-price movements (thus inferring that publication of data, and its subsequent use by investors, influences the movement in share prices by either confirming or rejecting prior expectations of share values, or helping to formulate new expectations of values).[3]

The generally consistent conclusions from these types of study (when related to large companies) are that data are used by investors in a 'feedback' role, most of the information about annual company profitability being anticipated prior to the annual report (mainly due to interim company reporting of the income), and that such anticipation is so accurate that there is little abnormal movement in share prices when annual income is reported, thus indicating that investors do take close cognisance of reported information when making their investment decisions. It also suggests that annually reported accounting information from companies has a relatively smaller part to play in investment decision-making than might be supposed initially, and that investors are relatively insensitive to annual reports of profitability and financial position since prior information of these factors is gleaned from other sources. This further supports the value of the 'feedback' role of accounting information, annual income statements in particular being used to confirm or reject prior expectations of profitability.

It also suggests that there are other sources of information which may have a more significant effect on investment decisions and share prices – particularly information contained in interim financial reports from companies. The usefulness of interim reports of profitability is supported by several research findings.[4] However, the conclusions of these studies indicate that, although interim reporting seems to be significant in investment decision-making, investors do not appear to mind the relatively lower level of credibility associated with interim reports (caused by the high degree of estimation required to produce them, as well as by the lack of auditing). This apparent lack of sophistication on the part of investors suggests that the relevance of information in interim reports (because it is relatively up to date) outweighs the need for its objectivity and verifiability. In other words, investors (and presumably other report users) place differing degrees of relevance on different types of information, and are willing to trade off other information characteristics in order to maximize on its relevance to their decisions.

A further group of studies in recent years has attempted to examine, at the level of the individual shareholder, the use which he or she makes of reported financial information.[5] Generally speaking, these studies are relatively consistent in their findings – that is, only those shareholders with knowledge and experience of accounting matters are making significant use of reported financial information; these users tend to make use of all sources of such information (including annual and interim statements, financial press reports, stockbrokers' reports, and various investment analysis services); of the detailed accounting statements, the income statement is the most used, followed by the balance sheet and the supporting notes to these statements; the funds statements and the auditor's report are, by comparison, little used; and, for the less 'sophisticated' shareholder, non-quantitative statements (such as the chairman's report) are a major and sometimes sole source of information about companies.

In other words, only institutional investors or private shareholders with an accounting 'background' appear to make substantial use of reported accounting information of the type being described in this text. Much of the problem is not so much the relevance or irrelevance of such information to investment decisions, but more the complexity and incomprehensibility of it to persons not trained to deal with it. Such a situation appears to negate the utility of financial reports – 'If they cannot be used, then why produce them?' is a reasonable question to ask. To date, legislators and the accountancy profession have done little to resolve the problem – the present system of company financial reporting assuming that all shareholders (and other users) are equally capable of making use of the reported statements.

Degree of use of information

Apart from the fundamental question of whether or not investors make use of published company financial statements, there are the related issues of (a) whether investors are likely to make greater use of one type of information as compared with other available types (the assumption being that some types of accounting information are more relevant than others with reference to investment decisions); (b) whether the use of one type of information leads to more effective investment decisions than does the use of other types; and (c) whether increasing the degree of disclosure of accounting information necessarily leads to more beneficial investment decisions. Here, again, the empirical evidence is scarce, and consequently inconclusive. The major problem is obviously the fact that the need for reliable information for investment decision-making depends on the investor involved (that is, whether he is a private or an institutional investor; whether he is a large investor or a small investor; whether or not he has financial knowledge and expertise; and so on); and the nature of the investment (whether it is risky or riskless; whether it is income or growth orientated). A major problem therefore facing the accountancy profession at the present time is how to make the current reporting package more relevant to the many different types of investor.

The efficient market

Over recent years, a belief has grown that the market in shares in companies is an efficient one in the sense that the prices of the marketed shares reflect, without bias, all the available information relevant to the share values concerned. A considerable number of studies have attempted to evidence this point,[6] and these have been used to derive certain conclusions relevant to company financial reporting – that (a) there is a strong relationship between reported information and share prices; (b) reported information is quickly and effectively impounded into these share values; and (c) the expert user of available information is the only important one because he cannot be fooled by such information.

Each of these points is questionable and raises considerable points of issue regarding the reporting process. First, it is difficult to isolate the specific effects of reported financial information from those of other sources when examining share prices. Secondly, there are too many company failures and investment mistakes to regard investors as being efficient in their use of information. Thirdly, the needs of the unsophisticated user of financial information ought to be catered for rather than ignored. Fourthly, accounting information contains too many problems and relies too much on subjective judgement for the investor to be left to assess its credibility.

In other words, it would appear that the evidence of efficient stock markets merely indicates the speed of use of available accounting and other information. It says little of the quality and effectiveness of information, and leaves legislators and the accountancy bodies with the continuing responsibility of ensuring that all investors are provided with useful and relevant accounting information. To fulfil this role, the individual needs and characteristics of investors must be considered.

Alternative types of information

It would appear to be wrong to think of useful and relevant information for investment decision-making solely in terms of the existing structure of statements of profitability and financial position, and based on the twin principles of historic cost and realization. Although such statements have been published and filed by companies for a great many years, and despite the apparent use of such statements by investors, there are other forms of information which appear to have relevance to the investor. For example, within the general reporting framework of historic-income statements, balance sheets and funds statements, the following suggestions or provisions have been made.[7] They are given here in relation to the needs of investors, but may also be of considerable relevance to other types of report user.

(a) A statement of value added, differentiating between employees, shareholders, lenders, government, and the company in terms of their proportionate shares in the value added produced during the reporting period concerned. This statement is increasingly being reported by companies, and has been described in detail in Chapter 3. It looks beyond the information needs of investors and should be of considerable interest to lenders, creditors, employees and government, as well as shareholders.

(b) An employment report detailing information relating to the nature, operations and management of the reporting company's employees. The various Companies Acts over the years have done little to supply shareholders with information about arguably the company's most important resource – its work force. This type of report, which is provided by a relatively few companies at the time of writing, is intended to fill this information gap, and to provide shareholders, employees and others with needed employment information. However, unlike most other reports described in this text, it is dependent on data which are outwith the traditional accounting function, and non-accounting experts may be required to produce it.

(c) A statement of future prospects, providing forecasts of income, financial position, etc. to aid investors and others to predict future company activity. Little or no information of this type is currently provided in company financial reports and, because of its subjectivity and potential to reveal corporate plans, may not be considered to be a suitable part of future company reports.

(d) A statement of company objectives, aiding shareholders and other report users to consider, when they are evaluating reported accounting information, what company management was trying to achieve, and what it is hoping to achieve in the future.

(e) A statement of money exchanges with government, including taxes and rates paid, and grants received, thereby providing report users with some indication of the part played by the reporting company in society, and its reliance on society.

(f) A statement of foreign exchange transactions, showing cash dealings of the reporting company between the UK and abroad. Such a statement would provide shareholders and others with an indication of the part played by the company in foreign trade, and its vulnerability to fluctuations in such trade.

Besides these amendments or additions to the existing structure of company financial reporting, other suggestions tend to advocate alternative structures. For example, one suggestion might be the separation of purely objective data from the more subjective value-based data so as to aid the investor when making decisions; the task of predicting being far more difficult when objective and subjective data are mixed, as in the present system of reporting. The minimization of subjectiveness in accounting measurements in this way could be achieved by the production of flow of funds statements based on cash movements alone.[8] Such a system would concentrate on the one key factor in company activity which is of primary importance to all persons and groups involved or interested in companies – cash. Without cash, companies cannot hope to survive and, more specifically, investors' expectations of dividends depend primarily on the availability of cash. Cash flow statements would provide all report users with a relatively straightforward provision of accounting data which reflected these vital issues but without the 'manipulations' which form such a major part of the present-day accounting function. The more subjective allocated data concerning income and financial position would also be reported but would not form the sole source of financial information concerning company performance and position.

The above list of recommended and suggested financial statements is not intended to be either exhaustive or detailed. It is given to remind the reader that the main financial statements, legally and professionally intended for shareholders, are not the only ones capable of satisfying the needs of such persons. Also, it suggests that the provision of useful and relevant information ought to look beyond the needs of the shareholders, and include those of lenders, creditors, employees, government and even customers.

Loan decisions and company financial statements

So far in this chapter, the objectives, uses and users of company financial statements have been discussed mainly within the context of the investor and his decision-making activities. However, there are other categories of potential users who should be mentioned, although many of their apparent information requirements tend to be similar to those of the shareholder-investor. Specifically, the needs of lenders (including bankers) appear to be relatively similar to investors. As with the investor, the lender is concerned with the company's ability to generate sufficient cash flow to provide a reasonable return on and, where relevant, repayment of the contracted financial sum. Unlike the investor, however, he is much more concerned with the risk of the company defaulting on its legal obligations to pay loan interest and repay capital.

Thus, lenders are assumed to be interested in reported data which will help them to evaluate a company's ability to repay the existing or proposed debt and any interest due thereon. No single factor about the company will aid the lender in this respect, although information relating to its liquidity and cash flow is of crucial importance, and the production of cash flow statements would appear to be of considerable relevance in this respect. In addition, profitability and overall financial position data appear to be of some value to the lender when assessing its financial strengths and weaknesses. The importance of the role of financial statements for this purpose, however, may well be considerably less than the corresponding one for investors.

Credit decisions and company financial statements

Suppliers to the company of goods and services on credit have a relatively obvious direct relationship with it which creates a need to receive formal financial information. Specifically, they need to know how capable the company is with regard to repaying the amounts due to them. Again, the assessment is one of the consequences of default, and the major point of attention would appear to be the availability of cash resources and cash flow for purposes of the required repayment. The interest of creditors is usually much more short-term than that of either shareholders or lenders. However, suppliers too are concerned with the long-term from the point of view of continuity of trade, and information about profitability and financial position may also be of interest when assessing the company's financial strengths and weaknesses.

Employees and company financial statements

A number of important matters ought to be of interest to a company's employees – that is, collective bargaining, employment prospects, and working conditions. Although much of these areas of concern will involve an assessment of company profits, cash flow and general financial position, it is unlikely that the existing type of financial statements can be of significant use in discussions concerned with settling wage claims, anticipating employment levels, and providing better working conditions. Income statements would not be needed to assess its liquidity in relation to meeting a wage claim. Future investment and operational plans will aid employment level and working condition factors better than income statements and balance sheets. Thus, employees may require specific information beyond that which is more designed for persons external to the company.

The importance of the employee in contemporary corporate activity in the UK is evidenced in Section 46, Companies Act 1980 which states that a company's directors, when carrying out their directorial functions, should take into account the interests of its employees as well as its shareholders, and that failure to do so could result in the company taking action against them. This part of the Act is exceedingly vague, but could be interpreted as including the financial reporting function – that is, the needs of employees may have to be taken into account when presenting financial statements.

Other uses of company financial statements

The other uses of the accounting information contained in the annual financial reports of companies are various. However, they mainly relate to the computation of corporate tax liabilities, government regulation of company activity, the relatively infrequent but major investment decisions concerning takeovers or mergers of companies, and the needs of company customers.

Taxation

The use of annual reported income data as a basis for computing tax due by companies to central government is well known. In the UK, Section 46(1), Finance Act 1965, states that corporation tax shall be based on the income of companies; income in this context meaning annual reported trading income and other gains. Section 53(1) of the same Act further states that taxable income is to be computed in accordance with the principles of income tax law and practice. In other words, the annually reported income figure for a company is suitably adjusted in a way compatible with tax law so as to produce a further figure of taxable income with which to compute the tax due. The nature of these adjustments is, in many instances, complex, but usually involves ensuring that all taxable revenues are included in the taxable income figure; and similarly, that all deductable business expenses are subtracted from it. However, such a process would be made far more difficult but for the prior measurement, admittedly for reporting purposes, of trading income.

Government regulation

Although companies operate within a so-called free-enterprise system, there is, and always has been, a certain amount of regulation and intervention by government in its workings to protect the public interest. This policing operation does, on occasion, involve annually reported accounting information, for the relevant financial statements contain data which are useful to government departments or quasi-governmental bodies concerned with such matters.

First, Section 1(7), Companies Act 1976, as amended by Sections 5 to 10, inclusive, Companies Act 1981, requires all companies registered in the UK to file their annual financial statements with the Registrar of Companies. Section 43(5) and (6), Companies Act 1980 also requires public companies basing their dividend distributions on initial or interim financial statements to file these with the Registrar (together with any relevant auditor's reports and statements). The files of the Registrar containing these documents are open for inspection to any member of the public for payment of a small fee, and thus annual (and, occasionally, interim) reported accounting information is available for public use.

Secondly, company financial statements may be used in a more particular way by specific governments or bodies monitoring company behaviour; by the Monopolies Commission when assessing possible monopoly practices by particular companies or industries; or by the Department of Trade and Industry when examining the case for government aid to vital companies or industries in need of financial support. More generally, governments will use financial statistics compiled in part from reported accounting information, when determining economic and fiscal policies and strategies.

Thirdly, although not specifically set up by government, the City Panel on Takeovers and Mergers, constituted by the Bank of England and other leading financial institutions in the UK, does make use of financial statements when monitoring and investigating the propriety of company acquisitions and mergers.

Finally, it has already been mentioned that the City Panel is responsible for overseeing company acquisitions on mergers in the UK. It does this by applying the rules and regulations of the *City Code on Takeovers and Mergers*, which has been designed specifically to cause companies to comply with a recognized code of behaviour in such matters. One of the major innovations of the *Code* is the suggestion that the acquiring or merging companies should provide an income forecast for their shareholders; that is, for what is usually a twelve-month period, but which may include part of the current accounting period.

The forecast (if produced) requires to be examined and reported on by the auditors or consultant accountants and financial advisers (if any) concerned in the situation. In this respect, although such forecasts obviously relate to managerial opinions and judgements regarding future business activity, cognisance must also be taken of past activity trends and, consequently, reported accounting information (particularly that relating to profitability) must be of potential use. It is also only fair to suggest that decisions leading to potential takeover bids must at some stage involve a scrutiny of reported financial results.

The needs of customers

Customers of a company are concerned with the continuity of supply of goods and services from it as well as, in certain circumstances, after-sales service. In these cases, the financial viability and profitability of the company must be of interest, and its annual financial statements could be of considerable use. The financial position and performance of the company should also be of concern in situations involving long-term contracts where the customer wishes to assess whether or not the company is financially capable of completing the contract.

The quality of company financial reports

The previous sections in this chapter have attempted to indicate the main uses to which company financial reports are or could be put. Hopefully, they have also indicated the main objectives of these reports. However, so far as reported accounting information is concerned, its overall usefulness, and therefore its potential to be used, depends on certain criteria being satisfied. Some are more obvious than others, and should require little elaboration. However, it will be noticeable that they can be divided into two main categories: those that predominantly relate to the measurement and reporting of the information concerned; and those that relate mainly to the use of it.

Measurement and communication criteria

Undoubtedly, one of the most basic qualities of reported accounting information is that it should be credible. The messages it contains should be capable of being believed by its users. If it is not credible, the probability is that it will not be used. Therefore, to maximize its credibility, the following further criteria are important to the reporting accountants:

(a) The information must be relevant; that is, it must be capable not only of describing the factors it purports to describe as realistically as possible, but must also have the capability of influencing its potential user's behaviour by reducing his uncertainty and aiding him in his decision function. As the previous sections in this chapter have attempted to indicate, satisfying this criterion is not easy – little is known of users and their decision functions, and much depends on the individual user and his personal circumstances – for example, his experience and knowledge of accounting information, whether or not he has other sources of information to influence his decisions, and so on. Accountants, however, must at all times attempt to adhere to this most difficult criterion.

(b) The information must be material; that is, it must be significant enough in relation to the factors it describes to be classified as relevant to its potential user. In other words, it must not be concerned with trivia. This is not just a question of size – of how big or small the figures are in relation to all other figures. It can also relate to the type of information – some information being material to the user whatever the size of figures concerned.

(c) The information must be fair; that is, it must be measured and reported with as much objectivity and neutrality as possible. It must be based on firm, verifiable evidence (wherever possible), and it must not be such as to tend to benefit a particular user (or group of users) to the relative detriment of others. Fairness in this sense must not be regarded as an absolute criterion. As previous parts of this text have indicated, the accounting process is one which can involve a great deal of personal, subjective judgement on the part of the financial reporter (for example, in the accounting allocation of data, and their matching with sales revenue to achieve periodic measures of income and end-of-period measures of financial position). It is therefore possible that a certain amount of fairness may have to be sacrificed in order to obtain relevant information.

(d) The information must be understandable; that is, it must be capable of being understood by its potential users, even allowing for the fact that accounting is an extremely complex language. This is one of the biggest problems facing accountants – the product of their work being received by a great many shareholders, employees and others who lack the accounting experience and training required to make adequate use of the available information.

(e) The information must be comparable; that is, it must be prepared in such a way as to be capable of being compared realistically with previous or similar information, remembering particularly that it is designed to aid users to make decisions which, by definition, involve comparisons of alternatives. In this respect, it is also necessary for the information to be prepared with some degree of consistency in methodology. If care is not applied in this area then users of reported information will be unable to differentiate between changes in figures from one period to the next, and between figures of one company and another, in order to assess whether such differences are operational or trading ones or merely due to different accounting practices being applied.

(f) The information must be timely; that is, it must be measured and communicated as quickly as possible to ensure that it is not so out of date as to be useless. If the information is out of date, it can no longer be regarded as relevant and therefore useful. This is one reason why, as mentioned earlier, interim financial statements appear to be of greater use to investors than annual reports – they contain the more timely information.

(g) The information must be complete; that is, the user of financial reports should be given a package of statements which is sufficient to provide him with all the information he requires either to assess management's stewardship or to make his decisions. This is an exceedingly difficult task to achieve, not only because of the current lack of knowledge about user decisions, but also because the provision of too much information may make an already complex package incomprehensible.

(h) The information must be reliable; that is, it must be of such a quality that its users can have the confidence to rely on its messages. This is normally achieved by means of the audit function, but much also depends on the credibility of the financial reporter. If the company and its management are not credible it is unlikely its financial statements will be so regarded by users.

These are put forward as the main measurement criteria applicable to company financial reports. There are others, but these appear to be the most significant. They are not given in any particular order of importance, for what is important in this respect is the balance achieved; the quality of reported information depends entirely on the circumstances of the company concerned and the nature of the information itself (whether it is, for example, historic or predictive). Relevance and materiality may have to be sacrificed in some measure to obtain a sufficient level of objectivity, or vice versa. Whatever balance is struck, however, will depend in general on the nature of the circumstances, and in particular on the information needs of the users. As the Trueblood Study Group concluded:

> The qualitative characteristics of financial statements, like objectives, should be based largely upon the needs of users of the statements. Information is useless unless it is relevant and material to a user's decision. Information should be as free as possible from any biases of the preparer. In making decisions, users should not only understand the information presented, but also should be able to assess its reliability and compare it with information about alternative opportunities and previous experience. In all cases, information is more useful if it stresses economic substance rather than technical form.[9]

User criteria

As previously mentioned, the reporting by companies of accounting information which describes aggregate measures of their financial progress and condition is primarily an attempt to aid potential users in their various decision activities. In this sense, it is a vitally important means of portraying the reality of company activity. It is therefore equally important that its users perceive that reality as accurately as possible if they are not to be misled or misinformed about the financial affairs of the company concerned. If company financial reports are to fulfil a meaningful role in society, they must not convey to their users messages of economic activity which do not reasonably conform to the reality of the situation. However, this is extremely difficult to guard against, for the process of perception is governed by a number of crucial factors:

(a) What people perceive, or are willing to perceive, is determined in part by their needs and personal values. Thus, if company financial reports are not regarded as relevant and useful by a potential user, the probability of their not being used will be high. Perception of a company's financial affairs would therefore not be gained through this medium.

(b) The degree of perception of objects, qualities and relationships depends on a person's capacity to perceive – only so much data can be absorbed at one time, and this, in turn, depends on the skill and experience of the person concerned. This is important in financial reporting since perceptual capacity may vary from one user to the next. There is also the attendant problem of disclosing more and more data in financial reports until a point is reached when additional data may prove to be a positive disadvantage by obscuring the main messages being reported.

(c) As mentioned in (b), perception is in part determined by the prior experience of the person concerned. In this respect, there are two main levels of perception: the level at which perception begins, and the more advanced level at which changes in the condition of the perceived objects, etc. are noted. This distinction has some importance in financial reporting because it must have some part to play in determining the materiality of data for reporting purposes. The problem for accountants, however, is one of trying to assess the ability of potential users to perceive what is material and what is relatively less material.

(d) There is a conditioning effect in perception. People can learn to perceive in a set way through familiarity – that is, as a process of learning. Thus, they can start to perceive what they expect or want to perceive rather than what they should perceive; this gives them security and avoids anxiety. If this happens, then it has implications for financial reporting; investors and others may become used to high levels of income or sound financial positions, and fail to notice changes quickly enough when they start to occur. (This last point is very much connected with that in (c) above.)

(e) Human attitudes, or the readiness to respond in a predetermined manner, underlie most of the previous points. Attitudes are formulated usually over long periods of time, and reflect personal values and biases. They create a rigidity of mind which, whilst not being enduring, can lead to preconception and can seriously affect judgements. This is important to any study of financial reporting practices because attitudes are inherent in both the processing and the use of accounting information. They can obviously influence the quality and credibility of both processes. It is therefore important that the attitudes and consequential influences are as favourable and fair-minded as possible.

These have been given as some of the more obvious psychological factors affecting company financial reports. They involve several important problem areas for accountants which remain as yet unexplored. They also indicate that the process of producing and presenting financial reports is not merely an exercise in computing and aggregating financial figures; it is as much a study of human behaviour – of both the reporter and the user.

General or specific-purpose information?

Arguably, the most fundamental point to emerge from any description of the objectives, uses and users of company financial reports is that the information contained in them must be capable of satisfying the needs of its users. However, this relatively uncomplicated point raises one of the most burning issues in accounting today: is the present system of providing a set of reports of a standardized nature for all potential users likely to achieve the objective of satisfying all their information needs? Company legislation has consistently assumed over the years that so-called general-purpose information is likely to do just that. Income statements and balance sheets for a company or group of companies as a whole have been assumed to be sufficient to satisfy the needs of its shareholders, irrespective of their various individual differences (for example, as between private and institutional shareholders). In addition, the separate needs of other potential users have been largely ignored; the assumption presumably being that information for shareholders ought to be of use to lenders, creditors, employees, government departments, etc. Likewise, it has been assumed, until very recent times, that income statements and balance sheets, based on the twin measurement principles of historic cost and realization, have a general relevance and usefulness to a variety of potential users.

The evidence to support the above assumptions is scant; but so too, is the evidence to contradict them. *A priori* reasoning, however, suggests that the needs of individual users may be better served by presenting specific-purpose information: information in a variety of forms suitable for use in a number of separately identifiable decision functions. Thus, the present need to explore more fully the decision functions of the various potential user groups described in this chapter. Meanwhile the present general-purpose system continues, and its problems will be examined in greater depth in the following chapters.

References

1 Accounting Objectives Study Group, *Objectives of Financial Statements*, American Institute of Certified Public Accountants, 1973; Accounting Standards Committee, *The Corporate Report*, 1975, pp. 15–60; and 'Inflation Accounting', *Report of the Inflation Accounting Committee*, HMSO, Cmnd 6225, 1975, pp. 42–55.

2 Accounting Objectives Study Group, op. cit., p. 25.

3 For example, studies such as G. J. Benston, 'Published Corporate Accounting Data and Stock Prices', *Empirical Research in Accounting: Selected Studies*, 1967, pp. 1–54; and R. Ball and P. Brown, 'An Empirical Evaluation of Accounting Income Numbers', *Journal of Accounting Research*, Autumn 1968, pp. 159–77.

4 For example, studies such as R. G. May, 'The Influence of Quarterly Earnings Announcements on Investor Decisions as Reflected in Common Stock Price Changes', *Empirical Research in Accounting: Selected Studies*, 1971, pp. 119–63; P. Brown and J. W. Kennelly, 'The Information Content of Quarterly Earnings: an Extension and Some Further Evidence,' *Journal of Business*, July 1972, pp. 403–15; and J. E. Kiger, 'An Empirical Investigation of NYSE Volume and Price Reactions to the Announcement of Quarterly Earnings', *Journal of Accounting Research*, Spring 1972, pp. 113–26.

5 For example, studies such as T. A. Lee and D. P. Tweedie, *The Private Shareholder and the Corporate Report*, Institute of Chartered Accountants in England and Wales, 1977.

6 See T. A. Lee, 'The Role of Accounting and Evidence of Efficient Markets,' *Accountant's Magazine*, June 1979, pp. 237–40 for a review of this matter and a supporting bibliography.

7 This owes much to the suggestions in *The Corporate Report*, op. cit., pp. 47–60.

8 For a review of this topic, see T. A. Lee, 'Cash Flow Accounting and Corporate Financial Reporting,' in M. Bromwich and A. Hopwood, *Essays in British Accounting Research*, Pitman, 1981, pp. 63–78.

9 Accounting Objectives Study Group, op. cit., p. 60.

Suggested discussion or essay topics

1 If company financial reports are to be used to portray the efficiency as well as the integrity of management, then the traditional form of financial statements will become increasingly inadequate. Discuss.

2 The philosophy of financial reporting should regard the disclosure of accounting information as a matter of economic importance to society as a whole. Discuss.

3 It has been stated that the approach to accounting objectives that assumes a set of unknown users of financial reports has also assumed that information regarding the past profitability and financial position of a company is relevant for the many data needs of these users. Comment and discuss.

4 Share prices reflect investors' expectations of future profitability, and these expectations are determined, at least in part, by investors' perceptions of the future. Comment on the validity of this statement, with particular regard to the role of accounting information in investment decisions.

5 Is there an efficient market so far as investor use of accounting information is concerned?

6 The importance of relating financial accounting information to the needs and requirements of its users (or potential users) is clearly evidenced in the general accounting objectives of information utility and its related concept of relevance. Discuss with particular emphasis on the importance of the information user in contemporary accounting thought.

7 No matter how well it is measured, accounting information is, at best, useless and, at worst, positively misleading, unless it is adequately communicated and timeously reported. Discuss.

8 What is meant by the general-purpose approach to company financial reporting?

9 The periodic accounting by a steward to his master is a concept of relevance to fifteenth-century estate management, but not to twentieth-century company activity. Comment and discuss.

10 What are the generally accepted objectives of company management and how do they relate to the objectives of company financial reports?

11 The information contained in annual financial reports is of little use to company management. Discuss the validity of this statement.

12 What is meant by accountability in relation to company financial reports?

13 Economic decisions about companies are made principally by present or potential investors, by creditors, and by managers and employees who invest time and effort. What role has the company financial report to play with regard to these decisions?

14 There is evidence to suggest that reported accounting information influences movements in share prices. Discuss.

15 What sources of information, other than company financial reports, could be said to aid investors and others in their decision activities vis-à-vis companies?

16 Accounting information must be credible. Explain and comment.

17 How much could the degree of risk in investment decision-making affect the degree of use made of company financial reports?

18 Too much accounting information is as bad as too little. Discuss.

19 The past is irrelevant to a decision-maker. Comment on the validity of this statement with regard to the use made of company financial reports.

20 Company financial statements are produced because not to do so would be illegal. They have only a limited use and this concerns the computation of tax liabilities. Discuss.

21 The one basic accounting assumption underlying company financial reports may be stated as that of fairness – fairness to all segments of the business community, determined and measured in the light of the economic and political environment, and the modes of thought and customs of all segments. Discuss.

22 What people perceive is determined partly by their needs, values, skills and experience, and partly by the quality of their information sources. Comment and discuss in relation to company financial reports.

Selected bibliography for Chapter 6

Note It has been particularly difficult to select a representative list of suitable additional readings for this chapter. This is mainly because of the relatively undeveloped nature of this aspect of company financial reporting. However, the following are suggested as providing useful additional material; writings on more detailed points can be found in the references to the text.

Accounting Objectives Study Group, *Objectives of Financial Statements*, American Institute of Certified Public Accountants, 1973. A study and review of the uses and users of company financial statements; also looks at statements of non-profit-making organizations.

Accounting Standards Committee, *The Corporate Report*, 1975. A UK study of financial reporting objectives, users and uses.

Arthur Andersen and Co., *Objectives of Financial Statements for Business Enterprises*, Arthur Andersen and Co., 1972. A detailed study and discussion of company financial statements; their objectives and users.

H. K. Baker and J. A. Haslem, 'Information Needs of Individual Investors', *Journal of Accountancy*, November 1973, pp.64–9. An attempt to identify the information requirements of investors.

B. Carsberg and T. Hope, *Current Issues in Accounting*, Philip Allan, 1977. Introduction to the subjects of accounting for shareholders (pp. 107–23); employees and their trade unions (pp. 124–40); society generally (pp. 141–52); and taxation (pp. 153–71).

Committee to Prepare a Statement of Basic Accounting Theory, *A Statement of Basic Accounting Theory*, American Accounting Association, 1966, pp. 4–30. A description of the main criteria underlying the measurement and communication of accounting information, and the importance of the information user in theory and practice.

M. W. E. Glautier and B. Underdown, *Accounting Theory and Practice*, Pitman, 1976, pp. 538–46. A brief introductory review of reporting objectives.

Inflation Accounting Committee, 'Inflation Accounting', *Report of the Inflation Accounting Committee*, Cmnd 6225, HMSO, 1975, pp. 42–55. A review of financial report users' needs in relation mainly to income measurement and asset valuation.

T. A. Lee, 'Utility and Relevance: the Search for Reliable Accounting Information', *Accounting and Business Research*, Summer 1971, pp. 242–9. The importance of identifying the user of accounting information and producing financial statements relevant to his needs.

K. Most, *Accounting Theory*, Grid, 1977, pp. 107–21. A critical review of US and UK reporting objectives.

G. J. Staubus, *Making Accounting Decisions*, Scholars Book Co., 1977, pp. 82–116. A study of the users and uses of accounting information.

7
Company financial reporting problems – 1

Introduction

The production of reportable financial information is not a straightforward matter of observing and collating suitable data and presenting them in suitable statements for the potential user. It is an extremely complex function and contains many significant problems. It is vital, therefore, for the producers and users of company financial reports to understand fully the nature of these problems (if only in general terms) so as to recognize that accounting information is not capable of being described in terms of accuracy and correctness.

The aggregate accounting data contained in financial statements can be regarded as no more than an expert impression or portrayal of aggregate company activity. As with any 'artistic' picture, its message depends on the techniques adopted to produce it; on the perceptions, attitudes and skills of its producer; and on the perceptions, attitudes and skills of its user. The aim of this and the following chapter is to provide the reader with an outline of the process of producing company financial reports as they are presently constituted, and thereby to give a necessary background to the criticisms and solutions which have been advocated in connection with them. The discussion, as previously mentioned, will centre on the information contained in annual financial statements.

Producing company financial reports

Before proceeding to the detail of the problems affecting the accounting function, it is useful to describe briefly the process undertaken to produce annual financial reports. The first point to make is that the primary responsibility for producing them lies, at least in the UK, with boards of directors. This duty is laid down in Section 1, Companies Act 1976. Directors are responsible for producing annually the required income statement and balance sheet with the supporting notes and explanations. The company's auditors are not, as might be supposed, charged with this primary responsibility. Their job is to verify and report on the way in which the reported information has been measured and disclosed, and their role, as such, is a supporting one to that of the directors. Nevertheless, the auditor may be involved in preparing financial statements without having the primary responsibility for them. This occurs in situations, particularly with small private companies, where a company does not have employee accountants, and the auditor is given the job of both preparing and auditing the statements. The task of preparing the accounting information, however, is a totally separate function from that of auditing. In other words, the auditor in these cases has to wear two hats: one as producer and one as verifier. Whatever the circumstances, the directors of the company remain ultimately responsible to the shareholders for the content of the financial statements.

The principal activity in producing the annual financial reports centres on the preparation and presentation of the income statement and balance sheet of the company. If it is a holding company, this will also involve similar tasks with regard to the relevant consolidated financial statements. In addition, the company may also publish a funds statement, current cost statements, and a value added statement. The production of these statements is a complex affair, and much of the work takes place throughout the company's financial year on a day-to-day basis. What follows is therefore only a brief description of the various stages involved. It assumes the traditional and existing system of annual financial reporting in the first instance.

Data processing

Every company is legally required in the UK to keep adequate and reliable accounting records from which annual financial statements can be prepared (Section 12, Companies Act 1976). These records, because of their nature and contents, are maintained on a day-to-day basis, and contain details of the daily transactions and activities of the company, most of which are expressed in monetary terms. This is the function of processing accounting data, and its objective is *inter alia* to gather together the data necessary to produce the required information on profitability and financial position.

The nature of data processing

Data processing (or bookkeeping as it is more normally termed) is the most objective and potentially accurate part of the entire process of producing company financial reports. It can, of course, contain errors, and there can be fraudulent manipulation of records to cover up theft or embezzlement. But, given a strong system of internal control, with adequate checks and counter-checks and a proper division of employee duties and responsibilities, data processing is a relatively straightforward activity. Transactions and activities capable of being measured and accounted for are observed and made the subject of data processing. This will include the buying and selling of goods and services, the manufacture of goods (where relevant), the administration of the business, and so on.

The processing can be handled manually, by machine, by computer, or, most probably, by a combination of these systems.

Data collection

The observed transactions or activities are documented in a standard form (for example, as invoices, statements, orders, wages sheets, stock cards, etc.) and these documents are filed until periodically recorded in permanent records. These records may be books and ledgers, machine cards or computer printouts, depending on the system operated. The recording can be undertaken daily, weekly or monthly, and in all cases will be completed following the generally accepted rules of double-entry bookkeeping. Data necessary for producing the required financial statements are therefore collated and aggregated ready for the following process of putting them in a form in which information on company income and financial position can be reported. It should be noted at this point that the data concerned are being reduced to manageable proportions and are expressed in terms of the monetary values which occurred at the time of the transactions and activities – in other words, this is the basis for the familiar historic cost reporting systems so widely practised throughout the history of companies.

Information processing

Whereas data processing is a relatively factual and routine function of accounting, the next stage of information processing can be extremely complex and subjective. Most of these topics have already been introduced in earlier chapters, but it is felt that the reader will benefit from a restatement and expansion of the main features of this aspect of financial reporting.

Information processing and realization

The primary aim is to put the recorded accounting data into a series of informational propositions which articulate with one another to form the annual financial statements. The information is traditionally based on the original values of the recorded transactions – the so-called historic cost principle, in which past sales revenues are matched against their related historic costs to produce a net surplus termed accounting income – and the remaining unallocated historic costs are carried forward in the balance sheet to be offset eventually against appropriate sales revenues in the future.

As introduced in Chapter 2, the main measurement principle adopted in this process is that of realization, now referred to in UK practice as the concept of prudence:

Revenue and profits are not anticipated, but are recognised by inclusion in the profit and loss account only when realised in the form either of cash or of other assets the ultimate cash realisation of which can be assessed with reasonable certainty; provision is made for all known liabilities (expenses and losses) whether the amount of these is known with certainty or is a best estimate in the light of the information available.[1]

In other words, traditional accounting practice generally follows the pattern that asset value increases and therefore positive income elements are not to be accounted and reported on until such time as they have been realized by sale of the assets concerned. On the other hand, decreases in asset value (negative income elements or losses) are required to be accounted and reported on as they can be recognized, even if this is prior to realization. (The Companies Act 1948 has taken this a stage further in Paragraph 12, Part II, Section A. In this provision, it is stated that companies must be prudent and can only include realized income in their income statements, and must make provisions for all liabilities and losses which have arisen or are likely to arise in relation to the current and previous financial years, and to the period between the balance sheet date and the date of signing of the latter by the directors. Section B goes on to prescribe certain historic cost accounting rules, although Section C permits the use of current cost accounting procedures. However, in law, companies are not permitted to produce an income statement without total commitment and application of the realization principle – even if current cost procedures are adopted.)

The overall result of this practice in income measurement and asset valuation (on a historic cost basis) is that the information processing function is concerned mainly with reporting income which has been realized during the defined period, irrespective of when it accrued. Thus reported income of the period is a heterogeneous mixture of income elements accruing in previous periods and realized in the current one, together with elements earned and realized during the current period. Balance sheet asset values are, as a consequence, expressed largely in historic cost terms, with the possible exception of cash and debtors. The balance sheet does not therefore usually reflect all the current values of the company's reported assets. On the other hand, if an asset's value falls below its original cost, the prudence concept dictates that provision be made for the unrealized loss by reducing the cost to its current value. This is particularly followed in stock valuations with the traditional accounting rule of value at the lower of cost or market value. This has already been demonstrated in a simple situation in Chapter 2 (Illustration 22), and Illustration 38 provides a further extended example.

Illustration 38 The realization principle – 1

A company has two assets, A and B. Asset A cost £1,000 at point t_0 and asset B cost £2,000 at the same time. During the period t_0 to t_1, the company continued to hold both assets and their realizable values at t_1 were £1,500 and £2,700, respectively. Asset A was sold during the period t_1 to t_2 for £1,800 but asset B continued to be held at t_2, when its realizable value was £3,100. During the period t_2 to t_3, asset B was sold for £3,500.

Following the realization principle, and assuming no other transactions, no taxation and an opening capital at t_0 of £3,000, the company's income statement and balance sheet figures would appear as follows:

Income statements	$t_0 - t_1$ £	$t_1 - t_2$ £	$t_2 - t_3$ £	Total £
Realized income for the period	— (a)	800(b)	1,500(c)	2,300

Balance sheets	t_0 £	t_1 £	t_2 £	t_3 £
Asset A	1,000	1,000	—	—
Asset B	2,000	2,000	2,000	—
Cash	—	—	1,800(d)	5,300(e)
	3,000	3,000	3,800	5,300
Opening capital	3,000	3,000	3,000	3,000
Retained income	—	—	800(f)	2,300(g)
	3,000	3,000	3,800	5,300

(a) No asset was realized during the period, therefore no income was recognized; (b) gain on the sale of asset A, £1,800 − 1,000; (c) gain on the sale of asset B, £3,500 − 2,000; (d) sale receipt for asset A, £1,800; (e) sale receipts for assets A and B, £1,800 + 3,500; (f) gain on sale of asset A, £800; (g) gains on the sale of assets A and B, £800 + 1,500.

This example reveals how the realization principle, and the related adherence to the valuation base of historic cost, leads to the reporting of income and asset value increases only after realization has taken place. Thus, the realization principle in income and value measurement can considerably affect the reportable income and capital of the periods concerned. It delays the reporting of unrealized income until it is realized, and it understates assets and capital, again until realization occurs. Users of traditionally measured accounting information cannot therefore be said to be informed about the earned income of a period or the current values of assets held at the period-end. Yet the income statement purports to disclose the former, and the balance sheet gives the impression, particularly to the non-accountant, that it contains the latter. Historic cost-based information does not therefore give an up-to-date or full picture of a company's financial affairs, and as a result could be misleading.

By way of contrast, the following figures use the same data but with a relaxation of the realization principle (Illustration 39).

Illustration 39 The realization principle – 2

Income statements	t_0-t_1	t_1-t_2	t_2-t_3	Total
	£	£	£	£
Income earned during the period	1,200[a]	700[b]	400[c]	2,300

Balance sheets	t_0	t_1	t_2	t_3
	£	£	£	£
Asset A	1,000	1,500	—	—
Asset B	2,000	2,700	3,100	—
Cash [d]	—	—	1,800	5,300
	3,000	4,200	4,900	5,300
Opening capital	3,000	3,000	3,000	3,000
Retained income	—	1,200[e]	1,900[f]	2,300[g]
	3,000	4,200	4,900	5,300

(a) Unrealized gains of the period on assets A and B, (£1,500 − 1,000) + (£2,700 − 2,000); (b) realized gain of the period on asset A, £1,800 − 1,500, plus unrealized gain of the period on asset B, £3,100 − 2,700; (c) realized gain of the period on asset B, £3,500 − 3,100; (d) as per Illustration 38; (e) income of period t_0 to t_1 £1,200; (f) income of the period t_1 to t_2 £700, plus retained income at t_1, £1,200; (g) income of the period t_2 to t_3, £400, plus retained income at t_2, £1,900.

Income statements	t_0-t_1	t_1-t_2	t_2-t_3	Total
	£	£	£	£
With the realization principle	—	800	1,500	2,300
Without the realization principle	1,200	700	400	2,300

Balance sheets: capital and retained income	t_0	t_1	t_2	t_3
	£	£	£	£
With the realization principle	3,000	3,000	3,800	5,300
Without the realization principle	3,000	4,200	4,900	5,300

By relaxing the restriction of the realization principle, the following reporting changes occur: (a) only income accruing during the period is reported, irrespective of when it is realized, thereby giving shareholders and other interested persons a measure of the earned rather than the realized income of the period; and (b) the balance sheet reflects up-to-date asset values rather than those occurring at the time of the original transactions. Financial report users are therefore in a better position to assess the recent financial progress of companies than if they used the existing historic cost-based system. The usefulness of the latter should nevertheless not be totally discounted given its long history of use.

Arguments for and against historic cost and realization

Financial reports which use historic costs have been defended on many occasions[2] and, indeed, it is only in recent years that there has been a sustained voice of opinion against the traditional system. The major argument for it is that it has stood the test of time and that there are no signs that investors or other users are ignoring it in their decision-making activities. In fact, as already mentioned, the empirical evidence to date is that investors do take cognisance of reported income figures compiled on a historic cost basis.

Another major argument is that historic cost information is firmly based on known business transactions and events capable of being evidenced and verified. In other words, it has an apparent objectivity which is not as evident in alternative valuation systems. It has also been argued that, because of this objective and factual base, the traditional system is open to less disputation than other systems thus minimizing the cost of time and effort in producing the information.

The arguments against historic cost concentrate particularly on its lack of relevance to the investment decision-making function; it does not report on the income earned during a defined period nor does it indicate contemporary values for assets. In other words, the traditional system is an accounting for what happened during the defined period, mainly in terms of cost movements suitably adjusted when allocation of data is necessary between periods. It singularly fails to recognize, on a continuous basis, the changing values of assets before realization.

Alternatives to historic cost

One alternative to reporting in past value terms is to use current values, or values existing at the date of reporting rather than at the dates of the original transactions. By using current values, not only are assets reported in contemporary terms, but income can include unrealized gain elements of the defined period, thereby ignoring the realization issue. The problem, however, is one of deciding which current value to adopt for measurement purposes.

There are four possible interpretations attributable to current value: economic value, replacement cost, net realizable value, and current cost (described as value to the business). Each is a description of the current value of an asset but each is different and therefore capable of producing a separate measure of periodic income. This indicates the somewhat elusive nature of income; its measurement depends on the particular values placed on the company's assets.

Economic value and periodic income

It can be argued that a conceptually correct value for a business asset is one which is based on the net revenues which, it is anticipated, will be received during its lifetime. In other words, the value to the company of an asset is determined by what the company would pay for the economic benefits which could be received from it. This involves forecasting the net revenues which could be earned from the use of each asset, with a discounting of each forecast at a suitable rate of interest. Once the economic value for each asset has been computed, the balance sheet position of the company can be evaluated at the beginning and end of the period concerned. Allowing for realized net revenues, dividends and share capital changes during the period, income is computed by measuring the periodic change in shareholders' equity based on these economic values. Illustration 40 outlines such a computation.

Illustration 40 Income and economic values

The aggregate economic value of the non-cash resources of a company at t_0 is estimated to be £25,000 (using discounted cash flow principles). At t_1, the corresponding figure is £37,000. During the period t_0 to t_1 cash resources increased from £5,000 to £12,000, of which £4,000 was received from shareholders subscribing to a new issue of shares. Income for the period t_0 to t_1 would then be (£37,000 − 25,000) + (£12,000 − 5,000) − £4,000 = £15,000, ignoring taxation.

Although theoretically valid, the use of economic value in the practice of income measurement is fraught with problems, not the least of them being the forecasting of future economic benefits to be derived from a company's assets. Apart from the extreme subjectivity of the exercise, there is the related problem of identifying particular revenues and costs with individual assets. There is also the question of which discount rate to use in the computations. An alternative approach would be to compute the economic value for the company as a whole rather than for its individual assets. However, this would involve the forecasting of total net revenues over the lifetime of the company. The impossibility of this task is relatively obvious. Therefore economic value is generally regarded as theoretically attractive but impracticable as an alternative to historic cost.

Replacement cost and periodic income

The measurement of periodic income and asset values using current replacement costs is now well known as an alternative to historic cost. It has been suggested on many occasions that, failing the use of economic values, the obvious choice is a current market value, and replacement cost seems appropriate because it reflects the continuity and indefinite life of the business. By using replacement costs for reporting purposes, it is possible to segregate income elements earned by selling assets from income elements earned by holding them. For both managerial and investment decision-making purposes, it is argued that such a segregation is useful when predicting future income elements: it helps distinguish income earned by deliberate managerial policy from income earned by luck and chance. Illustration 41 gives a brief example of this distinction.

Illustration 41 Income and replacement costs

At t_0, a non-manufacturing company held the following items of stock, with the appended values:

	Original cost	Replacement cost
	£	£
Item A	200	210
Item B	300	380
Item C	400	430

During the period t_0 to t_1, item A was sold for £270 (replacement cost at time of sale, £230), and item B was sold for £450 (replacement cost at time of sale, £430). Item C continued to be held at t_1 at a replacement cost of £460. In addition, a further item D had been bought during the period for £500 (replacement cost at t_1 was £530). Ignore taxation.

Operating income, period $t_0 - t_1$

		£
Item A	(£270 – 230)	40
Item B	(£450 – 430)	20
		60

Holding income, period $t_0 - t_1$

		£
Item A	(£230 – 210)	20
Item B	(£430 – 380)	50
Item C	(£460 – 430)	30
Item D	(£530 – 500)	30
		130

Total income, period $t_0 - t_1$ 190

The figures in the illustration reveal that, of the total income of £190 earned during the period, only £60 represented income from trading (sales revenue minus current replacement cost), the remainder being the result of rising replacement costs during the holding period. By way of contrast, traditional accounting practice would have measured income for the period as: item A (£270 − 200) + item B (£450 − 300) = £220, being the total realized income of the period.

The replacement cost alternative, however, has its problems. For example, what replacement cost should be used for each asset? With certain assets, there may not be a readily available replacement cost (for example, as with intangible assets such as goodwill). With other assets, the problem is whether the replacement cost should be that for an identical asset or for one giving equivalent services to the existing one. Technological changes can cause existing assets to be non-replaceable in identical form, and the problem is to find a suitable replacement cost for an equivalent asset. There is also the problem that not all assets will be replaced; the use of replacement costs assumes that this will occur in all cases. Similarly, replacement costs assume that the company will continue in business indefinitely and, with the exception of cash and near-cash resources, do not necessarily reflect the realizable value of its assets. The final problem relates to the treatment of holding gains – that is, whether or not they should be regarded as income. To exclude them from income would be to adopt an approach to capital maintenance based on a notion of physical capital (funds represented by the holding gains being retained in the company to meet the increased costs of replacing the physical assets concerned). The alternative approach of including holding gains in income would base the latter on a maintenance of financial capital without deliberate regard for the future replacement of physical assets. The current cost accounting described later in this chapter adopts the physical capital approach and thus leaves only realized operating gains within the income statement.

Realizable value and periodic income

The third alternative current value is net realizable value: what the company could realize for an asset if it were sold in an orderly liquidation. Based on the well-known economic concept of opportunity cost (the sacrifice the company is making by not having its assets in the next best alternative form of funds), it expresses the alternatives open to the company should its resources be liquidated. Obviously this is of particular concern to shareholders given that one of the decisions facing them is whether or not the company should continue in its present form. Therefore, although periodic income measures can be derived from this valuation base (by comparing opening and closing balance sheet positions, and allowing for dividends and share capital changes), the main emphasis is on producing relevant balance sheet data for report users. An example is given in Illustration 42.

During the stated period, and ignoring the question of taxation, the income of the company in realizable value terms is £10,000, though its total realizable resources have increased by £12,000. This gives shareholders and other interested persons a reasonable indication of the

---

Illustration 42 Income and realizable values

At t_0, a company had the following assets, all measures using net realizable values: fixed assets, £10,000; current assets, £35,000. Its current liabilities at the same date amounted to £15,000. At t_1, the corresponding realizable figures were: fixed assets, £12,000; current assets, £47,000. Its current liabilities were £17,000. During the period t_0 to t_1, the company paid a dividend for the period of £3,000 and received £5,000 from its shareholders for a new issue of shares.

Realizable income, period $t_0 – t_1$	t_0 £	t_1 £
Fixed assets	10,000	12,000
Current assets	35,000	47,000
	45,000	59,000
Less: current liabilities	15,000	17,000
	30,000	42,000
Less: financial position at t_0		30,000
Increase in realizable resources		12,000
Add: dividend paid for the period		3,000
		15,000
Less: share capital increase		5,000
Realizable income for the period		10,000

---

company's capacity to adapt, an aspect of its financial position which would not be possible with a historic cost or replacement cost balance sheet.

The balance sheet-orientated realizable value alternative to historic cost is nevertheless subject to the criticism that it concentrates too much on asset value changes, and not enough on the operational effectiveness of the company as depicted by its income measures. Apart from this, it can be argued that the use of realizable values implies that the assets of the company are to be liquidated (which may not be the case, at least in the short-term), or that the company has a definite life (which is extremely difficult to predict with any degree of certainty).

Current cost and periodic income

As mentioned in Chapter 3, *Statement of Standard Accounting Practice 16* introduced a formal system of current cost accounting to the UK corporate financial reporting function (at least in the first instance for large and usually public companies), and this is now legally acceptable (Section C, Part II, Schedule 8, Companies Act 1948). After several years of experimentation, it is a system of current values which attempts to account for the specific price changes affecting the reporting company's assets. Based on the concept of the value to the business (the maximum loss the company would suffer should it be deprived of the assets concerned), current cost accounting is mainly concerned with reporting asset values in current replacement cost terms, although, in certain limited circumstances, use may be made of net realizable values and future cash flows.

Current cost accounting has already been fully described in Illustrations 31 and 32 of Chapter 3 and, because it relies mainly on replacement costs, it contains most of the advantages and disadvantages of the latter system. It is not intended, therefore, to repeat these various explanations, although it will be useful to remind the reader of its main features – that is, the deduction from historic cost income of amounts required to provide for the increased cost of replacing fixed assets, stocks and monetary working capital; the limitation of the effect on income of these adjustments by a gearing factor; the revaluation of balance sheet assets in current cost terms; and the accumulation of current cost adjustments and revaluations in a current cost reserve. Each of these matters can be seen in the outline current cost statements provided in Illustration 43. It should be noted, however, that current cost accounting (as specified in the UK) does not completely abandon the realization principle – the income statement should not include unrealized gains. But realized holding gains are also excluded from the income statement, being taken to the current cost reserve in the balance sheet.

Illustration 43 Income and current costs		
Current Cost Income Statement for the Period $t_1 - t_2$		
	£	£
Historic cost profit before interest		100,000
Less: current cost adjustments:		
cost of sales	15,577	
monetary working capital	6,608	
depreciation	3,000	25,185
		74,815
Less: gearing adjustment	(8,681)	
interest	10,000	1,319
Current cost income before taxation		73,496
Less: taxation		40,000
Distributable current cost income		33,496
Less: dividends		20,000
		13,496
Add: income retained in previous years		100,000
Current cost income retained		113,496

Illustration 43 continued

Current Cost Balance as at t$_2$

	£	£	£
Fixed assets			
Tangible assets			
Land and buildings			120,833
Plant			161,000
			281,833
Current assets			
Stock		85,333	
Debtors		50,000	
Cash		10,000	
		145,333	
Creditors: amounts falling due within one year			
Creditors	40,000		
Taxation	40,000		
Dividends	20,000	100,000	
Net current assets			45,333
Total assets less current liabilities			327,166
Creditors: amounts falling due after more than one year			
Debenture stock			(100,000)
			227,166
Capital and reserves			
Called up share capital			50,000
Revaluation reserve			63,670
Profit and loss account (retained income)			113,496
			227,166

The alternatives compared

The periodic income of a company, together with its related balance sheet position, can be described in a number of ways, each depending on the particular valuation concept used. Historic cost produces a measure of income, based on the original values attributable to the underlying transactions, which aims to maintain intact the monetary value of shareholders' capital. In other words, allowing for new capital and capital repayments, as well as dividends, historic cost income is the difference between the opening and closing shareholders' equities in the traditional balance sheet. It cannot exist unless the opening equity figure has been maintained intact. However, in most instances, it ignores unrealized income.

Replacement cost income and current cost income, on the other hand, recognize unrealized gains (although they may not be included in the income statement), and are usually conceived as means of measuring income after attempting a maintenance of the productive capacity of the company's resources by valuing them in mainly replacement cost terms at the beginning and end of the period concerned. Similarly, realizable value income can contain unrealized gain elements, but income exists only after the maintenance of the company's capacity to adapt as represented by the aggregate realized values of its net assets.

Traditional historic cost income therefore has the income and value omissions brought about by the implementation of the realization principle. However, the three feasible current value alternatives, while partially or totally abandoning realization, may not necessarily produce income statements and balance sheets of complete relevance to their users. It may well be that these different systems (based on the same underlying operating and trading conditions) produce information of use to particular decision-makers in specific situations. Much work, however, has yet to be undertaken to confirm or reject this point.

The system of processing accounting information using the twin historic cost-realization principles is the generally accepted one in operation today, although the introduction of current cost accounting will reduce its former dominance in reporting. It is based on the convention of conservatism – that is, when measuring company profitability and valuing company assets, both for purposes of financial reporting, reasonable caution should be exercised by the accountant so as not to account for income which may not ultimately be realized. In other words, it is a sophisticated version of the old adage of not counting chickens before they are hatched. However, the problem of when to recognize revenue and, therefore, income, is not the only one associated with information processing.

The monetary unit problem

The discussion of measurement problems in financial reporting has so far been undertaken with the implied assumption that the monetary measurement unit (in this text, the pound sterling) has a stable value in terms of its generalized purchasing power. In other words, that there has been no inflation or deflation, and that value changes in company financial reports are entirely the result of specific price movements reflecting real rather than inflationary (or deflationary) changes in the values attributable to company resources. For example, if the reported value of stock and work-in-progress has increased from £100,000 to £150,000 over the period concerned, the assumption has been that the £50,000 increase is the result of either a 50 per cent increase in the quantity of stock held (assuming the specific prices of items have remained stable), or a 50 per cent increase in the specific prices of items (assuming quantities had remained stable), or a combination of both. The question of whether all or part of the value change has been because stock has become more expensive owing to the diminishing purchasing power of money has not been considered, and it is the purpose of this section to look at this question. The discussion will assume the more usual contemporary economic condition of inflation.

Accounting implications

Inflation is the term used by economists to denote the general movement upwards in prices of goods and services in an economy over a stated period. In other words, it is an economic factor resulting from all price movements, and as such represents the diminution in the generalized purchasing power of money rather than an increase in the specific value of goods and services. The effect of inflation is that the monetary unit loses value rather than the alternative of goods and services becoming more valuable. Thus, when a good's value increases during a period of inflation then part, all or even something in excess of the increase may be due to the fall in the purchasing power of money, the remainder of the change being the result of other economic factors, such as the demand for and supply of the goods concerned.

The fall in the value of money during a period of inflation has serious implications for financial accounting and reporting. Unless cognisance is taken of it, the reported data will be based upon monetary units with differing purchasing powers, each depending on the value of money at the date of each relevant transaction. By aggregating, allocating and matching data measured in differing purchasing power terms, the consequence would be to fail to report on the real profitability of companies since there will be a failure to exclude inflationary gains and losses which neither reflect real changes in asset values nor real changes in the physical resources underlying these values. Income would therefore be measured by a maintenance of capital in monetary rather than purchasing power terms.

For example, assuming no capital issues or repayments, and no dividends, income for the period t_0 to t_1 (unadjusted for inflation) was £10,000; being the difference between capital at t_0 of £25,000 and capital at t_1 of £35,000. Here opening and closing capitals have been measured in purely monetary terms to derive income for the period. However, if the concept of monetary purchasing power is introduced, it means that opening and closing capital (and therefore the underlying assets and liabilities) should be re-expressed in monetary units of the same purchasing power. This involves translating all asset and liability items at both t_0 and t_1 into current purchasing power terms. Thus, assuming these translations had been made, and opening and closing capitals were adjusted to £$_p$31,000 and £$_p$38,000 respectively, the inflation-adjusted income would be £$_p$38,000 − 31,000 = £$_p$7,000 (£$_p$ representing a unit of current purchasing power).

Data unadjusted for the effects of inflation can therefore be somewhat misleading to their users. Despite this, the traditional practice of accountants has been to assume that the monetary units with which they measure accounting information have a stable purchasing power. As a result, beside the problems created by the use of historic costs and the proliferation of accounting practices (to be dealt with in the next chapter), the measurement of income and financial position is affected by the monetary unit problem. The combination of all three factors obviously makes the traditional process of accounting measurement a questionable one, particularly from the point of view of users who require relevant and credible data for their decision and other activities.

There have been many arguments in the past against the monetary stability assumption in practice. As implied in the previous paragraphs, these arguments have been mainly in the area of historic cost-based financial statements, the claim being that not to adjust them for the effects of inflation produced misleading information about past profitability and financial position. However, the same argument applies equally to alternative valuation bases, such as current cost, replacement cost and net realizable value. Reporting in current value terms does not remove the additional necessity to account for the effects of inflation – that is, by removing the purely inflationary elements from income measured on the basis of current values. In other words, the nature of so-called inflation accounting is not, like the function of historic cost or current value accounting, a valuation process. Rather its purpose is to segregate the inflationary elements of the periodic capital value increase, leaving income to be reported in real terms.

The inflationary effect

Several professional accountancy bodies throughout the world have acknowledged the need to introduce inflation accounting, at least so far as historic cost data are concerned. For example, the UK professional accountancy bodies produced a provisional *Statement of Standard Accounting Practice* which require quoted companies to produce, in addition to their historic cost-based financial statements, inflation-adjusted income statements and balance sheets.[3] This has since been superseded by a system of current cost accounting which tends to ignore measuring income and capital in current purchasing power terms except so far as the current values used are in current purchasing power terms. Current cost accounting is not therefore a full system of accounting for inflation – only specific price changes are acknowledged; general price-level movements affecting the monetary measurement unit are not incorporated.

The process whereby historic cost statements are translated into terms of a monetary unit with a single purchasing power is relatively complex, and consequently difficult to explain fully within the context of this book. The following notes will help to give an introductory understanding of the process. The comments are explained solely within the context of the traditional system of historic cost reporting, although they also have a relevance to current value systems.

First, inflation accounting is akin to a translation process: the unadjusted historic cost data, expressed in monetary units of differing purchasing power, are translated into units expressed in terms of monetary purchasing power at the relevant period-end. The general effect of these adjustments is to inflate the reported data by the inflation factor, in both the income statements and the balance sheet, with the exception of those items which may already be reported in current purchasing power terms (if the relevant transactions have taken place near the period-end) or else cannot be translated for legal reasons (for example, cash and contracted liabilities).

Secondly, the translation process which is applied to historic cost data depends on the use of a relevant inflation factor for the period – that is, a suitable indicator of inflation for the period. In the UK, the recommendation was that the most suitable indicator available was the monthly retail price index which is published as a government document, and is based upon a statistical averaging of monthly (and, eventually, annual) price movements for certain consumer goods and services. The use of such an index as a guide to the annual rate of inflation in other areas of economic management is one of the main reasons for its use in inflation accounting. The other main reasons include its ready availability and its universality.

Thirdly, because the adjustments reflect translations, they ought not to be confused with valuations. For this reason, it is recommended that the sign for the measurement unit used in financial statements should not be the usual monetary one (for example, the £). Instead, a symbol denoting the translated purchasing power unit should be substituted (for example, $£_p$). This should prevent confusion regarding the meaning of the reported figures – particularly with regard to those which are historic cost-based. Report users should therefore be reminded that purchasing power translation does not eliminate the strengths and weaknesses of such a system.

Illustration 44 attempts to explain certain of the main adjustments for inflation which are necessary for the translation of the annual historic cost income figure. While these are not the only adjustments that need to be made to the annual financial statements, the information is intended to give an adequate picture within the limits of the present text.

Illustration 44 Inflationary effects in historic cost financial reports

A company bought goods costing £90,000 at t_0. It sold them at t_1 for £160,000. At t_0 it had cash in the bank of £23,000 and a debenture loan of £100,000. At t_1, cash at the bank was £30,000 (the additional £7,000 accumulating evenly throughout the period, and the debenture loan remaining at £100,000). In addition, the company had plant which cost £100,000 at t_0 and was being depreciated at 10 per cent on a straight-line basis with an estimated nil scrap value. Assume that retail prices increased in general by 15 per cent during the period, and ignore taxation.

Sale of Goods $t_0 - t_1$
Traditional historic cost accounting practice would measure income on these transactions at £160,000 − 90,000 = £70,000. However, assuming a 15 per cent rate of inflation, the adjusted cost of the goods sold at t_1 would be £90,000 + 3/20 × 90,000 = £$_p$103,500; and the adjusted historic cost income on the transactions would be £$_p$160,000 − 103,500 = £$_p$56,500. In other words, by measuring the transactions in terms of monetary purchasing power at t_1, the traditional income figure is composed of an inflationary element of £70,000 − £$_p$56,500 = £$_p$13,500 (not representing any real increase in resources available to the company), and £$_p$56,500 representing the 'real' historic cost gain (£$_p$ being used to denote the measurement unit used is a purchasing power unit and not a money unit such as a £).

Depreciation $t_0 - t_1$
Historic cost depreciation for the period would be 10 per cent of £100,000 = £10,000. However, to adjust it for inflation, the historic cost of the plant would need to be translated into t_1 purchasing power terms – that is, £100,000 + 3/20 × 100,000 = £$_p$115,000. Inflation-adjusted depreciation of the period would then be 10 per cent of £$_p$115,000 = £$_p$11,500. Thus, both the original cost of the plant, and its related periodic depreciation, would be re-expressed in current purchasing power terms.

Holding cash $t_0 - t_1$
Cash of £23,000 was held throughout the period, when its generalized purchasing power declined by 15 per cent. Thus, to maintain its purchasing power in terms of money at t_1, the company would require to have had cash resources of £23,000 + 3/20 × 23,000 = £$_p$26,450. Likewise, the £7,000 accumulated throughout the period has diminished in purchasing power by t_1 by an average rate for the period of $7\frac{1}{2}$ per cent. By t_1, an equivalent sum of £7,000 + 3/40 × 7,000 = £$_p$7,525 would be required to maintain the purchasing power of the accumulating cash. Thus, although the company held £30,000 at t_1, it should have held £$_p$26,450 + 7,525 = £$_p$33,975 to maintain the purchasing power of its cash resources during a period of 15 per cent inflation. It has therefore 'lost' £$_p$33,975 − 30,000 = £$_p$3,975 of purchasing power by holding cash during a period of inflation, and this effect is not accounted for in traditional accounting practice.

Long-term liability $t_0 - t_1$
A similar but opposite effect to holding cash occurs with long-term liabilities. During the period t_0 to t_1, the debenture loan remained at £100,000. But with inflation at 15 per cent, the purchasing power of the money to be repaid fell by such a percentage. Thus, the company could be said to have 'gained' by 15 per cent of £100,000 = £$_p$15,000 by 'holding' such a liability during t_0 to t_1. Again, traditional accounting practice ignores this inflationary effect.

Illustration 44 continued

Summary of effects $t_0 - t_1$

The traditional approach to accounting would measure income for the period t_0 to t_1 at £70,000 − 10,000 = £60,000 (the trading income after deduction of depreciation). By the way of contrast, inflation-adjusted income would be as follows:

	$£_p$	$£_p$
Adjusted trading income		56,500
Less: adjusted depreciation on plant		11,500
		45,000
Add: net gain on monetary items:		
gain on long-term liability	15,000	
Less: loss on holding cash	3,975	11,025
		56,025

References

1 As stated in 'Disclosure of Accounting Policies', *Statement of Standard Accounting Practice 2*, 1971, p. 3.
2 For example, A. C. Littleton, 'The Significance of Invested Cost', *Accounting Review*, April 1952, pp. 167–73; E. K. Kohler, 'Why Not Retain Historical Cost?', *Journal of Accountancy*, October 1963, pp. 35–41; and Y. Ijiri, 'A Defence of Historical Cost Accounting', in R. R. Sterling (ed.), *Asset Valuation and Income Determination*, Scholars Book Co., 1971, pp. 1–14.
3 'Accounting for Changes in the Purchasing Power of Money', *Provisional Statement of Standard Accounting Practice 7*, 1974.

Suggested discussion or essay topics; and selected bibliography

Because of the inter-relationship of topics in Chapters 7 and 8, this material is provided at the end of Chapter 8.

8
Company financial reporting problems – 2

The cost allocation problem

It has to be recognized that, despite the business activity of a company being a continuous affair, financial reporting of the activity must be divided into defined periods. This is done to provide shareholders and other interested parties with regular financial statements describing the financial progress of the company during the periods concerned. As Moonitz has commented:

> If economic activity occurs during specific periods of time, then accounting must be continuously concerned with the recognition and allocation of events. The problem of recognition and allocation is made more difficult because the 'events' often take longer to work themselves out than the reporting periods customarily in vogue. The results of operations for relatively short periods of time are tentative whenever allocation between past, present and future periods are required.[1]

In other words, certain of the transactions and activities completed during a defined financial period will have commenced during previous periods, and certain of the transactions and activities commencing in it will be completed in following periods. The problem for the accountant is therefore one of allocating accounting data of each period in such a way that they properly relate to the events which took place during each period. It is essentially a problem relevant to cost transactions.

Examples of the process of allocation are numerous. For example, not all goods bought or manufactured during a period are also sold during the same period. Thus a company normally has a stock of finished goods and/or semi-processed goods and/or raw materials on hand at the end of each financial period, and this has to be physically counted or measured and its relevant historic cost to date carried forward as unsold stock in the balance sheet, and eliminated (in the income statement) from the computation of income realized during the period on goods sold. Similarly, a company may purchase a fixed asset such as a motor vehicle with a limited useful life. At the end of each financial period, the accountant must measure that proportion of its original cost which has expired during the period due to use and treat it as depreciation when calculating the period's income.

The allocation problem involves decisions on whether expenditure of a defined period relates wholly to that period or whether it relates in part to the following periods owing to any unexpired usefulness in the services it provides. For example, replacements of major parts of plant and machinery may be regarded as repairs, and consequently written off in total against income of the period in which they were incurred; or they may be regarded partly as capital expenditure and treated as a fixed asset to be depreciated over its useful life. The same can be said of expenditure incurred on research and development or advertising. The problem is whether its service potential has expired completely during the period in which it was incurred or whether its usefulness is more long-term, thereby justifying an allocation in a similar manner to the depreciation of fixed assets.

Subjective judgement

The above examples are typical of the allocation problems facing the accountant when he processes data for reporting purposes. A great many involve subjective (albeit expert) judgements from persons such as engineers, chemists and production managers: for example, judgements on what is the useful life of a fixed asset for depreciation purposes; how much is in stock when production is a continuous process and flowing through the factory at speed; and how long-term are the benefits from a development programme or an advertising campaign. These judgements have to be made to allocate the recorded accounting data in such a way that they properly reflect the profitability and financial position of the company for a defined period.

However, judgements can vary, and different judgements can produce different income and financial position figures derived from the same data and economic events. Potentially, therefore, the financial affairs and results of a company could be reported in a variety of ways, each depending on the particular allocation judgements arrived at.

The historic cost valuation problem

The potential flexibility in historic cost information processing is added to by the further crucial function of valuation. The basic accounting data recorded throughout the accounting period are, as previously mentioned, stated in traditional practice in terms of their original values – that is, the actual revenues and costs which were transacted. However, these historic values require either to be allocated to relevant reporting periods (for reasons already discussed) or amended in light of existing circumstances which make them unsuitable for reporting purposes.

The valuation problems associated with accounting allocation are most serious in relation to fixed assets and stock. With fixed assets, the problem is one of deciding how much of the undepreciated original cost has expired during the period owing to use, and how much represents unexpired service potential to be used in following periods. Much obviously depends on the initial estimate of each asset's useful life and the subsequent estimate of its relative usefulness in each period of that life. But a great deal also depends on the method of depreciation applied to the asset in accordance with that earlier judgement. There are several methods available, each producing different periodic allocations of cost and therefore differing income statement and balance sheet figures. The reporting accountant has to decide which method appears most suitable in the circumstances. Other accountants, dealing with the same situation, could well decide to use other methods.

The valuation of stock and work-in-progress is yet another substantial problem area. Once stocks of raw materials and semi-processed and finished goods have been identified and physically counted at the end of the accounting period, there is the further process of placing a value on the total to represent its aggregate cost at that point. As with depreciation, this is a complex task which normally involves identifying past costs incurred in getting the stock to its existing state. However, there are many methods of computing such a cost, each capable of producing a different aggregate value for reporting purposes. There is also the problem of placing possibly subjective valuations on items of stock whose current value is less than their historic cost (thereby implementing the realization or prudence concept). Although these values may be determined by managerial experts or valuators, there is obviously potential for variation in the estimates, given that no asset value is certain until it is fully realized in cash.

Debtors, too, present valuation problems involving subjective judgements owing to the necessity to reduce the recorded values of certain debts when it is evident or possible that the amounts due will not be fully recovered. Very often, estimates of irrecoverable sums have to be made long before the position can be accurately determined.

The problem of cost allocation and asset valuation in traditional practice can be demonstrated in two simple examples – the first (Illustration 45) deals with allocating the cost of stock between periods, and the second (Illustration 46) with allocating the cost of fixed assets in the form of periodic depreciation.

Illustration 45 Accounting flexibility and stock valuations

Assume a company commences business at t_0 with capital subscribed in cash of £1,000. During the period t_0 to t_4, stock was bought on three occasions: at t_0, 100 units at £50 each; at t_1, 200 units at £60 each; and at t_3, 50 units at £70 each. During the same period, the following sales were made: at t_2, 150 units at £80 each; and at t_4, 100 units at £85 each. All transactions were in cash, and the question of taxation should be ignored.

The following possible income and financial position figures could be measured. The first set assumes unsold stock is valued at the latest possible cost; the second set assumes it is valued at the earliest possible cost; and the third set assumes it is valued at an average cost. Each of these bases is permissible (paragraph 27, Section B, Part II, Schedule 8, Companies Act 1948).

Illustration 45 *continued*

Income and financial position t_0–t_4 (alternative 1)

	£
Sales t_0–t_4 $(150 \times £80) + (100 \times £85)$	20,500
Less: cost of sales t_0–t_4 $(100 \times £50) + (150 \times £60)^*$	14,000
Income t_0–t_4	6,500
Stock at t_4 $(50 \times £60) + (50 \times £70)$†	6,500
Cash at t_4 $(£1,000 + 20,500) - (£5,000 + 12,000 + 3,500)$	1,000
Capital at t_4 $(£1,000 + 6,500)$	7,500

* Earliest possible costs; first-in, first-out basis
† Latest possible costs; first-in, first-out basis

Income and financial position t_0–t_4 (alternative 2)

	£
Sales t_0–t_4	20,500
Less: cost of sales $(t_0$–$t_4)$ $(150 \times £60) + (50 \times £70) + (50 \times £60)^*$	15,500
Income t_0–t_4	5,000
Stock at t_4 $(100 \times £50)$†	5,000
Cash at t_4	1,000
Capital at t_4 $(£1,000 + 5,000)$	6,000

* Latest possible costs; last-in, first-out basis
† Earliest possible costs; last-in, first-out basis

Income and financial position t_0–t_4 (alternative 3)

	£
Sales t_0–t_4	20,500
Less: cost of sales $(t_0$–$t_4)$ $(150 \times £56.67) + (100 \times £60)^*$	14,500
Income t_0–t_4	6,000
Stock at t_4 $(100 \times £60)$†	6,000
Cash at t_4	1,000
Capital at t_4 $(£1,000 + 6,000)$	7,000

* Weighted average cost at point of sale
† Weighted average cost at period-end

This illustration, though simplified, reveals that, by using three entirely permissible methods of stock valuation within the historic cost system of valuation, it is possible to produce three different income figures and three different capital figures. Yet the financial circumstances are identical in each case. It is obviously a situation ripe for confusion, for what is to be regarded as the 'right' or 'correct' figure: is income, for instance, to be measured at £5,000, £6,000 or £6,500?

What has happened in this case is reasonably typical of cost allocation problems – the company has purchased £20,500 worth of stock during the period t_0 to t_4 (100 at £50 each + 200 at £60 each + 50 at £70 each); a total of 350 units. It has sold 250 units for £20,500, and some decision has therefore to be made as to how much of the total cost of stock purchased has to be allocated to the 250 units sold during the period, and how much belongs to the cost of the 100 units of stock held at the period-end. Alternative 1 allocates £14,000 to cost of sales, and £6,500 to stock; alternative 2 allocates £15,500 to cost of sales and £5,000 to stock; and alternative 3 comes somewhere between these extremes, with £14,500 allocated to cost of sales and £6,000 to stock. Different allocations produce different valuations and income measurements, and these allocations are determined by judgements as to which allocation procedure to adopt. A similar problem involves depreciation of fixed assets (Illustration 46).

Illustration 46 Accounting flexibility and depreciation

Assume a company commences business at t_0 with capital subscribed in cash of £1,000. It purchased a depreciable fixed asset in cash for £800 (with an estimated four-period life, and a nil scrap value). Assume also, during the periods t_0 to t_1, t_1 to t_2, and t_2 to t_3, the cash operating surpluses were £500, £600 and £700, respectively. No other transactions are to be contemplated. Accounting allocation alternative 1 uses a straight-line basis for depreciation (that is, an equal amount is written off the asset's cost in each period of reporting; in this case, $\frac{1}{4} \times £800 = £200$ in each period). Allocation alternative 2 uses a reducing balance method (that is, a fixed percentage of the asset's undepreciated cost (or reducing balance) is written off; in this case, 50% – in period t_0 to t_1, 50% of £800 = £400; in period t_1–t_2, 50% of £400 = £200; in period t_2 to t_3, 50% of £200 = £100; and so on). The possible income and financial position figures under each alternative are as follows:

Income and financial position (alternative 1)

	t_0–t_1 £	t_1–t_2 £	t_2–t_3 £
Operating surplus (as given)	500	600	700
Less: fixed asset depreciation (as given)	200	200	200
Income (retained)	300	400	500

	t_1 £	t_2 £	t_3 £
Fixed asset (net of depreciation)	600[1]	400[2]	200[3]
Cash (opening cash plus cumulative operating cash surpluses)	700[4]	1,300[5]	2,000[6]
Capital (original capital plus cumulative income)	1,300[7]	1,700[8]	2,200[9]

Notes:
(1) £800−200; (2) £600−200; (3) £400−200; (4) £200*+500; (5) £700+600; (6) £1,300+700; (7) £1,000+300; (8) £1,300+400; (9) £1,700+500.

*Opening cash, £1,000 – purchase of asset, £800

Illustration 46 *continued*

Income and financial position (alternative 2)

	t_0-t_1 £	t_1-t_2 £	t_2-t_3 £
Operating surplus (as given)	500	600	700
Less: fixed asset depreciation (as given)	400	200	100
Income (retained)	100	400	600

	t_1 £	t_2 £	t_3 £
Fixed asset (net of depreciation)	$400^{(1)}$	$200^{(2)}$	$100^{(3)}$
Cash (as per alternative 1)	700	1,300	2,000
Capital (original capital plus cumulative income)	$1,100^{(4)}$	$1,500^{(5)}$	$2,100^{(6)}$

Notes:
(1) £800 − 400; (2) £400 − 200; (3) £200 − 100; (4) £1,000 + 100; (5) £1,100 + 400;
(6) £1,500 + 600.

By comparing the income, asset value, and capital figures under each alternative allocation method, it is clear that there are significant differences with each datum. Thus, the identical situation can be described in these different ways. Other alternative measurements of the same situation could also be produced – by varying the judgements as to the life of the asset concerned, or its eventual scrap or sale value, or by applying a different depreciation method. The measurement of income and capital under these circumstances can hardly be described as inflexible. The Companies Act 1948 (paragraph 18, Section B, Part II, Schedule 8) stipulates that depreciation should be provided for but makes no recommendation or requirement regarding the method to be adopted – other than that attention should be paid to the useful economic lives of depreciable assets.

The above examples have assumed that the issues of realization and allocation in traditional financial reporting practice are separate. This is far from the case, since both are essential parts of such practice. It is therefore essential that the reader can comprehend the combined effect of the two procedures. Illustration 47 attempts to do this in an admittedly somewhat artificial situation but, hopefully, highlights the considerable flexibility of traditional income measurement.

Illustration 47 Realization and allocation

ABC Ltd enters into a long-term contract with DEF Ltd to build a new factory. The terms of the contract are as follows:

The total contract price is £1 million, payable £300,000 at t_1, £300,000 at t_2, and £400,000 at t_3 (in each case subject to a 5% retention; the total retention being receivable at t_4). The contract costs are £250,000 (t_0 to t_1), £150,000 (t_1 to t_2), £300,000 (t_2 to t_3), and £30,000 (t_3 to t_4).

Assuming no further data, the following alternative accounting income figures can be contemplated:

Alternative 1
Revenues and costs recognized in total at the date of commencement of the contract.

	t_0-t_1 £	t_1-t_2 £	t_2-t_3 £	t_3-t_4 £	Total £
Revenue	1,000,000	—	—	—	1,000,000
Costs	730,000	—	—	—	730,000
Income	270,000	—	—	—	270,000

Alternative 2
Revenue recognized entirely at t_1 when the contract commenced; costs accounted for in the periods in which they were incurred; no allowance made for the retentions deducted from the revenue instalments.

	t_0-t_1 £	t_1-t_2 £	t_2-t_3 £	t_3-t_4 £	Total £
Revenue	1,000,000	—	—	—	1,000,000
Costs	250,000	150,000	300,000	30,000	730,000
Income	750,000	(150,000)	(300,000)	(30,000)	270,000

Alternative 3
Revenue recognized in the periods in which it was earned and mainly realized; costs accounted for in the periods in which they were incurred; no allowance therefore being made for retentions deducted from the revenue instalments.

	t_0-t_1 £	t_1-t_2 £	t_2-t_3 £	t_3-t_4 £	Total £
Revenue	300,000	300,000	400,000	—	1,000,000
Costs	250,000	150,000	300,000	30,000	730,000
Income	50,000	150,000	100,000	(30,000)	270,000

Alternative 4
Revenue recognized in the periods in which it was earned and realized; costs accounted for in the periods in which they were incurred; allowance therefore being made for the retentions deducted from each revenue instalment, and being finally received at t_4.

	t_0-t_1 £	t_1-t_2 £	t_2-t_3 £	t_3-t_4 £	Total £
Revenue	285,000	285,000	380,000	50,000	1,000,000
Costs	250,000	150,000	300,000	30,000	730,000
Income	35,000	135,000	80,000	20,000	270,000

Illustration 47 *continued*

Alternative 5
Revenue recognized entirely at t_4 when the contract was completed; costs accounted for in the periods in which they were incurred; no allowance being required for the retentions deducted from the revenue instalments.

	t_0-t_1 £	t_1-t_2 £	t_2-t_3 £	t_3-t_4 £	Total £
Revenue	—	—	—	1,000,000	1,000,000
Costs	250,000	150,000	300,000	30,000	730,000
Income	(250,000)	(150,000)	(300,000)	970,000	270,000

Alternative 6
Revenue recognized at the date of completion; costs matched in the same period; no accounting therefore being made for any transaction prior to that date.

	t_0-t_1 £	t_1-t_2 £	t_2-t_3 £	t_3-t_4 £	Total £
Revenue	—	—	—	1,000,000	1,000,000
Costs	—	—	—	730,000	730,000
Income	—	—	—	270,000	270,000

Summary of income

Income alternative	t_0-t_1 £	t_1-t_2 £	t_2-t_3 £	t_3-t_4 £	Total £
1	270,000	—	—	—	270,000
2	750,000	(150,000)	(300,000)	(30,000)	270,000
3	50,000	150,000	100,000	(30,000)	270,000
4	35,000	135,000	80,000	20,000	270,000
5	(250,000)	(150,000)	(300,000)	970,000	270,000
6	—	—	—	270,000	270,000

Each of the above alternatives adheres to the realization principle in a different way – from its complete rejection in alternatives 1 and 2 (in which revenue is recognized as soon as the contract is signed); through alternatives 3 and 4 (in which revenue is recognized when it is earned and realized – however, alternative 3 does not fully adhere to this because it recognizes 'retention' revenue prior to its realization); and, finally, to alternatives 5 and 6 (in which revenue is recognized only when the contract is complete). Thus, Illustration 46 again attempts to demonstrate that different interpretations of or attitudes to realization form the basis for different measures of periodic income. Traditional practice would adhere to some form of alternatives 3 and 4 with the earning and realization of revenue coinciding. In a short-term trading situation this would involve accounting for sales either when the sale was made (comparable to alternative 3) or when the sale proceeds were received (comparable to alternative. 4).

However, the recognition of revenue is not the only issue. The allocation of costs and their consequent matching with revenues is another problem highlighted in Illustration 47. The treatment of cost allocation varies from alternative 1 (recognition before they have been incurred – presumably by some form of budgeting); through alternatives 2 to 5, inclusive (when costs are allocated to the periods in which they are incurred); to alternative 6 (in which costs are carried forward until the completion of the contract). Each of these allocations, therefore, when coupled with the various revenue recognitions, is capable of producing a different periodic income measure. In practice, cost allocation procedures would normally be those used in alternatives 3, 4 and 6 (depending on when revenue was recognized). Thus, income in practice could be any of the trend of figures in alternatives 3, 4 and 6.

However, the main point about the illustration is the combined effect of the practices – the income of period t_0 to t_1 ranging from £750,000 to £(250,000); t_1 to t_2 from £150,000 to £(150,000); t_2 to t_3, from £100,000 to £(300,000); and t_3 to t_4, from £970,000 to £(30,000). It is this potential variability in measurement which is a major issue in contemporary financial reporting. (It should be noted that, although it is common practice in accounting to include a proportion of profit earned to date in work-in-progress, the relevant paragraphs in Section B, Part II, Schedule 8, Companies Act 1948 do not appear to allow this, nor does paragraph 12 of Section A permit unrealized profits on assets such as work-in-progress to be included in the income statement.)

Flexibility in accounting

The above paragraphs have attempted to give the reader some idea of the so-called flexibility problem in financial reporting. It is one which has given accountants increasing concern over the years, and it highlights a major dilemma for those persons faced with the task of producing financial statements – which accounting practices are the most suitable in the circumstances, and how can subjective judgements be minimized so as to produce reliable accounting information?

Although in the early days of financial reporting little formal guidance existed to help accountants, the position nowadays is relatively better. In the UK, the *Statements of Standard Accounting Practice* of the main professional accountancy bodies are intended to specify to practitioners the particular accounting methods which should be adopted in defined areas of accounting in addition to the general guidance given in Schedule 8, Companies Act 1948. These *Statements* are an attempt to narrow the areas of choice and difference in accounting, and thereby to create greater uniformity. A number of *Statements* have been produced to date and several more are in the process of preparation. Generally speaking, they tend to cover problem areas common to most companies; to prescribe a particular treatment; and to allow a certain amount of freedom for companies where there are reasonable grounds for departing from the standard practice advocated. Accountants responsible for the production of the relevant accounting information must ensure, however, that prescribed standards are adhered to by their companies when reporting to shareholders and other report users. If there is a departure from such a standard, then this must be fully disclosed in the financial statement concerned. In addition:

> The accounting policies . . . followed for dealing with items which are judged material or critical in determining profit and loss for the year and in stating the financial position should be disclosed by way of note to the accounts. The explanations should be clear, fair, and as brief as possible.[2]

Accounting flexibility, however, is not a new issue. It has confronted accountants throughout the decades during which company financial reporting has progressed and developed. The question is therefore why it has become such an important and, indeed, public issue in recent times. This will provide some necessary background to the accounting standards process mentioned above.

The answer would appear to be related to the increasing expertise of the main users of accounting information (including the financial press) and the increasing complexity of company activity, which demand a greater communication and use of accounting information. The first point is a relatively easy one to explain; as users become more knowledgeable about the nature and problems associated with accounting information, the problems inevitably become more public. The second is rather more difficult to explain, but it seems to revolve around the merger and acquisition activity of the 1960s.

During the late 1960s, the corporate sector of private enterprise developed to a considerable extent by means of merger or acquisition: companies had either combined to form larger entities created for the purpose (for example, British Motor Holdings Ltd and the Leyland Motor Corporation Ltd combining in 1967 to form British Leyland Motor Corporation Ltd); or one company had been taken over by another (for example, Schweppes Ltd acquired Cadbury Ltd in 1969). These activities created significant accounting and reporting problems, all of which have had (and still have) a bearing on the issue of flexibility.

First, with an acquisition or merger, the companies concerned can produce both historic and forecast data relating to profitability and financial position to help their shareholders decide whether or not to agree to the acquisition or merger. Because of the flexibility of accounting practice, particularly before the 1970s, one participant company could be using certain practices while the other could be using different practices. However, once the merger or acquisition is accomplished, a uniformity of practice may be established for both companies, which can render the comparison of pre- and post-merger or acquisition financial results extremely difficult. In addition, forecast data may be produced on the basis of one set of practices, with actual data prepared using a differing post-merger or acquisition approach; again, comparisons will be difficult. This situation is best demonstrated in the case of Associated Electrical Industries Ltd in 1967-8 where, because of a takeover bid from the General Electric Co. Ltd, an income forecast of £10 million was issued to its shareholders. The actual achievement, however, was a loss of £4.5 million. Of the difference of £14.5 million, £9.5 million was largely the result of differences in pre- and post-takeover accounting treatment.

Secondly, once a merger or acquisition has been completed, there arises a further accounting and reporting problem which is, again, caused by the inherent flexibility in accounting practice. At the present time, at least in the UK, there are two distinct methods of incorporating the net assets of acquired or merged companies for financial reporting purposes, each of which reflects an entirely different balance sheet position. The first is to account for the combination at so-called 'fair value'; thus, the net assets of the acquired or merger companies are incorporated into the financial statements of the combined entity at their current valuation (including a valuation of any goodwill which has been acquired at the time). The second is much less sophisticated, and is usually referred to as 'pooling of interests' or 'merger' accounting; the net assets of the ac-quired or merged companies are incorporated into the financial state-ments of the combined entity at their reported 'values' at the time of acquisition or merger. This means that, unlike 'fair value' accounting, report users are given little indication of the value of the net assets taken over, nor will goodwill be accounted for unless it happens to appear in the pre-takeover balance sheet of the acquired or merged company.

The above problem, reflecting flexibility in accounting practice and potentially serious differences for financial reporting purposes, despite similar circumstances, can be evidenced in recent company combinations in the UK. In 1968, the British Leyland merger took place on a pooling basis, as did the Cadbury Schweppes combination in 1969. Yet, in 1969, when General Electric combined with English Electric, 'fair value' accounting was used, resulting in a disclosure of acquired goodwill amounting to £167.13 million. The 1969 examples were large combina-tions, taking place at about the same time with all four companies profitable. Yet, in the former case, no account was taken for financial reporting purposes of the current valuation of combined net assets; nor was the existence of goodwill acknowledged. In the latter case, this was done, revealing a massive undervaluation of net assets in the companies, as well as considerable goodwill. Thus, it was situations such as these, made dramatic because of the size of the figures involved, which ap-peared to prompt the need for accounting standards in the UK and elsewhere by the end of the 1960s.

The need for accounting standards

An accounting standard can be defined as an agreed-upon criterion of what is regarded as best practice in a given set of circumstances, thereby allowing adequate comparisons and judgements to be made of periodic data. Thus, accounting standards are accepted as practical measures to improve the quality of reported financial information. They have evolved out of the concern and criticism which the flexibility in accounting practice has created. Standards exist to help the accounting practitioner to apply those accounting practices regarded as the most suitable for the circumstances concerned and, as such, they formalize the previously unwritten but generally acceptable practice, and enlarge on the general principles enunciated in Schedule 8, Companies Act 1948. In addition, they place individual companies and their managements in the position of having to justify whatever practices they adopt when producing their financial statements. Management should not be allowed to adopt any form of accounting it likes, for this type of anarchy could lead to significant doubts about the quality of reported accounting information, and thereby reduce its credibility and potential usefulness.

Without question, the main aim of accounting standards is to protect users of company financial statements by providing them with information in which they can have confidence. In so doing, this also helps to minimize the inherent flexibility in accounting practice by imposing a necessary but realistic uniformity on it. In this way, the individual information user can attempt adequate comparisons between companies and between periods for the same company through the use of reported financial statements.

Standardization is not therefore intended to put accounting in a straight-jacket. Rather it is an attempt to limit the theoretically possible flexibility and to give practitioners realistic working guidelines. If the individual circumstances of a particular company are such that an existing standard is not suitable, then alternative practices, regarded as more suitable, can be adopted. It is therefore possible to achieve both uniformity and flexibility in accounting practice. These two apparent opposites are not incompatible.

The accounting standards process

The need to formalize accounting practice by producing acceptable accounting standards has long been recognized in many countries. In both the UK and the US, the search for standards has been in progress since the 1930s, but only recently has any significant advance been made. Up to the mid-1930s, accounting practices developed in a relatively aimless manner, individual companies accounting usually as they thought fit. Any general acceptance in the process was derived through custom and habit. However, the proliferation of practices which tended to increase flexibility was eventually recognized by professional accountancy bodies and, from the 1930s to the early 1960s in the US, and by the late 1960s in the UK, accounting standards were formulated in particular problem areas and recommended for implementation by accountants and company management.

The period of standardization by recommendation did give practitioners some guidance, but because of lack of any mechanism to remove obsolete practices, as well as a lack of mandatory sanctions, the inherent flexibility in financial reporting continued (as did the consequential criticism). In the US, the recommended practices became mandatory on most qualified accountants from 1963 onwards, and a similar position was effectively reached in 1970 in the UK with the commencement of a programme to produce the now familiar *Statements of Standard Accounting Practice*.

Of particular concern to UK readers are these latter statements. They are produced mainly by a committee and, following a period of exposure and comment on the proposed practices, are mandatory for all relevantly qualified accountants involved in producing company financial statements. Such accountants must ensure that stated standards are implemented by the companies by whom they are employed, unless circumstances dictate that there should be a departure; in which case, this has to be fully disclosed in the published financial statements. Company auditors are also required to verify that companies have been following standard accounting practice and to report any disagreement with the departures made.

Despite these impositions on accountants, however, it must be said that *Statements of Standard Accounting Practice* are not mandatory on the persons ultimately responsible for the production and quality of financial statements (company directors), unless they also happen to be accountants to whom the *Statements* apply. Thus, it appears to be quite conceivable that company managements can deviate from the stated accounting standards, irrespective of the circumstances, though this will require to be verified by their auditors. In other words, professional statements of this kind do not appear to have the same force as those contained in statutory instruments such as the Companies Acts. The onus for implementation appears to be largely with individual accountants. However, the reader should be reminded that two matters have made these conclusions less relevant than they might otherwise have been – first, Sections 149 and 152, Companies Act 1948 provide that the requirement to give a 'true and fair view' in company annual financial statements overrides any other Companies Act reporting requirement – thus, *Statements of Standard Accounting Practice* intended to add to truth and fairness are effectively to be considered by the company and its management when preparing its financial statements; and secondly, Section A, Part II, Schedule 8, Companies Act 1948 contains most of the main accounting principles underlying the present series of *Statements of*

Standard Accounting Practice. In other words, those persons responsible for presenting company financial statements cannot ignore such a series.

Accounting standards problems

The process of trying to introduce a reasonable degree of uniformity into financial reporting practices is fraught with problems, many of which have not been fully recognized. This section attempts to outline certain of these problems, albeit briefly.

Uniformity and comparability

Accounting standards are designed specifically to reduce existing and potential flexibility in financial reporting practice. Hopefully, this is done to allow information users to make better use of the reporting data, and particularly to improve inter- and intra-company comparisons (especially for assessing alternatives in decision-making activities). However, no two companies are alike, despite apparent similarities in business activity. Therefore the danger is that standardization may impose a uniformity which creates a false comparability. In particular, it may obscure a company's 'personality' which can be assessed, in part, by the way in which its reported accounting information is measured and disclosed. There is a behavioural argument which suggests that the attitudes of company management can be partially evaluated from an analysis of the accounting practices it adopts (that is, dynamic and risk-taking or conservative and risk-avoiding). For example, a company writing off its research and development expenditure immediately against income can be said to be more conservative than another company which prefers to amortise it over its expected useful life. It may be suggested that this type of analysis would be impossible to make if a standard accounting practice was adopted which mandatorily required every company to write off such expenditure immediately.

The short term and the long term

The traditional system of financial reporting by companies is based upon historic cost values and the realization principle. The process of standardization attempts to reduce the flexibility of such a system. As such, it seeks to improve the quality of historic cost measures of income and financial position. But standardization does not, itself, provide answers to the long-term problems of accounting. In particular, it provides no direct answer to the question of what is the most relevant information to be reported to the potential users of company financial reports. It merely 'tidies up' one of the available alternative systems. The danger, therefore, is that the efforts to meet the short-term aims of the standardization process may very well divert attention away from the more long-term need to search for the best possible blend of accounting information for reporting purposes.

The need to reappraise

One of the major lessons to be learnt from a study of the history of financial reporting practices is that they have evolved largely in response to changes in the economic, social and technological environment of accounting. Thus, the Industrial Revolution introduced the problems of accounting for fixed assets; the development of stock markets created the need for greater disclosure of accounting information; and the social responsibilities of companies are now receiving attention in much of what is presently disclosed in financial reports.

It can be reasonably assumed that changes will continue to occur and to influence corresponding changes in the nature and quantity of information reported by companies. This means that the process of accounting standardization must always be regarded as a continuous one, with individual standards being the subject of continual reappraisal to assess their validity in light of changing circumstances. One of the faults of the previous 'recommendation' stage in accounting was that it did not contain a mechanism to remove invalid or obsolete recommendations, thereby helping to 'inflate' accounting flexibility. The danger with mandatory standards is that the same fault may be perpetuated.

Responsibility for standards

The question of who should be responsible for formulating and monitoring accounting standards is one of the biggest problems in the quest to minimize accounting flexibility. Accountants, and their professional bodies, have traditionally accepted this responsibility, with general support from statutory instruments such as the Companies Acts, and particular guidance from decisions upheld in courts of law. However, the existing system of mandatory standards has brought its attendant problems of responsibility.

Company management, in the form of boards of directors, has overall legal responsibility for the quality of published financial reports, but the mandatory accounting standards do not cover directly those directors who are not members of the professional accountancy bodies concerned. Therefore, although individual accountants may have a duty to ensure that prescribed standards are implemented, the mandatory scope of the prescribed standards does not appear sufficient to give them the same status as a Companies Act. However, as mentioned in an earlier section, the provisions of the Companies Act 1948 effectively bring *Statements of Standard Accounting Practice* within the scope of company law without the need to specify individual *Statements* in an Act of Parliament. Thus, directors have this indirect responsibility to adhere to them.

Extent of standardization

Business activity is rapidly becoming an extremely complex multinational affair, with a continuous movement towards bigger units and companies. The process of accounting standardization cannot, therefore, be thought of simply as a 'local' issue, affecting all companies in the locality concerned. In each such locality, there will exist small and large companies; some will trade nationally, and some will trade internationally; some will have large bodies of shareholders and other report users, and others will have a small number. These developments, which have existed for many years, raise important questions on the extent of standardization to be employed.

First, should mandatory accounting standards formulated by the professional bodies (and, where necessary, other interested groups) be applicable to all companies irrespective of size, nature of business, shareholder population, etc? Until recently in the UK and most other relevant countries, little attention was paid to these corporate differences, mandatory standards applying to all companies. Exceptions to this policy can be seen in Continental Europe, where several countries distinguish in their legislative requirements between different sizes of company (this being mainly determined by the size of subscribed share capital), and the recent EEC *Fourth Directive* (1978) now requires EEC member countries to distinguish between different sizes of company so far as financial reporting is concerned.[3] Although this mainly affects disclosure requirements, it is not unreasonable to suggest that it may be extended to include accounting standards. At the time of writing in the UK, only the Companies Act 1981 provisions concerning the delivery of modified annual financial statements to the Registrar of Companies, and those standards dealing with earnings per share computations, funds statements, and current cost statements make any differentiation between types of company to which the relevant standards apply.

Secondly, as individual countries develop their own accounting standards to deal with 'local' problems in financial practice, it is apparent that these problems are not as localized as they may seem and, indeed, many of them are common to most developed countries with an established investment market and company reporting system. It therefore seems sensible to bring about some degree of harmonization of accounting standards between countries, and of companies which trade in several countries. Once common international standards are adopted, investors and other report users have the assurance that reported information from different countries has been measured on a generally accepted basis. Companies, too, would not have to cope with conflicting standards of varying quality when consolidating accounting data from various countries for reporting purposes.

With these points in mind, it is interesting to see the formation taking place of international bodies of accountants to deal with cross-frontier harmonization of accounting standards: for example, the various Study Groups of the European Economic Community, the Accountants International Study Group, and the International Accounting Standards Committee (which has, since 1975, been issuing a number of *International Accounting Standards* in an attempt to introduce international standardization of reporting practice). But this proliferation of accounting standards bodies brings with it an attendant danger: the problem of various bodies producing different standards to deal with the same accounting problem. So far, those matters which have been standardized have not produced this potential divergence, but it could happen in the future, and what are companies to do when it does? Which standard should they adhere to? Should it be a national one, or an international one? Presumably national considerations should prevail, but this could mean a violation of an international standard, as in the case of a UK company following a *Statement of Standard Accounting Practice* which differed materially from an equivalent European Economic Community *Directive*, or an *International Accounting Standard*.

Summary of flexibility

Hopefully, the previous sections have given the reader some idea of the issues and problems associated with the inherent flexibility of financial accounting practice, many of which remain unresolved. It must in particular be made clear that, short of instituting legal provisions requiring all companies to measure and report accounting information according to a completely inflexible code of rules, it is impossible to envisage absolute uniformity in accounting practice, even with mandatory standards. The individual circumstances of each company, coupled with the degree of subjective judgement which is so necessary in accounting measurement, make it virtually impossible to envisage statements of accounting standards which can impose rigid uniformity. In other words, flexibility in accounting practice should never be eliminated completely; to do so is undesirable and liable adversely to affect the quality of financial reports.

The need for consistency

The allocating of accounting data between defined periods, the amendment of original valuations and the application of certain prescribed accounting methods, is a function which also involves a great deal of expertise, subjective judgement and explanatory disclosure. It is also a process where the methodology adopted must be implemented consistently if it is to produce information comparable from one period to the next (this is legally required in paragraph 11, Section A, Part II, Schedule 8, Companies Act 1948). Unless the methods adopted in producing the reporting information are the same from the period to period, it is conceivable that figures reflecting company profitability and financial position could increase or decrease from one period to the next, apparently portraying changes in the operational activities of the company but, in fact, resulting from the use of different accounting methods. For example, by changing the depreciation policy or method of valuing stock, inter-period income and financial position figures would change when company activity had remained unchanged.

However, consistency is a tool and not an immutable principle. It is essential for a proper comparison of information between periods but the information processor must change his methods of accounting when the circumstances of the company change materially enough to warrant it. In these cases, the change and its effect on the information concerned should be adequately disclosed.

Communicating the processed information

The communication process in financial accounting is concerned essentially with transmitting messages about the financial progress and position of a company to its external interests. The medium linking processor and user is, in general, the financial report, and, in particular, the financial statements. In this way, shareholders and other interested persons receive information about the company and thereby indirectly perceive its financial condition and investment potential. It is vital for these perceptions to correspond with the reality of the situation being reported, and company management has a major problem on its hands once the reportable accounting data have been suitably processed and aggregated. The problem is one of presenting it in the form of a financial report in such a way that it adequately compensates for the inability of its users to perceive directly the economic activity and events of the company to which it relates. In the UK, the main channels of communication are legally prescribed as the income statement and balance sheet (for the company and its subsidiaries, if any), together with the reports of the directors and auditors. However, this is not simply a matter of preparing these reports in a mechanical and routine fashion. There are other factors to be considered. Unfortunately, the standard formats for these financial statements contained in Part I, Schedule 8, Companies Act 1948 tend to negate these other factors because of the pro-forma nature of the prescribed statements. However, these factors ought to be considered by the reader.

Which data to be reported?

The financial accounting process produces, on a continuous basis, a great deal of data which are capable of being reported to shareholders and others. Consequently, because of their volume and range, management obviously has to select those which meet the needs of their users best. The needs of users, however, remain a somewhat indeterminate factor in

financial reporting at the present time. There are indications that reported income figures are of use in investment decisions; and there is
evidence that they can influence share price movement. Further, it can be
reasonably assumed and argued that certain data appear of considerable
use to particular users: for example, liquidity data contain information of
apparent use to lenders and creditors. Nevertheless, management is still
very much left on its own with regard to the selection of useful and
relevant reportable information, but with two important exceptions in the
UK.

First, as mentioned in the previous section, Part I, Schedule 8, Companies Act 1948 specifies a small number of prescribed formats for the
income statement and balance sheet for a single company (to be adapted,
where relevant, for a group of companies); and Parts II and III, Schedule
8, Companies Act 1948, contain certain mandatory accounting principles
and rules, and the current minimum disclosure requirements for annually
reported financial statements (the items of financial information which
must be disclosed, where appropriate, in the income statement, balance
sheet and directors' report). Secondly, Part III of the 1948 Act and the
Statements of Standard Accounting Practice of the major professional
accountancy bodies provide for the disclosure of explanations of the main
accounting practices adopted by companies when processing reportable
information.

Despite these guidelines, there remain significant judgements to be
made by management not only with regard to decisions concerning which
accounting numbers to report, but also with regard to the nature and
extent of any supporting explanations and comments on these figures. As
the complex nature of the accounting environment changes over time, so
too do user needs. In fact, the problem of delineating the boundaries of
accounting disclosure has been a vexed one throughout the history of
financial reporting: for example, the extent to which reported accounting
numbers should be supported by explanations in footnotes; and the
nature and extent of supplementary financial data which should be
supplied with the legally-required financial statements. What company
management has to take care over, therefore, is the identification of
matters which can and should be reported to conform with the required
qualities of truth and fairness, and to allow shareholders and other
interested persons to make meaningful decisions. The rider to this
general principle should not be ignored: that is, the disclosure of financial
information should not be detrimental to the company concerned (certain disclosures may be harmful if they reveal data of use to a competitor
in the field). The overall emphasis should nevertheless be to disclose
sufficient information to satisfy the needs of its users.

How should data be reported?

Communicating accounting information is not just a matter of deciding which data to disclose in the relevant reports. There is the related problem of presenting it with suitable wording. There can be no communication without understanding, and understanding depends on the information concerned both receiving the attention of its intended users and employing a language which is comprehensible and not subject to ambiguity. In other words, the reported financial statements must be presented in such a way that the user will give his attention to them in a reasonable way; and their information content must be given in terms which are understandable.

Attention to financial reports can be gained by sensible presentation and layout of the information, particularly with regard to the positioning and summarizing of data. Material information must not be placed in such a position that it is hard to find in the report, nor must it be summarized to such an extent that it creates more questions than answers for its user. On the other hand, it must be remembered that there is a limit to how much data can be absorbed and used by the user. This having been said, it must be remembered that the prescribed formats for financial statements in Schedule 8, Companies Act 1948 are not conducive to maximizing understanding as they require all companies to adhere to the same format – as if all companies could and should be reported on in this mechanical way.

Understanding reported financial information is a matter of considerable concern to accountants, largely because accounting involves a highly complex and sophisticated technical language capable of not being understood by non-accountants – or worse, of being mistakenly understood. The problem is that the accounting terms used may not have a common meaning to the processor and user alike, and may, indeed, not have a stable meaning to accountants (terms can vary in meaning when used in different circumstances). For example, the term 'depreciation' may represent an allocation of fixed asset cost to an accountant but a fall in the value of a fixed asset to a non-accountant. Thus, company management must be extremely careful when presenting accounting information in report form to use terms which are likely to be generally understood.

How quickly should data be reported?

The adage of old news being no news is pertinent to the function of company financial reporting because, particularly with annual financial statements, the information is mainly historical. Therefore, it is essential for it to be communicated as soon as possible after the end of the accounting period if its users are to obtain any benefit from it.

Unfortunately, the processing of accounting data can be a time-consuming activity, even when there is an efficient system of data collection. For example, management may have to count certain assets physically to obtain relevant data for incorporation in financial statements (as with stock and work-in-progress, or stores of tools and expendable equipment). It also has to adjust and value certain items of data to put them in reportable form (as with debtors, creditors, depreciable fixed assets, and stock and work-in-progress). This takes time and often cannot be undertaken until the end of the accounting period concerned. In addition, annual financial reports are normally required to be audited, and this particular process is also time-consuming, though it may be alleviated somewhat by a considerable amount of the routine audit verification work being conducted throughout the accounting period. The overall result, however, is that the annual financial report of a company is often inevitably delayed. Shareholders and other interested users therefore usually find that the information being communicated is becoming rapidly outdated not only because of its inherent nature, but also because of inevitable delays owing to its measurement and audit. This mainly affects annual reports and occurs to a lesser extent with interim reports, but it should not apply to forecast data because these, by definition, should not be dated.

Differences in perception

Possible variations in the way in which different financial report users perceive the same economic activity through the use of the same financial report is one of the least-explored areas of accounting, and it has distinct implications for the effectiveness of accounting communications. It is a well-known pyschological concept of human behaviour that, despite the reality of a situation, different people will manage to perceive it differently – whether the perceptions are direct (that is, via direct observation or contact with the object or persons being perceived) or indirect (that is, via some means by which the object or person is indirectly observed or contacted; as with newspaper accounts of people and events).

These perceptual differences can arise for a variety of reasons. For one thing, personal experience limits the ability to perceive reality (a person who has never observed or experienced the use of a chair is hardly likely to perceive its particular use on first observing or coming into contact with one). In other words, the more experienced or used to the perceived object or person the perceiver is, the more likely he is to arrive at a reasonably accurate perception.

On the other hand, irrespective of past experience, the perceiver can distort what he observes by his attitudes. His prejudices and biases can therefore lead him to see things which he wants to see, or to ignore things which he does not want to see, irrespective of what is actually there to see. Finally, it is possible for the reality of the objects or persons being perceived to be distorted in such a way that the perceiver fails to observe accurately (for example, as with a rusty motor car that has been resprayed to cover up structural defects when it is being offered for sale).

All the above points have some relevance to the communication of reportable accounting data, and therefore present problems in the financial reporting function. Company financial reports form a significant means by which shareholders and other interested parties can perceive the activities and affairs of companies. The nature and quality of these perceptions depend to a large extent on the experiences and attitudes of the users concerned. They also depend on how the data are communicated. In other words, the accuracy of user perception will increase the more the user is experienced in reading and analysing accounting information; the more open-minded he is when using the information (for example, his expectations of company performance should not be so inflexible that he perceives what he believes company performance ought to be); and the more objective is the process of producing and packaging the information in report form.

The major problem is thus one of ensuring objectivity and integrity in the communication process, so far as both the producer and user of information are concerned. This is something which obviously cannot be legislated for or regulated; it has to be worked at by all concerned. If this is not done, then a situation exists in which the report user could perceive company activity and performance inaccurately, with consequential disbenefits to himself from misguided decisions.

The audit of communicable accounting information

Certainly in the UK, and also in many other developed countries, company management must ensure that a suitably qualified accountant or firm of accountants has verified and reported on the quality of the reported information. In the UK, this is legally required for annual financial reports to shareholders; and is also required for prospectus and takeover and merger accounting reports. It does not apply at present to interim financial reports. As this text is mainly concerned with annual reports, the audit will be explained in that context.

In the UK, the board of directors of a company is legally responsible for producing the annual financial statements described in various parts of the text. As we have seen, the appointment of the auditor is intended to provide a measure of protection to company shareholders who are not normally in a position to verify the quality of the information personally.

The Companies Acts 1948, 1967, 1976, 1980 and 1981 require the auditor to give a considered opinion to the shareholders on the truth and fairness of the income statement and balance sheet. Although not defined by the Acts, this can be interpreted as meaning an opinion on the correspondence of the information to the economic activity it purports to describe, and on the objectivity which has been exercised by management when processing it. In other words, the major objective is to ensure that shareholders and other interested parties are presented with credible information which they can use with a reasonable assurance that it has been prepared honestly and with due care. In this respect, it is essential to verify that the accounting process has complied with any legal and professional regulations concerning the measurement and disclosure of accounting information.

Also, as mentioned on several occasions in this text, the UK auditor is expected to report on current cost-based financial statements (when these are published).[4] If they are the main financial statements, they will be subject to the provisions of the afore-mentioned Companies Acts, and the 'true and fair view' opinion should be adapted to relate to the current cost convention and practices.[5] However, if they are supplemental and unabridged, a similar type of opinion is recommended by the main professional bodies to be given to shareholders and others. Abridged or experimental current-cost statements, on the other hand, are recommended to be accompanied by an audit report stating that they comply with the relevant *Statement of Standard Accounting Practice.*[5]

Company audits at present appear to be legally intended for shareholders (and, only indirectly, the debenture holders who receive the annual report). This is despite the fact that annual financial statements of companies are available for use by any member of the public who cares to inspect the files kept by the Registrar of Companies. To date, courts have refused to allow damages to injured persons other than shareholders. (Injuries, in this sense, mean financial disadvantages caused through use of the reported information – for example, because of payment of dividends out of the reported income which has been inadequately measured, thereby causing financial hardship or disaster to the company concerned.)

There has been considerable debate on this point, but so far the legal decisions, and the attitude of the professional accountancy bodies, have been that annual financial statements are intended only for company shareholders. Third parties who make use of them, and are misled by them because of inadequate information, are not regarded as entitled to sue the directors or the company for damages. Indeed, shareholders can only sue for damages as a body, and only if injury has arisen out of inadequate stewardship on the part of the directors. It appears that injury to a single shareholder arising out of use of inadequate information for investment decision-making would not be acceptable for court action.

The conduct of the audit

The first stage of the audit is one of familiarization: the auditor acquires a knowledge of the general background to the company which is essential for an efficient audit. This involves a study of the nature and location of the business of the company, as well as its internal regulations and systems (including the accounting function). It also requires a knowledge of the management and employees of the company. With this knowledge, the various audit processes can be commenced. However, it is relatively obvious that familiarization of this kind will be more extensive when the auditor is appointed in the first instance, and that subsequent familiarization will be concerned with updating his existing knowledge.

The first stage of the audit concerns the process of validating the company's data–processing function to assess the accuracy and dependability of the data concerned. The auditor examines the system, judges its strengths and weaknesses, and, possibly by a sampling process, tests it by checking through it a number of transactions. This work is often conducted throughout the financial year, and once the auditor is satisfied with his tests, he can move on to the next stage of testing the information process. If he is not satisfied, he may conduct further tests or he may decide to report his findings to the shareholders if he believes these materially affect the truth and fairness of the financial statements.

The next stage in the audit concerns an examination of the process whereby the accounting data are put in a form which can be reported in the required financial statements. The auditor analyses and checks on the various accounting procedures used, paying particular attention to the application of Parts II and III, Schedule 8, Companies Act 1948, and relevant *Statements of Standard Accounting Practice* as well as to the crucial judgemental areas. He will also review the physical existence, ownership and condition of the company's assets described in the balance sheet. (A similar verification exercise takes place with its reported liabilities.) He will then verify that there has been adequate disclosure and presentation of the information in the financial statements, as required by law and best accounting practice. The auditor conducts these examinations on a test basis, the size of the samples depending on his confidence in the quality of the accounting system.

If he is satisfied with the results of these tests, he can then proceed to give his 'truth and fairness' report. If he is not satisfied, he will issue a report which will specify the nature and extent of his dissatisfaction. This can involve a qualified opinion (for example, that the information is 'true and fair' with the exception of one datum or more); or an adverse opinion (for example, that no opinion is being given because of the extremely poor quality of the information). In all cases where the opinion is not the straightforward positive one required by law, the auditor is professionally bound to explain fully the nature of the problem(s) and the reasons for his dissatisfaction.

The audit opinion

From the above brief summary of the nature of the audit function, it should be reasonably clear that the auditor is an expert accountant (or group of accountants) employed to give a professional opinion on the quality of company financial statements. As such, his opinion cannot be conceived as anything other than an expert appraisal and judgement. It is not a statement guaranteeing the accuracy of the figures concerned: this would be impossible, given the nature of the information being audited. Nor is it a statement that the auditor is in some way responsible for the quality of the reported financial statements: this is the responsibility of the board of directors, and the auditor is only responsible for the quality of his audit and opinion. If his opinion is not a correct one, or is misleading, then the shareholders can sue him for damage if financial injury has resulted from reliance on that opinion.

In this respect, it should be noted that the existence of a qualified audit opinion does not necessarily mean that the reported information cannot be relied on, or is, in some way, sub-standard. Nor does it mean that the company directors and managers are in any way dishonest. Qualifications may arise because the audit report is an opinion, and obviously the auditor can differ from the directors in his judgement of some accounting matter. As there is considerable room for such differences to exist in accounting, it is not surprising that they lead to qualified audit reports. The nature of the qualification must be read carefully, and its effect on the overall quality of the information thereby assessed.

Finally, it should be noted by the reader that the advent of current cost-based financial statements has introduced a form of audit report which contains something less than the traditional opinion on informational truth and fairness. In situations where current cost statements are abridged or experimental, the auditor is recommended to provide a 'compliance' report – that is, one which reflects a limited review of the reported data to the extent that they conform or comply with the provisions of a prescribed *Statement of Standard Accounting Practice*. In these cases, the auditor is not giving a professional opinion on the quality of the information – merely a statement that its measurement has been compatible with expected practice.

Auditing standards

The UK company auditor is now subject to prescribed principles and practices contained in a series of *Auditing Standards and Guidelines* published in 1980.[6] Members of the main professional accountancy bodies are expected to adhere to these standards, which are intended to provide all auditors with a framework within which the audit must be conducted. They also provide financial report users with a knowledge that certain prescribed audit standards are expected of all auditors when they undertake the audit function in relation to financial statements. The auditor is also subject to specific *Statements on Auditing* issued by the main professional accountancy bodies in areas requiring some degree of standardization.

Specifically, the company auditor in the UK is expected to (a) adequately plan, control and record his audit work; (b) ascertain the nature and adequacy of the company's accounting system as a basis for the production of its financial statements; (c) obtain sufficient relevant and reliable evidence to enable him to make reasonable conclusions concerning the quality of the company's reported information; (d) ascertain and test the adequacy of the company's systems of internal control; (e) conduct a review of the company's financial statements which is adequate enough to allow him, together with his other evidence, to form an opinion on them; (f) produce an audit report containing his 'true and fair view' opinion and a statement saying whether the financial statements on which this opinion is given have been audited according to approved auditing standards; and (g) refer in his report to all material matters about which he has reservations which, when relevant, have caused him to give a qualified audit opinion.

The management letter

Apart from his audit report, the auditor may produce a separate report to the board of directors which outlines any problem areas he has come across in the company and which, in his opinion, deserve managerial attention. This is called the management letter, and is produced on a purely voluntary basis with the aim of improving company systems of control, particularly as they affect the accounting function. These reports are not normally drawn to the attention of shareholders, except in so far as a particular problem area has also resulted in a qualification contained in the audit report.

The auditor

Lastly, a few comments on the auditor himself are appropriate. As already mentioned, 'he' is normally a firm of professionally-qualified accountants employing a number of accountants (at varying stages in their training and experience) to conduct the audit. Auditors are therefore professional people (highly skilled and trained), and subject to ethical rules governing their professional conduct and work. In particular, those employed on the audit must act with reasonable care, integrity and independence. The latter quality is particularly important as it is essential to the objectivity of the auditor's opinion. If it is not a balanced and unbiased opinion, then doubts may be created which affect the credibility of the audited financial statements. Auditor independence is therefore interpretable not only in terms of the auditor's attitude of mind but also in terms of his appearance of independence: he must not only be mentally independent but must also be seen to be independent. Thus, in the UK, the auditor is not permitted to be an officer or servant of the company (Section 161(2), Companies Act 1948).

The concept of professional independence has been further formulated in the *Statements of Professional Conduct 1*, issued in 1975 and revised in

1979.[7] In this, the implication is that the auditor is expected to be (and also to appear to be) free of any interest which is incompatible with his objectivity when conducting an audit – for example, he must not be too reliant for fee income on one client company; he must avoid personal relationships involving officers and employees of a client company; he should have no financial involvement with a client company (these including family, beneficial, trust, and nominee shareholdings); and he must avoid other conflicts of interest with client companies (for example, he should not be involved in decision-making, preparation of accounting records, and liquidations and receiverships for client companies where he has been or is acting as auditor). In other words, the UK auditor has very clear instructions from his professional body to be and be seen to be independent, and therefore to be capable of giving an objective opinion.

Summary

The preceding paragraphs in this and the previous chapter have attempted to indicate to the reader the main stages involved in the preparation of financial reports, particularly from the point of view of those which appear annually for company shareholders. The process involves the collection of suitable accounting data, its subsequent processing, by allocation and valuation, into relevant informational messages; and the final stage of communicating these messages in a suitable report form. In addition, the external auditor is required to verify and report on the credibility of each of these stages, prior to the information being presented to the shareholders (at least, so far as annual reports are concerned).

These descriptions have also outlined several of the major problems inherent in the present system of company financial reporting – particularly those of valuation, allocation, judgement and communication. Without a knowledge of these, the reader (and the user of financial reports) is inadequately prepared to enter the area of using reported information within various decision contexts. Hopefully, the reader is now prepared, and the following chapters deal with report usage.

References

1 M. Moonitz, 'The Basic Postulates of Accounting', *Accounting Research Study 1*, The American Institute of Certified Public Accountants, 1961, p. 33.
2 'Disclosure of Accounting Policies', *Statement of Standard Accounting Practice 2*, 1971, p. 3.
3 For a discussion of this issue, see *Company Accounting and Disclosure*, Cmnd 7654, HMSO, 1979, pp. 1–8.
4 'Auditors' Reports on SSAP 16 "Current Cost Accounting",' *Auditing Guideline 502*, The Institute of Chartered Accountants of Scotland, 1980.
5 'Current Cost Accounting', *Statement of Standard Accounting Practice 16*, 1980.

6 See *Auditing Standards and Guidelines*, Institute of Chartered Accountants of Scotland, April 1980.
7 'Ethical Guide for Members of the Institute of Chartered Accountants of Scotland', *Statements of Professional Conduct 1*, 1975 (1979), pp. 5 and 9–10b.

Suggested discussion or essay topics (covering Chapters 7 and 8)

1 Accounting accumulates and communicates information essential to an understanding of the activities of an enterprise. Discuss.
2 Comment on the suggestion that the measurement of financial accounting information of the type presently reported is as much based on subjective opinion as on objective evidence.
3 The choice of a time period of one year creates problems for the reporting accountant. Discuss.
4 Accountants and auditors adhere to the matching principle. What is meant by this term, and how significant is it in financial reporting?
5 Auditors do not certify or guarantee financial statements. Comment on the validity of this statement.
6 Financial accounting is concerned with obtaining a credible rather than an exact description of a company's financial affairs. Comment.
7 What is meant by the realization principle in accounting practice? Why has it survived for so long in accounting practice?
8 Accounting for periodic income is a relatively straightforward process of measuring revenues and costs and relating them to one another. Discuss this statement within the context of traditional income reporting.
9 The greater the lack of credibility in accounting information, the greater is the need to have such credibility established by the process of verification. Comment and discuss, particularly with a view to explaining the place of verification in contemporary accounting thought.
10 It should be emphasised that the financial statements of a company are prepared on the assumption that it will continue in business. Discuss the implications of this statement for financial reporting.
11 Discuss the importance of not delaying the reporting of financial information beyond certain tolerable limits.
12 The concept of audit care is based upon the prudent auditor – that is, the auditor who represents the average of his profession. What is meant by audit care, and how important is it to the quality of company financial statements?
13 The significance of independence in the work of the auditor is so well established that little justification is needed to justify its existence. Discuss.
14 The modern accountant can lay claim to the role of 'information technologist'. Explain what you believe this to mean in relation to the production of financial accounting information.
15 Arguably the most fundamental problem in financial reporting is valuation because different valuation measures produce different income measures. Discuss.
16 'Uniformity of accounting is said to be bad – that it stifles incentive and creative thinking, that it would bar experimentation in accounting. The uniformity bugaboo is a red herring that turns away and discourages searching inquiry into the problem. Seeking to improve or define accounting principles has been labelled as an attempt to establish uniformity, as seeking a strait-

jacket for accounting. Yet in simple truth, uniform accounting principles as applied to specific transactions foster reliability, quality performance and honesty, and require more original thinking than any of the so-called experimental practices we are now following.' Comment and discuss this statement on the problem of standardization of accounting practice.

17 There is a grave danger that increasing uncertainty as to the credibility and reliability of published financial statements will lead to potential users ignoring these sources of information and seeking others which they believe to be more reliable and relevant. Comment.

18 Why is it necessary to standardize accounting practices? What evidence exists to suggest that flexibility in such practice is a bad thing?

19 The type and amount of disclosure of accounting information in company financial statements depends, at least in part, on how expert the reader can be expected to be in interpreting accounting data. Comment on this statement in relation to the potential users of these statements.

20 The trouble with financial reports is that they disclose too much data rather than too little. Everything is distilled and aggregated into figures which obscure vital messages concerning the financial performance and conditions of companies. What is wanted is a reduction in disclosure, thus reversing the previous trend. Discuss.

Selected bibliography for Chapters 7 and 8

Accounting Standards Committee, *The Corporate Report*, 1975, pp. 61–73. A brief review of the main income and value models.

N. M. Bedford, *Extensions in Accounting Disclosure*, Prentice-Hall, 1973. The nature of accounting disclosures, and the main problems associated with them.

H. Bierman, 'Measurement and Accounting', *Accounting Review*, July 1963, pp. 501–7. The nature and problems of measuring reported financial accounting information.

S. L. Buzby, 'The Nature of Adequate Disclosure', *Journal of Accountancy*, April 1974, pp. 38–47. Determining what is required to be disclosed in the light of user needs.

B. Carsberg and T. Hope, *Current Issues in Accounting*, Philip Allan, 1977. The development of standard accounting practice (pp. 46–59); accounting and changing prices (pp. 72–86); and the modern audit function (pp. 87–106).

R. J. Chambers, *Accounting Evaluation and Economic Behaviour*, Prentice-Hall, 1966. An explanation of the accounting system (pp. 124–40); the nature of accounting information and its processing (pp. 141–65); and the process of communicating accounting information (pp. 166–85).

M. W. Glautier and B. Underdown, *Accounting Theory and Practice*, Pitman, 1976, pp. 591–609. An introductory review of the main current value accounting proposals.

E. S. Hendriksen, 'Disclosure in Financial Reporting', *Accounting Theory*, 3rd edition, Irwin, 1977, pp. 545–67. The theory and practice of financial statement communication.

J. R. Jordan, 'Financial Accounting and Communication', *The Price Waterhouse Review*, Spring 1969, reproduced in G. G. Mueller and C. H. Smith, *Accounting: A Book of Readings*, Holt, Rinehart and Winston, 1970, pp. 127–44. The communications aspect of the financial accounting process.

T. A. Lee, *Company Auditing*, 2nd edition, Gee & Co., 1982. The financial accounting function; and the company audit function (Chapter 1).

T. A. Lee, 'Accounting Standards and Effective Financial Reporting: A Review in

Principle', *Accountant's Magazine*, January and February 1975, pp. 25–30 and 73–81. A review of the accounting standards process; its nature, problems and objectives.

T. A. Lee, *Income and Value Measurement*, 2nd edition, Nelson, 1980. A full review and discussion of the various alternative income, value and capital maintenance models available for financial reporting purposes.

L. Spacek, *A Search for Fairness*, Arthur Andersen & Co., 1969. A book of readings by Spacek on the uniformity/flexibility issue in financial reporting.

E. Stamp and C. Marley, *Accounting Principles and the City Code: the Case for Reform*, Butterworth, 1970, pp. 129–40. An argument for uniformity and flexibility in accounting practice.

9

The context for using company financial reports

Introduction

The previous chapters have attempted to provide the reader with a broad understanding of the nature and problems associated with producing company financial reports. In particular, the main emphasis has been on the measurement and communication of relevant accounting information, with the intention of familiarizing the reader with financial reporting practice while remaining relatively uninvolved in the mechanics of the exercise.

However, financial reporting is not just a complex process of producing relevant accounting figures. It is also concerned with the use made of accounting data in economic activities of various forms. Thus, the aim of this and the following chapters is to attempt to describe the function of using the accounting information which has been reported. As such, the text will concentrate on the use made of financial reports by persons and bodies external to companies rather than by company managements.

Report analysis and decisions

In a perfect world, in which everyone had perfect knowledge, the need for a formal financial reporting system would not exist. The future would be known with absolute certainty, and decisions and actions could be taken in the security of such a certain future. However, the real world is an uncertain one in which knowledge is limited and information is a scarce commodity. Decisions and actions have to be taken in the face of a good deal of uncertainty, despite the existence of factual data relating to past activity. The company financial reporting system is intended specifically to provide such factual data on a regular basis, albeit occasionally supplemented by management's forecasts of future activity. As such, its fundamental purpose is to provide users with a knowledge of company activity which they did not have previously. Hopefully, this knowledge will be useful to them when assessing and formulating alternative courses of action in their various decision functions.

These decisions involve assessing what has to be given up so as to obtain some future benefit and, as such, reported information is an important input to the decision model concerned. What is equally clear, however, is that general-purpose information must be subjected to some form of analysis prior to incorporation into such a model; that is, it must be translated into specific-purpose data if it is to be capable of influencing the behaviour of the decision-maker. In this way, decision-making in a world of uncertainty is made more efficient and effective than it might otherwise be. The major problem is determining the analysed information relevant to a particular decision, and thus of determining the nature of the particular decisions to which the analysis must be directed.

The nature of decisions

People make decisions as part of the process of achieving certain defined objectives. In economic terms this involves the optimal use of scarce resources and, as already indicated, the need for reliable information in this exercise is relatively self-evident. It is therefore pertinent, when assessing the usefulness of different types and items of information, to look more closely than hitherto at the nature and characteristics of the decisions (and underlying objectives) to which the reported data may be applied. When this is done, the reasons and aims of report analysis become more apparent than may be the case by casual observation.

First, it is evident that decisions, no matter what their individual nature, concern assessments of the future. They must also concern assessments of alternative courses of action. Therefore, if reported information is to be of use in decision-making, it needs analysing to produce data capable of providing insights into the potential benefits and costs of alternative courses of action. The alternatives must likewise be identified to select relevant data for analysis. Once this is done, the relevance of the analysed information can be judged in terms of what is usually described as its predictive ability: its usefulness in enabling its users to forecast the future benefits and disbenefits associated with identifiable alternatives.

In other words, alternative courses of action will always involve potential benefits and sacrifices, for, when pursuing a certain course of action, benefits can only be derived by making certain sacrifices. For example, to obtain a future stream of income from his investment, an investor must be prepared not only to forgo a sum of money equivalent to the cost of that investment, but also to forgo the income streams obtainable from alternative investment sources to which the money could have been put. Likewise, a banker, when lending a sum of money to a company, is doing so in order to receive the interest and capital repayments due him in the future, and he is forgoing the opportunity of lending that sum to other company clients. It is therefore important for analysed data to have a bearing on identifying and assessing the various benefits and sacrifices associated with a particular decision and its related alternative courses of action; and predicting their future monetary value.

Secondly, decision-making is normally conducted with a certain strategy and objective(s) in mind, and it is reasonable to assume that, once a decision has been made and a particular course of action followed, the decision-maker will monitor events to ensure that his objectives are being achieved. In this way, he can further decide to continue with the existing course of action, to switch to an alternative course of action, or to amend his existing strategy and objectives. Whatever he does, he will require relevant data to aid him in this control function, and report analysis has a significant part to play identifying data useful in the monitoring of decisions.

In this respect, it is particularly important for the analysis to contain data relating to both actual and expected performance so that adequate comparisons can be made for control purposes. It is equally important that comparative data, if they are to be useful to the decision-maker, should be measured and analysed on the same basis. If this is not the case, then comparisons become at best difficult and at worst meaningless, the user never being quite sure whether differences are the result of economic and financial factors or differences in the methods used to measure these factors.

Report analysis objectives

It should be reasonably clear so far that the main purpose of report analysis is to provide financial statement users with data relevant to the predicting and controlling functions which constitute the decision process. In this sense, the aim of analysis is to refine and translate the reported data: to convert them from their general-purpose state to a specific-purpose form. The user can then make use of the analysed data to construct a profile of the company (its management, financial condition, income, dividends, liquidity, and so on). This provides part of the relevant background to the decision-maker's eventual decisions, remembering, of course, that company financial reports are not the only source of information about companies available to him. The required profile cannot be obtained from a casual observation of published financial reports, for this could only give a superficial impression of the important financial features of the company at one particular point in time. Analysis, on the other hand, particularly when conducted on a regular basis, provides a detailed description of these features over time as well as at particular points of time.

However, it must be noted that no matter how good the techniques of analysing financial reports, the quality and reliability of the analysed data are only as good as the financial reports themselves. If the latter are inadequately measured or ineffectively presented, these basic faults will not be remedied by detailed analysis. On the other hand, it is true to say that expert analysis can offset presentation faults, in the sense that once particular data have been chosen for analysis, the original presentation of financial reports becomes less important. Nevertheless, the effect of measurement faults will be carried through to the analysed data, and presentation faults can impede the selection of relevant data for analysis purposes. It is for this reason that the previous two chapters have concentrated on providing a general understanding of the main problems associated with the production of company financial reports. Unless the production process is of the highest possible quality, providing information of relevance to potential users, the stated objective of report analysis (the provision of relevant data for prediction and control in decision-making) cannot be achieved.

Types of decision

Having established that the main aim of analysing company financial reports is to provide a needed input to decisions to be made by their potential users, it is necessary to identify the main types of decision to which analyses are directed in practice. As previously mentioned, there are many uses to which company financial reports can be put, and these can be classified as internal and external uses.

Internal management uses

This particular grouping includes uses related to the legality of dividends and the prudence of dividend action, as well as to employee wage-bargaining procedures. In other words, data pertaining to company profitability (for example, the availability of income for dividend purposes) and financial position (for example, the liquidity position) will aid management in certain aspects of its financial policy and decision-making. Wage negotiators will also find it useful when discussing the merits and feasibility of wage claims, etc. However, these are uses with which this text is not primarily concerned, and are therefore excluded from further examination, though readers should note that they do suggest the practical usefulness of published accounting information, even to internal managements which have a continuous and detailed knowledge of company matters. The descriptions and explanations of financial statement analysis provided later in the text may well be of as much relevance to managerial and employee users as they are to investors and other external users. After all, such analyses provide a financial profile of the company concerned which ought to be of interest to anyone with a significant involvement in it.

External uses

The remaining uses relate to persons and organizations outwith the company who tend to rely on its formal financial reports as a major source of information about it, and who, because of the structure of the company, are unavoidably prevented from gaining an intimate knowledge of its activities through regular and close contact with its operations and management. They can be divided into two groups:

(a) *Governmental uses* The government is a major user of company financial reports, the uses including those concerned with fiscal policy, government supervision, price regulation and taxation. In the case of the latter function, the required information is contained in the annual financial report, and the analysis work involved with it is a relatively simple identification of individual items of revenue and expenditure which may or may not be incorporated in the measurement of the figure for annual income to be taxed. In this sense, the analysis is not an exercise conducted to refine the basic information and highlight specific characteristics of the company for purposes of decision-making; it is simply concerned with adjusting reported figures to conform with existing tax law.

Likewise, the remaining governmental uses relate to the collection of reported information for statistical purposes to provide governmental policy and decision-makers with aggregate data of use in their industrial, regional and national intervention and regulation activities.

As such, the analysis is not concerned with the characteristics of individual companies, except in occasional circumstances where government aid is being sought by a company, or when an individual company's trading activities are under investigation. In these circumstances, however, the use of information is akin to the investing category described next.

(b) *Investment uses* The remaining uses are primarily concerned with 'investment' in its broadest financial sense: the provision of short, medium and long-term finance to the company with the expectation of eventual repayment and a suitable financial return. 'Stewardship', for example, relates to the reporting of information which attempts to describe the effectiveness with which company management has employed the sources of finance invested in the company. Such information should therefore be potentially useful to shareholders, lenders and creditors of the company, particularly in the sense of 'feedback' data which can be used in the controlling or monitoring aspect of investment decision-making. However, to fulfil this role, the information contained in financial report form (particularly that contained in financial statements) must be subjected to detailed analysis if it is to identify the essential indicators of stewardship as well as decision-making.

The use of financial information by 'investors'

Investment in companies can be conveniently divided into two main categories: (a) short and medium-term investment by creditors, bankers and lenders; and (b) more long-term and permanent investment by shareholders. This section attempts to make this distinction.

Use by creditors

The function of granting credit can be interpreted as relating to decisions concerning the provision of existing or potential finance by suppliers of goods and/or services to the company, usually on a short or medium-term basis. The accounting information contained in company financial statements can, once suitably analysed, be used as an input to the types of decision made by such providers of finance. In particular, creditors are concerned with assessing a company's ability to repay its debts in accordance with the terms of the contracts and agreements concerned. The purpose of report analysis in this context is therefore the identification of financial factors relevant to assessments which are essentially concerned with expectations of cash receipts from the company to the providers of finance. Indicators of liquidity are obviously important, but an overall profile of the company is equally helpful, as its record of profitability and its financial structure will be factors which determine whether or not sufficient cash flow is generated to enable the repayment of sums due to take place on the agreed dates.

The above description of the credit function is necessarily brief for much will depend on the individual circumstances of the credit transactions concerned. Certainly, the creditor will rarely have any entitlement to the receipt of formal financial information about the company, and will require to make his forecasts of its liquidity, etc. from whatever source is available – for example, from its annual reports. However, terms of credit are usually short-term, and the credit transactions may well be regular. In that case, the creditor ought to be able to make some judgement of the short-term viability of the company from his recent experiences with it. Nevertheless, occasional reviews of its financial results by creditors could well prove useful in the long term, even from the point of view of the creditor.

Use by banks

Short to medium-term finance from banks is a familiar aspect of company activity. Bank overdraft facilities, originally intended as short-term sources of funding, often become long-term, almost permanent sources. In addition, banks may specifically lend long-term to companies. Whatever the means of lending, the essential issue to the banker is similar to that of the creditor – is there going to be a recovery of the sum lent on the due date of repayment and, where relevant, are the interest payments going to be met? These are obviously matters concerning company liquidity and cash flow – that is, whether or not there is likely to be sufficient cash to meet the amounts due. As with creditors, this is a study which involves the assessment of potential company failure to meet its obligations.

The banker, when making these decisions, must take much into account – first, the purpose for which the lending is required (this will determine whether it is short-term or long-term lending; it will also aid the assessment of the risk associated with the loan, and the probability of being repaid); secondly, whether the sum required is sufficient for the purpose (again, this will involve predicting future cash flows); and thirdly, following on from previous points, assessing fully the probability of being repaid, and receiving any interest sums when due.

Much of the process of assessment by the banker will involve an evaluation of the company and its management, but a great deal of assistance can be gained by him from an analysis of the available financial information (for example, its annual financial statements). In addition, the banker may be in a position to request forecast financial statements from the company when it is seeking funds. In these cases, such information is much more immediately relevant than past annual statements, although an analysis of the latter may also be useful in judging the validity of the projections contained in any forecast statement.

Use by lenders

Long-term lenders, such as debenture holders and mortgage holders, have information needs similar to two 'investment' groups – first, to bankers, because they are concerned with the problem of predicting the chances of the company defaulting over repayments (they are therefore as interested as bankers are in company liquidity – particularly, however, in the long term): and secondly, to shareholders, because of the long-term nature of their investment (many loans are quoted on the Stock Exchange in the same way as shares, and lenders are therefore as much interested as shareholders in company profitability and financial position). Analyses of available company financial information by lenders therefore ought to be similar to those of bankers lending long-term, and shareholders.

Use by shareholders

Existing and potential shareholders constitute the remaining group of investment users of company financial reports. They are primarily concerned with the value of company shares and the future flow of benefits to be derived from such investments. Buying shares involves the sacrifice of a sum of money (equivalent to their cost of purchase) in expectation of future dividends and realization proceeds whose aggregate present value is reckoned to be more than the purchasing value. Likewise, the holding of shares involves the sacrifice of a sum of money equivalent to their current realizable value. Existing and potential investors are therefore constantly weighing up the alternatives of having cash to consume presently or investing to receive cash for consumption at various future points of time. This gives rise to the familiar investment valuation identity of:

$$V_0 = \sum_{t=1}^{n} \frac{d_t}{(1+i)^t} + \frac{r_n}{(1+i)^n}$$

where V_0 is the present value of the investment at point t_0; d_t are the anticipated dividends receivable at points t; r_n are the anticipated sale proceeds of the investment if realized at point n; and i is the investor's personal rate of time preference, assumed to be constant throughout the period of investment t_0 to t_n.

This valuation model formally represents the value of shares of the individual shareholder (existing or potential), value being based on a discounting of the cash returns he anticipates during the period of investment. The discount rate is taken as the rate of return which the investor estimates he would be satisfied with as compensation for sacrificing present for future consumption. It is also usually taken to represent the degree of risk the investor associates with the shares concerned; the higher the anticipated risk, the higher the rate of discount necessary. The present value so calculated (albeit very informally in many cases in practice) is then available as a standard for comparison with the current market value of the shares. In other words, the potential investor's decision model is a comparison of his estimate of the shares' present value with their current purchase value; so long as there is a positive net present value, he will benefit from investment. For the existing shareholder, the comparison is between the shares' present value and current realizable value; and, again, so long as a positive net present value exists, the shareholder will benefit from continuing with his investment.

The above is necessarily a simplification of the investment decision, but it should reveal enough to explain the main features of the information needs of existing and potential shareholders which should be recognized in the process of report analysis. First, assuming that current market values are available to the individual shareholder (these are obviously more readily available in a quoted company than in any other), his major information requirements would seem to be data of use in predicting future receipts (this would appear to be concerned largely with company profits, but should also involve assessments of financial position, generally, and liquidity, particularly; dividends being dependent on the availability of profits and cash). Secondly, the investor may also require data to help him to evaluate the anticipated period of investment, the eventual realization proceeds, and the appropriate rate of discount (and, thus, the degree of risk associated with the investment).

These requirements suggest that the process of report analysis should be concerned largely with producing data with a maximum predictive capability. In particular, as in credit and loan decisions, it should be capable of enabling the decision-maker to discriminate between shares giving higher returns than others, thereby helping him to maximize his expected consumption over time. It should also be capable of reducing the uncertainties facing the decision-maker; if it does not do so, it cannot be said to be relevant information. However, given the predominantly historical nature of reported accounting information, it is difficult to envisage how relevant are such analysed data when predicting future dividend flows, realizable share values and the degree of risk attached to alternative investments. It is also difficult to prove the validity of the underlying assumption that decision-makers (of any kind) will act rationally by identifying the available alternative courses of action; evaluating the financial consequences of each (by making use of available accounting and other information); and selecting the alternatives which meet their preconceived strategies. There is little or no evidence of how decisions are reached, or by how much reported information specifically influences them. Report analysis assumes, therefore, that decision-makers will not only make use of the analysed data, but will also find it relevant.

Criteria for analysed data

Summarizing and expanding on the discussion in the preceding section, it is now possible to stipulate certain criteria which are useful guidelines in the analysis of accounting information contained in financial reports.

First, the analysed data must be relevant to the various decisions which information users are likely to make. This means that the decisions must be identifiable and the related information needs determinable. To date, however, accountants have paid relatively little attention to this aspect of report analysis; the assumption presumably being that the basic information and the analysed data are relevant to potential but largely unidentified users. As previous chapters have attempted to indicate, this is a largely untested assumption which is made even weaker by the several major faults contained in the traditional system of financial reporting. Thus, report analysis cannot be divorced from the problems of financial reporting; it is simply an extension of the latter function. In particular, it is clear that the general-purpose nature of financial statements must be countered when they are being analysed, the analysed data being prepared with the specific needs of the user in mind. It is therefore important for the analyst to be capable of identifying the accounting relationships specifically relevant to the individual user.

Secondly, examination of the decisions of potential users of company financial reports indicates that, irrespective of their individual identities, all are concerned with prediction and consequential monitoring of prior decisions. Thus, analysed data have a dual role to play: that of providing relevant information for forecasting company activities and financial results, as well as providing information of use when assessing the success or failure of prior decisions. However, it cannot be emphasized too often that the existing system of reporting accounting information is a mainly historical one (at least so far as regular periodic reporting is concerned), and even the suggestions for improving such a system (including improvements in the measurement process) are also conceived mainly within it. Therefore, within these constraints, financial report users are attempting to analyse their content to produce indicators of past performance which may provide guidelines to future performance. The following conditions are essential in these circumstances.

(a) That the analysed data used for predictive purposes are sufficient to provide their users with a reasonable basis for forecasting. In particular, this means the preparation of several years' data (where possible) to identify trends and fluctuations which may recur in the future. Such data must be measured, however, on the same accounting basis from one period to the next if they are to be comparable; and they must be free of any exceptional or non-recurrent items which, because of their nature, should not affect future financial results.

(b) That analysed data from financial reports are not regarded as the sole source of information for predictive and control purposes. Company financial reports are a major source of information, but they are not the only one and because of their mainly aggregate composition, they tend to obscure details of company operations and activities which may prove to be important influences on decisions. Companies operate within a very complex and ever-changing environment often causing their future to be somewhat different from their past. Aggregate figures for past profitability and financial position, even when supported by relatively detailed notes, are not necessarily suitable for assessing these vital decision-making factors.

(c) That it is understood that the availability of reported accounting and other information, and the relevance of analysed data, cannot eradicate the essential subjectiveness of decision-making. In other words, report analysis can only be regarded as a means of diminishing some of the uncertainty in decisions. Because the future cannot normally be forecast with accuracy, analysed data must be treated with a great deal of care and expertise in their application to decisions. This is particularly true of data relating to past activity: the decision-maker must exercise a considerable subjective judgement when translating measure of past performance into predictions of future activity.

The investment example

The analysis of company financial reports, and its relative importance, can best be put in context by looking more closely at the investment decision and the overall function of investment analysis (of which financial report analysis is only one part). This is not to minimize the analysis of such reports for credit or lending purposes. Much of what is described in the following sections on fundamental analysis is equally relevant to creditors, bankers and lenders.

Investment analysis is the process of analysing alternative investments so as to make certain decisions regarding buying or selling. The overall objective is to compute present values for shares which are being considered for sale or purchase – that is, for sale if they are already held, and for purchase if they are not already held. These intrinsic and highly subjective values are presented for comparison with existing market values for the shares concerned to determine whether sale or purchase is desirable as well as which shares should be bought or sold. As previously explained, present values are computed on the basis of forecast dividends and realization proceeds discounted at the investor's time preference rate. Illustration 48 provides a simple example of this process, the problems of taxation and inflation being ignored for the sake of simplicity.

It should be noted in the illustration, however, that the problem of risk in investment is one which cannot be dismissed completely in the simplicity of this example. Indeed, risk is an extremely complex factor which seriously affects the computation of financial values. For example, the latter are affected by risks related to the type of business being evaluated and the level of interest rates and inflation, as well as the risk associated with the marketability of the investments concerned. Generally speaking, the more risky the business, the higher the interest rates and inflation, and the less marketable the investment, the greater will be the risk associated with it. In addition, the risk factor is complicated by the natural aversion from risk by investors. They may well tend to opt for investments with smaller present values and returns because they are less risky than those with high values and returns. In the example below, investment A may be chosen because it is less risky than investment B, despite a higher net present value.

The figures used in Illustration 48 follow the traditional approach to investment values and decisions: the forecasting of dividends and realization proceeds, the assessment of risk and the application of the discounting technique. It is this approach which lends itself to what is normally described as fundamental analysis: the economic and statistical research-ing necessary to produce and identify factors which could provide guidelines to the future performance of a company and the present value of its shares.

Before proceeding to a detailed account of the fundamentalist ap-proach to investment evaluation, it will be useful to compare briefly the different approaches to the latter function, of which fundamental analysis is only one. In fact, there are two main approaches. First, there is the process of fundamental analysis which relies on the detailed use of all available information about the companies being evaluated. This is done to build up individual company financial profiles which can be used as foundations for investment decision-making (as previously mentioned,

---

Illustration 48 A simplified investment decision

Assume an investor has £1,000 available for investment in quoted ordinary shares, and he is considering shares in two companies, A and B. Shares in A are currently quoted at £10 a share, and the last dividend per share was £1. Shares in B are currently quoted at £8 a share, and the last dividend per share was 90p. The investor anticipates that A's dividends will increase annually by 10 per cent (the first being due in approximately twelve months' time); he anticipates that B's dividend will increase annually by 11 per cent (the first being due in approximately twelve months' time). He plans to sell his investment shortly after receiving his second dividend when he forecasts A and B's shares will have a market value of £15 and £13, respectively. He requires a yield of 6 per cent from an investment in A, and 7 per cent from B; in his opinion, A being less risky than B.

(1) *Present value of an investment in A: 100 shares*

Time	Estimated cash receipts £	Discount factor (6 per cent)	Present value £
End of year 1	110(a)	0.943	104
End of year 2	121(b)	0.890	108
Shortly after end of year 2	1,500(c)	0.890	1,335
			———
Present value			1,547
Total purchase price:			
beginning of year 1(d)			−1,000
			———
Net present value			547
			———

(2) *Present value of an investment in B: 125 shares*

Time	Estimated cash receipts £	Discount factor (7 per cent)	Present value £
End of year 1	124(e)	0.935	116
End of year 2	136(f)	0.873	119
Shortly after end of year 2	1,625(g)	0.873	1,418
			———
Present value			1,653
Total purchase price:			
beginning of year 1(h)			−1,000
			———
Net present value			653
			———

An investment in A produces a subjective net present value gain of £547 compared with a corresponding figure of £653 for B. Therefore, assuming these were the only alternatives open to the investor, he would invest in B, which could give him the higher return despite being the riskier investment.

(a) $100 \times £1 + 10\% \times £100$;   (b) $£110 + 10\% \times £110$;   (c) $100 \times £15$;   (d) $100 \times £10$; (e) $125 \times £0.90 + 10\% \times £112$; (f) $£124 + 10\% \times £124$; (g) $125 \times £13$; (h) $125 \times £8$.

such a technique of analysis may also be relevant to creditors, lenders and bankers – adapted where relevant to fit the needs of the particular decision). Secondly, investment decisions are often made on the basis of technical analysis – that is, by the examination of past share price movements to predict future movements. As such, this process does not depend on a detailed use of available information about individual companies as is the case in the fundamental approach. Each will be discussed separately in the following sections.

The fundamental philosophy

Because it is attempting to locate and isolate significant factors concerning the future of a company, fundamental analysis relies on an adequate information system from which indications of these factors can be drawn. A substantial part of the required information comes from analyses of company financial reports, but there are other sources of information available to the analyst, including aggregate national and international economic statistics and specific industry data as well as individual company information. From these various sources, the analyst attempts to construct detailed profiles of individual companies from which he can forecast future dividend and share realization flows. This provides him with a basis for computing present values for alternative shares, which can then be introduced into his investment decisions. Thus the emphasis is on forecasting future returns so as to compute intrinsic values for decision-making – that is, present values of shares. The fundamentalist approach is not, therefore, concerned primarily with forecasting share price movements.

This traditional approach to investment decision-making is open to the criticism that, despite the detailed analysis of available information, the decisions subsequently made can be no more successful than those made on the basis of a technical study of the past pattern of share price movements (that is, the process of technical analysis in which past share prices are analysed to predict future prices). However, this may be no more than a comment on the limitations of the information available to investors and the difficulties in using it for prediction purposes. In other words, the information used in the process of fundamental analysis is mainly historical, and it is extremely difficult to predict the future of companies on the basis of their past activity and performance. Nevertheless, information is available for analysis, no matter how imperfect it may be, and rational decisions would appear to dictate the use of such information so long as its imperfections are fully understood and great care is exercised in the analysis.

Sources of information for fundamental analysis

There are three main categories of information which can be analysed for purposes of forecasting dividends etc., and computing present values of shares: (a) company information; (b) industry information; and (c) general economic information.

Company information   When building up a profile of a company for decision-making purposes, the investor is obviously primarily interested in specific data about the company itself. Much of this emanates from the company, and has already been described in some detail in earlier chapters: annual financial reports, including statements of past profitability and financial position; interim financial statements (for quoted companies); and occasional prospectus and merger or acquisition reports, which can include short-term forecast data. These reports will come direct to individual shareholders but, particularly in the case of quoted companies, can be obtained by potential shareholders by application to the company. In addition, every company in the UK must deposit copies of its annual financial statements (in full or modified form) and prospectuses with the Registrar of Companies and these are open to public inspection for a small fee.

The Registrar is also required to receive from each company a copy of its memorandum and articles of association (giving details of its internal regulations); details of any legal charges secured over any of its assets; and its annual return giving details *inter alia* of its capital, directors, loans and changes in ownership during the year covered (the annual financial report is also attached to this return). The company is also legally required to keep registers of shareholders, debenture holders, directors and directors' shareholdings at its registered office, again for public inspection which can be made for a small fee.

Most of these information sources about a company can be assessed personally for analysis by the existing or potential investor. However, much of the data can also be obtained indirectly by him from organizations or entities which specialize in information analysis services for the investor. For instance, the Exchange Telegraph Co. Ltd provides a statistical service for quoted companies and this, on a card system, gives *inter alia* a detailed analysis of key accounting information over the last ten years, as well as brief comments on the history and background of the companies, with summarized financial statements for the last three years. It also gives details of their share price records over the last ten years.

Moodies Services Ltd operates a similar service, but can also provide analyses and forecasts of leading industry and commodity performances. Moodies also produces a quarterly investment handbook and an annual investment digest, both of which analyse, in a great deal of detail, the significant financial accounting figures and indicators for a large population of leading companies. In this sense, therefore, subscriptions to these services by investors avoid much of the detailed analysis work necessary to condense and refine all the available information for investment decision-making into manageable proportions.

Investors may also be able to obtain similar services from their stockbrokers, many of whom produce detailed analyses of accounting information derived from the published financial reports of individual companies. Of particular concern in these analyses are indicators of managerial performance and financial structure as well as income and dividend potential. A similar but far less detailed and extensive coverage of company performance is available in the serious financial press, including *The Investor's Chronicle*, *The Financial Times* and *The Times Business News Section*.

In other words, investors should never be short of analysed information about individual companies if they are unable to analyse it personally. It must be said, however, that the available analysed information is subject to two criticisms: first, there are very considerable doubts as to its relevance and usefulness (mainly because it is based largely on published accounting information which is subject to the doubts and problems discussed at length in the previous chapters); and secondly, it is often of a highly complex and technical nature, thereby raising doubts as to its usefulness to the private investor with little or no skill and experience with such material (this is particularly true of the services offered by such organizations as Exchange Telegraph and Moodies, which are mainly directed at the professional investor with the skills required to interpret it).

Industry and economy information   Although investors are primarily concerned with assessments of individual companies, they are also interested in the context in which these separate entities operate. For this reason, investors following the philosophy of fundamental analysis should be interested not only in the industries of which companies form a part, but also in the economy in general. In other words, the future of a company cannot be assessed adequately without considering the present and future state of the particular industry and the economy.

The nature and state of the industry in which a company operates seems to be of fundamental importance to the analyst, not only in an absolute sense but also as a point of comparisons of the company itself. The size and history of the industry; its past and potential growth; its profitability trend; the nature and size of its markets; the quality of its management and its labour force; its industrial relations – these are all factors which provide an essential background for the analyst assessing individual companies. He should provide himself with industry criteria (for example, sales, production, profitability and capital expenditure) with which to compare individual companies so as to assess whether their performance is above or below the industry average.

Sources of information about particular industries are varied, but can be divided into two main categories: (a) industrial and (b) governmental. Many industries and trade associations produce aggregate statistics which, when available, can provide interesting insights into industry trends. There are also occasional reports from the various industrial sub-committees of the National Economic and Development Council which give similar data on trends and prospects. Governmentally, industry information can be obtained in a number of ways. For example, the annual publication, *National Income and Expenditure*, contains tabulations of data concerning domestic consumption of goods and services, and capital expenditure in various industries, as well as aggregate industrial income. On a more regular basis, publications such as *Trade and Industry* contain data relating to orders, deliveries, production and stock in individual industries. The five-yearly *Census of Production* also gives aggregations of regional and industry production and capital expenditure.

Governmental publications provide useful background data for analysis and decision purposes. The state of the economy, and its future prospects, seem to be relevant features of any assessment of individual companies. The trend and prospects for national and international trade, unemployment, production, credit and banking facilities, interest rates, retail prices, monetary exchange rates, etc. are all matters which must impinge eventually on individual companies. It would, for example, be impossible to assess the future profitability and dividend prospects of a manufacturing company which was heavily involved in export sales without considering the state of international trade, the relative value of the pound sterling in relation to other currencies, the availability of bank and other credit facilities, the availability of skilled workers in the industry, and so on. The above-mentioned government publications all contain aggregate data of use in this context, but other publications are also available – including the *Monthly Digest of Statistics* and *Economic Trends*. In addition, the *Bank of England Quarterly Bulletins* provide useful summaries of many of these factors. Thus, the fundamental analyst who wishes to incorporate aggregate industrial and economy data into his computations appears well provided with sources of available information.

The process of fundamental analysis

Essentially, the share investment decision, when use is made of the process of fundamental analysis, is concerned with assessing the future prospects of individual companies, and particularly with their future profitability, dividend potential and share price. Given the mainly historical nature of the available information about an individual company, it is relatively obvious that past data trends will form a major part of the exercise of formulating these predictions. However, the latter can in no way be regarded as accurate because of the inherent uncertainty about the future. Nor is it possible to extrapolate a past trend of data and hope that such an analysis will provide reliable predictions. Although such trends may contain elements which remain relatively stable over the long term, there are other factors which are much more variable; for example, cyclical elements cause long-term fluctuations in trends and are relatively difficult to predict; and random factors, because of their 'once-and-for-all' nature, tend to be unpredictable.

It is for this reason that a thorough analysis of available information from all relevant sources should be undertaken so as, first, to establish past trends of significant data such as income and dividends which could be used as bases for estimating future data; secondly, to identify and segregate factors which are of a stable, cyclical or random nature so far as the company is concerned, and which are necessary ingredients in the process of adapting past trends to formulate future ones; and thirdly, to aid the analyst to assess the degree of risk and uncertainty associated with investment in a particular company. In all these matters, it is relatively clear that general industry and economy data should be relevant to the exercise of using specific company information to project future data of use in the investment decision. In addition, it should be remembered that not all of the information used in the processes of analysis and prediction will be of a quantitative nature. For example, chairmens' reports and reviews of prospects are more often than not couched in purely qualitative terms but can contain significant insights to the future of companies.

The major problem in fundamental analysis, therefore, is the translation of historical data into meaningful predictions of future company performance. The problem is accentuated the more the analyst is required to move into the future, and the more uncertain are the company, industry and general economic factors and conditions to be considered. For instance, an investor contemplating a twelve-month investment in shares of a relatively stable trading company in equally stable industrial and economic conditions would find the process of predicting for invest-ment decision-making purposes much easier than if he were contemplat-ing a five-year investment in a volatile company in times of great industrial and economic uncertainty and fluctuation.

In addition, in fundamental analysis, the investor making the analysis (or the person or organization making it on his behalf) is faced with predicting share prices as well as such factors as income and dividends; this being needed for his computation of the intrinsic values of the shares being assessed. In this respect, the analyst must not only make use of his predictions of income and dividends and related data on the financial position and condition of the companies concerned, but must also at-tempt to predict the predictions of other investors.

Although it would be wrong not to admit that guesswork is a significant ingredient to the investment decision, it must be stated that such guess-work should be of an expert kind. Fundamental analysis attempts to inject this expertise, and, as with the prediction of future income and dividends, the prediction of share prices should be made on the basis of a careful analysis of all available information, but particularly on industry and economy information.

Prediction and trend analysis[1]

Fundamental analysis is primarily concerned with processing data so as to make relevant predictions for share valuation purposes. Because of the historical nature of the data being processed, it is consequently concerned with analysing past trends of variables relevant to share valuation. Once these trends have been established, it is then possible to attempt to predict values for these variables so as to incorporate them into the share valuation model. The analyst uses trends as a starting-point for his projections which must, necessarily, incorporate factors which he believes will affect the absolute values of the variables in the future. In particular, he will require to identify the various components of trends to predict future movements in the variables being considered.

Trends can be composed of a number of factors, though not all of them may be apparent in particular time series of data. These components are, first, the secular component (T) caused by factors whose influence tends to be in the same direction over the long term; secondly, the seasonal component (S), which causes movements in the trends owing to seasonal variations; thirdly, the cyclical component (C), which causes movements owing to long-term cyclical fluctuations; and fourthly, the residual component (R), which causes movements owing to random factors of an *ad hoc* nature which are unpredictable.

The effect of these various components on actual data (A) can either be identified as their sum ($A = T + S + C + R$) or their product ($A = T \times S \times C \times R$). The first identity assumes that the effects on data are additive (which may be true over short periods), whereas the second identity assumes they are proportionate (which is more likely to be the case, particularly over long periods of time). Although the secular and residual components will appear in every trend, the other components may not be applicable. Where relevant, however, the purpose of trend analysis is to isolate these various components to enable reasonable predictions to be made.

The first stage in the decomposition of data is to estimate the secular component of the series. This can be done in a number of ways: for example, by graphically plotting the trend data and, by estimation, fitting a line which approximates to the trend; by calculation of moving averages; or by the least-squares method to derive a linear trend. It is not the purpose of this text to explain statistical techniques in detail, but Illustration 49 attempts to describe briefly each of the afore-mentioned techniques.

Illustration 49 Analysis of a trend of income

Assume a company with a time series of income as follows: period t_0-t_1, £2,000; period t_1-t_2, £6,000; period t_2-t_3, £8,000; period t_3-t_4, £5,000; period t_4-t_5, £7,000; period t_5-t_6, £6,000; and period t_6-t_7, £9,000.

(a) *Fitting a trend line*

By this method, income would be plotted against time, and a freehand trend line drawn.

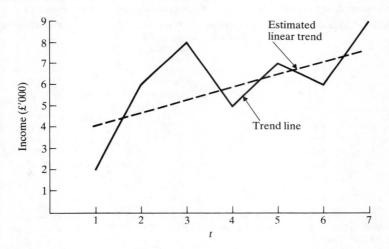

This method is very approximate indeed, and is subject to considerable judgement and estimation. It can only serve as a first estimate and indication of trend.

(b) *Calculating a simple moving average*

Assuming a three-period average, the following tabulation can be prepared:

Period	Actual income £	Sum of three periods £	Three-period average £
t_0-t_1	2,000		
t_1-t_2	6,000		5,333
t_2-t_3	8,000	16,000	6,333
t_3-t_4	5,000	19,000	6,667
t_4-t_5	7,000	20,000	6,000
t_5-t_6	6,000	18,000	7,333
t_6-t_7	9,000	22,000	

This methodology is a useful way of analysing the past, but it tends to have drawbacks regarding prediction, particularly its omission of average data at the beginning and end of the time series (the effects of these omissions are greater when the moving average is extended to cover larger series – for example, five or seven periods).

Illustration 49 continued

(c) *The least-squares approach*[2]

This method attempts to establish the trend line using the straight-line identity:

$$Y_{t_n - t_{n+1}} = a + b x_{t_n - t_{n+1}}$$

where Y is the dependent variable being analysed over time t (in this case, income); a is the linear constant equal to Y when $x = 0$ (the numerical difference between the origin and the point of intersection of the straight line and the y-axis); b is the linear constant equivalent to the value of the tangent to the angle formed between the straight line and the horizontal; and x is the independent variable being analysed (in this case, time).

Period	Actual income	Periods from beginning	Periods around median period			Trend line*
	y		x	x^2	xy	$y = a + bx$
	£				£	£
$t_0 - t_1$	2,000	0	-3	9	$-6,000$	4,001
$t_1 - t_2$	6,000	1	-2	4	$-12,000$	4,715
$t_2 - t_3$	8,000	2	-1	1	$-8,000$	5,429
$t_3 - t_4$	5,000	3	0	0	0	6,143
$t_4 - t_5$	7,000	4	1	1	7,000	6,857
$t_5 - t_6$	6,000	5	2	4	12,000	7,571
$t_6 - t_7$	9,000	6	3	9	27,000	8,285
	43,000			0 28	20,000	

*By placing the origin in the median period $t_3 - t_4$ so that $x = 0$, the normal least-squares equations reduce to: $\Sigma y = na$ (where $n =$ the number of observations of y) and $\Sigma xy = b \Sigma x^2$. Therefore

$$a = \frac{\Sigma y}{n}; \quad \text{and } b = \frac{\Sigma xy}{\Sigma x^2}$$

With values for x, y, xy and n, a and b can then be computed:

$$a = \frac{£43,000}{7} = £6,143; \quad \text{and } b = \frac{£20,000}{28} = £714$$

Therefore: $y = £6,143 + 714x$. And, for example, for period $t_0 - t_1$: $y = £6,143 + 714 (-3) = £4,001$.

Illustration 49 continued

These figures thus provide trend values for the complete series, and allow for easier projections to be made than is possible under the moving average approach (though the values derived under both systems are relatively similar). They can be depicted and compared graphically with the moving average and estimated linear figures, as follows:

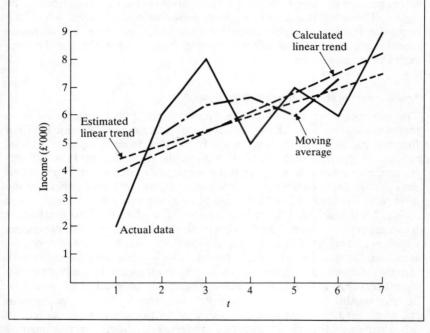

It can be seen from the graphs in the illustration that the estimated and moving average lines give little clear indication of the underlying trend of past figures, and it is for this reason that the mathematical least-squares approach is to be favoured.

The next stage in trend analysis is to use the moving average or linear trend values to estimate the remaining trend components, remembering that these trend values represent only the secular component. The other seasonal, cyclical and residual components also have to be identified for forecasting purposes, using the previously-defined identities of $A = T + S + C + R$ (if additivity is assumed) or $A = T \times S \times C \times R$ (if proportionality is assumed); that is, $A - T = S + C + R$ or $A/T = S \times C \times R$.

However, for purposes of investment analysis, and further assuming that investment forecasting is not so short-term as to require seasonal analysis and not so long-term to require cyclical analysis, then the data for trend analysis will require to conform to modified trend models; that is, either $A - T = R$ or $A/T = R$. In other words, annual time series will have no seasonal component and may well contain no cyclical component. Therefore, as R is, by definition, unpredictable, the main emphasis in investment analysis should be to determine T. Once this has been done, the analyst can then use the trend line as a basis for prediction, adjusting the underlying secular trend projections for factors which he believes will affect income dividends and share value prices in particular periods in the future. These adjusting factors will necessarily include values which will comprise residual components of future trends, and could, as previously mentioned, include seasonal and cyclical items, depending on the time series being predicted.

Trend analysis and fundamental analysis

The advantage of trend analysis, particularly if it is conducted on a mathematical basis, is that it makes use of past data in the forecasting of future data. Much of these data will be derived from company financial reports in general, and financial statements in particular. It is, for this reason, especially important that the accounting information used in this exercise be (a) measured on a consistent basis from one period to the next; and (b) free of any faults and biases in measurement which could make it unreliable for analysis purposes. The data used to establish a trend must not be affected by errors or changes in measurement practices which are likely to distort it. The analyst must therefore be fully conversant with the quality of the measured data he is using, and therefore with the methods of measurement used. For example, if there has been a significant change in the measurement practices adopted in a time series, he must be able to make some attempt at adjusting it so that it conforms to the same measurement practices throughout the periods concerned. In other words, before trend analysis is undertaken, the time series must be examined and, if necessary, suitably adjusted to conform with the principle of consistency.

So far as investment analysis is concerned, the fundamental approach would use trend analysis techniques with such data as income, dividends and share prices. Dividends are an essential ingredient of intrinsic valuation and are traditionally regarded as proportionally related to available income. In other words, forecasting future income from an analysis of a past income time series should provide valuable data for forecasting future dividends so long as there is some positive correlation between available income for dividend purposes and actual dividends distributed. This could be done by taking the current level of dividend and adjusting it appropriately for forecast changes in available income. Illustration 50 attempts to show some of the major considerations in this matter.

Illustration 50 Forecasting dividends for share valuation purposes

Assume the same situation and figures as in Illustration 49, excepting that the actual time series is reduced to more comparable proportions by describing income as 'earnings per share'; that is, the proportion of available income to each available ordinary share. Similarly, the equivalent past time series of dividends is expressed as 'dividends per share'. Both these measures will be explained in greater detail in Chapter 11. The available series is as follows (assuming 20,000 share units throughout):

Period	Earnings per share	Dividend per share
	p	p
t_0-t_1	10	5.0
t_1-t_2	30	12.5
t_2-t_3	40	17.5
t_3-t_4	25	12.5
t_4-t_5	35	17.5
t_5-t_6	30	17.5
t_6-t_7	45	20.0

(a) Coefficient of correlation: earnings to dividends

The first step would be to establish whether there is any significant relationship between dividends and earnings in this case. Using the Pearsonian coefficient of correlation:[3]

$$r = \frac{n\Sigma xy - \Sigma x \Sigma y}{\sqrt{[(n\Sigma x^2 - (\Sigma x)^2)(n\Sigma y^2 - (\Sigma y)^2)]}}$$

the following tabulation emerges (assuming x = earnings per share and y = dividend per share):

x	y	x^2	y^2	xy
10	5.0	100	25.00	50.0
30	12.5	900	156.25	375.0
40	17.5	1,600	306.25	700.0
25	12.5	625	156.25	312.5
35	17.5	1,225	306.25	612.5
30	17.5	900	306.25	525.0
45	20.0	2,025	400.00	900.0
215	102.5	7,375	1,656.25	3,475.0

$$r = \frac{(7)(3,475) - (215)(102.5)}{\sqrt{[(7)(7,375) - (215)^2][(7)(1,656.25) - (102.5)^2]}}$$

$$= \frac{2,287.5}{\sqrt{5,872,500}} = \frac{2,287.5}{2,423.3} = +0.94.$$

In other words, in this situation dividends and earnings are positively and significantly correlated.

Illustration 50 continued

(b) *Estimating future dividends*

The trend line, $y = a + bx$, in Illustration 48 revealed the following secular trend values for income, the origin of the series being taken as t_3-t_4:

Period	Trend line	Trend line as earnings per share
	£	p
t_0-t_1	4,001	20.00
t_1-t_2	4,715	23.57
t_2-t_3	5,429	27.14
t_3-t_4	6,143	30.71
t_4-t_5	6,857	34.28
t_5-t_6	7,571	37.85
t_6-t_7	8,285	41.43

Taking $y = £6,143 + 714x$, and with t_3-t_4 as the origin, it can be estimated that the trend of income and earnings per share for the next three periods will continue as follows:

	£	p
t_7-t_8	8,999	45.00
t_8-t_9	9,713	48.56
t_9-t_{10}	10,427	52.13

This establishes the secular trend forecast values, and these now need to be amended because of specific factors (seasonal, cyclical or random) which the analyst believes should be incorporated into his earnings forecasts. It is this aspect of fundamental analysis to which information analysis relates; that is, by analysing available data (including that contained in published financial reports), the analyst can provide himself with indicators of these special factors. Therefore it can be assumed that, forecasting such residual component adjustments, the forecasts of income and earnings per share in the next three periods are:

	£	p
t_7-t_8	9,500	47.5
t_8-t_9	12,000	60.0
t_9-t_{10}	11,500	57.5

The problem is then to forecast the dividends which it is anticipated will be distributed out of these predicted income figures. It has already been demonstrated that, in this case, income and dividends are significantly and positively correlated, and the analyst must therefore now estimate what the dividends per share will be in each of the three periods, knowing that his dividend forecasts can reasonably follow his income forecasts. The following table reveals the percentage of dividends per share to earnings per share during the previous seven periods.

Period	Earnings per share	Dividend per share	Percentage of dividends to earnings
	p	p	
t_0-t_1	10	5.0	50
t_1-t_2	30	12.5	42
t_2-t_3	40	17.5	44
t_3-t_4	25	12.5	50
t_4-t_5	35	17.5	50
t_5-t_6	30	17.5	58
t_6-t_7	45	20.0	44
	———		
	215		
	———		

Illustration 50 continued

The weighted average percentage dividend/earnings ratio is approximately:

$$\frac{10,240}{215} = 48\%$$

and therefore, applying this to the forecast earnings per share figures, produces the following anticipated dividends which could be incorporated into the share valuation model based on a discounting of future dividends.

Period	Anticipated earnings per share	Anticipated dividends per share
	p	p
t_7-t_8	47.5	22.8
t_8-t_9	60.0	28.8
t_9-t_{10}	57.5	27.6

Having been through the calculations shown in Illustration 50, the analyst will be in a position to incorporate his estimation of the eventual realization of shares concerned into the valuation model. This is an extremely subjective aspect of fundamental analysis, for the analyst is assessing not only the future prospects of the individual company, but also the attitude of other investors to its shares in the future. A mathematically-derived linear trend analysis of past share prices may be of some assistance in this respect, but the bulk of the analysis work will be concerned with examining all available information relating to the company, the stock market and the economy. The significance of forecasting the eventual realization price will vary, however. If the investment is to be short-term (say, less than a year), then the forecasting of such a price will assume primary importance because future dividends will not figure to any considerable extent in the present value calculation. On the other hand, if the investment is to be long-term (say, more than ten years), then the realization price for the shares is far less significant than the forecast flow of dividends, and any inaccuracies in it will be considerably minimized by the discounting process.

Technical analysis

In relative opposition to the philosophy of fundamental analysis is the process of technical analysis which, instead of aiming to produce forecasts of dividends for share valuation purposes, analyses trends of past share prices actually achieved so as to forecast future prices. It therefore assumes that fundamental analysis is, at best, a technique to be used to confirm forecasts of share price movements and, at worst, a useless technique which cannot add further information to that already taken into account in deriving past and present share prices. Technical analysis therefore uses the previously-mentioned technique of trend analysis, being concerned with long-term trends in prices (say, of more than one year) as well as short-term trends within the long-term fluctuation.

Illustration 51 gives a brief example of a long-term trend analysis of share prices for an individual company using the mathematically-based linear approach.

Illustration 51 Linear trend of share prices

Time	Share price (y) £	Time points	Points around median (x)	x^2	xy £	$y = a + bx^*$ £
t_0	1	0	−5	25	−5	2.05
t_1	2	1	−4	16	−8	2.42
t_2	4	2	−3	9	−12	2.79
t_3	3	3	−2	4	−6	3.16
t_4	2	4	−1	1	−2	3.53
t_5	5	5	0	0	0	3.90
t_6	6	6	1	1	6	4.27
t_7	7	7	2	4	14	4.64
t_8	4	8	3	9	12	5.01
t_9	3	9	4	16	12	5.38
t_{10}	6	10	5	25	30	5.75
	43		0	110	41	

$$^*a = \frac{\Sigma y}{n} = \frac{43}{11} = 3.9; \text{ and } b = \frac{\Sigma xy}{\Sigma x^2} = \frac{41}{110} = 0.37$$

Having established the secular trend line for this particular share, the technical analyst is in a position to decompose the data further so as to segregate any cyclical and residual trends. Ignoring the residual factors, which are, by definition, unpredictable, the analyst can take the secular and cyclical trend lines and use these as his basis for predicting future share prices. However, the major weapon in the technical analyst's armoury is the chart of graphical presentation of share price movements and trends. From an analysis of these charts, the analyst attempts to discern particular patterns of price changes. To eliminate the graphical distortions of absolute changes using an arithmetic scale, the usual procedure is to use logarithmic scales: by plotting the logarithms of the actual values, proportionate price changes are graphed, thereby giving the analyst a sounder portrayal of price trends. Illustration 52 outlines this approach to technical analysis.

Illustration 52 Arithmetic and logarithmic charts of share prices

Assume that the price of a particular share has moved as follows:

	£	
t_0	2.00	Log 0.3010
t_1	3.00	0.4771
t_2	4.50	0.6532
t_3	6.75	0.8293
t_4	10.12	1.0051

Illustration 52 *continued*

Plotting the absolute changes on an arithmetic scale, the graphical trend would appear in the following form:

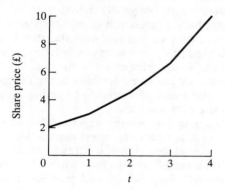

This gives the analyst little indication of the proportionate changes in the share's price, which, assuming an investor has a given sum to invest, is of much greater relevance than absolute changes. The following graph plots these proportionate changes, using a logarithmic scale.

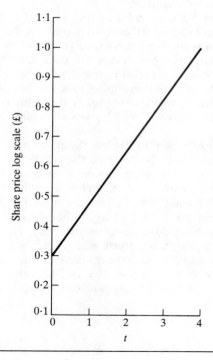

Therefore, by using logs, the straight-line proportionate trend can be readily discerned. This sort of technique can be adopted on a daily, weekly, monthly or yearly basis, depending on the particular trend regarded as important – daily and weekly trends being part of monthly trends which, in turn, are part of yearly trends.

In addition to graphical representation of share price movements and trends, the analyst is also concerned with the trend of the volume of shares traded, although this is not always available. When it is, it can be incorporated into the share price chart in the form of a bar chart. The trend of prices indicates what investors think about the future value of the shares concerned; the trend of volume of trading indicates what they think about the future of the shares.

The main problem in technical analysis is therefore the identification of trends and the taking of appropriate investment action quickly enough to benefit from the predicted direction of the trend – that is, buying when the predicted trend is upwards, and selling when the predicted trend is downwards. Obviously, the analysis and interpretation of short-term trends in this context is extremely subjective since fluctuations in price can be numerous and substantial, and consequently difficult to predict. The technical analyst is therefore looking for particular patterns to which he can apply specific investment decision rules, these rules having been devised for this type of analysis.

The most typical patterns to be found in charts of share price movements are 'head and shoulders' and 'triangles'. In the former, the share price rises until it meets some resistance (usually the volume of buying dropping off); the price then levels off until there is another surge upwards; there is then a reversal in trend with the price coming down, levelling off and then finally dropping to a low point which marks the beginning of another upward trend (again, the volume of trading usually follows this pattern). Illustration 53 gives an outline example of such a graphical pattern.

The graph in Illustration 53 depicts the point at which the pattern is said to be complete (that is, A), and the prediction would then be a downward trend in share price, assumed to be equal to the upward movement above the 'neckline'. The technical analyst therefore looks for the completion of this pattern to justify the selling of shares (they would not be held beyond point A), and to predict the end of the downward trend and the beginning of the next upward trend. The volume of trading is of help when analysing the pattern, since it indicates when buying is on the increase or decrease in the share concerned. The 'head and shoulders' pattern can also appear in reverse (that is, Illustration 53 would appear inverted) and would be used to support the prediction of upward trends and the buying of shares.

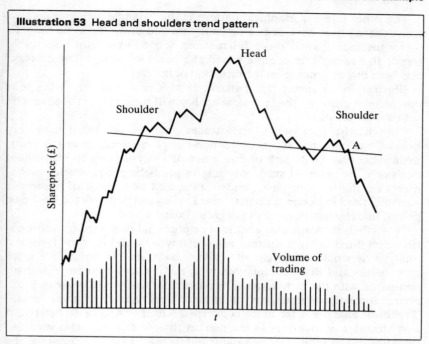

Illustration 53 Head and shoulders trend pattern

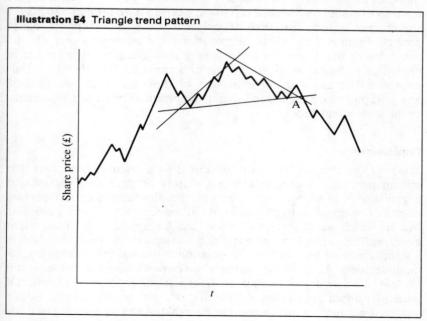

Illustration 54 Triangle trend pattern

The other familiar graphical pattern is the 'triangle' which is created when share prices have been fluctuating up and down for some time. In many instances, when these fluctuations settle down to a discernible trend, the triangle is complete and the point of investment decision reached; this depending on the direction of the trend.

Illustration 54 shows this pattern. In this case, once the triangle is complete at point A, the technical analyst will suggest that the shares be sold at that price.

The chartist approach to investment analysis, described here very briefly, has been the subject of a number of criticisms over the years, mainly because of its lack of fundamental analysis prior to investment decisions; its inherent subjectiveness in predicting future price movements on the basis of past trends established as a result of numerous variables; and its assumption that future prices can be predicted from past prices, thereby indicating some degree of dependence.

Nevertheless, despite its apparent or potential disregard for information contained in such sources as company financial reports, technical analysis depends on the use of relevant data; in this case, share price movements and share trading volumes, both related to time. However, compared with the techniques of fundamental analysis, the use of available information to support investment decisions is relatively small. Technical analysis is far more concerned with the aggregate behaviour and attitudes of investors in the market than in the characteristics and qualities of the individual company and its management. Certainly, the analysis of company financial reports appears to have little part to play in the process of technical analysis, unless it is used in a support role to confirm findings from chart computations and interpretations. On the other hand, there appears to be a very strong argument in favour of regarding technical analysis not just as a separate investment analysis approach but more as an extension of the process of fundamental analysis; past share price trends being important information ingredients to the investment decision.

Conclusions

Much of this chapter has been concerned with discussing the part that information has to play in aiding a variety of interested parties and organizations to assess the past and predict the future financial performance of companies. In particular, it has concentrated on one particular use to which available information can be applied: the investment decision. This example of potential information usage reveals that there is a significant role for analysed information in the making of share investment decisions. Logically, it can therefore be postulated that the same can be said of other decisions such as those relating to loans and credit. Of particular importance in the context of this book, therefore, is the role of analysed accounting information in the making and monitoring of decisions. The next three chapters will look specifically at this matter and will discuss not only the process and mechanics of analysing available accounting information, but also the significance of the analysed data when assessing the financial performance of companies.

References

1 It is not the purpose of this text to explain in detail the principles of trend analysis. However, the reader should refer to K. A. Yeomans, *Statistics for the Social Scientist: 1*, Penguin Books, 1968, pp. 208–44, for an introductory explanation of this topic. Much of what is explained in this section of Yeomans is used for the purpose of explaining trend analysis in relation to the investment decision.
2 For further details of this statistical technique, see ibid., pp. 170–81.
3 For further details of this statistical technique, see ibid., pp. 186–92.

Suggested discussion or essay topics

(*Note*   Unless specifically stated otherwise, the term 'investment decision' should be taken to include credit, banking and loan decisions).

1 Almost by definition, economic activity means the making and taking of decisions. It has been suggested that to undertake these functions without the use of available information would be foolhardy. Why should this be so?

2 What is meant by the analysis of available information in relation to economic decisions? Why is it necessary to analyse data for this purpose?

3 Many writers have pointed out the numerous faults and problems inherent in the measurement and communication of accounting information. Knowledge of them will therefore be of crucial importance to the analyst of company financial reports. Discuss.

4 By far the most significant use to be made of company financial reports is in relation to the investment decision. Describe what is meant by the term 'investment decision' and comment on the validity of the statement.

5 If future dividends are the most significant aspect of share investment decision-making, then historical financial reports of company profitability and financial position are largely irrelevant to this exercise. Discuss.

6 It has been suggested that one way of finding out whether or not published accounting data are useful to investors is to examine share price movements in relation to the publication of data. Describe, in general terms, this approach to assessing information utility, and comment on any doubts you may have with regard to such an association.

7 Rarely does the publication of financial statements have any important or lasting effect on share prices. Discuss.

8 Interim financial reporting appears to be more relevant to investment decision-makers than annual financial reporting. Explain why this should be the case.

9 What is meant by the intrinsic value of a share? Have company financial reports any part to play in its determination?

10 It has been stated that there is a need for financial data to be factual and objective if they are to be used by decision-makers as a guide to the future. Discuss.

11 The process of fundamental analysis utilizes data from a variety of sources. Define what is meant by fundamental analysis, and explain the relative importance of the major sources of information to the analyst.

12 Describe what is meant by trend analysis. How reliable is it as an investment technique?

13 Forecasts of company income, dividends and share prices have little value. The uncertainties of the company's world combined with those of the investment world produce substantial margins of error, and these margins increase with the length of the forecast. Comment.

14 Share investment appears to be more of a matter of flair, intuition and individual judgement than a precise science. The investor should therefore be more concerned with attempting to 'outguess' the decisions and judgements of other investors than in trying to evaluate the true worth of shares. Discuss.

15 Explain and comment on the debate and apparent conflict between the fundamental and technical analysts.

Selected bibliography for Chapter 9

B. V. Carsberg, *Analysis for Investment Decisions*, Accountancy Age Books, 1974. A thorough coverage of the investment decision.

D. A. Egginton, *Accounting for the Banker*, Longman, 1977, pp. 174–90. The information context for the lending banker.

P. Freeman, 'Some Aspects of Technical Analysis', *Investment Analyst*, October 1967, pp. 9–19. A useful description of the theory and practice of technical analysis.

K. V. Peasnell, 'The Usefulness of Accounting Information to Investors', *ICRA Occasional Paper 1*, 1973. An analysis of the predictive ability of accounting information compared with its use as feedback data.

G. H. Sorter, M. S. Gans, P. Rosenfield, R. M. Sharman and R. G. Streit, 'Economic Decision-Making and the Role of Accounting Information', in *Objectives of Financial Statements: Selected Papers*, American Institute of Certified Public Accountants, 1974, pp. 66–79. An analysis of decisions and their relationship to public accounting information. And J. Ronen, 'A User-orientated Development of Accounting Information Requirements', ibid., pp. 80–103. An analysis of information criteria from the point of view of using accounting information.

D. Weaver, *Investment Analysis*, Longman, 1971. A detailed account of the technical analysis function (pp. 108–21) and the forecasting of income (pp. 122–41).

10
The nature of financial ratios

Introduction

From the preceding chapter, the reader should now be aware that decisions dominate the use of company financial reports; that is, the information contained in them, coupled with other available sources of data, provides means by which various decision-makers can assess their alternative courses of action. The two main areas of activity to which financial reports can be brought to bear are prediction and control, the decision-maker typically having to adapt mainly historical data to formulate the predictions underlying his decisions, then using the same data to compare actual financial results with his previously formulated expectations.

It has also been suggested that, because of the predominantly historical nature of available information (including financial reports), it is important for the decision-maker to conduct a rigorous and a detailed analysis of data akin to the process of fundamental analysis in investment decision-making. This should provide him with a necessary background with which to evaluate the company concerned and predict future benefits to be derived from either his existing or his potential involvement in it. In this sense, financial report analysis is concerned with the construction of a financial profile of the company (preferably over a period of time) which will allow the decision-maker to assess its past, present and possibly future strengths and weaknesses. Of particular concern to him in this respect are the related problems of what future benefits he can expect from the company and, possibly most importantly, whether or not the company will survive in the future and thereby remain in a position to provide those expected benefits.

The accounting information contained in company financial reports can be used to build up this profile by providing the basis for prediction and consequent control through the process of ratio analysis, or the computation and interpretation of significant indicators of company progress and performance. These indicators take the form of ratios describing relevant relationships between individual data usually contained in published financial statements. The analyst therefore must be skilled and experienced enough to identify the relevant accounting data and to match them in such a way that meaningful indicators are made available for decision-making purposes. He must also be capable of interpreting the meaning of computed ratios and understanding the implications of material changes in them over time.

This suggests that ratio construction and analysis, as with the function of fundamental analysis of which it is a part, should be conducted by skilled professionals. Indeed, in practice, this tends to be the case, particularly in the decision-making of institutional investors (such as investment companies, unit trusts, insurance companies, pension funds and merchant banks) and banks which may employ teams of analysts to construct company profiles using such techniques as ratio analysis. However, it should also be said that ratio analysis and construction are not the sole prerogative of the employed analyst. So long as the user of published financial statements is fully aware of their nature and meaning, as well as their relative strengths and weaknesses, and so long as he is also aware of the nature and construction of the key relationships which can be derived from them, then he is in a position to use them in a way which facilitates his decisions.

This and the following chapter assume the knowledgeable user of company financial statements, and the remaining sections will attempt to describe and explain the process whereby published accounting information, together with other available data, is used to construct financial ratios useful for decision-making. As before, the emphasis will be on understanding rather than computation. It should also be noted at the outset that the process of financial ratio analysis is concerned mainly with the use of reported accounting information. There are other ratios which can be computed using other sources of information (such as industry data) but these are regarded as largely outwith the scope of a text mainly concerned with the use of company financial reports. On the other hand, certain financial ratios do make use of data derived from the Stock Exchange (for example, share prices), and these will be fully explained at appropriate stages in Chapters 11 and 12.

Objectives of financial ratios

The process of producing financial ratios is essentially concerned with the identification of significant accounting data relationships which give the decision-maker insights into the company being assessed. In particular, the aim of financial ratios is to provide indicators of a company's past performance (in terms of its operational activity and profitability) and near-present financial condition (for example, relating to its liquidity and financial structure) so as to give the decision-maker a basis for predicting future performance and financial condition. Provision of key ratios over a period of time can enable him to construct a pattern of company behaviour and condition which he can then incorporate into his decision model by formulating predictions of future dividends and so forth which make use of such a pattern.

For the purpose of this text, which is primarily concerned with external decision-makers to the company, the main financial ratio users appear to be existing and potential shareholders, lenders, bankers and creditors. Despite previous general descriptions in this text, the informational needs of each of these groups are difficult to specify in detail. For example, shareholders can be divided into different groupings: they can be holders of preferred, ordinary or deferred shares; institutional or private individuals; investing for income, capital value appreciation or a combination of both; willing to accept differing degrees of investment risk; and investing for short-term gain or long-term benefit. As yet, little is known of their precise informational needs except what is postulated in the accountancy literature.

The same remarks can be applied to lenders, bankers and creditors except that their assumed groupings appear to be less complex than those of investors. Lenders, bankers and creditors 'invest' for different periods of time with expectations of repayment on dates which are usually contractually agreed. It is therefore difficult to be precise as to what financial ratios are particularly relevant to each such group. However, the following very general indications can be given.

Financial ratios and investors

Chapter 9 described how investors are mainly concerned with the flow of future dividends which they predict will be attributable to their existing or potential investment. They are also interested in the ultimate realization proceeds for the particular investment being considered. From this, it can reasonably be assumed that investors are concerned with financial ratios which aid them in the prediction of dividends and share realization values. Therefore relevant ratios would appear to include those predicting company profitability (income being an essential ingredient in the computation of dividends, the latter usually being some proportion of available income); liquidity (dividends are usually paid in cash if there are sufficient liquid resources to allow distributions to be paid; and the long-term survival of the company as a going concern depends on the adequacy of its liquid resources); and capital structure (for example, the way in which the company is financed will have a significant part to play in determining investment risk; the more it relies on loans and credits, the more risk there is of falls in income levels and cash resources constraining the distribution of dividends).

Financial ratios and lenders, bankers and creditors

Because of their concern in the eventual repayment of monies due to them, together with any related interest payments, lenders, bankers and creditors would appear likely to use similar ratios to those of the investor. For example, interest payments will depend on the availability of income and liquid resources; and the latter are also essential to repayment of capital sums. Similarly, data on the capital structure of the company not only help the investor to assess his investment, but will also help the lender, banker or creditor to assess the risk he is taking when investing in the company.

Criteria for financial ratios

To be useful to the decision-maker, financial ratios should satisfy certain criteria. These may appear to be relatively self-evident, but should not be forgotten when preparing ratios. If they are neglected then, no matter how arithmetically correct the computed relationships, there is a very real danger that subsequent interpretations could be either misleading or erroneous. The following are the most obvious of these criteria.

Comparability

By definition, decisions are concerned with the assessment of alternative courses of action. This has certain implications for the use of information in the prediction and control phases of decision-making. First, prediction of future benefits for a number of alternatives requires the information used to be comparable; that is, that the information related to one alternative course of action be capable of being meaningfully compared with information related to another alternative. Secondly, when analysing information over time for predicting benefits related to a particular course of action, it is equally necessary to ensure that the data of one period can be compared with that of other periods. Thirdly, when monitoring the results of previous decisions, it is essential that the information pertaining to actual performance can be not only compared with predicted data, but can also be used for inter-period comparisons of actual performance.

Comparability is, in this sense, largely concerned with the measurement of the information used in financial ratio computation as well as in the measurement of the ratios themselves. Unless the information and the resultant ratios are measured on the same basis for purposes of comparisons at one point of time or over time, it is exceedingly difficult to deduce whether significant differences in comparisons are the result of differences in the underlying financial performance and condition or of differences in the measurement techniques employed. Thus, there is an obvious need for consistency in the accounting treatment of reported data which are going to be used for financial ratio purposes, not only between periods for the same company but also between companies within the same trade or industry.

The need for consistency in accounting is widely recognized by the accountancy profession. However, whereas comparability may well be achieved for the one company over time, it is a much more difficult task to achieve it between apparently similar companies. The major problem in this respect is that companies tend not to be identical even when they may appear, on the surface, to have similar features. Apparently similar companies tend to behave in different ways: the mix of their operations may vary; their managerial philosophy and practice may differ; and their operational environment may be dissimilar. The problem has become even more acute in recent years, the process of takeover and merger having created companies with widely-diversified interests and operations which make them difficult subjects for industrial classification.

The need for consistency in accounting practice to achieve comparability has been recognized in the programmes of accounting standardization which are now in operation in the UK and elsewhere, and in Section A, Part II, Schedule 8, Companies Act 1948. This is having the effect of improving the uniformity of accounting measurements for reporting purposes and, consequently, the computation and the use of financial ratios are being made more relevant to decision-making than before, owing to the gradual elimination of differences caused by accounting method rather than by economic activity.

However, it must be clearly stated that measurement differences still remain. For example, no two companies are absolutely identical and measurement differences may be entirely appropriate to reflect fairly the characteristics of each. Similarly, the circumstances and characteristics of individual companies tend to change over time, and this will cause changes in methodology from one period to the next. Finally, the programmes of standardization are continuous, long-term processes which attempt to minimize accounting flexibility. They cannot 'legislate' for every possible area of flexibility, particularly in those areas where subjective judgements by qualified experts are the bases for measuring accounting information. In other words, uniformity and consistency of practice are desirable properties of accounting information which is to be translated into ratio form for comparative purposes. However, the financial ratio user must be aware of the impossibility of achieving absolute uniformity, and thus of achieving absolute comparability.

Data limitations

Ratios describing an individual company's financial progress and position are very much a derivation of its published accounting information. As such, they are subject to the measurement limitations of the underlying information, the main features of which have been described in some detail in Chapters 7 and 8. The problems of valuation from the traditional use of the principles of realization and historic cost; together with the convention of conservatism, changing prices and price-levels, and significant resource omissions (accountants traditionally measuring on the basis of verifiable past transactions); as well as the flexibility issue due to accounting allocations – all affect the reliability and relevance of financial ratios. That is why it is so important for the decision-maker who makes use of financial ratios to be fully aware of the problems affecting the underlying accounting information. He must understand, for example, the limitations of ratios which rely on measures of accounting income based on the realization principle. They reflect realized rather than earned income of the period. Similarly, ratios utilizing asset valuations from a traditional balance sheet (for example, fixed asset or stock and work-in-progress values) should not be interpreted as indicating current values, or at least not in the normal case. Ratios are only as reliable and relevant as the accounting information upon which they are based.

Proliferation of ratios

As previously mentioned, and as will be shown in detail in Chapters 11 and 12, financial ratios are usually an expression of an assumed or known relationship between one accounting measure and another: for example, earnings per share describes the proportion of distributable periodic income attributable to each ordinary share unit of the company concerned. Within a typical set of financial statements (particularly annual statements), there is a very large number of measures available for ratio computation. However, the relevance of the latter process depends on recognizing pertinent relationships. It is perfectly feasible to relate all available reported data, and thereby to produce an extremely large number of ratios. But it is equally feasible to suggest that most of these ratios will be meaningless to the user, either because he has no use for them in his particular decision model or, more important, because the computed relationships are themselves meaningless because they do not convey or indicate important characteristics of the company's financial performance or condition.

In other words, there is a basic set of financial ratios which can be derived from financial statements, and which give all the data necessary to compute others if need be. This set contains the independent ratios from which other dependent ratios can be computed. The advantage of this approach is that it provides a set of relevant ratios which can be extended by the experienced analyst to include other ratios, but using the data in the original set to do so. This hopefully tends to cause the analyst to think of the relevance and usefulness of ratios before he computes them, and thereby tends to minimize the potential proliferation of unnecessary ratios.

The effect of extraordinary items

If, as has been explained throughout this text, the use of accounting information in decision-making is largely concerned with historical data from which predictions of future benefits are derived, it is extremely important to ensure that analysed past data are devoid of factors not likely to recur in the future. In accounting terms this refers particularly to so-called extraordinary gains and losses affecting the measurement of periodic income.

It is inevitable that a company will benefit or suffer financially from certain events or transactions which are of a non-recurrent nature; for example, gains or losses arising from the closing down of part of its trading operations; the sale of long-term investments; the confiscation of properties in a foreign country; and the major devaluation or revaluation of foreign currencies. The accounting treatment of these items for income reporting purposes has concerned accountants for many years, the alternative treatments being their separate disclosure, either in the balance sheet as movements in the company's reserves or in the income statement as adjustments to normal operating income. The latter has recently received professional approval in the UK,[1] its main aim being the separation of recurring and non-recurring income elements to aid the report user in his assessment of company performance over time. This particular approach is also required in the standard company financial statement formats prescribed in Part I, Schedule 8, Companies Act 1948. Therefore, the production of financial ratios using reported income data can be undertaken more easily, the non-recurrent items being ignored in the computation of comparable ratios for prediction purposes.

However, although ignoring extraordinary gains and losses in ratio computation and analysis seems entirely appropriate to the establishment of comparable data for decision-making, it does raise two related questions: first, what is an extraordinary item of a non-recurring nature, and secondly, assuming that these items can be identified, does their exclusion from computed ratios improve their predictive capability? The problem of what is a non-recurrent gain or loss has long vexed accountants and, despite the existence of professional standards, the situation remains largely unresolved. For example, what item of gain or loss can ever be regarded as absolutely non-recurrent? In other words, it may be more reasonable to regard these items as infrequent rather than non-recurrent.

This, however, raises the question of how infrequent they have to be to be treated as non-recurrent; is it to be recurring every two, ten, or fifty years? In addition, it is relatively self-evident that gains and losses may well be non-recurring for one company but not for another, the degree of recurrence depending on the nature of the business. Therefore, it is extremely difficult to standardize matters in this respect since there is a danger in so doing of imposing a uniformity in accounting practice which ignores the diversity of company activities and thereby produces meaningless comparisons. As yet there are no clear answers to these questions, and it is doubtful whether any are forthcoming.

So far as concerns improving the predictive capability of financial ratios by the exclusion of extraordinary items from income measures, logic appears to suggest that such exclusions will produce accounting relationships which provide more relevant comparisons of data both over time and between companies. However, it may well be that their segregation is not as vital as might first appear. Meanwhile, the problem does exist, and the computation of financial ratios would seem to benefit by the exclusion of extraordinary items. Therefore, the analyst must be capable of identifying potentially non-recurring items according to the circumstances of the individual companies concerned. This does not appear to be an area in which he can be guided in any detailed sense because of the differing circumstances of companies.

Materiality

Unquestionably, one of the most significant aspects of financial ratio computation and analysis is the materiality of the data being used. This has been defined in the following way by Dohr:

> A statement, fact or item is material, if, giving full consideration to the surrounding circumstances, as they exist at the time, it is of such a nature that its disclosure, or the method of treating it, would be likely to influence or to 'make a difference' in the judgment and conduct of a reasonable person. The same tests apply to such words as significant, consequential, or important.[2]

This is one of the most crucial aspects of accounting and, as such, it affects not only decisions regarding the data to be measured and communicated in financial reports, but also the data to be analysed. The producer of accounting information must ensure that he measures and discloses material data (in other words, that trivia should not be reported), while its users must equally ensure that the reported data selected for analysis purposes are material enough to be capable of influencing their decisions.

However, this poses a problem because there are no generally accepted guidelines to aid the analyst with regard to data materiality. The latter is very much a matter of personal judgement which has to be made in light of the surrounding circumstances at the time of judgement. It concerns not only the nature of the data being used, but also the size of the quantification, either in relative or absolute terms. For example, if the financial report contains information that the managing director has defrauded the company of a relatively small monetary sum then, irrespective of the insignificance of the sum involved, the nature of the item is important enough to have an influence on the behaviour of shareholders and others. On the other hand, if the analyst has computed the company's earnings per share and found the figure to be 0.5 per cent below what was generally expected for the period concerned then, irrespective of the relevance of the computation, the absolute size of the difference may well be regarded as immaterial when formulating subsequent decisions. The problem for the analyst in these circumstances is judging when an absolute or relative datum ceases to be immaterial and becomes relevant to the decisions under consideration.

References

1 'Extraordinary Items and Prior Year Adjustments', *Statement of Standard Accounting Practice 6*, 1974.
2 J. L. Dohr, 'Materiality – What Does It Mean in Accounting?', *Journal of Accountancy*, July 1950, p. 56.

Suggested discussion or essay topics; and selected bibliography

Because of the inter-relationship of the topics in Chapters 10, 11 and 12, this material is provided at the end of Chapter 12.

11
The computation and use of traditional financial ratios

Introduction

It is now appropriate to describe in some detail the main financial relationships which can be expressed in ratio form prior to use in a number of decision situations. The emphasis will be on meaning and interpretation, although necessary computations will be explained fully. The ratios with which this section will be concerned can be divided into three main groups: (a) 'internal' financial ratios (ratios comprising relationships of data derived entirely from published financial statements); (b) 'external' financial ratios (ratios comprising relationships of data from published financial statements and data from external sources such as Stock Exchange quotations of share prices); and (c) industrial financial ratios (ratios describing aggregate relationships of data comprising the financial results of industries as a whole). The first two categories make extensive use of published financial statements which, particularly for quoted companies, are readily available. The last category is not so accessible, though official government publications do contain ratios useful for comparative purposes.

Ideally, the use of computed financial ratios would be concerned with comparing those in the first two categories (both over time and between companies) with those in the third category. However, the comparability problem must be faced in this context. It is difficult enough to ensure consistency of accounting treatment over time for one company (for example, when comparing 'internal' and 'external' financial ratios in a time series). But it is more difficult to ensure consistency of accounting between companies (that is, when comparing 'internal' and 'external' ratios of comparable companies). The difficulties in the latter situation are multiplied when it is realized that, because of the complexity and diversity of industrial and commercial activity conducted within a single company or group of companies, it is virtually impossible to ensure absolute comparability. This latter problem is accentuated when either 'internal' or 'external' ratios are compared with their industrial equivalents. The complexity and diversity of activity within individual companies makes it extremely difficult to classify them industrially, therefore it is problematic whether the ratios of an individual company and its assumed industry classification are indeed comparable. For this reason, the undernoted ratio descriptions will concentrate on 'internal' and 'external' financial ratios, although the reader should note that industrial ratios are available, on occasion, for comparison should the analyst believe this to be relevant to the construction of his company profiles.

The ratios which will now be examined will be concerned with the following aspects of a company's financial profile: profitability, liquidity, and financial structure (including its market performance). These factors are believed to be the main ones which the analyst should be interested in when using published accounting information for assessing companies prior to making decisions. This proposition would appear to remain valid, no matter what the nature of the decision.

Profitability factors, in terms of measured income, dividend and retention levels, not only allow the analyst to assess potential dividends, but also to examine company financial success or failure (assuming it is accepted that income is a reasonable indicator of these matters). Liquidity factors are crucial to the future payment of dividends and interest, credit and capital repayments, and wage claims, as well as the long-term survival of the company. Assessments of a company's financial structure give important insights into the nature and quality of its financial management, and to the degrees of risk associated with the various sources by which it has been financed. Finally, indicators of market performance relate the performance of a company, as expressed in its published accounting information, to market assessments of that performance. They can be regarded as a separate category of ratios but, for purposes of this text, are discussed within the context of assessing the financial structure of a company.

The ratios to be computed, explained and discussed in this chapter will be based in the first instance on historic cost data. However, it is also intended to introduce the reader to two variations of this conventional analysis – first, to ratios based on equivalent current cost data and, secondly, to the effects on ratios of manipulating the basic historic cost data without contravening known accounting standards. Both these areas have been neglected in textbooks of this type to date, and a separate section of the following chapter will be devoted to each. The data used throughout this and the next chapter will be that contained in Chapter 2 – that is, from Illustration 25 (for historic cost balance sheet data), Illustration 26 (for historic cost income statement data) and Illustration 32 (for the equivalent current cost data). It should be assumed that the shares of Company Ltd are ordinary £1 units with a market value at t_1 of £2.50 and at t_2 of £2.40 The following is a summary of the basic historic cost data derived from the afore-mentioned illustrations (Illustration 55). The current cost data are given at the beginning of Chapter 12 (Illustration 78).

Illustration 55 Basic data for analysis

COMPANY LTD

Group Balance Sheet as at t_2

	t_1				t_2	
	£	£	£	£	£	£
Fixed assets						
Intangible asset						
Goodwill			200			200
Tangible asset						
Plant			400			5,300
			600			5,500
Current assets						
Stock		2,000			3,100	
Debtors		800			1,000	
Cash at bank		3,300			1,200	
		6,100			5,300	
Creditors: amounts falling due within one year						
Creditors	1,500			1,900		
Taxation	1,100			1,300		
Dividends	200	2,800		300	3,500	
Net current assets			3,300			1,800
Total assets less current liabilities			3,900			7,300
Creditors: amounts falling due after more than one year						
Bank loan			—			(2,000)
			3,900			5,300
Capital and reserves						
Called up share capital			2,000			3,000
Share premium account			500			—
Profit and loss account			1,400			2,300
			3,900			5,300

Illustration 55 continued

Group Income Statement for the Period t_1 to t_2

	t_0 to t_1 £	t_1 to t_2 £
Turnover	25,000	29,000
Change in stocks	(100)	1,100
Purchase of goods	(17,300)	(20,300)
Wages and salaries	(2,200)	(2,300)
Depreciation of fixed assets	(100)	(1,100)
Other business overheads	(2,600)	(3,200)
Loan interest paid	—	(200)
Income before taxation	2,700	3,000
Tax on income	(1,100)	(1,300)
Income after taxation	1,600	1,700
Dividend proposed	(200)	(300)
Retained income	1,400	1,400
Of which:		
Retained in holding company	1,300	1,200
Retained in subsidiary company	100	200
	1,400	1,400

A note on company taxation

The UK company tax system, which has been assumed for purposes of the illustration data, is the so-called imputation system. It is not the purpose of this text to discuss at length the details of company taxation within the context of financial reporting since this is a complex and technical matter which, if introduced at earlier stages, would have tended to obscure the crucial principles and problems of reporting. In addition, the system of assessing company taxation liabilities tends to vary considerably over time. In the UK prior to 1965, companies were subject to income tax and profits tax (both being based on company reported income), with dividends being paid to shareholders net of income tax, distributable profits having already borne income tax. Between 1965 and 1973, this system was replaced by corporation tax based on reported income: dividends being remitted to shareholders net of income tax, which companies then had to remit to the Inland Revenue in addition to their corporation tax liabilities. Since 1973, the imputation system has replaced the so-called classical system of corporation tax, and changes such as these make it extremely difficult to produce a textbook which will not date relatively rapidly. However, for purposes of computing meaningful financial ratios, the tax system must be explained, albeit briefly.

The main features of the imputation system are reasonably clear. A company is charged with corporation tax at a single rate (assumed for purposes of this text at 50 per cent). The basis for corporation tax is the company's reported income prior to taxation and distribution of dividends. However, if the company distributes part of its available income in the form of dividends, it is required to make a payment to the Inland Revenue equivalent to a proportion of the gross dividend distributed (the rate assumed for purposes of this text being taken as 30 per cent). This remitted tax is termed advance corporation tax, and is normally set against the company's total corporation tax liability (termed mainstream corporation tax) when assessing the payment to be made to the Inland Revenue for corporation tax. In other words, in the normal case, the company will suffer to the extent of its total corporation tax liability. However, if dividends are paid, it has to remit a proportion of this at the time of the distribution. The remainder is remitted some time after the end of the financial year concerned.

For purposes of financial statement presentation, the mainstream and advance corporation tax liabilities are aggregated and the total is then deducted from the figure for 'income before tax'. Dividends, paid net of advance corporation tax, are deducted from available income at the net figure. For example, taking the illustrated figures and assuming the tax rates mentioned above, the notes given in Illustration 56 support the given figures for corporation tax and dividends in the income statement.

Illustration 56 Corporation tax and dividends

(A) *Corporation Tax*	Periods	
	t_0 to t_1 £	t_1 to t_2 £
Corporation tax at assumed 50% rate*	1,100	1,300
Composed of:		
Advance corporation tax on gross dividends at an assumed 30% rate†	86	129
Mainstream corporation tax	1,014	1,171
	1,100	1,300

*It should be remembered that, although corporation tax is based on reported income, taxable income may differ considerably owing to the application of existing tax rules in its computation; for example, in period t_0 to t_1 reported income is £2,700 but taxable income is £2,200, assuming a 50% tax rate; the figures for period t_1 to t_2 are £3,000 and £2,600, respectively.

†The advance corporation tax, which is set against the total corporation tax liability to compute the mainstream corporation tax payment, is limited to a proportion of the company's taxable income (30 per cent thereof if a 50 per cent corporation tax rate is assumed). No such restriction is required in either of the periods in this example.

(B) *Dividends*	*Periods*	
	t_0 to t_1	t_1 to t_2
	£	£
Gross dividends declared of 14.3% of ordinary share capital	286	429
Less: advance corporation tax at assumed 30% rate	86	129
Net dividends as per income statements	200	300

Illustration 56 continued

There are additional complications in the imputation system because of such matters as investment income and foreign income received by the company, but these are ignored for the purposes of this text.

Financial ratios reflecting profitability on a historic cost basis

The aim of this group of ratios is to assess how successful the company has been in terms of income; that is, particularly in relation to the financial return achieved from the use of its resources. In other words, the achievement of periodic income is not of itself sufficient to assess operating and financial success or failure. Instead, it must be related to other relevant factors to indicate financial performance.

Return on investment

Often referred to as the income yield, this profitability indicator relates reported income to capital employed in the company. Because of problems in defining income and capital for this purpose, there cannot be said to be any one particular way of computing the yield or return which, in general terms, is as follows:

$$\frac{\text{Defined periodic income}}{\text{Defined capital employed}} \times 100$$

The traditional way of computing the yield (using the figures given at the beginning of the chapter) would be as in Illustration 57.

The first set of ratios (69.2 per cent and 56.6 per cent) indicates the financial return before tax on the recorded book value of the investment provided by shareholders. Investors and other interested persons looking at these figures can use them in an attempt to assess how well or badly the equity 'investment' in the company has been or could be used. This will require comparison with some predetermined standard, either with expected returns for the company or returns made by other similar companies. Comparability is improved by dealing with 'income before tax' data, thus avoiding the distortions which corporation tax deductions can cause (the computation of corporation tax depending on the tax law

239

Illustration 57 Return on investment

$$\frac{\text{Reported income before corporation tax but after deduction of interest for the period}}{\text{Reported share capital and premiums + retained income at the end of the period}} \times 100$$

$$= \frac{\pounds 2{,}700}{\pounds 3{,}900} \times 100 = 69.2\% \text{ (for period } t_0 - t_1 \text{); and}$$

$$= \frac{\pounds 3{,}000}{\pounds 5{,}300} \times 100 = 56.6\% \text{ (for period } t_1 - t_2 \text{);}$$

$$\frac{\text{Reported income before corporation tax and interest for the period}}{\text{Total assets at the end of the period}^*} \times 100$$

$$= \frac{\pounds 2{,}700}{\pounds 6{,}700} \times 100 = 40.3\% \text{ (for period } t_0 - t_1 \text{); and}$$

$$= \frac{\pounds 3{,}200}{\pounds 10{,}800} \times 100 = 29.6\% \text{ (for period } t_1 - t_2 \text{).}$$

*Fixed assets plus current assets.

---

of the day and the individual circumstances of the company, both of which can vary over time).

The second set of ratios (40.3 per cent and 29.6 per cent) concentrates on the financial return on the recorded book value of the total investment provided by shareholders, lenders and creditors, thus giving a wider and more general view of company profitability. In this case, to ensure that the numerator and denominator are related properly, it is necessary to use income data before deduction of loan interest; the latter being the bank's financial return. Therefore, whether it is the shareholder's investment or the total investment which is being used, the earnings yield gives a better insight into profitability than does a simple comparison of reported income levels. For example, reported income after deduction of interest, but before deduction of tax, has increased from £2,700 (in period t_0 to t_1) to £3,000 (in period t_1 to t_2); that is, by 11.1 per cent. But the income yield on shareholder investment has decreased from 69.2 per cent to 56.6 per cent; a decrease of 18.2 per cent. It would be wrong to draw any further inferences from these limited data, but it is clear that the function of information analysis benefits from the use of relative rather than absolute data.

It should be noted, however, that the denominator can also be taken as 'net total assets'; that is, total assets net of current liabilities (and, where relevant, provisions). Some would argue that this datum gives a more stable figure than the 'gross total assets' used for purposes of this example. Much depends on the business concerned, and whether it is subject to the volatility of seasonal and cyclical factors which could cause current asset data at each period-end to be either below or above the normal level for the period concerned. Netting with at least current liabilities in these cases would tend to minimize the effect of these distortions. Therefore, if business is volatile, the net figure would probably be more appropriate. It has been assumed for purposes of this example that such factors do not exist.

Provisions also create a problem in this respect. Within the context of UK company reporting law, they are defined as liabilities and losses which are likely or certain to be incurred but which are uncertain as to amount or date of settlement. In these circumstances, the analyst must decide whether it is more appropriate to treat it as a current liability, or as a long-term liability. Each of these treatments will provide different capital denominators in the returns ratios described in this section.

Alternative returns on investment

Before proceeding to examine other financial ratios of profitability, it is only proper to explain certain other variations of the return on investment, each of which is caused by a different interpretation of income and/or capital.

First, it could be argued that, because the numerator of the return refers to periodic income derived from the use of funds invested during the period, it would be more appropriate to use an average denominator of either shareholders' investment or total investment. For example, taking period t_1 to t_2, and assuming the computation of the return on the shareholders' average investment, the relevant ratio would appear as:

$$\frac{£3,000}{\frac{£3,900 + 5,300}{2}} \times 100 = 65.2\%$$

This compares with the previous year-end-based figure of 56.6 per cent and appears to reflect more fairly the financial return on the capital employed throughout the period rather than that existing at the end of it.

Secondly, as a result of the imputation system of company taxation, it can be argued that the income numerator in the return on investment ratio should be that which is the maximum available for distribution to shareholders. This is found by grossing up the figure for income after deduction of corporation tax by adding an amount equivalent to the advance corporation tax which would be payable if that income was distributed. For example, if income after deduction of tax was £500, then the maximum gross dividend the company could pay to its shareholders would be £714 (£500 + 3/7 × £500), assuming advance corporation tax at 30 per cent; that is, it could pay out a net dividend of £500.

Taking the figures given for Company Ltd, this approach would result in return on shareholders' investment figures as shown in Illustration 58, grossing up the relevant net income data.

Illustration 58 Maximum distributable income		
	Periods	
	t_0 *to* t_1	t_1 *to* t_2
	£	£
Income after corporation tax	1,600	1,700
Add: advance corporation tax assumed thereon 3/7	686	729
Maximum dividends distributable	2,286	2,429

These figures can now be used as the numerators of the ratio computation, with year-end equity as the denominators:

$$\text{Return on investment } (t_0 - t_1) = \frac{£2,286}{£3,900} \times 100 = 58.6\%$$

$$\text{Return on investment } (t_1 - t_2) = \frac{£2,429}{£5,300} \times 100 = 45.8\%$$

These ratios compare with those of 69.2 per cent and 56.6 per cent, respectively, using the traditional method. The advantage of the imputation-adjusted ratios, however, is that they attempt to reflect the distributable returns on investment, after allowing for corporation tax, but prior to any distribution of dividends. The traditional approach avoids the problem of taxation, and thus gives the analyst little indication of the maximum distributable return. It follows, too, that the imputation-adjusted return could be computed using an average capital employed figure as suggested previously.

Whichever approach to the computation of return on investment is used, it must remain a relatively imprecise reflection of company profitability for decision-making if it is assumed to be derived from accounting data measured on the historic cost–realization basis. It is subject to all the measurement problems previously mentioned in this text. The flexibility of accounting practice (despite mandatory provisions from the professional accountancy bodies) affects both the numerator and denominator of the ratio, as do the impact of price changes and different valuation bases. It is also possible to influence periodic returns by accelerating or decelerating transactions at period-ends. These matters, however, will be dealt with later in the next chapter.

Earnings per share

A test of profitability for the ordinary shareholders of a company can be found by measuring the reported income attributable to each ordinary share unit; that is, by measuring earnings per share. This particular ratio is normally taken as:

$$\frac{\text{Reported income after taxation and preference}}{\text{dividends, but before inclusion of extraordinary items}}$$

Number of ordinary share units issued by the company

In the case of income attributable to a group of companies, the numerator would also be after deduction of that proportion of net income attributable to minority interests; leaving earnings attributable to the shareholders of the holding company to be used in the computation. Assuming there are no complications with foreign income or unrelieved advance corporation tax owing to the latter exceeding the statutory limit under the imputation system, earnings per share would be as in Illustration 59, using the figures supplied at the beginning of this chapter.

Illustration 59 Earnings per share – 1		
	Periods	
	t_0 *to* t_1	t_1 *to* t_2
Reported income after tax	1,600	1,700
Number of £1 share units	2,000	3,000
= earnings per share	80p	56.7p

These figures are not on their own particularly useful. However, when taken as part of a trend analysis, or when compared with similar data for other comparable companies, they give some insight into future prospects for ordinary shareholders. If it is accepted that dividends are related to available income after deduction of tax (and this seems a reasonable assumption), then earnings per share data can help the investor to assess prospects for further dividends per ordinary share unit. In this respect, studies of earnings per share data are somewhat more meaningful than studies of the absolute 'income after tax' figures.

However, care must be exercised when interpreting such data. For example, in the circumstances used in this chapter, the ordinary share units in period t_1 to t_2 had increased from 2,000 to 3,000 because of a bonus issue. Thus, although reported 'income after tax' had increased by 6.3 per cent, earnings per share appeared to fall by 29.1 per cent, and appeared to have considerably reduced prospects for increased dividends per share, despite increased earnings. This reveals the importance of using relevant financial indicators when analysing available data. It also indicates the dangers which can arise unless the data are comparable. For example, the above figures indicate a significant fall in earnings per share from one point to the next. However, this resulted from the assumption of an increase in share units owing to a bonus issue. In these circumstances, the change is simply a restatement of share capital and involves no new shareholders or resources. To achieve proper comparability in earnings per share, it would be necessary to translate the share units of period t_0 to t_1 into share units of period t_1 to t_2 (see Illustration 60).

Illustration 60 Earnings per share – 2		
	Periods	
	t_0 to t_1	t_1 to t_2
Period income after tax	1,600	1,700
Number of £1 share units	3,000	3,000
= earnings per share	53.3p	56.7p

This restores the comparability of the data owing to an internal transfer which has not altered the dividend prospects of existing shareholders – that is, restated earnings per share have increased by 6.4 per cent.

Earnings per share calculations are subject to problems similar to those already discussed in relation to the return on investment. That is, the imputation system of taxation; price changes; flexibility in accounting practice; and transaction acceleration or delay can each affect the computation of earnings per share. Specifically, each influences the calculation of the earnings numerator in much the same way as for the return on investment. For example, taking the imputation system issue, it could be argued that a more reasonable measure of earnings per share (as an indicator of dividend potential) would be one in which earnings were computed on the basis of a maximum distribution. As previously explained, this would mean grossing up the income after corporation tax data at the advance tax rate (assumed for purposes of this chapter to be 30 per cent). This would give the earnings per share data for the two periods as in Illustration 61.

Illustration 61 Earnings per share – 3		
	Periods	
	t_0 to t_1	t_1 to t_2
	£	£
Reported income after tax	1,600	1,700
Add: advance corporation tax assumed thereon:		
3/7 of the net income	686	729
Maximum distributable earnings	2,286	2,429
Number of £1 share units	3,000	3,000
Earnings per share	76.2p	81p

As with the return on investment calculation which uses maximum distributable earnings, the answer seems to give a reasonable expression of this particular aspect of company profitability when expressed in traditional accounting terms – that is, the potentially distributable income to shareholders has increased by 6.3 per cent.

Income margins

One further aspect of company profitability which the analyst can examine as part of his construction of a company's financial profile is the income earned by the company as a proportion of its sales. This gives the analyst a fundamental indicator of managerial performance by looking at management's attempts to maximize sales revenues while also attempting to minimize related costs. However, it should be stated as well that any assessment of managerial performance which relies entirely on a study of income margins is incomplete and could be misleading. In particular, it ignores the question of the investment in resources to achieve the stated sales and income. For example, a significantly high level of income may have been earned on sales, but only after investment of such a level of resources that the return on investment was significantly small. In other words, ratios of income margins should be studied in conjunction with the related return on investment ratios, as well as with earnings per share data. Income margin ratios normally take the following form:

$$\frac{\text{Income before deduction of tax and interest}}{\text{Total sales revenues for the same period}} \times 100$$

This definition of income is usually used to assess managerial performance without any distortions caused by the taxation system and the financial structure of the company. It corresponds with the return on investment ratio of:

$$\frac{\text{Income before deduction of tax and interest}}{\text{Total assets at the end of the period}} \times 100$$

and could therefore be used in conjunction with it. However, income may also be defined in terms of income after deduction of tax and interest, or income after tax and interest but grossed up at the advance corporation tax rate (as explained in relation to the return on investment). Whichever approach is used, it should be on a consistent basis when relating it to return on investment data. For purposes of illustration, the definition of income before deduction of tax and interest is used, and the data in Illustration 62 emerge, applying the figures given at the beginning of the chapter.

Illustration 62 Income margin – 1		
	Periods	
	t_0 *to* t_1	t_1 *to* t_2
	£	£
Income before deduction of tax and interest	2,700	3,200
Total sales revenue for the period	25,000	29,000
= income margin (× 100)	10.8%	11%

From these figures, it is apparent that the margin on sales has increased slightly by 2 per cent between the two periods. These statistics could be used in any trend analysis, as well as in any comparative study either with data for other similar companies and industries or with return on investment data.

For example, taking the previously computed returns on total investment and the above income margins, the comparison in Illustration 63 can be made (all figures are stated as percentages, and income is before deduction of tax and interest).

Illustration 63 Returns and margins – 1		
Periods	*Return on total investment*	*Income margin*
$t_0 - t_1$	40.3	10.8
$t_1 - t_2$	29.6	11.0
Percentage change	−26.6	+2.0

These figures reveal that, whereas income margins have improved by 2 per cent, there has been a fall in return on total capital employed of 26.6 per cent, indicating less effective use of total company resources in period t_1 to t_2 than in period t_0 to t_1. This particular message would not have been available if the analyst had merely examined income margins.

It should be noted that income margins, as well as being affected by problems imposed on the definition of income by the imputation system of tax, price changes and valuation, accounting flexibility and transaction manipulation, can also be examined in a more specific sense from the point of view of the ordinary shareholder (instead of the company as a whole, as above). Thus, the income margin can be defined as:

$$\frac{\text{Income after deduction of tax and interest}}{\text{Total sales revenue for the period}} \times 100$$

Using the figures given at the beginning of the chapter, the relevant income margins would be as in Illustration 64.

Illustration 64 Income margin – 2		
	Periods	
	t_0 to t_1	t_1 to t_2
	£	£
Income after deducting tax and interest	1,600	1,700
Total sales revenue for the period	25,000	29,000
= income margin (× 100)	6.4%	5.9%

These statistics are now in a form to be used in conjunction with related return on investment and earnings per share data as shown in Illustration 65 (if income is after deduction of tax and interest, and investment is that of the shareholders only).

Illustration 65 A comparative analysis of income ratios			
Period	Income margin	Return on investment*	Earnings per share
$t_0 - t_1$	6.4%	41.0%	80.0p
$t_1 - t_2$	5.9%	32.1%	56.7p
Percentage change	−7.8%	−21.7%	−29.1%

*This particular set of data, using net income figures, has not been computed previously because returns are normally described in income-before-tax terms. The computations are £1,600/£3,900 and £1,700/£5,300 for the two periods respectively (using shareholders' equity data at each period-end).

This tabulation, using data produced on a comparable basis, begins to give the analyst an overall profile of company profitability over the two periods, in this case from the point of view of ordinary shareholders. Income margins on sales have deteriorated slightly, and the less effective use of company resources provided by shareholders has produced an even worse deterioration in their net of tax returns and earnings per share. The analyst could then compare these figures with those produced for earlier periods if he wished to use trend analysis techniques. He could also compare them with other companies or industry averages. However, it must be stated that, to achieve this sort of analysis, it has been necessary to ignore the effects of the imputation tax system, and to allow tax and interest deductions partially to distort the income measures used.

It should also be noted in this context that there is a significant relationship between the income margin and return on investment ratios which provides the analyst with data to help explain essential differences between businesses. The relationship is as follows:

$$\frac{\text{Income}}{\text{Total}} \times \frac{\text{Total}}{\text{Capital employed}} = \frac{\text{Income}}{\text{Capital employed}}$$
$$\frac{\text{(as defined)}}{\text{Total}} \times \frac{\text{sales revenue}}{\text{Capital employed}} = \frac{\text{(as defined)}}{\text{Capital employed}}$$
$$\text{sales revenue} \quad \text{(as defined)} \quad \text{(as defined)}$$

This identity reveals two major influencing factors in the determination of the return on investment: the income margin on sales and the number of times capital has been 'turned over' during a period to achieve that sales revenue. For example, to achieve a reasonably high return on investment, a company could afford to have a relatively low income margin, but only if it also has a rapid turnover of capital employed. Alternatively, a low capital turnover rate will require a high income margin.

In the example used in this chapter, and defining income as before deduction of tax and interest, and capital employed as gross total assets, the ratios given in Illustration 66 have been computed for the two periods.

Illustration 66 Returns and margins – 2		
	Periods	
	t_0 to t_1	t_1 to t_2
Income margin (1)	10.8%	11.0%
Return on investment (2)	40.3%	29.6%
$\therefore$ capital turnover $= \dfrac{(2)}{(1)}$	3.7	2.7

In other words, in period t_0 to t_1, the return on investment (as defined above) of 40.3 per cent was achieved by a combination of a relatively low income margin with a relatively high turnover of capital. Similarly in period t_1 to t_2, the deterioration in the return on investment to 29.6 per cent has been achieved by a slightly higher income margin at 11.0 per cent with a much slower turnover of capital at 2.7.

Much of the above data is obviously of direct concern to existing and potential investors in the company, in the sense that they are primarily interested in its profitability from the point of view of future dividend distribution. They are also concerned with the quality of managerial performance. Certainly, over the long term, the success of share investment in companies depends to a large extent on these matters. However, lenders, bankers, creditors and employees, must also be interested in these factors, for the ability of the company to meet its obligations is determined in part by how profitable it is and how well it is managed. If it is not profitable or well managed, then insufficient cash resources will be generated to meet their claims.

Financial ratios reflecting liquidity on a historic cost basis

The next group of financial ratios is used by the analyst who is concerned with assessing a company's ability to meet its financial obligations. It is vital that companies should be able to pay their way by repaying liabilities as and when they become due. In other words, a company must be profitable and liquid if it is to be successful over the long term. It can be highly profitable yet unable to meet its obligations and, if this is the case, its chances of remaining in existence in the long term are fairly remote unless its liquidity position can be improved.

Generally speaking, measures of liquidity involve comparisons of a company's relatively immediate liabilities with those assets available (or potentially available) to meet them. The following are offered as the most frequently used of these measures.

Working capital

The most general of the available liquidity ratios is working capital. This statistic is based on the relationship of total current assets to current liabilities:

$$\frac{\text{Current assets}}{\text{Current liabilities}}$$

The ratio is measured to assess the cover available to meet the existing current liabilities, these being assumed to require repayment in the relatively near future. In other words, current liabilities contain known and quantifiable obligations which are due almost immediately but also contain other items due at various times over a period of a year (if the Schedule 8, Companies Act 1948 definition if adopted). Likewise, current assets contain resources already in cash or near-cash form, as well as items which, at varying times over a period of a year or more, will be converted into cash resources (for example, stock and work-in-progress, and debtors). Therefore, given the time lags in both the numerator and denominator of the ratio, it can be argued that working capital is a reasonable measure of a company's ability to meet its known, short-term obligations. In addition, however, it can be argued that the ratio should reflect a surplus of current assets over liabilities, indicating a margin of safety to allow for the differing rates of maturing current assets and current liabilities, as well as meeting unexpected obligations.

Using the figures given for Illustration 55, the working capital data emerge as in Illustration 67.

Illustration 67 Working capital ratio

	Time	
	t_1	t_2
	£	£
Current assets	6,100	5,300
Current liabilities	2,800	3,500
= working capital ratio	2.18	1.51

Thus, from a position with a considerable surplus of current assets at t_1, the company has produced a less healthy surplus by t_2, indicating a deterioration in its liquidity position. From a study of the detailed figures in the illustration, much of this results from the decrease of £2,100 in cash resources. Therefore, although the previous section has indicated that the company was increasingly profitable over the two periods, its overall ability to meet its financial obligations has deteriorated; although obviously not disastrously. The information is of considerable interest to existing and potential creditors and lenders whose immediate concern is the availability of cash to meet their claims. It is also of interest to investors, who wish to see the company continue to prosper and develop, pay dividends and obtain further funds from lenders and creditors to finance its future operations.

The computation and use of the working capital ratio, however, is subject to four major problems, each of which makes it a somewhat imperfect indicator of company liquidity – first, its credibility depends to a large extent on the proper classification of assets and liabilities (particularly between fixed and current assets, and long-term and short-term liabilities) – wrong classifications can produce misleading ratios; secondly, the flexibility of accounting practice affects the valuation of stock and work-in-progress, and can therefore affect the ratio; thirdly, the ratio as described is based on the historic cost–realization principles, and thus avoids the problems of unrealized price changes and valuation; and, fourthly, it is possible to manipulate the ratio by accelerating or delaying working capital transactions at period-ends in order to improve or reduce it. As with the income ratio, each of these problems will be examined in the next chapter.

The quick ratio

One of the major drawbacks of the working capital ratio is that it does not fully reflect the current ability of a company to meet its financial obligations: the current assets immediately available to cover current liabilities. In other words, the working capital ratio does not, of itself, answer the question of what would happen if all the company's current liabilities had to be met in the relatively near future. The quick ratio has been designed to attempt to do this, and comprises the following relationship:

$$\frac{\text{Current assets – stock and work-in-progress}}{\text{Current liabilities}}$$

By ignoring the relatively less realizable stock and work-in-progress data, current liabilities are therefore compared with the most realizable of the available current assets. This also avoids the valuation problem which particularly affects stock and work-in-progress, and thereby makes the quick ratio much more comparable than the working capital ratio, both over time and between companies. Using the figures given for Illustration 55, the quick ratios are given in Illustration 68.

Illustration 68 Quick ratio		
	Time	
	t_1	t_2
	£	£
Current assets – stock and work-in-progress	4,100	2,200
Current liabilities	2,800	3,500
= quick ratio	1.46	0.63

Thus, as with the working capital ratio, the liquidity position of the company appears to be worsening – by 57 per cent between t_1 and t_2. In fact, the overall position at t_2 is particularly weak, although it must be remembered that the company would not require to meet all its obligations at one time, and that there is a continuous flow of stock into debtors into cash. Nevertheless, the company has little 'cushion' available to cope with the repayments of current liabilities and the financing of future transactions, thus indicating possible future liquidity problems. It should be noted that the quick ratios are liable to 'window-dressing' treatments in much the same way as working capital ratios.

Other liquidity measures

Working capital and quick ratios constitute the most popular means of assessing company liquidity. However, other statistics can be produced to complete the liquidity profile. These relate, first, to how much stock and work-in-progress the company is holding and thus having to finance; and secondly, to how quickly it is paying its creditors and how quickly its debtors are paying it back. In other words, the ratios relating to these factors are intended to give the analyst some insight into the quality of financial management in the company, especially in relation to funds tied up in the form of stock and credit terms given and received. They attempt to go behind the aggregate data in the liquidity ratios, and the following paragraphs describe each of them briefly.

Stock turnover ratio

Particularly in manufacturing companies, stock and work-in-progress is an important financial item. Considerable funds can be employed by the company to finance stock, and it may well be that reductions in stock levels could lead to the release of funds needed for other more pressing purposes. One indication of how much stock is being held can be obtained from the stock turnover ratio which measures the average time stock is held during a period:

$$\frac{\text{Cost of sales for the period}}{\text{Stock at the end of the period}}$$

This ratio attempts to describe the number of times stock has been 'turned over' and replaced during the period and, by dividing the answer into the number of days in the period, it indicates the average holding time for stock. An alternative would be to relate the figure for the period's purchases of goods to the closing stock held – this would provide data on the proportion of the period's purchases which is held in stock; rather than the proportion of the period's sales volume which is so held. However, in published reports, unless a value added statement is provided, the figure for purchases may not be available and the cost of sales datum should be used instead. In addition, if the figures for purchases or cost of sales are not available because of the lack of disclosure in the financial statements, it is usual to use the sales revenue figures as a surrogate.

It is also acceptable to obtain an average stock figure for the period to avoid distortions in the calculation should closing stock not be typical of the normal stock level held throughout the period. (In practice, because of lack of information about stock throughout the period, this figure is calculated by averaging opening and closing stock data.) Using the cost of sales figures given for Illustration 55 (that is, change in stocks plus purchase of goods), it should be assumed that stock at t_0 was £2,100 and the ratios can then be computed as in Illustration 69.

Illustration 69 Stock turnover ratio

	Periods	
	t_0 to t_1	t_1 to t_2
	£	£
Cost of sales for the period	17,400	19,200
Average stock for the period	2,050 *	2,550 †
= stock turnover ratio	8.49	7.53

$$* \left[\frac{£2,100 + 2,000}{2} \right] \qquad † \left[\frac{£2,000 + 3,100}{2} \right]$$

By dividing these ratios into 365 (assuming each period to be one year of 365 days), it is found that the average holding time for stock in each period is 43 days for period t_0 to t_1, and 48.5 days for period t_1 to t_2. These statistics are then available for comparison with similar data for other periods and for other comparable companies and industries.

The reasonableness of such statistics will depend entirely on the nature of the business; aircraft manufacturers, for example, will obviously require to hold stock and work-in-progress for far longer periods than, say, a retail food supermarket. It must be realized, however, that the ratio's validity depends, first, on a consistency of accounting measurement for both the numerator and the denominator over time; secondly, on a similar consistency of treatment between comparable companies and industries to avoid misleading variations arising from the flexibility of accounting practice; and, thirdly, on an absence of 'window-dressing' of the type previously mentioned in working capital calculations. In other words, as in the case with the previously described ratios, the frailties of the accounting measurement process can significantly affect the 'value' of the statistic, and great care must be taken in its computation and analysis.

Debtor collection

A further indicator of liquidity can be found by measuring the average collection period for debtors; in other words, the average period of credit given by the company to its customers. Obviously, the shorter the period of credit, the speedier will be the receipt of cash to be used in continuing operations. This is particularly important in times of inflation when money is losing its purchasing power over time. The ratio, in its most general form, is as follows:

$$\frac{\text{Credit sales for the period}}{\text{Debtors at the end of the period}}$$

By dividing the turnover into the number of days in the period, the average collection time can be obtained. However, as with the stock turnover rate, it is advisable to use an average denominator for the period so as to avoid a period-end figure which is unrepresentative of the typical figure for the period. Using the sales figures stated at the beginning of the chapter, and also assuming debtors were £700 at t_2 (for averaging purposes), the ratios take the form shown in Illustration 70.

Dividing these ratios into 365 (assuming each period to be a year of 365 days), the average collection period, or period of credit allowed to customers, is found to be 11 days for period t_0 to t_1 and 11.3 days for period t_1 to t_2. This indicates stability in the collection of customer cash in both periods, although the relative merits of the figures will only be established by comparison with those of other past periods, similar companies and comparable industrial statistics.

Illustration 70 Debtors turnover ratio

	Periods	
	t_0 to t_1	t_1 to t_2
	£	£
Sales for the period	25,000	29,000
Average debtors for the period	750*	900†
= debtors turnover ratio	33.33	32.22

$$ * \left[\frac{£700 + 800}{2} \right] \qquad † \left[\frac{£800 + 1,000}{2} \right] $$

It should also be noted that the problem of 'window-dressing', by acceleration or delay of transactions affecting credit sales, can affect the validity of debtors turnover ratios. So, too, can the valuation issue, particularly with regard to the provision of doubtful debts (that is, debts due which are regarded as potentially irrecoverable). Finally, in practice, although the ratio ought only to be concerned with credit sales, it will not be possible to separate these from the total sales reported in the income statement. Thus, the latter figure is usually adopted in the above type of computation.

Creditor payments

The above ratio for debtors can be repeated for creditors, giving the average period of credit allowed by suppliers of goods and services to the company. The ratio can take the following form:

$$ \frac{\text{Credit purchases for the period}}{\text{Creditors at the end of the period}} $$

As with sales, the figure for purchases ought to relate only to credit transactions. However, in circumstances where it is possible to obtain it (as from a value added statement), it may not be possible to distinguish credit from cash transactions, in which case the total figure should be used. In situations where not even this is possible due to lack of disclosure, the cost of sales figure may be used as a surrogate for purchases. In addition, it should be noted that the denominator, as with other turnover ratios, should be the average creditors for the period to avoid any year-end unrepresentativeness. Taking the cost of sales figures given for Illustration 55 (and adjusting for stock at t_0 £2,100, t_1 £2,000 and t_2 £3,100) and assuming creditors were £1,200 at t_0, the creditors' turnover ratios in Illustration 71 can be produced.

Illustration 71 Creditors turnover ratio

	Periods	
	t_0 to t_1	t_1 to t_2
	£	£
Purchases for the period	17,300	20,300
Average creditors for the period	1,350 *	1,700 †
= creditors turnover ratio	12.81	11.94

$$* \left[\frac{£1,200 + 1,500}{2} \right] \qquad † \left[\frac{£1,500 + 1,900}{2} \right]$$

Thus creditors have turned over nearly 13 times in period t_0 to t_1, and nearly 12 times in the next period. By dividing these ratios into 365 (again assuming annual periods), the average period of credit given to the company by its suppliers can be ascertained. In period t_0 to t_1, this amounted to 28.5 days, and in period t_1 to t_2 to 30.6 days. This indicates a slight relaxing of credit conditions by suppliers over the two periods, the average payment period being increased by 7.4 per cent. This would, of course, require comparison with other comparable statistics, but reveals a potential source of support for company liquidity if cash for creditor repayments is forthcoming more slowly than previously.

Summary

Summarizing on the above turnover ratios for stock, debtors and creditors, it seems reasonable to suggest that they can give important insights into the liquidity position of the company: the average holding time for stock indicates funds 'tied up' in stock and work-in-progress; the average collection period for debtors indicates the time taken to collect cash from customers; and the average payment period indicates the time taken to repay suppliers. In the above example, the company holds, on average, about 46 days' stock throughout the two periods while allowing, on average, approximately one month's credit to customers. The reasonableness of these data, in terms of financial efficiency, would very much depend on the nature and conditions of the trade concerned. However, allowing for this, they should provide users of the financial statements with necessary information regarding assessments of the company's future liquidity positions.

Lastly, from the various comments which have been made at different stages in these sections on liquidity, it is obvious that all such ratios are liable to window-dressing and valuation problems which could distort them and lead to misleading portrayals of liquidity. Obviously, the audit function can alleviate many of these potential problems, but the analyst must understand the frailties of the data and, particularly, the problems of comparison over time and between companies. In other words, they are no more than rough indicators of liquidity and should not be regarded as accurate measurements. Further attention will be paid to these frailties in the next chapter.

Financial ratios on a historic cost basis, and indicating financial structure and performance

A company finances itself from a variety of external sources: by issuing shares to investors; by borrowing from lenders and bankers, either on a long-term or a short-term basis, or both; and by obtaining trade credit from suppliers. The latter source has already been dealt with in the section on liquidity and, on the grounds of simplicity and availability of space, will not be the main issue for discussion here. Trade credit by its very nature tends to be a relatively temporary and short-term, but extremely important, source of finance to any company. However, its availability depends on the conditions of trading, which can vary considerably from period to period; and its cost to the company can generally be regarded as free, unless it is losing substantial cash discounts by not paying suppliers immediately.

The main aim of this section is therefore to examine the more permanent sources of finance available to the company (that is, shares and long-term loans) and, by the use of financial ratios, to assess the financial returns to investors and lenders, and the relative degrees of risk taken by these suppliers of capital. Such ratios are consequently of interest not only to investors but also to lenders, both from the point of view of assessing the risk associated with their investment and the suitability of the returns intended to compensate for such risks.

Capital yields

This is a somewhat complex aspect of investment appraisal and it should be noted at the outset that, within the context of this book, all that can be done is to adopt a 'broad-brush' approach to the subject. The yield on capital is, in general terms, equivalent to the financial return expected by the investor or lenders on his 'investment'. It is therefore also the cost to the company of financing itself either by shares or long-term loans.

At a conceptual level, capital yield can usually be regarded as the yield expected by the investor or lender on the current market value of his shares or loan stock. This, again in general terms, is the approximate relationship between the expected dividend or interest rate and the relevant current market price:

$$r = \frac{c}{p}$$

where r is the yield, c is the expected dividend or interest rate, and p is the current market price of the share or loan stock. However, given that there is a great deal of uncertainty in forecasting future dividends (loan interest rates usually remain constant throughout the period of the loan), the yield computation for shares can be based on a value for c which is equivalent to the current or immediate past dividend rate, with r being increased by a suitable percentage equivalent to the expected rate of increase in future dividends; that is,

$$r = \frac{c}{p} + g$$

where r and p are as defined above, c is the current dividend rate, and g is the estimated dividend growth rate.

It is these basic models, and adaptations of them, which will now be examined, using data provided in Illustration 55. (There is no loan capital in this example, and therefore no interest yield has been computed – although such a computation is relatively straightforward.)

Yield on share capital

The calculation of yields on ordinary shares is somewhat complex owing to the variability of the dividend rate. As mentioned above, to obtain some predictive content to the ratio, it is possible to use the current rate and supplement it with an estimated growth factor. However, the normal procedure is to relate the current dividend rate and market price of the share concerned. In this respect, the dividend rate is usually taken as the dividend per ordinary share, and the ratio is multiplied by 100 to reduce it to a percentage. Again, to avoid the variability of personal taxation, dividends per share would be expressed before deduction of tax and, using the figures supplied at the beginning of the chapter, the yields in Illustration 72 would result.

Illustration 72 Dividend yield		
		Time
	t_1	t_2
Net dividends per financial statements	£200	£300
Add: advance corporation tax, assumed to be 30% of gross dividends	86	129
Dividends before tax (1)	£286	£429
Number of ordinary shares of £1 each (2)	2,000	3,000
Dividends per £1 share unit [(1) ÷ (2)]	14.3p	14.3p
Market price of £1 share unit	£2.50	£2.40
= dividend yield (× 100)	5.72%	5.96%

Therefore, in our example, over the two periods the financial return to ordinary shareholders has increased by 4.2 per cent. The increase seems to indicate a slightly greater uncertainty and risk associated with the ordinary shares, but this would need to be compared with yields of previous periods, similar companies and alternative types of investment (such as loan stock). Estimations of future dividend yields would need to incorporate estimates of future dividends per share and market prices, but calculations based on historic cost data provide a basis for this further exercise.

Earnings yield

An alternative indicator of the financial return to the ordinary shareholder, which does not limit itself to the distributed dividend returns, is the earnings yield. This ratio relates earnings per ordinary share to the current market price of the shares concerned:

$$\frac{\text{Earnings per ordinary share}}{\text{Market price per ordinary share}} \times 100$$

Alternatively, this is more usually described in its reciprocal form as the price–earnings ratio; that is:

$$\frac{\text{Market price per ordinary share}}{\text{Earnings per ordinary share}}$$

The above ratio includes the distributable earnings per share as a measure of the financial return for investment in ordinary shares. For this purpose, it is recommended that, because of the complexities of the imputation tax system, earnings should be calculated on the basis of reported income after deduction of corporation tax and (where relevant) preference dividends. Therefore, it is not recommended that, as previously demonstrated for return on investment and earnings per share calculations, the earnings denominator in the price–earnings ratio should be grossed up at the advance corporation tax rate.

In essence, the price–earnings ratio reflects the multiple of the latest reported earnings which investors are willing to pay for the ordinary shares – the higher the multiple, the greater the periodic earnings for which investors are willing to pay. Using the data provided for Illustration 55, the price–earnings ratio can be computed as in Illustration 73.

Therefore, whereas at t_1 (and assuming the periods are annual) investors were willing to pay for a little over three years' earnings, at t_2 they were willing to purchase rather more than four years' earnings. This indicates an apparent increase in confidence in the company and rise in the estimation in which it is held by investors. This can be seen in another way by converting the ratio into its reciprocal: the earnings yield. At t_1 the yield was $100/3.13 = 31.9$ per cent, and at t_2 it was $100/4.23 = 23.6$ per cent.

Illustration 73 Price–earnings ratio

	Time	
	t_1 £	t_2 £
Market price per £1 share unit	2.50	2.400
Earnings per £1 share unit	0.80 *	0.567 †
= price–earnings ratio	3.13	4.23

$$*\left[\frac{£1,600}{2,000}\right] \qquad †\left[\frac{£1,700}{3,000}\right]$$

In other words, investors seemed to be seeking a financial reward for the degree of risk they were taking, thereby revealing that they regarded an ordinary share investment in the company as more risky at t_1 than at t_2. However, comparisons with other periods and companies would need to be conducted before these conclusions could be built into the financial profile being constructed for the company. As with other financial indicators, the reliability of the inherent data (for example, with regard to the measurement of periodic income underlying earnings per share), and its variability owing to uncontrollable factors (for example, with regard to market prices for shares), make price–earnings ratios useful, though rough, guidelines to investment behaviour. In addition, they are mainly historically based, and their users must make some attempt to amend them to allow for predictions of future changes in the basic ingredients.

Finally in this section, it should be of interest to note the difference in orientation between the two main yields; dividend and earnings. Basically, this highlights a major difference in investor objectives: some investors are interested mainly in the receipt of income from their investments (thus being concerned with dividend yield) and some are interested mainly in capital growth (thus being concerned with earnings yields as a basis for predicting future earnings, and present and future share valuations). The relative emphasis placed on each will therefore depend very much on the objectives investors are attempting to achieve.

Risk indicators on a historic cost basis

Because they indicate financial returns or rewards, the afore-mentioned yield ratios also indicate indirectly the relative risks the various providers are taking when investing in a company. A further group of ratios is specifically designed to look at this aspect of its financial structure and performance. These are as follows:

Gearing

Gearing, or leverage, is the term used to denote the relationship between ordinary share capital (with its inherent uncertainty as to dividends and capital repayments) and long-term preference share capital and loans (usually with a known and fixed dividend or interest rate and repayment terms). The higher the level of fixed rate capital to that of variable rate capital, the higher the gearing and the greater the risk of ordinary shareholders receiving diminished dividends if available income drops. Conversely, if income levels rise, the greater the chance of ordinary shareholders benefiting through increased dividends. The same sort of argument applies to capital repayments: the higher the gearing, the greater the risk of ordinary shareholders not being repaid on a liquidation. Fixed-rate capital is also affected by these propositions: the smaller the fixed-rate capital, and the lower the gearing, the greater the chance of interest and capital repayments being met when due. In other words, gearing ratios go to the heart of risk evaluation from the point of view of lenders and investors.

Gearing can be computed in two main ways; first, by comparing the relevant capital figures; and secondly, by comparing the relevant income figures. The following sections describe each approach.

The capital approach

Under this method, gearing can be defined as:

$$\frac{\text{Long-term loans} + \text{preference shares}}{\text{Ordinary shareholders' funds}}$$

(ordinary shareholders' funds being taken to mean ordinary share capital plus retained income and other relevant reserves, but excluding provisions). The numerator can also include bank overdrafts and certain provisions if these have become a permanent source of finance for the company. The ratio can be expressed either in terms of reported data (that is, based on data derived from the historic cost system) or in terms of current market prices of the loans and shares (if available). Given the significant problems of measuring accounting data, the market-based approach seems to have merit (though market-determined prices cannot be said to be fully reliable because they tend to fluctuate from day to day).

The ratio describes the relationship between funds with a fixed rate of interest or dividend, and funds provided by the ordinary shareholders: the higher the proportion of the former to the latter, the higher the so-called gearing, and the higher the risk ordinary shareholders are taking by investing in the company. If profitability is poor, the chances of income being available for the distribution of ordinary share dividends are diminished because of the high level of interest charges. Similarly, if the company were forced into liquidation, the repayment of a high level of fixed interest capital would equally diminish the ordinary shareholders' chances of capital repayment. The reverse applies if the gearing is low because of smaller interest charges and so forth.

Taking the data supplied for Illustration 55, the gearing ratios can be determined using the capital approach (Illustration 74) and the income approach (Illustration 75), both of which use reported rather than market data.

It is clear that this particular company is relatively highly geared at t_2 – there being no long-term borrowing at t_1. However, the important issue in relation to gearing is the stability of income levels so far as the company is concerned. If income is stable from period to period, then high gearing

---

Illustration 74 Gearing – 1

	Time	
	t_0	t_1
	£	£
Bank loan	—	2,000
Share capital + retained income	3,900	5,300
= gearing ($\times$ 100)	—	37.74%

---

does not indicate the same degree of risk as in a situation where income levels are liable to fluctuate from period to period. Thus it is important for the analyst to incorporate his gearing ratios into his company profile, particularly in relation to his analysis of income trends. The nature of the latter, coupled with gearing, will provide him with an indicator of the degree of risk associated with ordinary share investment. In addition, the same points apply to assessing risk *vis-à-vis* preference or loan capital: the higher the gearing and the more unstable the income levels, the greater the risk of fixed interest rate and capital repayments not being met when due.

The income approach

The alternative method of computing gearing is to relate fixed interest or dividend payments to reported income available for such payments. In other words, gearing would be defined as:

$$\frac{\text{Gross interest payments}}{\text{Income before interest and tax}} \quad (for fixed interest capital)$$

and

$$\frac{\text{Ordinary dividends}}{\text{Income available for ordinary dividends}} \quad (for ordinary share capital)$$

Taking the figures given at the beginning of the chapter, this would result for fixed interest capital in the ratios given in Illustration 75.

This means that, in the period t_1 to t_2, interest payments were covered 16 times ($100 \div 6.25$). Therefore, with income at these particular levels, the degree of risk associated with possible non-payment of interest is

---

Illustration 75 Gearing – 2

	Periods	
	t_0 to t_1 £	t_1 to t_2 £
Loan interest	—	200
Income before interest and tax	2,700	3,200
= interest cover ($\times$ 100)	—	6.25%

---

relatively small. Ordinary shareholders, too, would be interested to see this high interest cover since it indicates that the risk of non-payment of ordinary dividends is small in view of the comparatively high level of distributable income after deduction of interest payments.

The particular 'risk' ratio for ordinary share capital is normally referred to as the dividend cover, and represents the proportion of available income distributed in the form of ordinary share dividends. It therefore also indicates the margin by which available income would have to fall before it leads to a reduction in the current level of distributed ordinary share dividends. Owing to the effects of the imputation tax system in the UK, it is suggested that the income denominator in the ratio be grossed up at the effective rate of advance corporation tax, thereby giving an income figure which is the maximum distributable for the period. This would then be compared with the gross dividend before deduction of the relevant advance corporation tax, both numerator and denominator being expressed in 'before tax' terms. The alternative treatment which could be adopted involves using (a) income after deduction of corporation tax, loan interest and preference dividend payments; and (b) ordinary dividends after deduction of advance corporation tax. Taking the figures provided in Illustration 55, the ratios in Illustration 76 apply for ordinary share capital.

Illustration 76 Dividend cover

	Periods	
	t_0 to t_1 £	t_1 to t_2 £
Ordinary share dividend (gross)*	286	429
Available income grossed up at the advance corporation tax rate†	2,286	2,429
= dividend cover ($\times$ 100)	12.51%	17.66%

*for period $t_0 - t_1$, £200 + 86; and for period $t_1 - t_2$, £300 + 129; assuming an advance corporation tax rate of 30 per cent.

†for period $t_0 - t_1$, £1,600 + 686, and for period $t_1 - t_2$, £1,700 + 729; again assuming a tax rate of 30 per cent.

These ratios reveal that ordinary dividends were covered 8 times $(1.000 \div 0.1251)$ in the first period, and 5.66 times $(1.000 \div 0.1766)$ in the second period. The figures indicate a 'margin of safety' for ordinary shareholders in both periods, the margin decreasing somewhat in the second one. In other words, available income would need to fall by approximately 87 per cent in period t_0 to t_1 $(100-13$ per cent) and by 82 per cent in period t_1 to t_2 $(100-18$ per cent) before the ordinary dividends paid for these periods could not be distributed from the available income for the period. It also indicates that 87 and 82 per cent, respectively, of the available income of the two periods has been retained in the company, thereby aiding its maintenance and development.

A summarized profile of the company on a historic cost basis

The major ratios which could be used to construct a profile of a company for decision-making purposes have now been explained. It is useful to gather these together so as to comment on any profile which emerges. The ratios selected for this purpose are those measures using recommended and traditional practices, and allow for the present system of company taxation. It should also be noted that the profile is a limited one owing to the data being restricted to two periods. For this reason, it would be difficult to apply trend analysis techniques to such a limited series. Illustration 77 contains the summary of ratios computed in the previous sections of this chapter (all figures have been taken to one decimal place).

Given the limitations of the data available, the analyst should be able to discern the following points which could affect the nature of the decisions to be taken:

First, the profitability of the company seems to be deteriorating in terms of the return on investment but not in terms of earnings per share and income margins obtained on sales revenue (which have both improved slightly). Overall, management during the second period does not appear to have made more profitable use of the company's resources than in the first period. If this lack of progress were maintained, it would not augur well for shareholders, lenders, creditors and employees alike, in the sense that increasing profitability is a major factor contributing to the long-term success and survival of the company.

Secondly, in addition to its lack of progress in terms of profitability over the two periods, the company's liquidity position has deteriorated. Although its working capital position at the end of both periods reveals an excess of current assets over current liabilities, its quick ratio has decreased by 57 per cent. This should be of some concern to all interested groups, but particularly to existing and potential creditors and lenders. Repayment of their claims depends on the availability of liquid resources to meet them.

The worsening liquidity position can be seen in the more detailed figures, with stock levels being maintained throughout at a fairly high

Illustration 77 A summarized financial profile

	Periods	
	t_0 to t_1	t_1 to t_2
Profitability		
Return on investment	58.6%[a]	45.8%[a]
Earnings per share	53.3p[b]	56.7p[b]
Income margin	10.8%[c]	11.0%[c]
Liquidity		
Working capital	2.18	1.51
Quick ratio	1.46	0.63
Stock turnover	8.49	7.53
Debtors turnover	33.33	32.22
Creditors turnover	12.81	11.94
Financial structure		
Dividend yield	5.7%	6.0%
Price-earnings ratio	3.13	4.23
Gearing	— %[d]	37.7%[d]
Loan interest cover	— %[e]	6.3%[e]
Dividend cover	8.00[f]	5.66[f]

Notes

(a)   Income after deduction of corporation tax, grossed up at the advance corporation tax rate, and related to shareholders' equity.

(b)   Income after deduction of corporation tax, related to ordinary share units.

(c)   Income before deduction of interest or corporation tax, related to sales revenue.

(d)   Debenture capital related to shareholders' equity as reported.

(e)   Gross debenture interest related to income before deduction of interest and corporation tax.

(f)   Gross ordinary dividend related to income after deduction of corporation tax but grossed up at the advance corporation tax rate.

level, debtors being given slightly more time to pay, and creditors having to be paid less quickly. The long-term survival of the company depends on its ability to meet its obligations and, if the position at t_2 continues to deteriorate in the future, there is the danger of the company in the longer term being less and less able to pay creditors, repay the bank loan or pay interest and dividends (despite its increasing profitability). In the long term, creditors may cease to give credit; lenders may cease to lend; and shareholders may cease to receive dividends. The above figures give all concerned some indication of that possibility occurring unless the company can stabilize or improve its liquidity by rigorous financial management of working capital.

Thirdly, the yield on share capital has changed relatively slightly over the two periods. The significance of this change and the absolute figures are difficult to comment on since there is a lack of data relating to such yields in general and to interest rates in the economy as a whole. However, the substantial increase of 35 per cent in the price–earnings ratio indicates an improvement in the stock market's estimation of the earnings potential of the company; at t_1 it was prepared to pay for earnings of approximately three periods, but by t_2 it was willing to pay for much more than four periods' earnings. Thus, despite apparently worsening profitability and liquidity records, it seems that investors have a higher opinion of its future at t_2 than was the case at t_1. Thus, either the company's shares may have been under-priced at t_1, for reasons other than its financial condition (and the t_2 price reflects a correction of this), or the shares may be over-priced at t_2 for similar reasons. Readers are reminded of earlier comments about investor behaviour and stock market prices (in Chapter 6) which tend to make indicators, such as the price–earnings ratio, somewhat difficult to interpret. Movements in it, as well as the absolute figures, would require to be compared with ratios for comparable companies – as for the interest and dividend yields.

Fourthly, somewhat in contradiction to the price–earnings situation, the degree of risk being taken by the shareholders in the company seems to have somewhat increased over the two periods. The dividend cover has been reduced significantly, although still providing indications of substantial 'cushions' of income to maintain existing levels of interest and dividend distributions in the future. In addition, a gearing position has been introduced in period t_1 to t_2, thereby increasing shareholders' risk. However, the latter factor still remains at a relatively low level at t_2, and can be presumed to be a contributing factor to the increasing price–earnings ratio (which, when looked at in its reciprocal form, is the earnings yield: the earnings return on the market value of the shares). That is, an increasing price–earnings ratio indicates a lower earnings yield which, in turn, indicates that investors are looking for a lower return on their investment to compensate for the degree of risk they believe they are taking.

And fifthly, in summary, the company appears to be a relatively profitable one with a deteriorating liquidity position and a degree of risk associated with ordinary share investment. These factors, assuming they are examined over a longer period of time and compared with those of other similar companies, would appear to provide useful data for incorporation in the decision models of shareholders, lenders and creditors, as well as being of interest to other users of the company's financial statements.

Selected discussion or essay topics; and selected bibliography

Because of the inter-relationship of topics in Chapters 10, 11 and 12, this material is provided at the end of Chapter 12.

12
Extensions to financial ratio analysis

Introduction

The above descriptions of the main financial ratios which can be derived mainly from reported accounting information ignore the limitations of the historic cost and realization principles upon which they are based; and the potential flexibility of accounting practice. In particular, they pay no heed to the possibility of (a) producing financial ratios while accounting for the increased cost of replacing the company's assets, and of allowing for the maintenance of its capital in physical rather than monetary terms; and (b) manipulating financial ratios through accounting practice variations.

In Chapters 7 and 8, the major problems in accounting were outlined and explained. The main principles of current cost accounting were introduced in Chapter 3 – that is, adjustments being made in the income statement to allow for the increased cost of replacing working capital and fixed assets (having also allowed for the incidence of long-term borrowing in the future to partly finance this); and further adjustments being made in the balance sheet to enable it to be described in terms mainly of current replacement costs. Chapter 8 also discussed the need to reduce accounting flexibility by means of the process of standardization. This chapter takes each of these issues and relates them to the production and use of financial ratios – mainly to reveal the effects that current cost accounting and accounting flexibility have on such derived data. The first section will deal with current cost accounting information and ratios.

Current costs and financial ratios

The summarized current cost statements of the company being analysed in this chapter are given in Illustration 78. The intention in this section of the book is to produce and describe certain of the main financial ratios based on current cost data. Because of the newness of the latter topic, much of the computations and descriptions must be regarded as tentative. The ratios, and the basis of computation, are similar to those described above in the various illustrations in Chapter 11.

Illustration 78 Basic data for analysis

COMPANY LTD
Group Current Cost Income Statement for the Period t_1 to t_2

	t_0 to t_1 £	t_1 to t_2 £
Historic cost income before deduction of interest and taxation	2,700	3,200
Less: current cost operating adjustments:		
additional cost of sales	900	800
provision for increase in monetary working capital	50	60
total provision for increased cost of working capital	950	860
additional depreciation of fixed assets	20	140
	970	1,000
Current cost operating income	1,730	2,200
Add: gearing adjustment	—	300
Less: loan interest paid	—	200
	—	100
Current cost income before taxation	1,730	2,300
Less: taxation on group income for the period	1,100	1,300
Current cost income attributable to shareholders	630	1,000
Less: dividend proposed for the period	200	300
Current cost income retained	430	700

continued overleaf

Illustration 78 continued

Group Current Cost Balance Sheet as at t_2

	t_1			t_2		
	£	£	£	£	£	£
Fixed assets						
Intangible asset						
Goodwill			200			200
Tangible asset						
Plant at valuation		840			7,560	
Less: aggregate depreciation		360	480		1,650	5,910
			680			6,110
Current assets						
Stock		2,100			3,400	
Debtors		800			1,000	
Cash at bank		3,300			1,200	
		6,200			5,600	
Creditors: amounts falling due within one year						
Creditors	1,500			1,900		
Taxation	1,100			1,300		
Dividends	200	2,800		300	3,500	
Net current assets			3,400			2,100
Total assets less current liabilities			4,080			8,210
Creditors: amounts falling due after more than one year						
Bank loan			—			(2,000)
			4,080			6,210
Capital and reserves						
Called up share capital			2,000			3,000
Share premium account			500			—
Revaluation reserve			1,190			2,670
Profit and loss account			390			540
			4,080			6,210

Profitability ratios

The first ratio is to examined is the return on investment – the numerator being current cost income after deduction of corporation tax, grossed up at the advance corporation tax rate, and related to shareholders' equity which is also expressed in current cost terms (Illustration 79).

Illustration 79 Current cost return on investment

		Periods	
		t_0 *to* t_1	t_1 *to* t_2
		£	£
Current cost income after tax		630	1,000
Add: advance corporation tax: 3/7		270	429
Maximum dividends distributable		900	1,429
Return on investment =	Maximum dividends	900	1,429
	Shareholders' equity	4,080	6,210
		22.1%	23%

(all expressed in current cost terms)

Thus, despite the 'revaluation' of shareholders' equity in current cost terms at t_1 and t_2, the returns on investment are considerably less than the equivalent historic cost data (which were 58.6 per cent and 45.8 per cent, respectively, for periods t_0 to t_1 and t_1 to t_2). The main reason for this is due to the current cost deductions for additional cost of sales, monetary working capital and depreciation (all net of the gearing factor). In other words, when taking into account specific price inflation, the company is far less profitable than seems to be the case with historic cost data. This can also be seen when the current cost earnings per share data are produced (Illustration 80).

Illustration 80 Current cost earnings per share

	Periods	
	t_0 *to* t_1	t_1 *to* t_2
Current cost income after tax	£630	£1,000
Number of £1 share units*	3,000	3,000
= earnings per share	21p	33.3p
*allowing for the bonus issue in t_1-t_2		

The above figures compare with the historic cost equivalents of 53.3p (period t_0 to t_1) and 56.7p (period t_1 to t_2).

Current cost accounting produces similar reductions in these performance ratios when income margins are examined (Illustration 81).

Illustration 81 Current cost income margin		
	Periods	
	t_0 to t_1 £	t_1 to t_2 £
Current cost income before deduction of interest and tax	1,730	2,500
Total sales revenue for period	25,000	29,000
= income margin ($\times$ 100)	6.9%	8.6%

In summary, therefore, the various current cost adjustments appear to have done much to disturb the relativity of these ratios – over the two periods, the return on investment has increased by 4 per cent (the historic cost change was a decrease of 22 per cent); earnings per share have increased by 58.6 per cent (the historic cost increase was 6.4 per cent); and the income margin has increased by 24.6 per cent (the historic cost increase was 1.9 per cent). Thus, the relative picture has changed significantly using this basis. But so too has the absolute position. In all cases for each period, the current cost ratios have considerably lower absolute values than their historic cost equivalents because of the required current cost adjustments.

The reduction in absolute amounts was to be expected – companies are not as profitable as they seem during times of inflation, unless some attempt is made to adjust the somewhat misleading historic cost figures. However, as in this case, when the absolute figures are reduced dramatically by the current cost adjustments, then any relative movement in them from period to period is accentuated – in other words, current cost accounting can increase the volatility of the reporting company's income measures.

Again, this should not be surprising – for example, with the return on capital employed, the current cost accounting process reduces the income numerator (because of the various current cost adjustments) and decreases the capital denominator (because of the transfer of these adjustments and further unrealized asset valuations to reserve). With the income adjustments, for every £ deducted in arriving at the income numerator, a £ can be added to the capital denominator.

Liquidity ratios

The overall ratio of liquidity is the working capital ratio comparing current assets with current liabilities. The effect of current cost accounting on this ratio is mainly to change the historic cost-based current asset numerator by the amount that stock and, where relevant, work-in-progress have been revalued in current cost terms. Using the figures provided in Illustration 78, the current cost-based working capital ratio is as follows (Illustration 82).

Illustration 82 Current cost working capital ratio

	Time	
	t_1	t_2
	£	£
Current assets	6,200	5,600
Current liabilities	2,800	3,500
= working capital ratio	2.21	1.6

Thus, due to the upwards revaluations of stock at t_1 and t_2, the working capital ratio has slightly improved in current cost terms compared with historic cost terms – that is, current liabilities appear to be better covered. This could be argued to mean little, given that the improvement has come about as a result of the revaluation of an asset which may not be available immediately to cover such obligations. However, it could also be argued that the current cost figure which is included in the working capital ratio is a useful surrogate for the realizable value of that stock and, therefore, that the current asset figure is a reasonable description of the liquid or potentially liquid resources available to meet known short-term liabilities. Much, however, will depend in the saleability of stock and, thus, as in conventional analysis, the quick ratio may be preferred to the working capital one.

The quick ratio is not affected by current cost accounting because it excludes stock and work-in-progress from its computation. Similarly, the sales turnover ratio contains no figure usually affected by current cost adjustments. Thus, in the liquidity area, the remaining ratios which could be influenced by the latter are (a) the stock turnover ratio; and (b) the creditors turnover ratio.

The usual stock turnover ratio is based on a comparison of periodic cost of sales, and closing or average stock and work-in-progress, in order to determine on average how many times stock was replaced during the period (or the number of days of stock held on average by the company before it was replaced). The current cost equivalent of this ratio would be as follows (Illustration 83) using the current cost data supplied in

Illustration 83 Current cost stock turnover ratio

	Periods	
	t_0 to t_1	t_1 to t_2
	£	£
Historic cost of sales + additional current cost of sales adjustment	17,400 + 900	19,200 + 800
Average current cost stock for the period	$\dfrac{2,150 + 2,100}{2}$	$\dfrac{2,100 + 3,400}{2}$
= current cost stock turnover ratio	8.6	7.3

Illustration 78 (assume the current cost of stock held at t_0 was £2,150).

The average holding time for stock (in current cost terms) was therefore $365/8.6 = 42$ days (period t_0 to t_1) and $365/7.3 = 50$ days (period t_1 to t_2). Conversion of the basic historic cost data into current cost terms puts the numerator and denominator on the same price basis – the average current cost for the period. It therefore avoids the problem of using outdated historic cost data as in the conventional ratio. With the numerator and denominator both in the same terms, the comparison tends to reflect the frequency of replacing stock during the periods concerned in terms of current prices, and thereby avoids distorting the ratio by comparing prices of different periods.

Using current costs in this example, stock was replaced on average every 42 days in period t_0 to t_1 and every 50 days in period t_1 to t_2 – thus suggesting that the average period for holding stock in current cost terms increased by 19 per cent between the two periods. However, these figures do not necessarily differ significantly from the figures obtained for the historic cost data (mainly because both the numerator and the denominator have been adjusted by relevant current cost measurements during the periods concerned). The period of holding stock using historic cost data increased by 13 per cent between the two periods – from 43 to 48.5 days.

The creditors turnover ratio relates purchases to creditors to ascertain the average number of days of credit being obtained from suppliers. If purchases data are being used, then current cost accounting ought not to distort the ratio – both numerator and denominator being expressed in average current cost terms. However, if the cost of sales figure is being used as a surrogate for purchases, it will be required to be upgraded to current cost terms by the appropriate current cost of sales adjustment, thus arguably giving a numerator expressed in the same price terms as the creditor figure. Using the data in Illustration 78, and assuming creditors at t_0 of £1,200, Illustration 84 provides such a ratio.

Illustration 84 Current cost creditors turnover		
	Periods	
	t_0 to t_1	t_1 to t_2
	£	£
Historic cost of sales + additional current cost of sales adjustment	17,400 + 900	19,200 + 800
Average creditors for the period	1,200 + 1,500	1,500 + 1,900
	2	2
= creditors turnover ratio	13.6	11.8

Thus, for period t_0 to t_1, the average terms of credit have been nearly 27 days ($365/13.6$) and for period t_1 to t_2, they have been nearly 31 days

(365/11.8) – an extension of 15 per cent in these terms. This compares with the historic cost, purchases-based figures (Illustration 71) of 12.8 and 11.9, respectively – a decrease of 7 per cent. This reveals that augmenting the historic cost of sales by a current cost adjustment does not necessarily provide a reasonable surrogate for the purchases figure which ought to be used as the numerator of the ratio.

Capital yields

It is to be expected that, once current cost data become more widely available, then investors will 'build' this information into market prices. Indeed, it could be argued that existing market prices already allow for these data as a result of the workings of the so-called 'efficient' market. However, at the present time, the use of market values in relation to current cost data (particularly in the price–earnings ratio) could be misleading. The calculation for the latter ratio is exactly as before (Illustration 73) except the earnings per share numerator is in current cost terms (as per Illustration 80). The dividend yield remains as per Illustration 72 because the calculation of dividend per share is unaffected by current cost adjustments.

Gearing

The final group of ratios concerns the gearing of the company. Using the capital approach, it is relatively apparent that the comparison of long-term borrowing with shareholders' equity in current cost terms will decrease the gearing factor because of the increase in reserves resulting from the revaluation of assets to allow for unrealized value changes or holding gains. It can be argued in these circumstances that failure to allow for these revaluations in the historic cost gearing ratio, tends to overstate the gearing because of the understatement of shareholders' equity. This can be seen in Illustration 85 which is based on the data in Illustration 78 (only period t_1 to t_2 is covered because of the lack of long-term borrowings in period t_0 to t_1).

Illustration 85 Current cost capital gearing	
	Time
	t_2
	£
Bank loan	2,000
Share capital and reserves	6,210
= gearing ($\times$ 100)	32.21%

The above ratio compares with that of 37.74 per cent using historic cost data, and reflects the possible overstatement of gearing due to the omission of current values for assets in the traditional reporting system.

Gearing can also be reflected in the interest and dividend cover ratios. By relating interest and dividend payments (or proposals) to income available to cover such figures, it is possible to assess how much of a 'cushion' there is available to cover these items. Both are affected by current cost accounting because of adjustments to the covering income – that is, if income is taken as current cost income before interest and tax (for interest) and current cost income grossed up at the advance corporation tax rate (for dividends), the two 'cover' figures can be demonstrated to be different from their historic cost equivalents. Using the current cost data supplied in Illustration 78, the relevant ratios are as follows (Illustrations 86 and 87).

Illustration 86 Current cost interest cover

	Period t_1 to t_2 £
Loan interest	200
Current cost income before interest and tax	2,500
= interest cover ($\times$ 100)	8%

There was no interest payment in period t_0 to t_1 but the current cost figures for period t_1 to t_2 reveal that the relevant interest payment has been covered 12.5 times ($100 \div 8$) compared with 16 times ($100 \div 6.25$) for historic cost data. In other words, the current cost adjustments reduce the income available to cover interest.

Illustration 87 Current cost dividend cover

	Periods	
	t_0 to t_1 £	t_1 to t_2 £
Ordinary share dividend (gross)*	286	429
Available current cost income grossed up at the advance corporation tax rate†	900	1,429
= dividend cover ($\times$ 100)	31.78%	30%

*For period t_0–t_1, £200 + 86; and for period t_1–t_2, £300 + 129; assuming an advance corporation tax rate of 30%.
†For period t_0–t_1, £630 + 270; and for period t_1–t_2, £1,000 + 429; again assuming a tax rate of 30%.

The current cost cover for dividends has increased slightly between the periods – from 3.15 times ($100 \div 31.78$) to 3.33 times ($100 \div 30$). But this compares unfavourably with the historic cost equivalents of 8 and 5.66 times, respectively (Illustration 76) – again revealing the effect of current cost accounting: far less income being available to cover dividends than is the case with traditional accounting.

Summary

Illustration 88 summarizes the above results using the data provided and compares them with their historic cost equivalents (HCA = historic cost data and CCA = current cost data).

Illustration 88 Comparative summary of ratios

	t_0 to t_1		t_1 to t_2	
	HCA	CCA	HCA	CCA
Profitability				
Return on investment	58.6%	22.1%	45.8%	23.0%
Earnings per share	53.3p	21.0p	56.7p	33.3p
Income margin	10.8%	6.9%	11.0%	8.6%
Liquidity				
Working capital	2.18	2.21	1.51	1.60
Quick ratio	1.46	1.46	0.63	0.63
Stock turnover	8.49	8.60	7.53	7.30
Debtors turnover	33.33	33.33	32.22	32.22
Creditors turnover	12.81	13.60	11.94	11.80
Financial structure				
Dividend yield	5.7%	5.7%	6.0%	6.0%
Price–earnings ratio	3.13	N/A	4.23	N/A
Gearing	— %	— %	37.7%	32.2%
Loan interest cover	— %	— %	6.3%	8.0%
Dividend cover	8.00	3.15	5.66	3.33

The following ratios are relatively unaffected by current cost accounting – the quick ratio, debtors turnover and dividend yield. The price–earnings ratio cannot be computed until market prices can be said to allow for reported cost data. The remaining ratios, however, are affected by the latter. In this case, the primary indicators have been considerably reduced in each period – whatever the type of indicator. In the liquidity section, the working capital, stock turnover, and creditors turnover figures have also been affected; although not as dramatically as in the income area. A similar analysis can be made of the financial structure area – the gearing ratio being changed by CCA but not as much as the income-orientated interest and dividend cover figures. In other words, CCA adjustments affect most ratios – some more extensively than others. Those most affected are those involving income; those least affected are those involving mainly balance sheet items. Considerable thought and experience, however, will require to be applied to the computation and use of CCA-based ratios. The above analysis can only be regarded as a first attempt.

Accounting flexibility and financial ratios

Unless accounting standards are prescribed in the most rigid way (that is, no choice being given), it is always possible to describe the financial results of a company in different ways. Different interpretations of standards, as well as subjective judgements, create this flexibility, and it is therefore relatively obvious that the potential flexibility of accounting measurements affects ratios as well as reports. It is the aim of this section of the text to demonstrate briefly and simply how different measures of the same activity can be used to compute different ratios for analysis purposes. Rather than concentrate on different interpretations of pre-scribed accounting standards (which tend to change over time), the examples which follow will be concerned with variations in matters of subjective judgement when financial reports are prepared. Certain of the main financial ratios described in this and the previous chapters will be dealt with in this way to demonstrate the flexibility issue.

Return on investment

In Illustration 55, new plant purchased during period t_1 to t_2 for £6,000 was depreciated on a straight-line basis over a 6 year life – that is, in t_1 to

---

Illustration 89 Return on investment and flexibility

	Period t_1 to t_2 £
Income after straight-line depreciation and taxation (as per Illustration 55)	1,700
Less: additional reducing balance depreciation (40% × £6,000−1,000)	1,400
	300
Add: advance corporation tax assumed thereon 3/7	129
Maximum dividends distributable	429
Capital employed (as per Illustration 55)	5,300
Less: additional depreciation written off plant	1,400
Amended capital employed	3,900

$$\text{Return on investment} = \frac{£429}{£3,900} = 11\%$$

---

t_2, £1,000 was deducted from profits in arriving at the post-tax income of £1,700. Illustration 89 describes what the return on investment for period t_1 to t_2 would be if a 40 per cent reducing balance method of depreciation had been adopted instead (40 per cent being the approximate rate required under the latter method to write off most of the cost of the plant over 6 years).

The new return of 11 per cent compares with that of 45.8 per cent using the straight-line basis. In other words, although the basic operational features of the situation have not changed the return on investment has fallen by 76 per cent from 45.8 per cent to 11 per cent merely by the use of an alternative and acceptable method of depreciation. As the cost of the plant is finite, however, the two methods of depreciation would produce the reverse effect in later years of its life – for example, in year 5 of its life, straight-line depreciation would be £1,000 and its reducing balance equivalent would be £311 – thus resulting in a higher return on investment using the latter, compared with using the former.

Earnings per share

A similar effect can be obtained in the earnings per share ratio. Using the same data as above for period t_1 to t_2, and assuming the situation in Illustration 55, the ratio is amended in Illustration 90.

Illustration 90 Earnings per share and flexibility	
	Period t_1 *to* t_2 £
Income after straight-line depreciation and taxation (as per Illustration 55)	1,700
Less: additional reducing balance depreciation (see Illustration 89)	1,400
Amended earnings after tax	300
Number of £1 share units	3,000
Earnings per share $= \dfrac{£300}{3,000} = 10\text{p}$	

Thus, because of a perfectly acceptable alternative method of depreciation, earnings per share can be described as 10p per share instead of 56.7p. Again, it is only fair to say that these variations would be reversed over the useful life of the asset, but the point is that the trend of figures (in ratio terms) would be completely different over that time – being higher under straight-line accounting in the early years, and lower in the later years.

Extensions to financial ratio analysis

Income margin

The income margin would be influenced in precisely the same way as demonstrated in the above example (using depreciation accounting as the variable). This section examines similar manipulations by varying the stock valuations. Assume for this purpose that, at t_1, the stock valuation was estimated at £1,500 (instead of £2,000 as in Illustration 55), certain stock being regarded as potentially unsaleable. Illustration 91 contains the income margin computation for periods t_0 to t_1 and t_1 to t_2 (based on those in Illustration 62).

Illustration 91 Income margin and flexibility

	Periods	
	t_0 to t_1	t_1 to t_2
	£	£
Income before deduction of tax and interest	2,700	3,200
Less (add): reduction in original stock		
valuation at t_1 (£2,000–1,500)	500	(500)
*Amended income after tax**	2,200	3,700
Sales revenue	25,000	29,000
Income margin $\dfrac{£2,200}{£25,000}$; $\dfrac{£3,700}{£29,000}$	8.8%	12.8%

*The reduction in stock at t_1 has the effect of reducing income for period t_0 to t_1, and increasing income for period t_1 to t_2 (in the latter case because cost of sales is reduced by the decreased opening stock at t_1).

When the stock valuation at t_1 was £2,000, the income margins were 10.8 per cent and 11 per cent, respectively, for periods t_0 to t_1 and t_1 to t_2. The £1,500 stock valuation changes these margins to 8.8 per cent and 12.8 per cent, respectively, thus transforming the trend of margin and the way in which the performances of these two periods can be compared – one stock valuation showing the first period's performance to be similar to that of the next; but the other valuation revealing the first period's performance to have improved by 45 per cent in the next.

Working capital

The comparison of current assets and liabilities in the working capital ratio can also be influenced by accounting flexibility. Taking the stock example used in the previous section, the working capital ratios for the two periods are as follows (taking the stock valuation at t_1 to be £1,500 instead of £2,000) (Illustration 92).

Illustration 92 Working capital ratio and flexibility

	Time	
	t_1 £	t_2 £
Current assets as per Illustration 55	6,100	5,300
Less: adjustment to reduce stock to £1,500	500	—
Amended current assets	5,600	5,300
Current liabilities as per Illustration 55	2,800	3,500
Working capital ratio $\dfrac{£5,600}{£2,800}$; $\dfrac{£5,300}{£3,500}$	2	1.51

Thus, the ratio appears to have deteriorated by 24.5 per cent between the two periods (compared with 30.7 per cent using the £2,000 valuation). In other words, yet again, a matter of judgement can alter key indicators of the company's performance and position.

Quick ratio

The quick ratio would not be affected by the above stock example, but could be influenced by, say, a judgement on debtors valuation. For example, using the data supplied in Illustrations 55 and 68, assume debtors at t_1 are reduced by a provision for doubtful debts of £200 and, at t_2, of £300 (Illustration 93).

Illustration 93 Quick ratio and flexibility

	Time	
	t_1 £	t_2 £
Current assets minus stock	4,100	2,200
Less: doubtful debt provision	200	300
Amended quick assets	3,900	1,900
Current liabilities	2,800	3,500
Quick ratio $\dfrac{£3,900}{£2,800}$; $\dfrac{£1,900}{£3,500}$	1.39	0.54

These figures are somewhat different from the originals of 1.46 and 0.63, respectively, and display a deterioration of 61 per cent between the periods (compared with the original reduction of 57 per cent).

Note The other liquidity ratios can also be achieved by different accounting judgments – for example, (a) in the stock turnover ratio, any change to stock valuations (as in Illustration 92) will alter the cost of sale numerator and the stock denominator (using the £500 valuation reduction in Illustration 92, the t_0 to t_1 ratio would be 9.67 compared with the original figure of 8.49 in Illustration 69); and (b) in the debtors turnover ratio, any change in debtors will alter it (for example, using the £200 and £300 reductions in Illustration 70, the ratios for the periods t_0 to t_1 and t_1 to t_2 become 38.46 and 44.62, respectively, compared with 33.33 and 32.22, respectively, for data without the provisions for bad debts).

Earnings yield

Although the dividend yield is unaffected by accounting judgements, the earnings yield is so influenced. Because it relies on the earnings per share datum, the price–earnings ratio can be altered by the particular methods applied to the measurement of earnings. For example, assuming the t_2 share price given in Illustration 55, and the amended earnings per share figure in Illustration 90, the earnings yield is as follows (Illustration 94).

Illustration 94 Price earnings ratio and flexibility	
	t_2
	£
Market price per £1 share unit	2.40
Amended earnings per £1 share unit	0.10
= price–earnings ratio	24

Of course it can be argued that the market may adjust the share price to accommodate the anticipated earnings based on the different depreciation policy (the efficient markets hypothesis would assume such an ability). However, it is doubtful if the share price could properly reflect a future accounting judgement, and the above ratio can be seen to be totally different from the original at t_2 of 4.23.

Gearing

The important financial indicator of gearing is affected by accounting flexibility – in the capital version, because the retained income figure in the denominator can be altered; and in the income version, because the income denominator can be so influenced. For example, assuming the additional depreciation deduction of £1,400 (in Illustration 89), and the gearing data in Illustration 74 and 75, the following gearing and cover measures can be prepared (Illustration 95).

Both these ratios are considerably different from the originals in Chapter 11 (which were 37.7 per cent and 6.3 per cent, respectively). The changed depreciation method has appeared to reduce materially the

Illustration 95 Gearing and flexibility

	Time t_1 £
Bank loan	2,000
Share capital + retained income*	3,900
= gearing ($\times$ 100)	51.3%

*minus additional depreciation of £1,400

	Period t_1-t_2 £
Loan interest	200
Income before interest and tax*	1,800
= gearing ($\times$ 100)	11.1%

*minus additional depreciation of £1,400

income cover for loan interest payments, and to heighten the company's gearing to a more serious level. Yet it is basically the same company; the same operations, only different accounting.

Dividend cover

Finally, and following on from the previous section, it is reasonably obvious that the dividend cover ratio can be altered by alterations to the income denominator. For example, taking the stock change of £500 at t_1 (in Illustration 91), the data in Illustration 76 can be changed as follows (Illustration 96).

Illustration 96 Dividend cover and flexibility

	Periods	
	t_0 to t_1 £	t_1 to t_2 £
Ordinary share dividend grossed up at the advance corporation tax rate	286	429
Income grossed up at the advance corporation tax rate	1,571*	3,143†
= dividend cover ($\times$ 100)	18.2%	13.6%

*£1,600 − 500	= £1,100	†£1,700 + 500	= £2,200
add: 3/7 × £1,100	= 471	*add*: 3/7 × £2,200	= 943
	£1,571		£3,143

The above cover compares with the equivalent figures of 12.5 per cent and 17.7 per cent, respectively, using the alternative stock valuation of £2,000. The influence of different accounting practices is once again demonstrated, the periodic data being reversed.

Summary

Each of the above illustrations in this section has sought to demonstrate how different accounting judgements in making accounting measurements can produce materially different data for purposes of producing key financial ratios. Thus, if it is assumed that ratios are a useful input to a variety of decisions, it can also be reasonably assumed that, at least in the short term, decision makers could have their decisions altered simply by the use of different accounting judgements by the producers of financial reports. Despite the existence of prescribed accounting standards, the inherent flexibility of accounting practice must be guarded against by anyone making use of reported accounting information.

Suggested discussion or essay topics (covering Chapters 10, 11 and 12)

1 The main aim of financial ratio analysis is to construct a financial profile of the company being examined. What is the general nature of this profile; what are its constituent parts; and why is it so important to the analyst?
2 If, as Henry Ford stated, 'all history is bunk', why should decision-makers find financial ratios useful when, as is generally the case, they are based on historical data?
3 The use of a single indicator of company profitability, liquidity or financial structure for investment or other decision-making purposes could be extremely misleading. Explain, and outline an alternative approach to the use of financial ratios.
4 Financial ratios are only as good as the accounting information upon which they are based. Discuss.
5 The return on investment is an example of the difficulty of attempting to assess company profitability by using financial ratios. What are the main problems involved in relation to such returns?
6 Assuming return on investment ratios as comparisons of income before deduction of tax and loan interest with total assets, you are required to comment on the significance of the following comparative returns (all figures are percentages), particularly with regard to those of the individual company:

Period	Individual company	Manufacturing companies* Quoted	Unquoted
$t_0 - t_1$	22	15	19
$t_1 - t_2$	29	17	20
$t_2 - t_3$	20	17	18

*These data would be averages taken from government statistics.

7 Current investment practice places considerable emphasis on company earnings per share. Discuss why this should be so, indicating the problems associated with its computation.

8 The price–earnings ratio of a company increases from 8 to 10. Explain the significance of this change to the potential investor, and its possible impact on his investment decision. Also comment on these matters if the ratio had fallen from 8 to 5.

9 Indicators of company liquidity are of vital interest to all concerned with assessing company performance. Discuss.

10 The working capital ratio was the sole indicator of company performance during the early part of the twentieth century. Discuss the use to which it was put; its limitations (if any); and the reasons why it has not remained as the primary indicator.

11 A company can be profitable and yet become bankrupt because of lack of liquid resources. Explain how this can be so, and the relevance of financial ratio analysis in providing indicators of such a potential situation.

12 A company's working capital ratio at three successive points of time has been 1.0, 0.6 and 0.2, respectively. Explain the meaning of these ratios; the significance of the trend; the possible reasons for the trend; and the implications of the figures for the investor, lender and creditor.

13 What is meant by the term 'yield' in relation to share and loan investment, and what significance does it hold for the investor and lender?

14 The dividend yield on the ordinary shares of a quoted company was 9 per cent at a time when the yield on its debenture stock was 12 per cent and the average yield on irredeemable government loan stock was 15 per cent. Explain the possible reasons for the difference in these yields, assuming that they were not untypical of differences in similar investments at the time.

15 Your stockbroker advises you that a company you are contemplating investing in is highly geared. Discuss what is meant by this statement, and what influence it should have on your investment decision, assuming this would be in ordinary shares. What difference would it make to your decision if the company had a low gearing?

16 The decision-maker is as much interested in using financial ratios to predict company failure as he is to predict company success. Comment and discuss.

17 The data given below relate to a company in which a client has invested.

	Periods	
	t_0 to t_1	t_1 to t_2
	£	£
Income from trading	40,000	50,000
Less: loan interest paid	1,000	4,000
	39,000	46,000
Less: corporation tax	23,000	20,000
	16,000	26,000
Less: dividends on:		
preference shares	1,120	1,120
ordinary shares	4,500	5,250
	5,620	6,370
Income retained	10,380	19,630

Extensions to financial ratio analysis

	Time	
	t_1	t_2
	£	£
Share capital:		
Preference shares: £1 units, fully paid	20,000	20,000
Ordinary shares: 50p units, fully paid	50,000	50,000
	70,000	70,000
Retained income	75,710	95,340
Loan capital: debenture stock	10,000	40,000
	155,710	205,340

From this data the client has produced the ratios noted below, using the figures as stated.

	Periods	
	t_0 to t_1	t_1 to t_2

(a) *Return on investment*

$$\frac{\text{Income after deduction of tax, interest and dividends}}{\text{Share and loan capital employed}}$$

$$\frac{£10,380}{£155,710} \; ; \; \frac{£19,630}{£205,340} \; ; (\times 100) = \qquad 6.7\% \qquad 9.6\%$$

(b) *Earnings per share*

$$\frac{\text{Income from trading}}{\text{Ordinary share capital}}$$

$$= \frac{£40,000}{£50,000} \; ; \; \frac{£50,000}{£50,000} = \qquad 80p \qquad £1$$

(c) *Dividend yield*

$$\frac{\text{Total dividends}}{\text{Total share capital and retained income}}$$

$$= \frac{£5,620}{£145,710} \; ; \; \frac{£6,370}{£165,340} \; ; (\times 100) = \qquad 3.9\% \qquad 3.9\%$$

(d) *Earnings yield*

$$\frac{\text{Earnings per share (as above)}}{\text{Total ordinary share capital and retained income per share}}$$

$$= \frac{£0.8}{£1.3} \; ; \; \frac{£1.0}{£1.5} \; ; (\times 100) = \qquad 61.5\% \qquad 66.7\%$$

He further comments from these computed data that it is difficult to assess the investment potential of the company; its return on investment, despite a significant increase over the two periods, remains relatively low; earnings per share have improved, but dividend yield remains stable and low; and the earnings yield, apparently at a high level, appears to be inconsistent with the other indicators of potential.

You are asked to comment on his figures, and to point out any changes to them which you believe to be necessary. (Assume any other data to them which you believe to be relevant.)

Selected bibliography for Chapters 10, 11 and 12

Past writings on financial ratios have tended to concentrate on the mechanical aspects of the topic under discussion in these three chapters, and therefore it has proved exceedingly difficult to provide a suitable bibliography to support their content. The following publications are regarded as being the most suitable; readers interested in pursuing individual points should find useful readings in the list of references.

P. Bird, *Understanding Company Accounts*, Pitman, 1979, pp. 56–78. An introduction to financial statement analysis.

S. Dev, 'Ratio Analysis and the Prediction of Company Failure', in H. Edey and B. S. Yamey, *Debits, Credits, Finance and Profits*, Sweet and Maxwell, 1974, pp. 61–74. A very readable analysis of the use of financial ratios as predictors of failure, giving brief accounts of the existing empirical evidence in this area.

J. O. Horrigan, 'A Short History of Financial Ratio Analysis', *Accounting Review*, April 1968, pp. 284–94. Content as indicated by title.

B. Lev, *Financial Statement Analysis: A New Approach*, Prentice-Hall, 1974. The most authoritative study to date of the nature and use of financial ratios; examines areas in which financial ratios can be applied, including predicting future income and company failure, loan risk evaluation, and credit evaluation by banks.

L. Revsine, *Replacement Cost Accounting*, Prentice-Hall, 1973, pp. 170–88. A discussion of financial ratios using replacement cost data.

D. Weaver, *Investment Analysis*, Longmans, 1971, pp. 26–84. A detailed and expert account of traditional ratio analysis.

13
Some unresolved issues in company financial reporting

The problem of satisfying user needs

At a relatively complicated level, but nevertheless of vital importance to the practice of financial reporting, is the question of establishing a blend and quality of accounting information likely to meet the needs and requirements of potential users of financial reports from companies, including shareholders, lenders, bankers, creditors, employees, government agencies and financial analysts. As previously mentioned, if financial reports do not satisfy their users, then the accounting function is not being fulfilled. It is therefore essential that accountants should continuously reappraise their financial reports (annual, interim and occasional) to ensure that, as best as can be determined, the consumer is satisfied.

The present-day system of company financial reporting is centred on annual statements of income and financial position, measured in accordance with the historic cost and realization principles. These annual statements are now supplemented, in certain cases, by funds statements, current cost accounting statements, value added statements and interim income statements. However, all present-day financial information which is reported on a regular basis is historical in outlook, concentrating on past profitability and financial position. Only rarely do companies report forward-looking data in the form of income forecasts when making a new issue of shares for public subscription, or when acquiring or merging with other companies.

On the whole, therefore, the major part of the total information flow is contained in general-purpose reports of a historical nature, intended primarily for existing shareholders and debenture holders so as to satisfy stewardship requirements but, in practice, used by a number of differing groups of individuals with different needs. In particular, these needs appear to relate to the making of decisions, and therefore to an assessment of future prospects *vis-à-vis* the companies concerned.

Users, decisions and the future

If users of financial reports are mainly concerned with making decisions and assessing the future, then it would seem appropriate to question the relevance of historically-based financial statements to these activities. In particular, it seems necessary to question the validity of historic cost-based information. Is information relating to past company activity and performance necessarily useful to persons interested in future activity and performance? And, even if it is, should it concentrate on income and capital measurements based on historic costs or current costs?

Certainly it is debatable whether historic cost-based information on income and capital is relevant to a variety of users concerned with the future. As previously discussed, this does not give an adequate impression of current values for company assets, nor does it give a reasonable portrayal of income earned by a company during a specified past period (concentrating, as it does, on income realized during the period). Thus, report users are deprived of realistic information about asset values and income performance which, even if related to the past, could be of relevance to their assessments and ultimate decisions through extrapolation.

However, it is possible to produce income and capital measures using current costs (usually based on replacement costs), thus giving up-to-date data on asset values and periodic earned income. But this system is not presently required to be reported legally (although it is legally permissible), nor is it professionally required for a great many companies (being intended only for large companies as defined in *Statement of Standard Accounting Practice 16*). In any case, it is a relatively new system of reporting, and has yet to be judged as to whether it provides more relevant and useful information about company performance and position than does the traditional system based on historic costs. In particular, although it attempts to avoid the problems of changing prices so poorly attempted in the latter system, current cost accounting remains a system reflecting past company activity to decision-makers anxious to predict future activity.

Forecast data

By definition, a decision-maker looks to the future. In financial reporting, the present emphasis is on past performance and position. Therefore can the future be adequately assessed through the use of historical data, given the rapidly-changing circumstances of modern industry and society? Do past figures form an adequate basis for prediction? Answers to these questions are difficult; it is not easy to dismiss the past in any assessment of the future since it may contain vital clues for prediction. On the other hand, the past need not repeat itself and trends may not continue. The answer is possibly a compromise: that the past is of some use, but that some data relating to the future could be extremely beneficial.

With this last point in mind, the company financial reporting function has had some experience of the formal communication of forecast or budgeted data in relation to share issues and takeovers and mergers in the UK. These limited and infrequent exercises have given rise to suggestions that companies should provide regular information of a predictive nature as supplements to historical data. These have mainly concerned the forecasting of company income for up to one year ahead. From a study of the relevant literature, there seems to be little general resistance to the idea in principle: it does appear that predictive data are believed to have relevance in providing report users with information likely to satisfy their needs.[1] There also appears to be agreement that publication of forecasts should not be made mandatory, since a general concern exists that the average report user may misinterpret the significance of a published forecast.

In other words, report users may believe forecasts to be more accurate and objective than they are or can be. Indications of the potential range of differences between forecasts and actual data were found in a recent study of income forecasts in company prospectuses.[2] In particular, it was found (perhaps not surprisingly) that forecasting inaccuracies appeared to be greater in industries and businesses in which there was an inherent trading uncertainty. However, far from being a disadvantage, these forecast data could give report users clearer insights into the risks and uncertainties associated with companies, and thereby improve the quality of accounting communications. Nevertheless, the following associated problems must be recognized.

Managerial opposition

It is clear that, at a very practical level, there is opposition from company management to the idea of publishing forecast data, the main reason for opposition seeming to be the danger of injuring the competitive advantage of companies by disclosing their future plans, particularly those affecting international markets.[3]

Managerial manipulation

Because published forecasts of income, sales turnover and so forth could be used by report users to measure managerial effectiveness (by comparing them with actual results), it could be suggested that management would deliberately manipulate budgeted data so as to appear to meet their goals successfully. This, of course, would provide misleading data and comparisons for the report user.

It could also be envisaged that manipulation might take place in order to influence share prices in the short term by causing investors' expectations to change – for example, falsely inflated income predictions could cause investors to believe shares to be undervalued and, through consequent purchasing, to inflate prices over the short term, though obviously not over the long term. It has already been mentioned that historical data, when published, have an influence on share prices; it is not unreasonable to assume that forecast data would have a similar effect. However, forecast data are far more subjective than traditional information, and consequently the opportunities for managerial manipulation are much greater. Forecasting could therefore introduce the problem of undue managerial influence on the financial reporting function, to the potential detriment of the report users.

These problems, however, could be offset, first, by the separation in financial reports of the effects of poor prediction from those of trading when comparing forecast and actual data; secondly, by the reporting of a statement of the trading and commercial assumptions underlying forecast data; and thirdly, by an expert verification and audit report on the quality of forecasts and their assumptions.

Forecasting inaccuracies

Financial reports of a predictive nature are, by definition, subjective and capable of including material inaccuracies from forecasting errors. The future is not known, and uncertainty is bound to be a major factor in predictive data. If forecasts are published on a widespread and regular basis, it must be remembered that these inaccuracies will occur, and report users must be made fully aware of this when using the data.

Verification of forecasts

The subjectiveness and scope for managerial manipulation which forecast reports contain make it essential for their credibility to be tested and reported on if they are to be issued to shareholders and others. This is at the moment done in the UK when income forecasts are included in financial reports published in the process of an acquisition or merger, and a guidance statement for accountants reviewing income forecasts has been issued by the main professional accountancy bodies.[4]

An expert and independent assessment of forecast data is therefore possible. But the main emphasis is not on the overall accuracy of the figures. Rather, it is concerned with the reasonableness of the underlying trading and other assumptions made, as well as the appropriateness and consistency of the accounting standards adopted. In this sense, reporting accountants are not auditors and do not themselves have any responsibility for the forecasts. Their liability is therefore limited to reviewing and reporting on the means by which the data have been computed.

Feasibility of reporting forecast data

The commentary in the previous sections has looked at some of the main problems associated with reporting forecast data, particularly from the point of view of reporting it on a regular basis to meet the predictive needs of investors and others. These problems have already been experienced in the UK in relation to occasional acquisition and merger forecasts of income. This experience raises the question of the feasibility of reporting predictive data; that is, whether their relevance to report users exceeds their inherent subjectiveness and inaccuracy.

If forecasting inaccuracies were too large, then such data would fail to give their users anything worthwhile upon which to base their assessments and decisions. On the other hand, inaccuracies can be permissible if kept within certain tolerable limits and if users appreciate that this is the case. It may be that some criterion of accuracy in forecasting is necessary, based on the concept of materiality – that is, inaccuracies of less than an agreed percentage would be acceptable in such a financial reporting system. However, while forecast data for reporting purposes may appear attractive so far as information relevance is concerned, because of inaccuracies they may not be as practically suitable, at least until forecasting techniques improve.

The relevance of income

No one would deny the importance of measures of income in company financial reporting, particularly over the last thirty to forty years. It has become central to most assessments of company performance over time. However, there are several problems associated with its measurement which raise doubts about its relative high position of importance in accounting thought. Whether these doubts are serious enough to cause income to lose its prestigious position has yet to be proved conclusively. That doubts do exist, however, is reason enough to examine them to assess their seriousness. It is also important to look at other reporting concepts which may have been ignored or neglected over the years simply because attention has been directed mainly at developments and improvements in the income concept. In other words, the quest for information to satisfy the varying needs of investors and others may have been too concerned with solutions in terms of measures of periodic income rather than with a range of alternative concepts.

The elusive concept of income

Arguably the most serious fault of the income concept is its elusive nature. What it attempts to do is to encompass, in aggregate form, all of the activity of a company over a period of time which is capable of being described in monetary terms. Essentially, therefore, it is a distillation of a myriad of transactions, events and activities. Yet, despite the reality of a given company situation, numerous measures of income, each one different from the next, can be produced to describe it. Different valuation bases (for example, historic cost, replacement cost or realizable value) will produce different income measures.

In addition, further variations in income can be seen because of the inherent flexibility in accounting practice due mainly to the cost allocation process: even with the advent of professional statements on accounting standards, it is likely that flexibility will continue to exist because of the subjective personal judgements which enter into the accounting process and which cannot be standardized. On top of all this, it is clear that income is a less than perfect measure of company performance since it is, more often than not, produced omitting significant company resources from the relevant accounting data: accounting capital does not usually include important and valuable intangible resources (normally classified as goodwill) nor does it include human resources. Instead, it concentrates mainly on tangible resources and, consequently, the resultant measures of income take no cognisance of movements in the value of the omitted resources.

The meaning of income

Since income measures tend to be complex aggregations of company activity over defined periods of time, they encompass much of what goes on within a company: the good and bad, the successes and failures, the desirable and undesirable, and so on. The problem is therefore one of deciding what income measures really represent *vis-à-vis* the company and its management. In other words, what does the report user look for when income measures are communicated to him? Does he regard income as simply a quantified measure of the increase in company capital (this depending on the valuation basis adopted); or is it an indicator of company or managerial success or failure; or is it merely a basis for determining shareholders' dividends; or is it the figure from which the company's taxation liabilities can be derived; or should it be used as a basis for employee wage claims?

Income can certainly be interpreted as the periodic movement in valued capital. However, care must be exercised when looking at it in this way. Capital value may have changed, but this depends on the valuation adopted, the accounting standards used and the subjective judgements employed, as well as on the resources accounted for, or not accounted for. In other words, income, as a measure of the change in company capital, seems to be subject to too much potential and actual variation to be of much use in assessing aggregate value movements. This is particularly so when historic costs are the basis for measurement.

Income can also be regarded as a means of determining dividends and taxation. Certainly, case law reveals that income has played a substantial part in the determination of gains available for distribution. However, given the inherent, if reducing, flexibility in accounting practice, it is hard to regard reportable income as an accurate indicator of dividend levels. In addition, so long as original subscribed share capital is not being repaid by payment of excessive dividends, it is difficult to justify the retention of income reporting specifically for this purpose. Dividends are, after all, dependent on the availability of cash as much as income, although relatively recent examples of companies satisfying dividends by issuing further shares instead of paying by cash make this argument less strong than it once was. Taxation, too, need not depend entirely on income measures. At present, the usual basis is annual income, but this need not be so since it is not the only basis available: taxes could be levied on sales turnover or dividends distributed. Wage settlements, too, depend not so much on income but on the availability of cash, employee productivity and so on.

In summary, therefore, what the above paragraphs have briefly tried to indicate is that income is used frequently in a variety of capacities to indicate some financial or economic factor, whether taxable capacity, dividend proposals, managerial success or wage capacity. But income measures are subject to a great deal of flexibility which renders them somewhat less than precise indicators. And, in any case, they are not entirely essential or relevant to assessments of the factors concerned. Therefore, the question raised is whether income justifies the high importance it has been given in company financial reporting over many years.

The alternatives to income

The previous section has outlined doubts about the general and particular usefulness of income. It has been used extensively for a variety of purposes and, subject to a lack of evidence to the contrary, appears to have established itself as a significant financial indicator. Much attention has therefore been given to ways of improving the quality of income measurements over the years, culminating in the UK and other countries in various programmes for the standardization of accounting practices. Most of the work in this direction has concentrated on improvements in the historic cost-based concept of income, and only recently has much attention been paid to alternative valuation bases for income purposes. Little or no effort has therefore been given to the task of exploring alternatives to income, the implicit assumption being that it is the most relevant reporting concept on which to concentrate.

Despite the apparent reluctance of the accountancy profession to look at alternatives to income reporting, there are signs of proposals being put forward, and it is appropriate at this stage to examine the main ones briefly. The following paragraphs attempt to do so.

Funds flow and cash flow reporting

One definite indication of a de-emphasizing of income reporting is the gradual increase in the publication of funds statements by companies (already commented on in this book). Thus the requirement to report on all financial flows over a period of time is satisfied by this additional statement in a way which the traditional income statement and balance sheet cannot do. The income statement reflects the periodic income inflow and dividend outflow, but does not indicate other financial flows. The balance sheet is, by definition, static, and therefore cannot of itself reveal flows. The funds statement, which is basically a derivation of the latter two statements, can do so.

However, funds flows are subject to certain problems already discussed. They incorporate the periodic measure of income and rely, in most cases, on the flexible accounting practice necessary to the measurement of income. They also depend considerably on the particular valuation basis adopted because they incorporate data derived from the traditional balance sheet. In other words, funds statements are an extension of traditional income and financial position reporting, and therefore contain and involve most of the valuation and flexibility problems associated with the production of income statements and balance sheets. They provide additional information about companies for interested readers, and have without doubt helped to improve the quality and relevance of company financial reports. Nevertheless, they cannot break away from the problems of income reporting and do not, as such, provide a distinct alternative to the existing system of reporting.

One alternative is that the apparent relevance of funds flow reporting should continue to be identified, but that these problems should be segregated from flow measurements to produce a funds statement which gives a factual account of the company's financial transactions with the outside world. In other words, it would describe the company's cash and credit transactions without the subjectiveness and flexibility of stock valuations, depreciation and other cost allocations, as well as other asset valuation problems. Income and balance sheet reporting need not necessarily be excluded from this system; the segregated funds statement would simply attempt to present factual data separate from the somewhat more subjective data of the traditional type.

The importance of accounting for financial flows can also be recognized in the alternative form of cash flow reporting – that is, statements expressed in pure cash terms and not, therefore, including credit transactions. The simplicity of cash flow is its lack of involvement in measurement problems, and its relevance to investors and others concerned with assessing future cash benefits to be derived from investment, can be advanced as significant reasons for concentrating on this aspect of a company's financial affairs.

It can also be argued that, despite its inherent problems, the financial report should continue to contain statements of income and financial position since these reveal data of apparently great significance to report users. But there is one economic factor which is crucial to a proper assessment of the dividend potential etc. of the company, and this is its capacity to survive as an enterprise – indeed, it could be argued that survival should be the primary corporate objective. If the company does not survive over the long term, there will be no flow of dividends, no payments of interest, no repayment of loans and other amounts due, and no wage settlements. Therefore, it can be argued that investors and other interested parties require information which enables them to assess and predict the development and progress of the company over time; its capacity to survive over time; and its capacity to pay its dividend, interest, and repayment commitments over time. Ideally, the information required should be expressed as a flow of funds in order to reflect these factors. In particular, it should also be measuring the one resource which indicates progress, survival and the ability to provide returns on investments – that is, cash. A company cannot survive, progress, repay loans and other debts, or pay dividends without cash.

A system of cash flow reporting could include the publication of actual cash inflows and outflows over a number of years; forecast cash flows for possibly one or two years ahead; statements of the assumptions upon which these forecasts have been based; explanations of the differences between actual and forecast data; and an independent audit report on the credibility of the published data. Thus the main emphasis would be on supplying report users with relevant data which are alternatives to the present income-orientated system, and which attempt to avoid the flexibility and subjectiveness of such a system without abandoning it.

Illustration 97 provides an example of a very simple cash flow statement. It is derived from the funds statement explained in Illustration 27, and reveals how the latter type of statement can be 'manipulated' by the report analyst to produce cash flow equivalent data. The main adjustment involves the setting off of the working capital changes against the trading profit in order to obtain an operating cash flow figure free of items of stock and credit.

Obviously much depends on the ordering of the case data in order to arrive at the change in the company's resources. However, it does provide information additional to that contained in the conventional funds statement – that is, the amount of cash flow generated from company operations for the period, and available to meet its tax and distribution commitments and to aid the financing of replacement and new investment. It should be noted that, for the experienced analyst, even if the required data in the funds statement are not available, it ought to be possible to compute them from the reporting company's balance sheet and income statement.

Cash flow accounting proposals are subject to some criticisms. Among them is the comment that they tend to ignore the problems of income measurement by presenting an over-simple portrayal of a company's financial affairs (this need not be the case if cash reports are published as well as other traditional reports). Then there is the criticism that cash flow forecasts are subject to all the problems and difficulties mentioned above in the forecasting section (this is undeniable, but the balance of relevance and feasibility has yet to be decided with regard to any form of forecast; at least cash forecasts avoid certain of the subjective judgements contained

Illustration 97 Producing a cash flow statement

Assume the following data:

COMPANY LTD
Group Funds Statement for Period t_1 to t_2

	£
Sources of funds included:	
Trading profits realized	4,100
Bank loan received	2,000
Additional credit given by suppliers	400
	6,500
The *uses* to which these funds were put included:	
Payment of taxation	1,100
Payment of dividends	200
Purchase of plant	6,000
Replacement of stock	1,100
Additional credit given to customers	200
	8,600
Resulting in a *reduction* of cash resources of	2,100

By adding the additional credit given by suppliers of £400, and deducting the increase in stock (£1,100) and credit given to customers (£200) to and from the trading profit of £4,100, the operating cash flow surplus for period t_0 to t_1 becomes £4,100 + 400 − 1,100 − 200 = £3,200. This adjustment having been made, the remainder of the above data can be rearranged to produce a 'surplus' statement in cash flow terms.

COMPANY LTD
Group Cash Flow Statement for Period t_0 to t_1

	£
Operating cash flow surplus	3,200
Less: taxation paid	1,100
Distributable cash flow surplus	2,100
Less: dividends paid	200
Cash flow surplus retained	1,900
Add: bank loan received	2,000
Cash flow available for investment	3,900
Less: purchase of new plant	6,000
Reduction of cash resources	2,100

in income forecasts because of the avoidance of problems such as the forecasting of certain valuations and cost allocations).

Human resources reporting

It has been mentioned in this text that the traditional system of company financial reporting tends to concentrate on accounting for tangible resources for which transactions have taken place. Little or no account is usually taken of intangible resources which can include the skills and experience of the company's labour force, including its management. Presumably because human beings in industry and commerce are 'rented' or 'leased' for their services rather than purchased outright (as in slavery), they have not been treated for reporting purposes as measurable assets.

Nevertheless, it is possible to conceive of a system of financial reporting involving the incorporation of human resource values to the traditional reporting system. The concept involves the identification of historic costs incurred on expenditure relating to human resources employed by the company which, it is estimated, will have an expected value stretching beyond the period in which the outlay took place. This would include costs incurred on recruiting, training and developing skills of employees; and would be treated for accounting purposes in much the same way as a fixed asset, with a gradual amortization of the 'capitalized' aggregate cost over its estimated useful life (as with depreciation of fixed assets).

As such, this does not seem to represent an alternative to the present system of reporting. However, in a conceptual sense, it is a positive attempt to break away from accounting for the physical resources of the company, and thus approaches the economist's concept of entity value, which is concerned to value it as a whole, including all its resources: tangible and intangible, human and non-human. It should be stated, however, that the system is subject to the major criticisms that (a) it utilizes a rather crude cost allocation process to determine human asset values; (b) it also involves a great deal of subjective judgement in the subsequent process; and (c) it is presently conceived within terms of the traditional historic cost-based system of reporting, and therefore does little to alleviate the latter's inherent faults and problems.

Events reporting

Arguably the most extreme proposal as an alternative or supplement to income reporting is the so-called 'events' accounting process, which concentrates on the crucial events (internal, environmental and transactional) which affect the company. Thus the 'events' approach recognizes the need in financial reporting to provide users with information relevant for predictions and decisions. The major argument is that the present traditional system is essentially concerned with valuation (that is, to produce income statements, balance sheets and funds statements), and that this results in several faults detrimental to users concerned with predicting: for example, (a) a loss of information occurs in value accounting owing to aggregation (because of the process of distilling data into a relatively few figures, such as with periodic income, crucial information about events affecting the future of the company is hidden from the user); (b) not all relevant events affecting the future of the company are reported in the value-based system because they are not capable of being valued conventionally (for example, resources which are leased rather than purchased, as well as the problem mentioned earlier of human resources); (c) the factual and verifiable nature of events accounted for is obscured by the accountant's valuation procedures which allocate and match accounting data based on his rather than the user's prediction of the company's future.

In other words, the events approach is mainly directed against any interference by accountants in the reporting process which tends to obscure matters crucial to predicting the company's future – that is, by avoiding the accountant's subjective judgements of that future. The report users thus are left hopefully at less of a disadvantage in attempting to make their own personal judgements. The events approach ignores valuation and, consequently, income; it favours historical reporting and rejects forecasting in reports; and, as a result, gives far more detailed information about the basic events affecting the financial life of the company. This would include data which need not necessarily be capable of measurement in financial terms. It would be fair to say, however, that events accounting is at present very much at the theory stage.

Employment reporting

Following recent suggestions from the main professional accountancy bodies and government in the UK,[5] financial reports of companies occasionally contain employment statements – that is, reports pertaining to the management of the company's employee resources. Presently conceived as a statement of how effective such management has been, the employment report is yet another example of the move away from the orientation in financial reports to measures of income and financial position. It recognizes the primary importance of employees in the company, and is an attempt to report on and to employees (although other users, such as shareholders and lenders should obviously be concerned with receiving information about the corporate management of the work force).

Not to be confused with employee statements of simplified financial data (discussed in a later section of this chapter), employment reports are a relatively new form of reporting for which there are no prescribed rules or standards for measurement and disclosure. When produced by companies on the present voluntary basis, they usually contain data relating *inter alia* to employee numbers, employment and training policies, collective bargaining arrangements, industrial disputes, pension and pay arrangements, and disabled employee numbers. Much of this information appears to go beyond the traditional limits of financial information and disclosure and, as with human resources reporting and events reporting, it reveals how the company financial reporting function is expanding.

Socio-economic reporting

Traditional financial reporting systems tend to concentrate on the financial and economic consequences of corporate activity. However, recent pressures for companies to recognize their duty to be accountable to society in general have given rise to the development of socio-economic accounting. In its broadest sense, this aspect of the reporting function is concerned with the measurement and communication of both the economic and the social effects of corporate behaviour, thus extending the conventional reporting system. Socio-economic accounting statements are intended to report on such matters as the company's contribution to the arts and education; the community in which it is located; safety standards; the reduction of its pollution of the environment; and so on. As such, these statements go much beyond the traditional function of the accountant as a reporter, and will inevitably involve other experts within the company. They evidence the development of the financial reporting function beyond the hitherto rather narrow confines of accounting and finance.

Simplifying the financial message

As previously mentioned in this text, there is a major problem in financial reporting, and this concerns the communication of needed data about company progress and performance in a complex language and structure which may be beyond the powers of comprehension of most non-accountant users. Financial reporting should be as much about communication as it is about measurement. Unfortunately, however, two factors have combined to act counter to the communication objective – first, as the network of financial report users has increased over the years (including shareholders and employees), and the financial affairs of companies have become of considerable public interest, more and more persons with no financial or accounting experience or training have been exposed to financial reports; and, secondly, the need to increase the scope and content of financial statements has undoubtedly made them exceedingly complex documents.

Thus, on the one hand, the potential untrained readership of financial reports has increased when, on the other hand, their complexity and potential incomprehensibility has increased. The obvious answer to this dilemma is to produce simplified financial statements for non-accounting users. However, this process is not as easy as it looks.[6] There is a practical experience of simplified statements in the form of summarized reports of income and financial position to employees (diagrammatic and illustrative material often being used by the companies concerned). There is a great deal of variety in these reports, and the level of comprehension is not always improved by producing summaries of figures. The essential issues remain, as always, the identification of the needs of the users to whom the reports are directed, and the production of the needed data in a form and language which is comprehensible. The essential features of the annual financial statements are therefore not necessarily what is required by shareholders, employees and others who have little financial or accounting background. Much has yet to be done by the main professional accountancy bodies in order to resolve this problem.

Problems for the auditor

As mentioned several times throughout this text, it has been a traditional requirement for reported company accounting information to be audited by a suitably qualified and independent accountant. In the UK, this is the case with annually reported financial statements of profitability and financial position (both for single companies and groups of companies) as well as with occasional prospectus or acquisition and merger reports. With historical data, the auditor's main task is to examine and verify reported information so as to report on its quality in terms of the familiar 'true and fair view' opinion, thereby establishing its credibility for shareholders and other interested users. In the case of predictive data, mainly because of its inherent total subjectiveness, the audit emphasis is on establishing and reporting on the credibility of the accounting practices used rather than the underlying trading assumptions (this latter aspect of auditing is usually conducted by non-accountants acting as financial or banking advisors to the company concerned with making the forecast). Interim financial reports, even though of a historical nature, are not at present required in the UK to be audited prior to publication.

This section seeks to outline the main problem areas facing the auditor when verifying the quality of reported information – that of to whom and for what he is responsible. Hopefully, this will give the reader an understanding of problems in company financial reporting other than the measurement and communication ones which are usually commented on.

Auditor responsibility

It is a fundamental postulate of auditing financial statements that the auditor can be held accountable for the quality of his work and the nature of his opinion on the accounting information in the company's financial statements. In other words, the auditor has a duty of care to those to whom he is responsible. If he is negligent in his work, he must be capable of being held accountable. If this were not the case then no one could rely upon his verification work and audit report, and his services would not be sought. This topic is a complex one, but it does deserve some comment in the context of this chapter, and the following are given as indicators of the main problem areas of responsibility facing the auditor today.

To whom is the auditor responsible?

From previous sections and chapters, it can be seen that the auditor of company financial statements in the UK (and many other countries) is legally responsible to the shareholders of a client company. This means that if he is negligent, and is found to have damaged the shareholders because of such negligence, he can be sued by them, collectively, for damages. This is supported in the judgment in such cases as *London and General Bank (No. 2)* (1895) 2 Ch. 673, *The London Oil Storage Co. Ltd* v. *Seear, Hasluck and Co.* (1904) 31 Acct, L.R.1., and *Candler* v. *Crane, Christmas & Co.*, C.A. (1951) 2 K.B. 164; (1951) 1 All E.R. 426; (1951) 1 T.L.R. 371. The last-mentioned case went one stage further and decided that, even if the auditor were negligent and damaged persons other than the shareholders, he would not be legally responsible to those third parties.

It is this last point which is of so much concern to company auditors for, as other parts of this text have made clear, company financial statements are of potential interest and use to many groups of persons and bodies other than shareholders. It is therefore quite conceivable that the auditor could, if negligent, harm third parties. Therefore, is the auditor legally responsible or not to these other persons and bodies? The answer so far has been in the negative, despite a recent non-accounting case, *Hedley, Byrne and Co. Ltd* v *Heller and Partners Ltd* (1963) 2 All E.R., 575; (1963) 3 W.L.R. 101; (1964) A.C. 465, in which the judgment suggested that third-party responsibility for practitioners such as accountants did exist. However, Counsel's advice at the time was that:

> ... third parties entitled to recover damages under the *Hedley Byrne* principle will be limited to those who by reason of accountants' negligence in preparing reports, accounts or financial statements on which the third parties place reliance suffer financial loss in circumstances where the accountants knew or ought to have known that the reports, accounts or financial statements in question were being prepared for the specific purpose or transaction which gave rise to the loss and that they would be shown to and relied on by the third parties in that particular connection. There is no general principle that accountants may be liable for damages if a report or statement which proves to have been prepared negligently by them is shown casually or in the course of business to third parties who suffer loss through reliance on the report or statement.[7]

This statement was taken at the time to mean the exclusion of third parties from the legal responsibility of auditors. But nowadays, with a greater awareness of the various potential uses to which audited financial statements can be put, auditors must realize that shareholders are not the only persons who could be damaged through use of negligently audited information. Therefore, although no specific third-party responsibility has been outlined in a legal sense, the auditor must have at least a moral responsibility to all potential users of company financial reports, and must take this into account when conducting his verification procedures and formulating his audit opinion.

For what is the auditor responsible?

In the UK, the Companies Acts 1948, 1967, 1976, 1980 and 1981 effectively charge company directors with the responsibility for producing the required financial reports and statements. The directors are collectively responsible for the nature and quality of accounting information contained in these documents. The auditor, on the other hand, is responsible for the nature and quality of his expert opinion on the information which is required to be audited. He is not responsible, in his capacity as auditor, for the quality of the information he audits. The main problem facing the auditor in this connection is one of what exactly he is responsible for in his audit work and opinion.

First, it is clear on the basis of decisions in past court cases that the auditor cannot be held responsible for searching out and reporting on fraud or errors which have been committed within a client company. Such may have been the purpose of auditing at the turn of the century but, nowadays, the emphasis is very much on establishing the creditability of reported information. The cases of *Irish Woollen Co. Ltd* v. *Tyson and Others* (1900) 26 Acct. L.R. 13, *Henry Squire (Cash Chemist) Ltd* v. *Ball, Baker and Co.* (1911) 44 Acct. L.R. 25, and *S. P. Catterson & Sons Ltd* (1937) 81 Acct. L.R. 62 have conclusively shown that the auditor's responsibilities for searching out fraud and error are limited to those occasions when his suspicions about such matters are sufficiently aroused in the course of his audit to cause him to ensure that company management is aware of the situation and doing something about it. Besides this, however, should his audit techniques be inadequate and fail to arouse his suspicions regarding fraud and error, he could be held to be negligent (as in the case of *Thomas Gerrard & Son Ltd* (1968) Ch. 455; (1967) 2 All E.R. 525).

Therefore the auditor has a limited responsibility for searching out fraud and error. But the size of companies and the volume of their transactions would make such a task an impossibly time-consuming and costly operation. If undertaken, it would considerably delay the publication of company financial reports to the detriment of shareholders and other report users. The words of Lord Justice Lopes in the case of *Kingston Cotton Mill Co. (No 2)* (1896) 2 Ch. 279 are pertinent:

> Auditors must not be made liable for not tracking our ingenious and carefully laid schemes of fraud where there is nothing to arouse their suspicion, and when those frauds are perpetrated by tried servants of the company and are undetected for years by the directors. So to hold would make the position of an auditor intolerable.

Secondly, arising out of several relatively recent US cases (*Escott et al.* v. *Barchris Construction Corporation et al.* (1968) 283 F. Suppl. 643, 703, S.D.N.Y.; and *United States* v. *Simon* (1968) United States District Court, S.D.N.Y.), it is clear the US auditors are being expected to adhere to higher standards than ever before. In fact, it appears that US courts are setting standards before they gain general acceptance within the accountancy profession. In the *Barchris* case, it was decided that the auditor has a duty continuously to reappraise past audits of financial statements to ensure that subsequent circumstances have not invalidated their original audit opinions. This occurs mainly with accounting information contained in annual reports which are subsequently used for prospectus purposes. In the other case, usually referred to as *Continental Vending*, the decision concerned how far an auditor must go to establish the reliability of reported accounting information. The implication of the decision to finalize reporting was such that the court expected auditors to seek audit evidence much more widely than is presently the case. Thus, auditors are faced with the potential problem not only of meeting generally accepted standards of the day but also of possibly attaining standards beyond those presently appearing to receive general acceptance.

Lastly, auditors in many countries are now faced with verifying the implementation of mandatory accounting standards by companies; in the UK, for example, these are contained in *Statements of Standard Accounting Practice*. This could well present auditors with serious problems. These are not impossible to face when a client company departs from a published standard, and the auditor has a duty to verify the nature of the departure. However, there may be cases where an auditor disagrees with the prescribing standard, irrespective of whether the client company implements it or not. Does he then state this in his report and give his reasons for doing so? Or does he accept that the mandatory standard is regarded as generally acceptable and hide his personal views in the matter? The problem has not been resolved and reflects the relatively unstable state of the art of accounting at the present time. However, it does not appear unfair to say that for auditors publicly to state their disagreement with prescribed practice would undermine the credibility of that practice as well as financial statements. In other words, by working through their professional bodies, auditors should seek to improve accounting standards rather than to undermine public confidence in published financial statements.

Verification problems

The practice of auditing financial statements is not a straightforward matter of checking figures and documents. There are several major problems facing the auditor in this area, and this brief section can do no more than outline the main ones.

The first problem has already been discussed: verification that the financial statements concerned have been produced in accordance with recognized accounting practice. In the UK, this refers specifically to the implementation of mandatory *Statements of Standard Accounting Practice*. The main issue facing the auditor in this context is the decision on whether or not a company's departure from a recommended standard is valid. His duty is to report on such a departure should he disagree with it. He must therefore be extremely careful in coming to his decision so as not to create doubts and suspicions in the minds of report users *vis-à-vis* the credibility of the information. In particular, he must ensure that he has objectively reviewed the circumstances of the company, the nature of the relevant prescribed standard, and management's reasons for departure.

Secondly, the auditor will inevitably be faced with giving an expert opinion on a mass of data which have to be aggregated and reported in financial statement form. Given the constraints of time and cost, it is relatively obvious that he cannot personally examine every figure, transaction or document. This would be an impossible task to undertake, especially in large companies or groups of companies. Therefore he must verify data on a test basis, having first established the various strengths and weaknesses in the accounting system. The more confident he is of the reliability of the system, the smaller will be his tests and checks. The opposite is true for a weak system. Statistical sampling techniques could be used in this connection. The auditor's problem is assessing the strength of the system and the size and nature of his samples so as to provide sufficient evidence of the quality of the data on which he has to report.

Thirdly, as previously explained in various parts of this text, the process of producing reportable accounting information inevitably involves a great deal of managerial opinion, particularly relating to the allocation and evaluation of accounting data. This presents an enormous problem for the auditor since he has to examine the credibility of these subjective judgements to determine his own personal opinion of the credibility of the aggregate information. It is extremely difficult for an accountant to judge the quality of a judgement made by an engineer, chemist, lawyer, surveyor or whatever. In most instances, unless he can seek an independent assessment from a suitably qualified expert, he must rely on the integrity of the managers concerned. This explains why auditors of predictive data such as income forecasts confine their attention to the accounting practices used rather than the underlying trading and commercial assumptions.

In conclusion, therefore, it should be clear from the above paragraphs that the auditor, when he reports on company financial statements, is not guaranteeing their accuracy or credibility. He is giving an expert opinion on the basis of tests he has conducted. Given the flexibility of accounting, reported information cannot be regarded as completely accurate. There can be no such thing as complete accuracy in financial accounting, given the many different ways of reporting the same economic and financial circumstances. This is true whether the basic data are historical or predictive; and obviously more so with the latter than with the former.

Conclusions

The contents of this chapter have attempted to remind the reader that the function of company financial reporting contains many unresolved issues for the reporting accountant and auditor. The production of financial statements is an immensely complex activity, and has developed continuously since its early beginnings in the nineteenth century. It continues to develop at a pace, new practices and statements being added to those of a traditional nature. Each creates issues awaiting resolution. Hopefully, the reader should now be aware of the extent of these problems and the current 'state of play' regarding the financial reports of companies.

References

1 R. Schattke, 'Expected Income – A Reporting Challenge', *Accounting Review*, October 1962, pp. 670–6; W. W. Cooper, N. Dopuch and T. F. Keller, 'Budgeting Disclosure and Other Suggestions for Improving Accounting Reports', *Accounting Review*, October 1968, pp. 640–7; and C. R. Tomkins, 'The Development of Relevant Published Accounting Reports', *Accountancy*, November 1969, pp. 815–20.

2 S. Dev and M. Webb, 'The Accuracy of Company Profit Forecasts', *Journal of Business Finance*, Autumn 1972, pp. 26–39.

3 K. F. Skousen, R. A. Sharp and R. K. Tolman, 'Corporate Disclosure of Budgetary Data', *Journal of Accountancy*, May 1972, pp. 50–7.

4 'Accountants' Reports on Profit Forecasts', *Statements on Miscellaneous Matters*, Institute of Chartered Accountants of Scotland, November 1978.

5 See, respectively, E. R. Thomson and A. Knell, *The Employment Statement in Company Reports*, Institute of Chartered Accountants in England and Wales, 1979; and *The Future of Company Reports*, Cmnd 6888, HMSO, 1977.

6 See A. E. Hammill, *Simplified Financial Statements*, Institute of Chartered Accountants in England and Wales, 1979.

7 'Accountant's Liability to Third Parties – the Hedley Byrne Decision', *Accountancy*, September 1965, p. 829.

Suggested discussion or essay topics

1 The amazing thing about published accounting information is that it is predominantly concerned with the past. Yet its readers use it as if it was describing the future. Comment on this apparent inconsistency.

2 The future is not known, and therefore there can be no reliable information produced to describe it. Predicted data are not information; they are guesswork, no matter how expertly guessed. Discuss this statement in the context of producing forecast data for financial reporting purposes.

3 What reasons can be given to justify the predominant position in company financial reports of measures of periodic income?

4 Income is the end-result of an aggregation and collation process which

attempts to squeeze the entire economic activity of a company into one figure. Comment on the validity of this criticism.

5 Funds flow accounting is simply an extension of income accounting. It has often been confused with cash flow accounting. Explain.

6 Human resources are an essential and extremely valuable contribution to economic activity. Yet they are ignored by companies when producing their financial statements. Comment on the validity of this statement.

7 In economic decision-making, it is better to be able to predict events than to know the financial consequences of past events. What relevance has this statement got for company financial reporting?

8 What effect would there be on investor behaviour with regard to company financial statements if the independent audit function were withdrawn and data were published in unaudited form?

9 It has been suggested that the accountancy profession is evolving in the direction of regarding the public as the primary client of the auditor. Might such a development resolve a good deal of the confusion that now surrounds the matter of legal liability, and what would the auditor's standard of liability become under such circumstances?

10 Unless the company auditor satisfies himself as to the existence of fraud or error in the accountancy function, he cannot given an opinion on the quality of the reported financial statements. Discuss.

Selected bibliography for Chapter 13

R. L. Brummet, E. G. Flamholtz and W. C. Pyle, 'Human Resource Measurement – A Challenge for Accountants', *Accounting Review*, April 1968, pp. 217–28. An introduction to human resource accounting.

D. R. Carmichael, 'Reporting on Forecasts: a UK Perspective', *Journal of Accountancy*, January 1973, pp. 36–47. A useful description of the problem of reporting forecast data.

D. Y. Causey, 'The Emerging Standards of Auditor Responsibility', *Accounting Review*, January 1976, pp. 19–30. The modern standard of care expected of the auditor.

D. Flint, 'The Role of the Auditor in Modern Society: An Exploratory Essay', *Accounting and Business Research*, Autumn 1971, pp. 287–93. An analysis of the widening responsibilities and duties of the auditor.

A. E. Hammill, *Simplified Financial Statements*, Institute of Chartered Accountants in England and Wales, 1979. The first study of this complex topic.

T. A. Lee, 'A Case for Cash Flow Reporting', *Journal of Business Finance*, Summer 1972, pp. 27–36. A reasoned argument for cash flow reporting and a description of such a system.

T. A. Lee, 'Enterprise Income: Survival or Decline and Fall?', *Accounting and Business Research*, Summer 1974, pp. 178–92. A detailed criticism of the concept of income for company financial reporting purposes.

R. K. Mautz and H. A. Sharaf, *The Philosophy of Auditing*, American Accounting Association, 1961, pp. 111–57. The most comprehensive conceptual analysis of auditor responsibility.

R. A. Rayman, 'Is Conventional Accounting Obsolete?', *Accountancy*, June 1970, pp. 422–9. A critique of traditional financial reporting concepts and the advocation of funds flow accounting.

G. H. Sorter, 'An "Events" Approach to Basic Accounting Theory', *Accounting Review*, January 1969, pp. 12–19. An introduction to events accounting.

Some unresolved issues

E. R. Thomson and A. Knell, *The Employment Statement in Company Reports*, Institute of Chartered Accountants in England and Wales, 1979. A detailed study of employment statements.

C. R. Tomkins, 'The Development of Relevant Published Accounting Reports', *Accountancy*, November 1969, pp. 815–20. A case for disclosure of budgeted data.

Appendix
Outline solutions to exercises at end of Chapter 3

1(a)

AB LTD

Balance Sheet as at t_1

	£	£	£
Fixed assets			
Shop premises			4,000
Shop fittings			450
			4,450
Current assets			
Stock		800	
Debtors		120	
Cash		20	
		940	
Creditors: amounts falling due within one year			
Trade creditors	350		
Bank overdraft	960	1,310	
Net current assets			(370)
Total assets less current liabilities			4,080
Creditors: amounts falling due after more than one year			
Mortgage loan			(2,500)
			1,580
Capital and reserves			
Share capital			1,000
Reserves			580
			1,580

1(b)

CD LTD

Balance Sheet as at t_1

	£	£	£
Fixed assets			
Motor van			500
Current assets			
Stock		1,150	
Debtors		1,250	
Cash		85	
		2,485	
Creditors: amounts falling due within one year			
Trade creditors	225		
Taxation	200		
Bank overdraft	195	620	
Net current assets			1,865
Total assets less current liabilities			2,365
Creditors: amounts falling due after more than one year			
Mortgage loan			(600)
			1,765
Capital and reserves			
Share capital			1,000
Reserves			765
			1,765

1(c)

EF LTD

Balance Sheet as at t_1

	£	£	£
Fixed assets			
Plant and machinery			2,900*
Current assets			
Stock and work-in-progress		4,907	
Debtors		2,000	
		6,907	
Creditors: amounts falling due within one year			
Trade creditors	880		
Bank overdraft	6,350	7,230	
Net current assets			(323)
Total assets less current liabilities			2,577
Capital and reserves			
Share capital			200
Profit and loss acount			2,377†
			2,577

*The cost of £6,500 and accumulated depreciation of £3,600 would be disclosed in a note to the financial statements.
†£9,500 − (5,500 + 1,200 + 83 + 240 + 700) + 600

XY LTD

Draft Income Statement for Period t_1 to t_2

	£
Turnover	116,400
Cost of goods sold	(97,040)*
Depreciation of fixed assets	(1,090)
Other business overheads	(4,940)†
Retained income	13,330

*Change in stock and purchase of good figures not available
†£3,340 + 1,600

Balance Sheet as at t_2

	£	£
Fixed assets		
Property, plant and equipment		11,060*
Office equipment		260†
		11,320
Current assets		
Stock	19,000	
Debtors	16,730	
Cash in bank and on hand	3,800	
	39,530	
Creditors: amounts falling due within one year		
Trade creditors	6,800	
Net current assets		32,730
Total assets less current liabilities		44,050
Creditors: amounts falling due after one year		
Loans		(6,000)
		38,050
Capital and reserves		
Share capital		20,000
Profit and loss account		18,050‡
		38,050

*The cost of £26,100 and accumulated depreciation of £15,040 would be disclosed in a note to the financial statements.
†The cost of £530 and accumulated depreciation of £270 would be disclosed in a note to the financial statements.
‡£4,720 + 13,330

PQ LTD

Income Statement for Period t_1 to t_2

	£
Turnover	2,455,422
Change in stocks	61,307
Purchase of goods	(914,152)
Wages and salaries	(300,888)
Depreciation of fixed assets	(86,926)
Other business overheads	(290,763)
Loan interest paid	(1,347)
Income before taxation	922,653
Tax on income	406,751
Income after taxation	515,902
Dividend proposed	74,256
Retained income	441,646

Balance Sheet as at t_2

	£	£	£
Fixed assets			
Land and buildings			504,371
Plant and equipment			391,508*
			895,879
Current assets			
Stock and work-in-progress		753,431	
Debtors		1,220,114	
Investments		21,865	
Bank and cash balances		527,540	
		2,522,950	
Creditors: amounts falling due within one year			
Trade creditors	455,872		
Bank loan	1,281		
Tax payable	518,283		
Dividend payable	74,256	1,049,692	
Net current assets			1,473,258
			2,369,137
Capital and reserves			
Called up share capital			416,000
Revaluation reserve			298,196
Profit and loss account			1,654,941†
			2,369,137

*£908,602 − 517,094
†£1,213,295 + 441,646

4

ST LTD

Funds Statement for Period t_1 to t_2

	£
Sources of funds	
Income before taxation	21,000
Add: depreciation of fixed assets	17,000
Funds from operational activity	38,000
Sale of investments	3,000
Sale of plant	27,000
Long-term loan	30,000
	98,000
Application of funds	
Payment of tax	8,000
Payment of dividends	4,000
Purchase of plant	120,000
Increase in working capital*	7,000
	139,000
Resulting in:	
A decrease in bank balance of	41,000
*Increase in stock	12,000
Increase in debtors	10,000
	22,000
Less: increase in trade creditors	15,000
Net increase in working capital	7,000

5

VW LTD

Funds Statement for the Period t_1 to t_2

	£
Sources of funds	
Income retained including depreciation	920
Increase in mortgage loan	500
	1,420
Application of funds	
Purchase of premises and fittings	2,100
Increase in working capital*	160
	2,260
Resulting in an increase in bank overdraft of	840

*Increase in stock, £100 + increase in debtors, £10 + decrease in trade creditors, £50.

6

XY LTD

Funds Statement for the Period t_1 to t_2

	£
Sources of funds	
Income retained including depreciation	28,000
Sale of factory and plant	115,000
	143,000
Application of funds	
Purchase of plant	40,000
Purchase of investments	10,000
Increase in working capital*	27,000
Repayment of mortgage loan	60,000
	137,000
Resulting in an increase in cash resources of	6,000

*Increase in stock, £26,000 + increase in debtors, £12,000 − increase in trade creditors, £11,000.

7

PQ LTD

Current Cost Income Statement for Period t_1 to t_2

		£
Income before tax on the historic cost basis		922,653
Less: current cost adjustments:		
additional cost of sales	94,060	
provision for increase in monetary working capital	16,329	
	110,389	
additional depreciation of fixed assets	47,187	157,576
Current cost operating profit		765,077
Less: taxation		406,751
Current cost income after tax		358,326
Less: dividends		74,256
Current cost income retained		284,070*

*To be aggregated with the previous years' retained income of £1,213,295.

Appendix

Current Cost Balance as at t_2

	£	£	£
Fixed assets			
Land and buildings			721,000
Plant and equipment			531,628*
			1,252,628
Current assets			
Stock and work-in-progress		848,201	
Debtors		1,220,114	
Investments		24,766	
Bank and cash balances		527,540	
		2,620,621	
Creditors: amounts falling due within one year			
Trade creditors	455,872		
Bank loan	1,281		
Tax payable	518,283		
Dividend payable	74,256	1,049,692	
Net current assets			1,570,929
			2,823,557
Capital and reserves			
Called up share capital			416,000
Revaluation reserve			910,192†
Profit and loss account			1,497,365
			2,823,557

*£1,236,345 − 704,717

†*Revaluation Reserve*

Increase in value of:		
land and buildings	216,629	
plant and machinery	140,120	
stock and work-in-progress	94,770	
investments	2,901	
	454,420	
Current cost adjustments to income	157,576	
	611,996	
Previous period's balance	298,196	
	910,192	

ABC LTD

Current Cost Income Statement for Period t_1 to t_2

	£	£
Historic cost income		9,000
Less: additional cost of sales	2,600	
monetary working capital provision	700	
	3,300	
additional depreciation	300	3,600
Current cost operating profit		5,400

Current Cost Balance Sheet as at t_2

	£	£
Fixed assets		
Plant		60,200*
Investments		20,000
		80,200
Current assets		
Stock	7,500	
Debtors	26,500	
Cash	27,000	
	61,000	
Creditors: amounts falling due within one year		
Trade creditors	6,400	
Net current assets		54,600
		134,800
Capital and reserves		
Called up share capital		50,000
Revaluation reserve		19,400†
Profit and loss account		65,400‡
		134,800

*£86,000 − 25,800

† Revaluation surplus on plant		6,000	
Less: aggregate depreciation thereon		1,800	(24/80 × £6,000)
		4,200	
Revaluation surpluses on:			
stock	1,600		
investments	10,000	11,600	
Current cost income adjustments		3,600	
		19,400	

‡ Historic cost retained income	69,000
Less: current cost income adjustments	3,600
	65,400

LM LTD

Value Added Statement for Period t_1 to t_2

	£	£
Sales revenue for period		204,000
Less: bought-in materials and services	134,000	
depreciation of fixed assets	21,000	155,000
		49,000

	£	%
Distributed as follows:		
To employees for wages	26,000	53
To government for taxation	11,000	22
To shareholders for dividends	4,200	9
For reinvestment in the company	7,800	16
	49,000	100

Index